THRIVING IN COMMUNITY COLLEGE & BEYOND

A Customized Textbook for Anne Arundel Community College

Kendall Hunt
publishing company

Cover images Courtesy of Anne Arundel Community College

www.kendallhunt.com
Send all inquiries to:
4050 Westmark Drive
Dubuque, IA 52004-1840

Brief Contents

Contents

Chapter 5: Higher-Level Thinking
Moving beyond Basic Knowledge to Critical and Creative Thinking 101

Chapter 6: Learning Style 127

Chapter 7: Improving Memory and Reading 149

Chapter 12: Health and Wellness
Body, Mind, and Spirit 315

Chapter 13: Educational and Career Planning and Decision Making
Making Wise Choices about Your Courses, Major, Degree, and Career Plans 357

Welcome to Anne Arundel Community College! Since you are reading this, I know you have made a very wise decision to enroll in ACA 100 Student Success. The course is aptly named because the content will provide you with the tools to be a successful student. As an ACA 100 student, it is my expectation that you will increase your knowledge and skills, as well as your ability to think critically by applying and integrating information you are learning. In this course, you can expect to be involved with lively discussions, activities, and challenging assignments, and you should know that support is available to you from your instructor and many others at AACC. Data from across the United States and locally at AACC show that students who complete this course are more successful and more likely to reach their academic goals, which is exactly my wish for you. It is also my hope that if you actively participate in this course, you will build a foundation allowing you to experience success now and in the future.

Colleen Eisenbeiser, PhD
Director, TEACH Institute
Anne Arundel Community College

College History

On Jan. 2, 1961, the county Board of Education established Anne Arundel Community College, a comprehensive community center of higher learning. The college opened in September that year for 270 students in late-afternoon and evening classes in temporary quarters at Severna Park High School. Dr. Andrew G. Truxal became our first president. The college moved to its own 165-acre Arnold campus in September 1967. The Middle States Association of Colleges and Secondary Schools, now known as the Middle States Commission on Higher Education, awarded the college full accreditation in April 1968.

Anne Arundel Community College has built a tradition of more than 50 years of bringing innovation and excellence to the community. With 225 programs and more than 3,500 courses, it's easy to find your passion in the credit offerings, enhance your career through professional and workforce training or challenge yourself to do something new in personal enrichment classes.

Mission Statement

With learning as its central mission, Anne Arundel Community College responds to the needs of a diverse community by offering high quality, affordable, and accessible learning opportunities and is accountable to its stakeholders.

College Vision

Anne Arundel Community College is a premier learning community whose students and graduates are among the best-prepared citizens and workers of the world.

Philosophy

Anne Arundel Community College strives to embody the basic convictions of our country's democratic ideal: that individuals be given full opportunity to discover and develop their talents and interests; to pursue their unique potentials; and to achieve an intellectually, culturally and economically satisfying relationship with society.

Counseling, Advising AND Retention Services (CARS)

CARS offers services and resources to support students in:

- Developing and clarifying career goals and educational plans
- Course selection
- Interpretation of academic rules and regulations
- Administration and interpretation of career assessments
- Pathways to Success workshops on study skills, time management, major selection and more
- Crisis intervention and referral
- Academic tracking and intervention
- Services for students with disabilities
- Transfer planning
- Job search assistance
- Accessing The Career and Transfer Resource Center in the Advising Office on the Arnold Campus

All degree and certificate-seeking students are assigned to an advising team on the Arnold campus, AMIL, GBTC, and Fort Meade locations based on the type of program the student is seeking. Your team will communicate with you throughout each term via your MyAACC student email account, and we encourage you to establish a relationship with an advisor on your team. If you are a student who is interested in transferring to a four-year institution, you are strongly encouraged to meet with a transfer advisor. If you are an undeclared student, you are strongly encouraged to take advantage of career advising. For additional information, students are encouraged to go to www.aacc.edu/advising.

Pathways to Success Workshop Series

Every term, a series of workshops entitled "Pathways to Success" is offered to focus on study skills, self-exploration, career decision-making, transfer planning, job searching, and online college resources. The workshops are free; however, some do require registration. For a current schedule of workshops, please visit www.aacc.edu/advising and link to *Workshops*.

Counseling (Personal)

AACC's personal counseling services allow you to speak individually with a counselor about an issue that concerns you and may lead to academic difficulties. Counseling services are time-limited to a maximum of three visits, 50 minutes each, and are provided without charge to currently registered AACC students. Licensed counselors provide personal counseling services and make referrals for continued counseling or other community-based resources as necessary. Additional self-help services and community resources can be found at www.aacc.edu/advising, under counseling services.

Career and Transfer Resource Center

The Career and Transfer Resource Center is open to all students and alumni, and services include:

- Resume development
- Career assessment and guidance
- Job search assistance
- Transfer school applications
- Resource materials related to transferring, internships, career planning, and job seeking
- Workshops
- Transfer and career advice
- Preparation for AACC Job Fair

AACC's Career and Transfer Resource Center provides in-person career assessments to students who can meet with a career counselor. The available assessments include:

- Myers Briggs Type Indicator (personality assessment);
- Self-Directed Search (interest inventory); and
- Strong Interest Inventory.

The Career and Transfer Resource Center also provides access to the ARTSYS Program. The ARTSYS Program is the computerized articulation system for the University System of Maryland, designed to assist with course selection for students transferring from Maryland Community Colleges to a University System of Maryland institution and other participating institutions. Students can use ARTSYS even if they do not plan to earn a degree at AACC. More information regarding transfer services can be found at www.aacc.edu/transfer

The Career and Transfer Resource Center also offers many free online services via the web, at www.aacc.edu/careers, such as:

- AACC's *JobConnection* database is powered by College Central Network and provides job search assistance and free employer job postings that students can access to connect with employers. Resumes posted at the site can be reviewed by employers who will then contact students for interviews.

- *Optimal Resume* is an extremely innovative online resume site where students can create, present, and style up to five resumes and interact with a Career Counselor to have resumes reviewed and approved quickly. Resumes can be displayed in traditional MS Word or as personal websites in Flash. (Please note that your MyAACC email is required to use this service).

- Online guides are provided for *Resume Writing, Interviewing, Dressing for Success, Negotiating Salaries,* and *Portfolio Development.* Students will have access to useful links for additional/updated information at the end of each guide.

- There is also a *Calendar of Events* linked to *Career Fair* and *Recruiting Events* at AACC and throughout the metropolitan area.

- *DISCOVER* is an online career-planning system that students can access from any computer. A token from AACC's Career and Transfer Resource Center is needed to use *DISCOVER.* Using *DISCOVER,* students can:

  - Explore career options
  - Take interest, abilities and values inventories
  - Search for majors and colleges
  - Prepare resumes
  - Research interview preparation.

- *FOCUS 2* is an online career-planning system that students can access from any computer once they have been assigned an access code by an advisor. Using *FOCUS 2,* students can:

  - Explore career options
  - Take interest, abilities and values inventories
  - Search for majors and colleges

Disability Support Services

The Disability Support Services (DSS) office, under the federal Americans with Disabilities Act (ADA), advocates for students with disabilities in support of AACC's commitment to make all students the best citizens and workers of the world. The DSS office strives to provide equal access to educational opportunities for qualified students with disabilities and to promote full participation of all students in college life.

In order to receive classroom accommodations, all self-identified students must provide current documentation, and DSS advisors are available to meet with students to discuss the procedures necessary to obtain appropriate documentation and to identify accommodations for which a student is eligible.

Disability Categories at AACC:
- Learning Disabilities
- Psychological Disabilities
- Hearing Impairment
- Deaf
- Visual Impairment
- Blind
- Traumatic Brain Injury
- Attention Deficit Hyperactivity Disorder
- Chronic Medical
- Autism
- Intellectual Disability
- Speech or Language Impairment
- Mobility/Orthopedic Impairment

A primary goal of Anne Arundel Community College's mission is to promote full participation of all students in college life. The services listed below seek to provide equal access to educational opportunities for persons with disabilities. Before any accommodation can be made, however, all self-identified students must provide current documentation of their disability.

DSS checklist for services:

- Schedule an appointment with the DSS office.

- Bring a comprehensive evaluation report that provides a diagnosed disability or a Disability Verification Form completed by a physician, psychologist, or other certified clinician to your appointment with the DSS office. If you do not have documentation and do not have a resource for evaluation, call the DSS office for referral resources.

- At your appointment, the DSS advisor will discuss the course accommodations for which you are eligible based on the documentation and information you provided. Appropriate accommodation forms will be completed.

- Students should then take the accommodation forms to their professors and/or to Testing and Assessment Services. The student and instructor must sign and date the forms. The student must return a copy of the signed forms to the DSS office.

*Potential Accommodations** for students with documented disabilities include:
*Note: Accommodations provided are based on a student's individual case. Not all accommodations are available to all students.

- Applications and registration assistance
- Note takers, readers, and/or scribes
- Testing modifications
- Books on tape
- Lab assistants
- Sign language interpreters
- Amplification systems
- Voice Synthesizer
- Computers equipped with software: Dragon Dictate, (voice recognition system for dictation), Zoom Text (system for enlarging test), Kurzweil Reader (system for scanning and producing text verbally), JAWS (computer screen reader)
- Chair lift in the Humanities building
- Swimming pool lift to enter and exit the pool
- Special parking areas equipped with curb cuts and ramps located close to classroom buildings (license tags for those with disabilities are obtained through the Maryland Motor Vehicle Administration (MVA).

For more information, students are encourage to go to www.aacc.edu/disability/

Student Services

Tutoring

The Tutoring Office helps students with diverse learning styles enhance their academic experience by providing individualized academic support. Every student enrolled at AACC is encouraged to use AACC Student Success Services. All of our services are designed to be flexible and free of charge. AACC's Tutoring Program is nationally certified by the College Reading and Learning Association. Students can request a peer tutor for any AACC class. www.aacc.edu/tutoring

Math Tutoring

Math labs are located on both the Arnold and Arundel Mills campuses. The Math labs offers professional and peer tutoring in various levels of mathematics, including arithmetic, basic math, trigonometry, business math, statistics, algebra and calculus.

The Math FIRS3T Lab offers focused individualized resources to support student success with technology. This fully-staffed lab provides instructional and tutoring support on a walk-in basis primarily for students enrolled in computer-intensive developmental mathematics courses, but all mathematics students are welcome.

Reading Tutorial Lab

The reading labs are also located on both the Arnold and Arundel Mills campuses. The labs provide student supports in reading comprehension, study skills, and critical thinking. Students can receive individualized instruction on topics such as test taking strategies, organizational skills, note taking, outlines, and other academic skills.

Science Tutoring Center

The science tutoring center is located on the Arnold campus. The center provides drop in tutoring support for students taking classes in anatomy and physiology, environmental science, microbiology, physical science, astronomy, ecology, meteorology, veterinary science, biology, genetics, oceanography, zoology, chemistry, geology, and physics.

Business/Accounting Lab

The business/accounting lab is located on the Arnold campus. The lab offers drop in support for students taking business and accounting classes, such as business statistics, business law, accounting, and economics.

English as a Second Language Lab

The English as a Second Language program offers tutoring to students enrolled in the program on the Arnold campus.

For additional information regarding labs and tutoring supports, go to www.aacc.edu/tutoring

Supplemental Instruction

Supplemental Instruction (SI) is a learning enhancement program that offers a series of free group study sessions conducted by peer student leaders for specific classes in science, accounting and social science. Students can compare notes, discuss assignments, and learn skills and strategies. Additional information can be found at www.aacc.edu/si

The Writing Center

The Writing Center provides continuous help to students from all disciplines by providing one-on-one tutoring on a walk-in basis. English department faculty tutors are happy to assist in preparing written assignments, offer help in understanding errors on graded papers, and provide additional training in grammar, punctuation, and usage. For more information, visit www.aacc.edu/writingcenter

Services Provided
What tutors will do:
- Read **some** of your work and indicate problems in unity, coherence, grammar, punctuation, and mechanics.
- Teach you how to repair errors.
- Guide you through the process of developing a thesis statement.
- Share proofreading strategies that you can employ on your own.
- Help you assess if you have documented your research-based paper correctly (APA or MLA style).
- Raise questions regarding conformity with assignments.

What to expect:
- A 30-minute individual session with a tutor (during peak times you might need to wait for the next available tutor)
- The tutor to go through **some** of your paper with you, focusing on the area(s) that you indicated on the intake form (thesis/topic sentences, style, organization, grammar/punctuation, documentation, or other) online follow-up activities for skill development, if applicable and desired.

The Virtual Writing Center

The Virtual Writing Center offers the same high quality tutoring experience as our face-to-face Writing Center locations in a synchronous, voice-interactive online environment. It is open to all enrolled AACC students and can be accessed using Canvas and Blackboard Collaborate.

Tutoring options available through The Virtual Writing Center:

Welcome to the Virtual Writing Center!

Click on **Modules** (located on the left) to begin or to schedule an appointment.

- Individual appointment with a writing tutor
- Individual appointment with a research librarian
- Drop-in Open Discovery session (research)

Enrolling in The Virtual Writing Center is completed through Canvas. Additional information and directions can be found at www.aacc.edu/writingcenter

SMARTTHINKING

SMARTHINKING is an online tutoring service that is available to currently enrolled AACC students. SMARTHINKING provides tutoring in a variety of subjects, some of which are available 24 hours a day, 7 days a week!

AACC students have access to 15 hours of free tutoring through SMARTHINKING. com. If more time is needed, contact the Tutoring Coordinator.

Live E-structors (tutors) provide tutoring in:

- Math: basic, algebra, geometry, trigonometry, calculus I-III, differential equations, linear algebra, discrete math, and statistics
- Business: statistics, accounting, micro and macroeconomics, introduction to finance,
- Sciences: chemistry, biology, physics, introduction to anatomy and physiology, organic chemistry
- Foreign Language - Spanish grammar and essay
- Online Writing Lab for all subjects.

For more information on SMARTHINKING, please visit www.aacc.edu/tutoring/smarthinking/ SMARTHINKING is located in the MyAACC Self Services Quick Links under the Self Services tab.

Testing Department

The Testing Department provides a wide range of testing and assessment services including:

- Providing assessment testing for incoming students
- Interpreting test results
- Providing make-up and distance learning testing.
- Assisting student in acquiring financial resources to facilitate access and achieve their educational goals through the administration of Ability to Benefit Tests.
- Providing testing accommodations to students with special needs.
- Providing certification exams and credit by examination.

Additional information can be found at www.aacc.edu/testing

Computer Labs

The Technology Learning Center (TLC) Lab and Computer Commons (CC) Lab provide our diverse community with a welcoming environment that offers access to state-of-the-art computer resources and individually targeted technical support for the purpose of helping individuals to attain their personal and academic goals. Additional information can be found at www.aacc.edu/tlclab and www.aacc.edu/computercommons

College Bookstore

The AACC Bookstore carries new, used, and digital books (subject to availability). The bookstore also offers new and used text- book rentals on select titles (inquire with staff for details). In addition to being your one-stop-shop for textbooks, the AACC Bookstore offers a variety of products and services including computers and software at special academic prices, study aids, school and office supplies, art, engineering and drafting materials, freshly prepared sandwiches and salads, snack foods, greeting cards, postage stamps, AACC sportswear and gift cards. www.aaccbooks.com

Health Services

Health Services is staffed by Registered Nurses and provides assistance with basic health concerns by offering non-prescription medications, first aid, health and wellness information, stress management resources, and affordable health care referrals for insured and uninsured individuals.

- Free services include:
- Blood pressure screening
- First aid
- Health information and counseling
- Health insurance information
- Health care referrals
- Non-prescription medications
- StressLess Room
- Lactation Room
- Gender Neutral Restroom
- Tobacco Cessation Counseling & Nicotine Patches or Gum
- HIV testing

Fitness Center

The Fitness Center at AACC features two rooms with state-of-the-art cardiovascular fitness and weight training equipment for use in classes and during open-hour workouts. Fitness center open hours are designated each semester for AACC students currently enrolled in any credit courses and employees of the college. There is also a pool available for student use. Additional information can be found at www.aacc.edu/healthfitness

Child Development Center

Child care is available to students at AACC's Child Development Center in Arnold, during the day and in the evening. Need-based partial scholarships for child care are available. Contact the center for information and an application. www.aacc.edu/cdc

Student Achievement and Success Program (SASP)

The Student Achievement and Success Program is a support and retention program at Anne Arundel Community College designed to increase the academic success, retention, graduation and transfer of students who traditionally may have more barriers and challenges to overcome in order to realize their goals. In addition, these students are traditionally first generation students, low income, under prepared and minority students. Services provided included incentive scholarships up to $1,000 an academic year, walk-in tutoring, life skill/study strategy workshops, and cultural activities, campus visits, informal interactions with faculty/staff and academic monitoring. The specific programs of the Student Achievement and Success Program are:

- First Year Experience
- Summer Bridge
- Adelante Bridge Program
- Black Male Initiative

You can join SASP if you meet any (1 or more) of the following criteria:

- Your parents do not have a bachelors degree
- AACC requires you to take at least one developmental class
- Your FAFSA shows you qualify for financial aid
- You belong to a minority group

Additional information can be found at www.aacc.edu/sasp

Military/Veteran Support Services

Military/Veteran Support Services provides AACC wide transition assistance and support for all AACC active duty military, veterans, guard, reserve and dependents with emphasis on academics, career, and life skills to support the academic success, transfer and graduation of military and veteran students. The Military/Veterans Retention Advisor facilitates the development of an educational plan, monitors and documents academic progress, completes follow-up contacts, and makes referrals for other student support services, such as the Veterans Resource Center and community resources specific to Military/Veteran student needs.

Additional information can be found at www.aacc.edu/military/

The Sarbanes Center

The Sarbanes Center helps students gain real world experience. The Center connects students with the community. Activities with government agencies, schools, businesses and nonprofit organizations are designed to be mutually beneficial, and a win-win for all.

Sarbanes Center programs include:
- Center for Learning through Service
- Center for the Study of Local Issues (CSLI)
- Institute for the Future (IF @ AACC)
- Internship Office
- Office of Travel Study and Global Engagement

Some classes require service learning and the Sarbanes Center can provide support for course-related projects.

Additional information can be found at www.aacc.edu/sarbanescenter

Library Services

The Andrew G. Truxal Library supplements classroom instruction with additional resources. Students are encouraged to use library services to reach their full academic potential in each course. The Library has a collection of over 150,000 books, 202,000 electronic books, 6,000 print and electronic periodicals, and 9,000 audiovisual items selected to meet the needs of our students. The Library maintains the audiovisual (AV) collection of CD, DVD, audiobook, and videocassette materials on a wide variety of topics and makes new purchases based on the college community's educational needs.

Students can access the library catalog, databases and services by going to the library on the Arnold campus or off campus using their student ID. For more information go to www.aacc.edu/library

Tutorials

Truxal Library offers several online Tutorials and Tutors to help you become more acquainted with our resources and services and to teach you information retrieval skills.

General Library Tutorial - a 15-30 minute tutorial on all aspects of the library. You will receive a 'Certificate of Completion' at the end of the tutorial, which you may wish to print as proof of completion (HINT: many instructors assign this tutorial as homework).

Discipline-specific Web Tutors - these 30-minute tutors are designed to help you become proficient at evaluating information sources retrieved from the Internet in selected discipline areas. The following discipline web tutors are available at www.aacc.edu/library
> Green Architecture
> History
> Science
> Social Sciences

Research Support

The Truxal Library provides both online and in person support to students conducting research. A research guide is available that offers information on each of the following steps of the research process:

1. Select a general topic
2. Develop search vocabulary
3. Find background information
4. Narrow or broaden the topic
5. Focus your research
6. Find current and specific information: Library databases
7. Find detailed and historical information: Library catalog
8. Find current and specific information: The Internet
9. Cite sources

Research assistance is also available at the reference desk in the Truxal Library or through the Virtual Writing Center. The Virtual Writing Center allows students to make an appointment with a Truxal Reference Librarian for help with finding, evaluating, and citing sources (MLA or APA form). Additional information can be found at www.aacc.edu/writingcenter

Student Engagement

The Office of Student Engagement encourages students to engage in learning by providing opportunities that allow for growth and development within and beyond the classroom setting. The office promotes engaged learning and assists students with connecting to college resources and programs including student activities, student organization development, leadership development, new student programs, service learning, diversity and multicultural education. The Office of Student Engagement also partners with faculty members to develop strategies and projects that promote student engagement.

The Office of Student Engagement services include:
- Advising the Student Association, Campus Activities Board, and all clubs and organizations
- Facilitating New Student Orientation.
- Facilitating the Leadership Challenge Program.
- Providing a food pantry for students in need
- Providing free passes to the MD Science Center and National Aquarium (by reservation)
- Providing discounted tickets to Bow Tie Cinema, Cinemark Theatre, and Regal Cinema
- Coordinating and planning events for the college community
- Developing publications such as the Student Handbook, Student Engagement Newsletter, and Student Planners.
- Providing information to students such as housing opportunities.
- Facilitating Connect U

The Office of Student Engagement offers the Connect U program to connect a new student with a returning student. The returning student can help answer questions about the college for the new student. The new student will also receive invitations to all of the special campus events.

Passport To Success Program

All new students received a Passport to Success card at their orientation session. Passes can also be obtained in the Office of Student Engagement. The program is designed to encourage new students to get involved in activities that will support their success. The student completes the following activities to be eligible for prizes.
- Attend a New Student Orientation.
- Attend a Welcome Week Activity.
- Attend a Pathways to Success Workshop.
- Pick up a student discount card.
- Get a student ID at the bookstore.
- Complete a Degree Map with an advisor.

For more information, visit www.aacc.edu/studentengagement

Clubs and Organizations

Student Association
Campus Activities Board
American Sign Language
Architecture
Art Association
Arundel Fund Investment Club
Astronomy
Biology and Environmental
    Science
Ceramics-Keramos Society
Chemistry Club
Criminal Justice
Center for the Study of Local
    Issues
Cyber Security Club

Student Education Association
    (SEA)
Economics Club
Engineering
Entrepreneurs Club
Epsilon Chi Honor Society
Game Development Club
Graphic Arts & Design Club
HCAT Chefs Club
Health and Wellness Club
History
Human Services
Interior Design -A.S.I.D.
Japanese Language Club
Mathematics Club

Medical Lab Technician
National Kitchen and Bath
    Association
Paralegal
Philosophy Club
Phi Theta Kappa Honor Society
Photography
Physical Therapist Assistant
Physician Assistant
Printmaking
Psychology and Psi Beta
Radiological Technology
Sculpture Spanish Club

Performing Groups

Concert Band
Concert Choir
Symphony Orchestra

Dance Company
Jazz Band

Opera
The Theatre at AACC

Recreational Groups

Adventure Society

Arundel Gaming Association

Communications Groups

Amaranth Literary Magazine

Campus Current

Special Interest Groups

Amateur Radio Club
Arabic Club
Black Student Union
Cru Hip Hop Dance Club
International Students
    Association
Maryland Defense Force
NexGen Students Talking About
    Tobacco
To Write Love on Her Arms

Anime Club
Athletic Club
Bonsai Club
Enclave
Improvisational Music
    Committee
Gay/Straight Alliance
Meditation Club
SPEAR Student United Way
World Music Club

Apostolic Campus Ministry
Baptist Campus Ministry
Circle K
Hands of Harmony Club
Improvisational Society
Latino Club
Muslim Student Association
Student Veterans Association
Students Organized for Disability
    Awareness

Athletic Teams

Men's Baseball
Women's Cross Country
Women's Lacrosse
Women's Softball

Men's Basketball
Men's Golf
Men's Soccer
Women's Volleyball

Women's Basketball
Men's Lacrosse
Women's Soccer

MyAACC Information

MyAACC is AACC's Web Portal for students. If you are a new student, you must activate your MyAACC portal and college computer accounts to use college computers, access the learning management system to view courses and course materials, check college email, view grades and more. You must use your AACC ID# to complete the College Account Request Form. Once the form is processed, you will receive an email and information on how to login and use the Password Management Tool. Additional information on this process can be found at www.aacc.edu/myaacc/help

You can access MyAACC from the tab at the top right of the college main page (www.aacc.edu) or directly at https://portal.aacc.edu

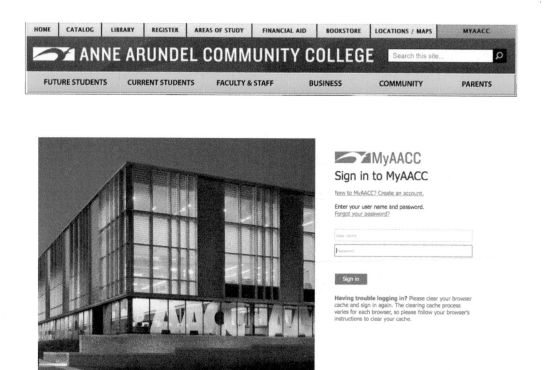

Student Tab

The Student tab provides access to information regarding quick links to frequently used services, campus announcements, help topics, student email and class access.

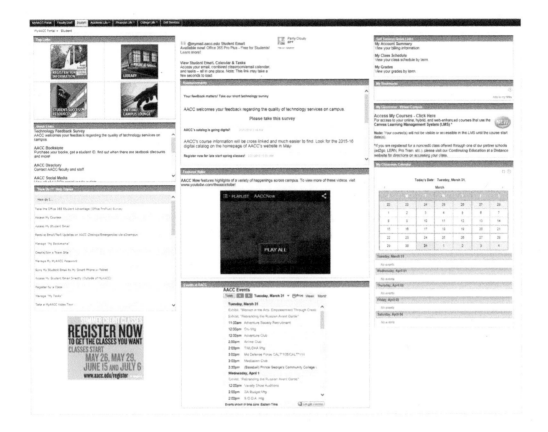

Students have the ability to access their email through MS Office 365 by clicking on the message following the envelope icon, on the Student tab. MS Office 365 is the student email interface. The functions of your AACC email account are similar to other kinds of email such as Hotmail, Gmail, Yahoo, etc. Your email address is your AACC username and the college's student email domain name @mymail.aacc.edu . For example, Joe C Bob would have the email address, jcbob@mymail.aacc.edu. Students can set up their college emails to be forwarded to a personal email account.

Canvas

Canvas is the learning management system used to deliver all credit (and some non-credit) online, hybrid, and web-enhanced courses.

Online courses start and end according to the published schedule of classes. The syllabus, instructional materials, and assignments are posted within the course site. Learner-learner and learner-faculty interactions take place online. Learners submit assignments electronically according to due dates established by the instructor; learners may, however, be required to take exams or assessments at a testing center or in a proctored setting. This should be noted in the course syllabus and students who have concerns about this should communicate them to the instructor within the first day of the course in case it becomes necessary to drop the course in a timely manner. For more information on AACC's online courses and to determine if you are ready for online learning, got to www.aacc.edu/vitualcampus

Hybrid courses combine the learning formats of in-class instruction and convenient, online computer-based learning, resulting in a reduction of the amount of time spent in the classroom. Students registered in hybrid courses must attend required campus meetings, as printed in the AACC Schedule of Credit Classes. Students should access the online portion of the course on the course start date.

Web-enhanced courses meet on campus according to the schedule published in AACC's Schedule of Classes. Selected tools and features of a learning management system are used to supplement and/or expand on-campus instruction and activities.

Access your courses in Canvas by logging into the college portal, MyAACC. Next click on the link "Access my courses" under the "My Classroom – Virtual Campus" web part (located on the right side of the page).

My Classroom - Virtual Campus

Access My Courses - Click Here
For access to your online, hybrid, and web-enhanced courses that use the **Canvas Learning Management System (LMS).***

NEW

The Dashboard is the first thing you will see when you access Canvas. The Dashboard helps you see what is happening in all your courses and allows you to figure out what to do next. You will navigate to your course(s) using the Dashboard. Select the course you want to open by hovering over the Courses* link on the Global Navigation bar.

Introduction

Congratulations and welcome! We applaud your decision to continue your education. You've made it to college, also known as "higher education," where you'll be learning and thinking at a higher level than you did in high school and work situations. You're about to begin a new and exciting journey in your life, joining approximately 12 million students who are now enrolled at more than 1,000 community colleges in the United States today. America's community college system embodies the nation's ideal of equal educational opportunity for all people, regardless of their age, gender, race, ethnicity, prior educational history, family history, or family income. Community colleges in the United States represent the most diverse system of college education in the world. (See Snapshot Summary I.1 for a list of community college students in America today.)

It's probably safe to say that after your college experience, you'll never again be a member of an organization or community with as many resources and services that are intentionally designed to promote your learning, development, and success. Your time in college has the potential to be the most enriching experience of your life. If you capitalize on the numerous resources available to you and use effective college-going strategies (such as those suggested in this book), you can create an experience that will transform your life.

Snapshot Summary

I.1 Student Diversity in America's Community Colleges

- There are 13 million students currently enrolled in approximately 1,150 community colleges in the United States; they account for almost half of all first-year college students in America today.
- More than 630,000 community college students will earn an associate degree this year, and more than 425,000 will earn a certificate.
- Most first-year community college students are employed either part or full time and attend college part time.
- The average age of the American community college student is 28.
- Almost 42 percent of all community college students are the first in their family to attend college.
- More than 37 percent of community college students are members of minority racial or ethnic groups.

- Close to 6 percent of international students attend America's community colleges.

Source: American Association of Community Colleges (2012).

There are two other groups of students that are growing in number and adding to the student diversity found in America's community colleges:

- Veterans returning from the war in the Middle East who have been afforded the opportunity to attend college with the help of generous financial aid provided by a GI Bill passed in 2009.
- Displaced workers over the age of 20 who have lost full-time jobs due to job layoffs and company closings triggered by the current economic recession.

Personal Experience

There are some challenges us vets do face when we get out and go to college. There is that natural gap in maturity [between] the regular college student versus the veteran student. While some students come in late on a regular basis, veteran students are often early to class. Also some students talk during a lecture, while a veteran student gives the instructor the utmost attention. But these are things that are drilled into our heads being raised in the military. Things like loyalty, respect, and integrity.

— *Veteran student*

"The scariest thing for me to have done was to get out [of the military] and not have a plan. I firmly believe that you have to plan for success. Success doesn't just happen; you have to work for it."

—First-year veteran student

Personal Experience

Many of these new students [displaced workers] feel that going back to school was the best thing that they have ever done. They feel better about themselves because of the daily challenges, making contacts and developing new relationships with classmates, and the thrill of learning helps them to believe in themselves and feel successful. I hear these comments: "This is a wonderful opportunity for me." "I realized what was important to me." "I've wanted to go back to school for a long time."

— *Community college counselor*

"I am very impressed by the displaced workers who are returning to school. While one would expect the workers to be down and depressed, most of them are viewing this as an opportunity to pursue an opportunity [and] a dream delayed."

—Community college counselor

Ready for take off,
On my adventure today,
As I take a seat in my chair
And clear the way.
Eager people around,
With destinations to go,
As a woman at the front says,
"Please find a seat in any
     row."
Some people are anxious,
Waiting to take flight,
To soar above the rest
With aspirations in sight
Our first day of college,
A chance to start anew,
To find out who we are,
And learn what is true.

—"Waiting to Take Flight," a poem by Kimberly Castaneda, first-year student

Your previous enrollment in school was required; however, your decision to continue your education in college is entirely your choice. You have made a choice that will improve the quality of your life for the remainder of your life. (See **Snapshot Summary I.1** for a list of the multiple lifetime benefits of a college education and college degree.)

Think About It — Journal Entry **I.1**

1. How did you feel on your first day of college?

    _____

    _____

    _____

    _____

2. Why did you feel this way?

    _____

    _____

    _____

    _____

Snapshot Summary

1.2   Why College Is Worth It: The Economic and Personal Benefits of a College Education

Less than 30 percent of Americans have earned a four-year college degree (U.S. Census Bureau). When individuals who attend college are compared with people from similar social and economic backgrounds who did not continue their education beyond high school, research reveals that college is well worth the investment. College graduates experience multiple benefits, such as those summarized in the following list:

1. **Career Benefits**
   - Security and stability—lower rates of unemployment
   - Versatility and mobility—more flexibility to move out of a position and into other positions
   - Advancement—more opportunity to move up to higher professional positions
   - Interest—more likely to find their work stimulating and challenging
   - Autonomy—greater independence and opportunity to be their own boss
   - Satisfaction—more enjoyment of their work and the feeling that it allows them to use their special talents
   - Prestige—higher-status positions (i.e., careers that are more socially desirable and respected)

"A bachelor's degree continues to be a primary vehicle of which one gains an advantaged socioeconomic position in American society."

—Ernest Pascarella and Patrick Terenzini, *How College Affects Students*

2. **Economic Advantages**
   - Make better consumer choices and decisions
   - Make wiser long-term investments
   - Receive greater pension benefits
   - Earn higher income

The gap between the earnings of high school graduates and those of college graduates is growing. Individuals with a bachelor's (or baccalaureate) degree now earn an average annual salary of about $50,000 per year, which is 40 percent higher than that of high school graduates, whose average salary is less than $30,000 per year. When these differences are calculated over a lifetime, families headed by people with a bachelor's degree take in about $1.6 million more than families headed by people with a high school diploma.

"I am coming from a household that does not have a high standard of living—I want to do better than just getting by."

—First-year student (Franklin, 2002)

"If you think education is expensive, try ignorance."

—Derek Bok, former president of Harvard University

3. **Advanced Intellectual Skills**
   - Greater knowledge
   - More effective problem-solving skills
   - Better ability to deal with complex and ambiguous (uncertain) problems
   - Greater openness to new ideas
   - More advanced levels of moral reasoning
   - Clearer sense of self-identity and greater awareness and knowledge of personal talents, interests, values, and needs
   - Greater likelihood to continue learning throughout life

4. **Better Physical Health**
   - Better health insurance—more comprehensive coverage and greater likelihood of being covered
   - Better dietary habits
   - More regular exercise
   - Lower rates of obesity
   - Longer and healthier life

5. **Social Benefits**
   - Higher social self-confidence
   - Better understanding and more effective communication with others
   - Greater popularity
   - More effective leadership skills
   - Greater marital satisfaction

Student Perspective

"I noticed before when I wasn't going to college, they [my family] didn't look at me as highly as a person. But now since I have started college, everybody is lifting me up and saying how proud they [are] of me."

—First-year student (Franklin, 2002)

6. **Emotional Benefits**
   - Lower levels of anxiety
   - Higher levels of self-esteem
   - Greater sense of self-efficacy and belief that they have more influence and control over their lives
   - Higher levels of psychological well-being
   - Higher levels of personal happiness

7. **Effective Citizenship**
   - Greater interest in national issues, both social and political
   - Greater knowledge of current affairs
   - Higher voting participation rates
   - Higher rates of participation in civic affairs and community service

(continued)

8. **Higher Quality of Life for Their Children**
   - Less likelihood of smoking during pregnancy
   - Better health care for their children
   - More time spent with their children
   - More likely to involve their children in educational activities that stimulate their mental development

- More likely to save money for their children to go to college
- More likely that their children will graduate from college
- More likely that their children will attain high-status and higher-paying careers

Student *Perspective*

"My 3-month-old boy is very important to me, and it is important that I graduate from college so my son, as well as I, live a better life."

—First-year student responding to the question "What is most important to you?"

Student *Perspective*

"Being a first-generation college student, seeing how hard my parents worked these past 18 years to give all that they can to get me to where I am now, I feel I cannot let them down. It is my responsibility to succeed in school and life and to take care of them in their old age."

—First-year college student (Nunez, 2005)

Sources: Astin (1993); Bowen (1977, 1997); College Board (2006); Dee (2004); Feldman & Newcomb (1969/1994); Pascarella & Terenzini (1991, 2005); Tomasho (2009); U.S. Census Bureau (2008).

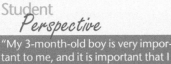

Think About It ———————— *Journal Entry* 1.2

1. Why have you decided to attend college?

   So I can get my associates degree, without the "big college" experience and expense.

2. Why are you are attending the college you're enrolled in now?

   Proximity and so I can earn college credits while Im still in high school.

The Importance of the First Year of College

Your movement into higher education represents an important life transition. Somewhat like an immigrant moving to a new country, you're moving into a new culture with different expectations, regulations, customs, and language (Chaskes, 1996). (See the Glossary and Learning the Language of Higher Education: A Dictionary of College Vocabulary at the end of this book for translations of the new language that is used in the college culture.)

The first year of college is undoubtedly the most important year of the college experience because it's a stage of *transition.* During the first year of college, students report the most change, the most learning, and the most development (Doyle, Edison, & Pascarella, 1998; Flowers, Osterlind, Pascarella, & Pierson, 2001; Light, 2001). Other research suggests that the academic habits students establish in their first year of college are likely to persist throughout their remaining years of college (Schilling, 2001). When graduating seniors look back at their college experience, many of them say that the first year was the time of greatest change and the time during which they made the most significant improvements in their approach to learning. Here is how one senior put it during a personal interview (Chickering & Schlossberg, 1998, p. 47):

Interviewer: What have you learned about your approach to learning [in college]?

Student: I had to learn how to study. I got to the university and there was no structure. No one checked my homework. No one took attendance to make sure I was in class. No one told me I had to do something. There were no quizzes on the readings. I did not work well with this lack of structure. It took my first year and a half to learn to deal with it. But I had to teach myself to manage my time. I had to teach myself how to study. I had to teach myself how to learn in a different environment.

In many ways, the first-year experience in college is similar to surfing or downhill skiing; it can be filled with many exciting thrills, but there's also a risk of taking some dangerous spills. The first year is also the stage of the college experience during which students experience the most stress, the most academic difficulties, and the highest withdrawal rate (American College Testing, 2009; Bartlett, 2002; Sax, Bryant, & Gilmartin, 2004). The goal of surfing and downhill skiing is to experience the thrills, avoid the spills, and finish the run while you're still standing. The same is true for the first year of college; studies show that if you can complete your first-year experience in good standing, your chances for successfully completing college improve dramatically (American College Testing, 2009).

In a nutshell, your college success will depend on taking advantage of what your college does to help you and what you do to help yourself. You'll find that the research cited and the advice provided in this book point to one major conclusion: Success in college depends on *you*—you make it happen by what you do and how well you capitalize on resources available to you.

After reviewing 40 years of research on how college affects students, two distinguished researchers (Pascarella & Terenzini, 2005, p. 602) concluded the following:

The impact of college is largely determined by individual effort and involvement in the academic, interpersonal, and extracurricular [cocurricular] offerings on a campus. Students are not passive recipients of institutional efforts to "educate" or "change" them, but rather bear major responsibility for any gains they derive from their postsecondary [college] experience.

"What students do during college counts more than who they are or where they go to college."

—George Kuh et al., *Student Success in College* (2005)

Compared to your previous schooling, college will provide you with a broader range of courses, more resources to capitalize on, more freedom of choice, and more decision-making opportunities. Your own college experience will differ from that of any other college student because you have the freedom to actively shape or create it in a way that is uniquely your own. Don't let college happen *to* you; make it happen *for* you—take charge of your college experience and take advantage of the college resources that are at your command.

"Some people make things happen, while others watch things happen or wonder what has happened."

—Author unknown

Think About It ———————————— *Journal Entry* **1.3**

To succeed in college, what do you think you'll have to do differently from what you've done in the past?

_____

_____

_____

_____

_____

_____

Importance of a Student Success Course (a.k.a. First-Year Experience Course)

If you're reading this book, you are already beginning to take charge of your college experience because you are probably enrolled in a course that's designed to promote your college success. Research strongly indicates that new students who participate in student success courses (such as the one that's using this text) are more likely to stay in college, complete their degrees, and achieve higher grades. These positive effects have been found for:

Student
Perspective

"Every first-semester freshman needs a class like this—whether they think so or not."

—First-year student evaluating a first-year seminar (college success course)

- all types of students (underprepared and well prepared, minority and majority, residential and commuter, male and female);
- students at all types of colleges (two- and four-year, public and private);
- students attending colleges of different sizes (small, midsized, and large); and
- students attending colleges in different locations (urban, suburban, and rural).

Sources: Barefoot, Warnock, Dickinson, Richardson, & Roberts (1998); Boudreau & Kromrey (1994); Cuseo & Barefoot (1996); Fidler & Godwin (1994); Glass & Garrett (1995); Grunder & Hellmich (1996); Hunter & Linder (2005); Porter & Swing (2006); Shanley & Witten (1990); Sidle & McReynolds (1999); Starke, Harth, & Sirianni (2001); Thomson (1998); Tobolowski (2005).

"I am now one of the peer counselors on campus, and without this class my first semester, I don't think I could have done as well, and by participating in this class again (as a teaching assistant), it reinforced this belief."

—First-year student evaluating a first-year seminar (college success course)

There has been more carefully conducted research on student success and college success courses, and more evidence supporting their effectiveness for promoting success, than for any other type of course in the college curriculum. You're fortunate to be enrolled in this course, so give it your best effort and take full advantage of what it has to offer. If you do, you'll be taking an important first step toward thriving in community college and beyond.

Enjoy the trip!

Introduction Reflection

After reading the Introduction, how do you feel this course can benefit you?

List and explain three things you hope to learn or accomplish as a result of successfully completing this course.

1.

2.

3.

The Game Plan

Appropriate Online and In-Class Behavior

| THOUGHT STARTER | *Journal Entry* **1.1** | LEARNING GOAL |

LEARNING GOAL

To equip you with a set of fundamental skills that all college students need to get off to a fast and good start in college and that will ease your adjustment to college.

1. What are the differences between college and high school?

_____

_____

_____

_____

2. What tools do you have that will help you succeed in college? Explain.

_____

_____

_____

_____

_____

Think About It ———————————————— *Journal Entry* **1.2** ✳

Look at the list of differences between high school and college in Snapshot Summary 1.1. Which differences were you most unaware of or most surprised to see?

- the academic year is divided into quarters
- You have to study 2-3 hours/1hour in class

_____

_____

_____

(continued)

From *Thriving in the Community College & Beyond*, Second Edition by Joseph B. Cuseo, Aaron Thompson, Julie A. McLaughlin, and Steady H. Moono. Copyright © 2013 by Kendall Hunt Publishing Company. Reprinted by permission.

Why?

_____

_____

_____

_____

_____

_____

_____

Snapshot Summary

1.1 Birds of a Different Feather: High School vs. College

High School	College
Your classes are mostly arranged for you.	You arrange your own schedule in consultation with your advisor. Schedules tend to look lighter than they really are.
Your time is structured by others.	You manage your own time.
You go from one class directly to another, spending six hours per day—30 hours per week—in class.	You have free time between classes; class times vary throughout the day and evening; and you spend 12–16 hours each week in class if you are a full-time student.
The school year is 36 weeks long; some classes extend over both semesters, and some do not.	The academic year may be divided into separate semesters or quarters.
Teachers monitor class attendance.	Professors may not formally monitor class attendance; you're expected to have the self-discipline to show up and get down information that's presented in class.
Teachers often write information on the board for you to put in your notes.	Professors may lecture nonstop, expecting you to identify and write down important information in your notes. Notes that professors write on the board are used to supplement or complement the lecture, not to summarize or substitute for the lecture.
Teachers provide you with information you missed when you were absent.	Professors expect you to get information you missed from classmates.
You are given short reading assignments that are then discussed, and often reviewed, in class.	You're assigned substantial amounts of reading and writing that may not be directly addressed in class.
You seldom need to read anything more than once, and sometimes listening in class is enough.	You need to review class notes and read material regularly.
Teachers present material to help you understand the textbook.	Professors may not follow the textbook, but you may be expected to relate class sessions to textbook readings.

You may have studied outside of class for zero to two hours per week.

You need to study for at least two to three hours outside of class for each hour spent in class.

Teachers remind you of assignments and due dates.

Professors expect you to consult the course syllabus for assignments and deadlines.

Source: Southern Methodist University (2006).

Think About It ——   *Journal Entry* **1.3**

1. How do you think college will be different from high school?

_____

_____

_____

_____

_____

2. What do you think it will take to be successful in college? (What personal characteristics, qualities, or strategies do you feel are most important for college success?)

_____

_____

_____

_____

_____

3. How well do you expect to do in your first term of college? Why?

_____

_____

_____

_____

_____

Time Spent in Class

Since the total amount of time you spend on learning is associated with how much you learn and how successfully you learn, this association leads to a straightforward recommendation: Attend all class sessions in all your courses. It may be tempting to skip or cut classes because college professors are less likely to monitor your attendance or take roll than your teachers were in high school. However, don't let this new freedom fool you into thinking that missing classes will have no effect on your grades. Over the past 75 years, many research studies in many types of courses have shown a direct relationship between class attendance and course grades—as one goes up or down, so does the other (Anderson & Gates, 2002; Devadoss & Foltz, 1996; Grandpre, 2000; Launius, 1997; Moore, 2003, 2006; Moore, et al., 2003; Shimoff & Catania, 2001; Wiley, 1992; Wyatt, 1992). Figure 1.1 represents the results of a study conducted at the City Colleges of Chicago, which shows the relationship between students' class attendance during the first five weeks of the term and their final course grades.

FIGURE 1.1

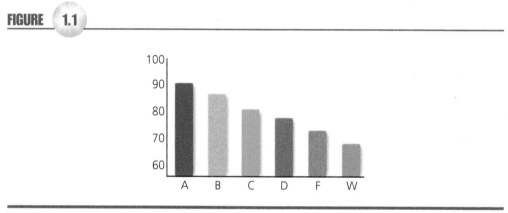

Percentage of Classes Attended and Final Course Grades

Time Spent on Coursework outside the Classroom

You will spend fewer hours per week sitting in class in college than you did in high school. However, you will be expected to spend more time on your own on academic work. Studies clearly show that when college students spend more time on academic work outside of class, the result is better learning and higher grades. For example, one study of more than 25,000 college students found that the percentage of students receiving mostly A grades was almost three times higher for students who spent 40 or more hours per week on academic work than it was for students who spent between 20 and 40 hours. Among students who spent 20 or fewer hours per week on academic work, the percentage receiving grades that were mostly Cs or below was almost twice as high as it was for students who spent 40 or more hours on academic work (Pace, 1990a, 1990b).

Unfortunately, less than 40 percent of beginning college students report having studied for six or more hours per week during their final year in high school (Pryor et al., 2012), only one-third expect to spend more than 20 hours per week preparing for class in college (National Survey of Student Engagement, 2009), and less than 10% say they will study at least two hours out of class for every hour spent in class—which is what most college faculty believe is necessary to do well in college (Kuh, 2005). This has to change if new college students are to earn good grades. Just as successful athletes need to put in time and often work hard to improve their physical performance, successful students need to do the same to improve their academic performance.

Think About It ——————————————— *Journal Entry* **1.4**

How are you going to make sure you have the time needed to study in college?

I'm going to use the Study Time Calculator™ to help me stay on track.

If you need further motivation to achieve good grades, keep in mind that higher grades during college result in higher chances of career success after college. Research on college graduates indicates that the higher their college grades, the higher:

- The status (prestige) of their first job;
- Their job mobility (ability to change jobs or move into different positions); and
- Their total earnings (salary).

The more you learn, the more you'll earn. This relationship between college grades and career success exists for students at all types of colleges and universities regardless of the reputation or prestige of the institution that the students are attending (Pascarella & Terenzini, 1991, 2005). In other words, how well you do academically in college matters more to your career success than where you go to college and what institutional name appears on your diploma.

Student
Perspective

"In high school, you were a dork if you got good grades and cared about what was going on in your class. In college, you're a dork if you don't."

—College sophomore (Appleby, 2008)

Think About It ——————————— *Journal Entry* 1.5

In high school, how many hours per week did you spend on schoolwork outside of class during your senior year? What do you think you will need to do differently in college?

I'm a senior in HS, but at AACC
I spend around 6-7 hours on
school work per day.

Author's Experience

When I went to college, I had to work to assist my family and to assist in paying for college. Although I was an 18-year-old, I came from a very poor family and it was part of my obligation to assist them financially, while it was more important for me to go to school and graduate so I could have a higher standard of living in comparison to my mother and father. Juggling my work life and school life quickly became a reality to which I had to adjust. Thus, I made sure I made the time to study and attend class as my first priority and worked with my employer to adjust my work hours around my classes. By placing my future above my immediate present, I was able to get my college degree and increase my earnings substantially beyond the earnings I had in college and way beyond my parents' earnings.

———— Aaron Thompson

Classroom Basics (or Fundamentals)

You are now in college and there will be expectations for appropriate behavior both in and out of the classroom. Depending on what kind of course (traditional face-to-face, online, technology-enhanced, or hybrid) you are taking, there will be different expectations for which you are held responsible. Other than a few exceptions (i.e., you can wear pajamas in your house to do an online course but you should not in class), most of the following expectations apply to all.

Snapshot Summary

1.2 Types of Classrooms

Traditional (face-to-face) instruction classrooms offer students and instructors an opportunity to see each other and have interaction. This kind of classroom setting and experience enhances the opportunity for collaborative and social learning.

Technology-enhanced courses use traditional (face-to-face) instruction but also use some Web-based learning tool (i.e., Blackboard) to enhance the course. You are expected to attend all class sessions and also to check the course Web site regularly. You may even be required to do some of your assignments through the course Web site.

Online courses are designed to bring campus-based classes to students' computers. The instructor provides information posted on a course Web site that guides the student through course content, prompts discussions, and helps students keep pace with assignments. Online courses offer flexibility for many working adults; they can offer an accelerated opportunity to a certificate and/or degree. However, they provide less face-to-face social interaction and fewer degree options in comparison to traditional face-to-face classrooms. You will need to pay special attention to when assignments are due and where to turn them in for the instructor's review. In addition, you may have to go to a central location to take proctored exams or do other assessments (e.g., placement tests). Students who are not disciplined often struggle in online courses. These courses are not as easy as many commercials make them out to be. Sometimes an online class can be more difficult than a traditional course.

Web-hybrid (blended) courses blend on-campus instruction with Web-based instruction. Students meet on campus according to the published schedule of classes with approximately half of the course instruction and/or activities occurring online. The hybrid classroom incorporates characteristics from both the traditional and the online classroom: hybrid classrooms have access to the Internet in order to enhance the learning process. Students have the benefit of having face-to-face interactions along with having assignments available to them online at any time. Web-hybrid courses create flexible learning options while allowing students to meet face-to-face with instructors and other students.

Source: http://www.csmd.edu/OnlineLearning/WhatisOnlineLearning.htm

No matter how you take your classes, the first day of class is often the most important and is full of hustle and bustle. There are students of all ages, ethnicities, races, and genders walking with backpacks and energy drinks, looking for their classrooms, or sitting down in front of the computer. Most of these students will be like you, full of newfound curiosities and apprehensions. Questions are being asked of new faces and soon new friends. When you find your classroom (in person or virtually), hopefully the first person you sit next to will become a new friend or study partner. Here you go on your college trip, so please enjoy the ride!

Classroom Top Strategies

1. **Adopt a seating location that maximizes your focus of attention and minimizes sources of distraction.** Many years of research show that students who sit in the front and center of class tend to earn higher exam scores and course grades (Benedict & Hoag, 2004; Rennels & Chaudhair, 1988; Tagliacollo, Volpato, & Pereira, 2010). These results are found even when students are assigned seats by their instructor, so it's not just a matter of more motivated and studious students tending to sit in the front of the room: instead, the better academic performance achieved by students sitting in the front and center of the room likely results from a learning advantage provided by this seating location. Front-and-center seating benefits students' academic performance by improving their vision of

material written on the board or screen and their ability to hear the instructor's lectures. In addition, this seating position allows for better eye contact with the instructor, which can increase students' level of attention, reduce their feeling of anonymity, and heighten their sense of involvement in the classroom. Sitting in the front of class can also reduce your level of anxiety about speaking up in class because, when you speak, you will not have numerous classmates sitting in front of you turning around to look at you while you speak.

2. **Sit by people who will enable (not disable) your ability to learn.** Intentionally sit near classmates who will not distract you or interfere with the quality of your note taking. Attention comes in degrees or amounts; you can give all of your attention or part of it to whatever task you're performing. Trying to grasp complex information in class is a task that demands your undivided attention.

3. **Adopt a seating posture that screams attention.** Sitting upright and leaning forward increases your attention because these bodily signals will reach your brain and increase mental alertness. If your body is in an alert and ready position, your mind tends to pick up these physical cues and follow your body's lead by also becoming alert and ready (to learn). Just as baseball players assume a ready position in the field before a pitch is delivered to put their bodies in position to catch batted balls, learners who assume a ready position in the classroom put themselves in a better position to catch ideas batted around in the classroom. Studies show that when humans are mentally alert and ready to learn, greater amounts of the brain chemical C-kinase are released at the connection points between brain cells, which increases the likelihood that a learning connection will form between them (Howard, 2000).

There's another advantage to being attentive in class: you send a clear message to your instructor that you're a conscientious and courteous student. This can influence your instructor's perception and evaluation of your academic performance, which can earn you the benefit of the doubt at the end of the term if you're on the border between a lower and higher course grade.

Expectations: Classroom Behavior

Research indicates that one key characteristic of successful learners is that they monitor or watch themselves and maintain self-awareness of the following:

- Whether they are using effective learning strategies. For example, they're aware of their level of attention or concentration in class.
- Whether they comprehend what they are attempting to learn. For example, they're aware of whether they're understanding it at a deep level or merely memorizing it at a surface level.
- How to self-regulate or self-adjust their learning strategies to meet the different demands of different tasks or subjects. For example, when reading technical material in a science textbook, they read more slowly and stop to test their understanding more frequently than when they're reading a novel (Pintrich, 1995; Weinstein, 1994; Weinstein & Meyer, 1991).

For instance, studies show that students who self-monitor their thought processes when solving math and science problems are more effective problem solvers than those who just go through the motions (Resnick, 1986). Effective problem solvers ask themselves such questions as "How did I go about solving this problem correctly?" and "What were the key steps I took to arrive at the correct solution?"

"For success, attitude is equally as important as ability."

—Walter Scott

"Successful students know a lot about themselves."

—Claire Weinstein and Debra Meyer, professors of educational psychology, University of Texas

Snapshot Summary

1.3 Reading and Understanding a Syllabus

What's in a syllabus? A course syllabus is a document created by instructors that will probably be given to you on the first day of class. The syllabus has been called a contract between the student and the instructor. Please pay careful attention to all parts of the syllabus and make a copy to keep with you at all times. You are responsible for adhering to this contract. However, your instructor can change the syllabus as he/she deems necessary. A syllabus usually contains the following components (not necessarily in this order):

1. Course department, prefix, number, title, credit hours, semester and year, and course reference number.
2. Meeting times and location, instructor information (name, office location, office hours, contact information).
3. Catalog course description, including prerequisites and/or corequisites (courses students need to have taken before this one or at the same time); prerequisite skill sets (e.g., programming languages, familiarity with software).
4. Text(s) with dates, supplemental text(s), other required readings, and references readings (books, reserve readings, course readers, software, and supplies with information about where they can be obtained). You are expected to have these on the first day or soon after the first day.
5. Student learning outcomes and/or course objectives (this is what the instructor is telling you that he or she will work the lectures around, and you will have learning opportunities around them throughout the course). The tests, quizzes, papers, etc., are based on these objectives.
6. Skills and knowledge students will gain. These are the new items you will have learned after the course is completed. You may hear these referred to as competencies.

7. Course organization. This tells you step-by-step how this course will be taught.
8. Explanation of the topical organization of the course. This will give you an idea of the specific topics that will be covered in class.
9. Course requirements (what students will have to do in the course: assignments, exams, projects, performances, attendance, participation, etc.). Usually the nature and format of assignments and the expected length of written work, as well as due dates for assignments and dates for exams, will be explained.
10. Evaluation and grading policy: what grades are based on, especially your final grade. Always keep up on what grade you have in class and discuss how to improve it with the instructor on a regular basis.
11. Course policies and expectations: may include policies on attendance, participation, tardiness, academic integrity, missing homework, missed exams, recording classroom activities, food in class, laptop use, cell phone use, etc.
12. Other expectations such as student behavior (e.g., respectful consideration of one another's perspectives, open-mindedness, creative risk-taking).
13. Course calendar/schedule (sometimes the instructor will put "tentative" before these words, letting you know it is subject to change). However, this is a class-to-class breakdown of topics and assignments (readings, homework, project due dates).

As a college student, you are responsible for knowing the contents of the course syllabus. It is not the instructor's responsibility to go over it with you. Be sure you read and understand your syllabi for all your courses. If you have any questions, be sure to ask your instructor right away.

You can begin to establish good self-monitoring habits now by getting into a routine of periodically pausing to reflect on how you're going about learning and how you're "doing" college. For instance, consider these questions:

- Are you listening attentively to what your instructor is saying in class?
- Do you comprehend what you are reading outside of class?
- Are you effectively using campus resources that are designed to support your success?

- Are you interacting with campus professionals who can contribute to your current success and future development?
- Are you interacting and collaborating with peers who can contribute to your learning and increase your level of involvement in the college experience?
- Are you effectively implementing the key success strategies identified in this book?

Inappropriate Classroom Behaviors

The following behaviors indicate to the instructor and to your fellow classmates that you are not as committed to your education as they are. In addition, they create confusion in the classroom and disturb the education process. More specifically, they cut down on your opportunity to learn all that you could.

- Coming in class late and/or leaving early
- Walking in and out of the classroom during class
- Talking with classmates while the instructor is lecturing
- Disregarding the deadlines set by your instructor or study partners
- Interrupting class with electronic devices or other distractions
- Disrespecting your classmates and/or instructor
- Acting uninterested or sleeping during class
- Working on homework during class
- Cheating on tests, quizzes, papers, or other homework

> "Behavior is a mirror in which everyone displays his own image."
>
> —Johann Wolfgang von Goethe

Technology Is for Learning

Guidelines for Civil and Responsible Use of Personal Technology in the College Classroom

Technology as a Partner

- Turn your cell phone completely off or leave it out of the classroom. In the rare case of an emergency when you think you need to leave it on, inform your instructor.
- Don't check your cell phone during the class period by turning it off and on.
- Don't text message during class.
- Don't surf the Web during class.
- Don't touch your cell phone during any exam, because this may be viewed by the instructor as a form of cheating.

Insensitive Use of Personal Technology in the Classroom: A Violation of Civility

Behavior that interferes with the rights of others to learn or teach in the college classroom is a violation of civility. Listed below are behaviors illustrating classroom incivility that involve student use of personal technology. These behaviors are increasing in college, as is the anger of college instructors who witness them, so be sure not to engage in them.

Student Perspectives

"I wasn't sure what this class was about. Now I understand this class and I really like it. I learned a lot about myself."

"In the start of the semester I thought this class would be a waste of time and busy work. But I realized it is an important way of learning who and what you are . . . I underestimated this class."

—Comments made by first-year students when evaluating their first-year experience course

Using Cell Phones

Keeping a cell phone on in class is a clear example of classroom incivility because if it rings, it will interfere with the right of others to learn. In a study of college students who were exposed to a cell phone ringing during a class session and were later tested for their recall of information presented in class, they scored approximately 25 percent worse when attempting to recall information that was presented at the time a cell phone rang. This attention loss occurred even though the material was covered by the professor before the cell phone rang and was projected on a slide during the call. This study also showed that students were further distracted when classmates frantically searched through handbags or pockets to find and silence a ringing (or vibrating) phone (Shelton, Elliot, Eaves, & Exner, 2009). These findings clearly suggest that the civil thing to do is turn your cell phone off before entering the classroom or keep it out of the classroom altogether.

Sending and Receiving Text Messages

Just as answering a cell phone during class is a violation of civility because it interferes with the learning of other members of the classroom community, so too is text messaging. Although messaging is often viewed as a quick and soundless way to communicate, it can momentarily disrupt learning if it takes place when the instructor is covering critical or complex information. Text messaging while driving a car can take your eyes and mind off the road, thereby putting yourself and others in danger. Similarly, messaging in the classroom takes your eyes and mind off the instructor and any visual aids being displayed at the time. It's also discourteous or disrespectful to instructors when you put your head down and turn your attention from them while they're speaking to the class. Finally, it can be distracting or disturbing to classmates who see you messaging instead of listening and learning.

Correct Use of the Internet

There are common rules for the use of the Internet (see Snapshot Summary 1.4), colloquially referred to as *netiquette* [nétti kèt]. These rules hold true for social media sites such as Facebook, LinkedIn, or MySpace.

Plagiarism: A Violation of Academic Integrity

What Is Plagiarism?

Plagiarism is deliberate or unintentional use of someone else's work without acknowledging it, giving the reader the impression that it's your own work.

Various Forms of Plagiarism

1. Submitting an entire paper, or portion thereof, that was written by someone else
2. Copying sections of someone else's work and inserting it into your own work
3. Cutting paragraphs from separate sources and pasting them into the body of your own paper
4. Paraphrasing (rewording) someone else's words or ideas without citing that person as a source; for examples of acceptable paraphrasing versus plagiarism, go to www.princeton.edu/pr/pub/integrity/pages/plagiarism.html

Student *Perspective*

"My intent was not to plagiarize. I realize I was unclear [about] the policy and am actually thankful for now knowing exactly what I can and cannot do on assignments and how to prevent academic dishonesty in the future."

—First-year student's reflection on a plagiarism violation

Snapshot Summary

1.4 Top 20 Rules to Follow for Appropriate Netiquette

1. The Internet is not private. What goes out on the airwaves stays on the airwaves! Do not post pictures to the Internet that you would not want your mom or younger cousin to see.
2. Avoid saying anything that could be interpreted as derogatory (e.g., no cursing).
3. Do not say harsh or mean things to someone over e-mail or text (this could be considered cyber bullying) and do not post nasty, mean, or insulting items about someone.
4. Do not respond to nasty e-mails sent to you.
5. Do not break up with a significant other via text or e-mail.
6. When you receive an e-mail that says to forward it to everyone you know, please don't.
7. Do not use ALL CAPITALS. IT IMPLIES YOU ARE SHOUTING!!!
8. When you send messages online, make sure you proofread and correct mistakes before sending.
9. Do not forward other people's e-mails without their permission.
10. Do not forward virus warnings. They are generally hoaxes.
11. Ask before you send huge attachments.
12. Keep your communications short and to the point.
13. Do not leave the subject field blank in e-mails.
14. Avoid posting personal messages to a listserv.
15. Avoid using texting language for e-mails or social media sites (use correct spellings and correct language mechanics).
16. Remember to treat others online as you would like to be treated.
17. Use the Internet in ways that do not take away from your learning, but add to it.
18. Allow an appropriate amount of time for a person to respond to a message (24–48 business hours).
19. Be sure to have an appropriate salutation (i.e., *good morning, hello*) and closing (i.e., *goodbye, see you tomorrow*, etc.) in your e-mails.
20. Avoid slang (i.e., *wha's up, yo,* etc.) and acronyms (*btw, lol*, etc.)

> "To err is human. To really foul things up requires a computer."
> —Unknown

> "The best thing about the Internet is that it makes everyone a publisher. The worst thing about the Internet is that it makes everyone a publisher."
> —Unknown

Student Perspective

> "When a student violates an academic integrity policy no one wins, even if the person gets away with it. It isn't right to cheat and it is an insult to everyone who put the effort in and did the work, and it cheapens the school for everyone. I learned my lesson and have no intention of ever cheating again."
> —First-year student's reflection on an academic integrity violation

5. Not placing quotation marks around someone else's exact words that appear in the body of your paper
6. Failing to cite the source of factual information included in your paper that's not common knowledge

Note: If the source for information included in your paper is listed at the end of your paper in your reference (works cited) section but is not cited in the body of your paper, this still qualifies as plagiarism.

Sources: Academic Integrity at Princeton (2003); Pennsylvania State University (2005); Purdue University Online Writing Lab (2004).

Think About It ———————————— *Journal Entry* 1.6

Look back at the definition and forms of plagiarism. List any form of plagiarism contained in that box that you were not already aware of.

_____

_____

_____

_____

_____

_____

People with integrity have the courage to admit when they're wrong and when they haven't done what they should have done. They don't play the role of victim and look for something or someone else to blame; they're willing to accept the blame and "take the heat" when they're wrong and to take responsibility for making it right. They feel remorse or guilt when they haven't lived up to their own ethical standards, and they use this guilt productively to motivate them to do what's right in the future.

Summary and Conclusion

Research reviewed in this chapter points to the conclusion that successful students are able to:

1. Understand the differences between high school and college;
2. Understand responsible classroom personal behaviors;
3. Understand the dos and don'ts of Internet usage; and
4. Understand the syllabus and class policies.

Student *Perspective*

"I understood what I did was morally wrong and now I have to overcome it and move on living morally and ethically. It's really amazing that integrity is in everything we do in our lives."

—First-year student's reflection on an academic integrity violation

Learning More through the World Wide Web
Internet-Based Resources for Further Information on Academic Integrity

For additional information related to the ideas discussed in this chapter, we recommend the following Web site:

www.academicintegrity.org/useful_links/index.php

Chapter ① Exercises

1.1 Personal Traits of a Responsible Student

Construct a master list of personal traits you need to be a responsible student.

1. _____

2. _____

3. _____

4. _____

5. _____

1.2 Is It or Is It Not Plagiarism?

Following are four incidents that were actually brought to a judicial review board to determine if plagiarism had occurred and, if so, what the penalty should be. After you read each case, answer the questions listed below it.

Case 1. A student turned in an essay that included substantial material copied from a published source. The student admitted that he didn't cite the sources properly, but argued that it was because he misunderstood the directions, not because he was attempting to steal someone else's ideas.

Is this plagiarism?

How severe is it? (Rate it on a scale from 1 = low to 10 = high)

What should the consequence or penalty be for the student?

How could the suspicion of plagiarism have been avoided in this case?

Case 2. A student turned in a paper that was identical to a paper submitted by another student for a different course.

Is this plagiarism?

How severe is it? (Rate it on a scale from 1 = low to 10 = high)

What should the consequence or penalty be for the student?

How could the suspicion of plagiarism have been avoided in this case?

Case 3. A student submitted a paper he wrote in a previous course as an extra-credit paper for a course.
Is this plagiarism?

How severe is it? (Rate it on a scale from 1 = low to 10 = high)

What should the consequence or penalty be for the student?

How could the suspicion of plagiarism have been avoided in this case?

Case 4. A student submitted a paper in an art history course that contained some ideas from art critics that she read about and whose ideas she agreed with. The student claimed that not citing these critics' ideas wasn't plagiarism because their ideas were merely their own subjective judgments or opinions, not facts or findings, and, furthermore, they were opinions that she agreed with.

Is this plagiarism?

How severe is it? (Rate it on a scale from 1 = low to 10 = high)

What should the consequence or penalty be for the student?

Looking back at these four cases, which of them do you think are the most severe and least severe violations of academic integrity? Why?

Crime and Punishment: Plagiarism and Its Consequences

In an article that appeared in an Ohio newspaper, titled "Plagiarism Persists in Classrooms," an English professor is quoted as saying, "Technology has made it easier to plagiarize because students can download papers and exchange information and papers through their computers. But technology has also made it easier to catch students who plagiarize." This professor's college subscribes to a Web site that matches the content of students' papers with content from books and online sources. Many professors now require students to submit their papers through this Web site. If students are caught plagiarizing, for a first offense, they typically receive an F for the assignment or the course. A second offense can result in dismissal or expulsion from college, which has already happened to a few students.

Source: Mariettatimes.com (March 22, 2006).

Discussion Questions

1. Why do you think students plagiarize? What do you suspect are the primary motives, reasons, or causes?

2. What do you think is a fair or just penalty for those found guilty of a first plagiarism violation? What is fair for those who commit a second violation?

   How do you think plagiarism could be most effectively reduced or prevented from happening in the first place?

Chapter 1 Reflection

List and describe at least five principles discussed in this chapter that you can use to be a successful college student.

1. Be sure to use correct citations

2. Use good "Net equette"

3. Be considerate of others in classroom

4. Sit where there are the least amount of distractions

5. Refer to the Syllabus

Now explain HOW you can put these principles into practice.

I will put the principles into Practice by remembering to use all the campus resources, internet, office hours to clarify my questions. I shall also do my best to be considerate to others and to sit where there are the fewest distractions.

Sam Hernández

Touching All the Bases

An Overview and Preview of the Most Powerful Principles of Community College Success

LEARNING GOAL

To equip you with a set of powerful success strategies that you can use immediately to get off to a fast start in college and use continually throughout your college experience to achieve success.

1. What concerns do you have about starting college?

_____

_____

_____

_____

_____

2. What excites you about starting college?

_____

_____

_____

_____

_____

The Most Powerful Research-Based Principles of Community College Success

Research on human learning and student development indicates four powerful principles of college success:

1. Active involvement
2. Use of campus resources
3. Interpersonal interaction and collaboration
4. Personal reflection and self-awareness (Astin, 1993; Kuh et al., 2005; Light, 2001; Pascarella & Terenzini, 1991, 2005; Tinto, 1993).

FIGURE 2.1

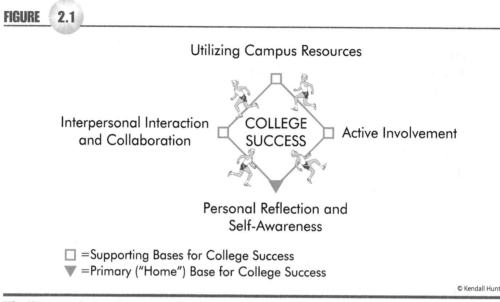

Utilizing Campus Resources

Interpersonal Interaction and Collaboration   COLLEGE SUCCESS   Active Involvement

Personal Reflection and Self-Awareness

□ =Supporting Bases for College Success
▼ =Primary ("Home") Base for College Success

© Kendall Hunt

The Diamond of College Success

These four principles represent the key bases of college success. They are introduced and examined carefully in this chapter for two reasons:

1. You can put them into practice to establish good habits for early success in college.
2. These principles represent the foundational bases for all success strategies recommended throughout this book.

The four bases of college success can be represented visually by a baseball diamond (see Figure 2.1).

Touching the First Base of Community College Success: Active Involvement

Research indicates that active involvement may be the most powerful principle of human learning and college success (Astin, 1993; Kuh, 2005). It could be considered the first base of college success, because if it's not touched or covered, you can't advance to any other base. This principle is the gateway to implementing all other principles of college success. The bottom line is that to maximize your success in college, you cannot be a passive spectator: you need to be an active player in the learning process.

The principle of active involvement includes the following pair of processes:

* The amount of personal time you devote to learning in the college experience
* The degree of personal effort or energy (mental and physical) you put into the learning process

Think of something you do with intensity, passion, and commitment. If you were to approach academic work in the same way, you would be faithfully implementing the principle of active involvement.

"Tell me and I'll listen. Show me and I'll understand. Involve me and I'll learn."
—Teton Lakota Indian saying

Student *Perspective*

"You don't have to be smart to work hard."
—24-year-old first-year student who has returned to college

One way to ensure that you're actively involved in the learning process and putting forth high levels of energy or effort is to *act* on what you are learning. Engage in some physical action with respect to what you're learning. You can engage in any of the following actions to ensure that you are investing a high level of effort and energy:

- **Writing.** Express what you're trying to learn in print.
- Action: Write notes when reading rather than passively underlining sentences.
- **Speaking.** Express what you're trying to learn orally.
- Action: Explain a course concept to a study-group partner rather than just looking over it silently.
- **Organizing.** Group or classify ideas you're learning into logical categories.
  Action: Create an outline, diagram, or concept map to visually connect ideas.

The following section explains how you can apply both components of active involvement—spending time and expending energy—to the major learning challenges that you will encounter in college.

Active Listening and Note Taking

You'll find that college professors rely heavily on the lecture method: they profess their knowledge by speaking for long stretches of time, and the students' job is to listen and take notes on the knowledge they dispense. This method of instruction places great demands on the ability to listen carefully and take notes that are both accurate and complete.

Remember

Research shows that, in all subject areas, most test questions on college exams come from the professor's lectures and that students who take better class notes get better course grades (Brown, 1988; Kiewra, 2000).

The best way to apply the principle of active involvement during a class lecture is to engage in the physical action of writing notes. Writing down what your instructor is saying in class "forces" you to pay closer attention to what is being said and reinforces your retention of what was said. By taking notes, you not only hear the information (auditory memory) but also see it on paper (visual memory) and feel it in the muscles of your hand as you write it (motor memory).

Remember

Your role in the college classroom is not to be a passive spectator or an absorbent sponge that sits back and simply soaks up information through osmosis. Instead, your role is more like that of an aggressive detective or investigative reporter who's on a search-and-record mission. You need to actively search for information by picking your instructor's brain, picking out your instructor's key points, and recording your "pickings" in your notebook. See Do It Now! 2.1 for top strategies on classroom listening and note taking, which you should put into practice immediately. Compared to high school, achieving academic success in college will require you to work harder (by investing more time and energy) and to work smarter (by using more effective learning strategies). Academic success will depend not only on the quantity of your work time, but also on its quality; you need to work hard and you need to work smart—by using effective learning strategies and methods (such as those discussed in this text) that enable you to learn more efficiently and more deeply.

2.1

Top Strategies for Listening and Note Taking

One of the tasks that you will be expected to perform at the start of your first term in college is to take notes in class. Studies show that professors' lecture notes are the number one source of test questions (and test answers) on college exams. So, get off to a fast start by using the following strategies to improve the quality of your note taking:

1. **Get to every class.** Whether or not your instructors take roll, you're still responsible for all material covered in class. Remember that a full load of college courses (12 units) only requires that you be in class for about 12 hours per week. If you consider your classwork to be a full-time job that only requires you to show up for about 12 hours a week, that's a sweet deal, and it's a deal that allows more educational freedom than you had in high school. To miss a session when you're required to spend so little time in class per week is an abuse of your educational freedom. It's also an abuse of the money you pay, your family pays, or taxpaying American citizens pay to support your college education.

2. **Get to every class on time.** The *first few minutes* of a class session often contain valuable information, such as reminders, reviews, and previews. It is also rude and disruptive to come in late.

3. **Get organized.** Arrive at class with the right equipment; get a separate notebook for each class, write your name on it, date each class session, and store all class handouts in it. Bring your textbook, a writing utensil, paper to take notes, and the right attitude.

4. **Get in the right position.**
   - The ideal place to sit—front and center of the room, where you can hear and see most effectively
   - The ideal posture—upright and leaning forward, because your body influences your mind: if your body is in an alert and ready position, your mind is likely to follow
   - The ideal position socially—near people who will not distract you or detract from the quality of your note taking

5. **Get in the right frame of mind.** Get psyched up; come to class with attitude—an attitude that you're going to pick your instructor's brain, pick up answers to test questions, and pick up your grade.

6. **Get it down (in writing).** Actively look, listen, and record important points at all times in class. Pay special attention to whatever information instructors put in writing, whether it is on the board, on a slide, or in a handout.

7. **Don't let go of your pen.** When in doubt, write it out; it's better to have it and not need it than to need it and not have it.

> **Remember**
>
> *Most college professors do not write all important information on the board for you: instead, they expect you to listen carefully to what they're saying and write it down for yourself.*

8. **Finish strong.** The *last few minutes* of class often contain valuable information, such as reminders, reviews, and previews.

9. **Stick around.** As soon as class ends, don't immediately bolt: instead, hang out for a few moments to briefly review your notes (by yourself or with a classmate). If you find any gaps, check them out with your instructor before he or she leaves the classroom. This quick end-of-class review will help your brain retain the information it just received.

Note: More detailed information on listening and note taking is provided in Chapter 5.

Finish class with a rush of attention, not a rush out the door!

"Learning is something students do, NOT something done to students."
—Alfie Kohn

Think About It ———————————— Journal Entry 2.2

1. When you enter a classroom, where do you usually sit?

_____

_____

_____

_____

2. Why do you think you sit there? Is it a conscious choice or more like an automatic habit?

_____

_____

_____

_____

Active Class Participation

You can become actively involved in the college classroom by arriving at class prepared (e.g., having done the assigned reading), by asking relevant questions, and by contributing thoughtful comments during class discussions. When you communicate orally, you elevate the level of active involvement you invest in the learning process because speaking requires you to exert both mental energy (thinking about what you are going to say) and physical energy (moving your lips to say it). Thus, class participation will increase your ability to stay alert and attentive in class. It also sends a clear message to the instructor that you are a motivated student who takes the course seriously and wants to learn. Since class participation accounts for a portion of your final grade in many courses, your attentiveness and involvement in class can have a direct, positive effect on your course grade.

Active Reading

Writing not only promotes active listening in class, but also can promote active reading out of class. Taking notes on information that you're reading, or on information you've highlighted while reading, helps keep you actively involved in the reading process because it requires more mental and physical energy than merely reading the material or passively highlighting sentences with a highlighter. (See Do It Now! 2.2 for top strategies for reading college textbooks that you should put into practice immediately.)

2.2   DO IT NOW

Top Strategies for Improving Textbook Reading Comprehension and Retention

If you haven't already acquired textbooks for your courses, get them immediately and get ahead on your reading assignments. Information from reading assignments ranks right behind lecture notes as a source of test questions on college exams. Your professors are likely to deliver class lectures with the expectation that you have done the assigned reading and can build on that knowledge when they're lecturing. If you haven't done the reading, you'll have more difficulty following and taking notes on what your instructor is saying in class. Thus, by not doing the reading you pay a double penalty. College professors also expect you to relate or connect what they talk about in class to the reading they have assigned. Thus, it's important to start developing good reading habits now. You can do so by using the following strategies to improve your reading comprehension and retention.

Student Perspective

"I recommend that you read the first chapters right away because college professors get started promptly with assigning certain readings. Classes in college move very fast because unlike high school, you do not attend class five times a week but two or three times a week."

—Advice from a first-year student to new college students

1. **Come fully equipped.**
    - **Writing tool and storage.** Always bring a writing tool (pen, pencil, or keyboard) to record important information and a storage space (notebook or computer) to save and later retrieve information acquired from your reading for use on tests and assignments.
    - **Dictionary.** Have a dictionary nearby to quickly find the meaning of unfamiliar words that may interfere with your ability to comprehend what

you're reading. Looking up definitions of unfamiliar words does more than help you understand what you're reading: it's also an effective way to build your vocabulary. Building your vocabulary will improve your reading comprehension in all college courses, as well as your performance on standardized tests, such as those required for admission to graduate and professional schools.

- **Glossary of terms.** Check the back of your textbook for a list of key terms included in the book. Each academic subject or discipline has its own special vocabulary, and knowing the meaning of these terms is often the key to understanding the concepts covered in the text. Don't ignore the glossary; it's more than an ancillary or afterthought to the textbook. Use it regularly to increase your comprehension of course concepts.

2. **Get in the right position.** Sit upright and have light coming from behind you, over the opposite side of your writing hand. This will reduce the distracting and fatiguing effects of glare and shadows.

3. **Get a sneak preview.** Approach the chapter by first reading its boldface headings and any chapter outline, summary, or end-of-chapter questions that may be provided. This will supply you with a mental map of the chapter's important ideas before you start your reading trip and provide an overview that will help you keep track of the chapter's major ideas (the "big picture"), thereby reducing the risk that you'll get lost among the smaller, more specific details you'll encounter along the way.

4. **Use boldface headings and subheadings.** These are cues for important information. Turn these headings into questions, and then read to find their answers. This will launch you on an answer-finding mission that will keep you mentally active while reading and enable you to read with a purpose. Turning headings into questions is also a good way to prepare for tests because you're practicing exactly what you'll be expected to do on tests—answer questions.

5. **Pay special attention to the first and last sentences.** Absorb those in sections of the text that lie beneath the chapter's major headings and subheadings. These sentences often contain an important introduction and conclusion to the material covered within that section of the text.

6. **Finish each of your reading sessions with a short review.** Recall what you have highlighted or noted as important information (rather than trying to cover a few more pages). It's best to use the last few minutes of reading time to "lock in" the most important information you've just read because most forgetting takes place immediately after you stop processing (taking in) information and start doing something else (Underwood, 1983).

Remember

Your goal while reading should be to discover or uncover the most important information contained in what you're reading; when you finish reading, your final step should be to reread (and lock in) the most important information you discovered while reading.

Touching the Second Base of Community College Success: Use of Campus Resources

Your campus environment contains multiple resources designed to support your quest for educational and personal success. Studies show that students who use campus resources report higher levels of satisfaction with college and get more out of the college experience (Pascarella & Terenzini, 1991, 2005).

Remember

Involvement with campus services is not just valuable, it's free; the cost of these services has already been covered by your college tuition. By investing time and energy in campus resources, you not only increase your prospects for personal success but also maximize the return on your financial investment in college—that is, you get a bigger bang for your buck.

"Do not be a PCP (Parking Lot → Classroom → Parking Lot) student. The time you spend on campus will be a sound investment in your academic and professional success."

—Dr. Drew Appleby, professor of psychology

Your Key Campus Resources

Using your campus resources is an important, research-backed principle of college success, and it is a natural extension of the principle of active involvement. Successful students are active learners inside and outside the classroom, and this behavior extends to active use of campus resources. An essential first step toward putting this principle into practice is to become fully aware of all key support services that are available on campus. You can find this information in three major forms:

1. **In print.** Information published in written form. For in-print information on campus resources, consult your college catalog (also known as the college bulletin) and your student handbook. If you do not have a copy of the college catalog, you should be able to obtain one from the Office of Admissions or Center for Academic Advising. If you do not have a copy of the student handbook, you should be able to obtain one from the Office of Student Life or Student Affairs.

2. **Online.** Information posted electronically on the Internet. For online information on campus resources, check your college's Web site. Your college may have its entire catalog and student handbook available online.

3. **In person.** Information communicated directly to you by a knowledgeable person. For in-person information on campus resources, speak with professionals in different offices or centers on your campus, such as those listed here:

   - **Academic Support Services (Tutoring/Writing Center).** Ask about the type of support the tutoring center provides for improving course learning and increasing academic success (e.g., study and test-taking strategies).

   - **College Library.** Ask about the type of support the library provides for finding information and completing research assignments (e.g., term papers and group projects). Librarians are professional educators who provide instruction outside the classroom. You can learn from them just as you can learn from faculty inside the classroom. Furthermore, the library is a place where you can acquire skills for locating, retrieving, and evaluating information that you may apply to any course you are taking or will ever take.

   - **Academic Advisement.** An academic advisor is a personal resource who can help guide you through the educational planning and decision-making process. Studies show that college students who have developed clear educational and career goals are more likely to continue their college education and complete their degrees (Willingham, 1985; Wyckoff, 1999). However, most beginning college students need help clarifying their educational goals, selecting an academic major, and exploring careers (Cuseo, 2005; Frost, 1991). As a first-year college student, being undecided or uncertain about your educational and career goals is nothing to be embarrassed about. However, you should start thinking about your future now. Connect early and often with an academic advisor to help you clarify your educational goals and choose a field that best complements your personal interests, talents, and values.

   - **Student Development Services (Student Affairs).** Ask about the type of support provided on issues relating to social and emotional adjustment, involvement in campus life outside the classroom, and leadership development.

   - **Disability Services.** If you have a physical or learning disability that is interfering with your performance in college, or think you may have such a disability, Disability Services would be the resource on your campus to consult

Student Perspective

"Where I learn the material best is tutoring because they go over it and if you have questions, you can ask, you can stop, they have time for you. They make time."

—First-year college student (Nunez, 2005)

"The next best thing to knowing something is knowing where to find it."

—Dr. Samuel Johnson, famous English literary figure and original author of the *Dictionary of the English Language* (1747)

for assistance and support. Programs and services typically provided by this office include:

- Assessment for learning disabilities;
- Verification of eligibility for disability support services;
- Authorization of academic accommodations for students with disabilities; and
- Specialized counseling, advising, and tutoring.

- **Financial Aid.** If you have questions concerning how to obtain assistance in paying for college, the staff of your Financial Aid Office is there to guide you through the application process. Upon first glance, the materials that need to be submitted may seem confusing or overwhelming. Don't let this intimidate you; seek assistance with this process from the knowledgeable staff in this office on your campus.

- **Counseling Center.** Counseling services can provide you with a valuable source of support in college, not only helping you cope with college stressors that may be interfering with your academic success but also helping you realize your full potential. Personal counseling can promote your self-awareness and self-development in social and emotional areas of your life that are important for mental health, physical wellness, and personal growth.

Think About It ———————————— *Journal Entry* **2.3**

Take a minute to look back at the major campus resources that have been mentioned in this section, and identify two or three of them that you think you should use immediately. Briefly explain why you have identified these resources as your top priorities at this time. Consider asking your course instructor or academic advisor for recommendations about what campus resources you should consult during your first term on campus.

> - College Library – for research projects and to ask for help for resources, study rooms.
> - Academic Advisement – to get help on future class advisement, and college planning

---

Touching the Third Base of Community College Success: Interpersonal Interaction and Collaboration

Learning is strengthened when it takes place in a social context that involves interpersonal interaction. As some scholars put it, human knowledge is socially constructed, or built through interaction and dialogue with others. According to these scholars, your interpersonal conversations become mentally internalized (represented in your mind) and are shaped by the dialogue you've had with others (Bruffee,

1993). Thus, by having frequent, intelligent conversations with others, you broaden your knowledge and deepen your thinking.

Four particular forms of interpersonal interaction have been found to be strongly associated with student learning and motivation in college:

1. Student-faculty interaction
2. Student interaction with academic advisors
3. Student interaction with a mentor
4. Student-student (peer) interaction

Student-Faculty Interaction

Studies repeatedly show that college success is influenced heavily by the quality and quantity of student-faculty interaction *outside the classroom*. Such contact is associated with the following positive outcomes for college students:

- Improved academic performance
- Increased critical thinking skills
- Greater satisfaction with the college experience
- Increased likelihood of completing a college degree
- Stronger desire to seek further education beyond college (Astin, 1993; Pascarella & Terenzini, 1991, 2005)

These positive results are so strong and widespread that we encourage you to seek interaction with college faculty outside of class time. Here are some of the most manageable ways to increase your out-of-class contact with college instructors during the first year of college:

1. **Seek interaction with your instructors immediately after class.** This is when you may be interested in talking about something that was just discussed in class, and it may be when your instructor is interested in discussing it with you. Furthermore, interaction with your instructor immediately after class can help the professor get to know you as an individual, which should increase your confidence and willingness to seek subsequent contact.
2. **Seek interaction with your course instructors during their office hours.** One of the most important pieces of information on the course syllabus is your instructor's office hours. Make specific note of these office hours, and make an earnest attempt to capitalize on them. College professors spend most of their professional time outside the classroom preparing for class, grading papers, conducting research, and serving on college committees. However, some of their out-of-class time is reserved specifically for office hours, during which they are expected to be available.

   You can schedule an office visit with your instructor during the early stages of the course. You can use this time to discuss course assignments, term-paper topics, and career options in your instructor's field. Try to make at least one visit to the office of each of your instructors, preferably early in the term, when quality time is easier to find, rather than at midterm, when major exams and assignments begin to pile up.

   Even if your early contact with instructors is only for a few minutes, it can serve as a valuable icebreaker that helps your instructors get to know you as a person and helps you feel more comfortable interacting with them in the future.

Student *Perspective*

"I wish that I would have taken advantage of professors' open-door policies when I had questions, because actually understanding what I was doing, instead of guessing, would have saved me a lot of stress and re-doing what I did wrong the first time."

—Advice to new students from a college sophomore (Walsh, 2005)

3. **Seek interaction with your instructors through e-mail.** Electronic communication is another effective way to interact with an instructor, particularly if that professor's office hours conflict with your class schedule, work responsibilities, or family commitments. If you are a commuter student who does not live on campus, or if you are an adult student who is juggling family and work commitments along with your academic schedule, e-mail communication may be an especially effective and efficient mode of interaction for you. If you're shy or hesitant about "invading" your professor's office space, e-mail can provide a less threatening way to interact and may give you the self-confidence to seek face-to-face contact with an instructor.

Student-Advisor Interaction

An academic advisor can be an effective referral agent who can direct you to, and connect you with, campus support services that best meet your needs. An advisor can also help you understand college procedures and help you navigate the bureaucratic maze of college policies and politics.

> **Remember**
>
> *An academic advisor is not someone you see just once per term when you need to get a signature for class scheduling and course registration. An advisor is someone you should visit more regularly than your course instructors. Your instructors will change from term to term, but your academic advisor may be the one professional on campus with whom you have regular contact and a stable, ongoing relationship throughout your college experience.*

Your academic advisor should be someone whom you feel comfortable speaking with, someone who knows your name, and someone who's familiar with your personal interests and abilities. Give your advisor the opportunity to get to know you personally, and seek your advisor's advice about courses, majors, and personal issues that may be affecting your academic performance.

Think About It ————————————— *Journal Entry* **2.4**

1. Do you have a personally assigned advisor?

   _No_

   _____

   _____

   _____

   _____

   _____

(continued)

2.　If yes, do you know who this person is and where he or she can be found?

_____

_____

_____

_____

_____

_____

3.　If no, do you know where to go if you have questions about your class schedule or academic plans?

_____ *Yes* _____

_____

_____

_____

_____

_____

If you have been assigned an advisor and you find that you cannot develop a good relationship with this person, ask the director of advising or academic dean if you could be assigned to someone else. Ask other students about their advising experience and whether they know any advisors they can recommend to you.

If your college does not assign you a personal advisor but offers advising on a drop-by or drop-in basis, you may see a different advisor each time you visit the center. If you are not satisfied with this system of multiple advisors, find one advisor with whom you feel most comfortable and make that person your personal advisor by scheduling your appointments in advance. This will enable you to consistently connect with the same advisor and develop an ongoing relationship.

Interaction with Peers (Student-Student Interaction)

Studies repeatedly point to the power of the peer group as a source of social and academic support during the college years (Pascarella, 2005). One study of more than 25,000 college students revealed that when peers interact with one another while learning, they achieve higher levels of academic performance and are more likely to persist to degree completion (Astin, 1993). In another study that involved in-depth interviews with more than 1,600 college students, it was discovered that almost all students who struggled academically had one particular study habit in common: they always studied alone (Light, 2001).

2.3   DO IT **NOW**

Top Strategies for Making Connections with Key Members of Your College Community

Here is a list of 10 tips for making important interpersonal connections in college. Start making these connections now so that you can begin constructing a base of social support that will strengthen your performance during your first term and, perhaps, throughout your college experience.

1. Connect with a favorite peer or student development professional that you may have met during orientation.
2. Connect with peers who live near you or who commute to school from the same community in which you live. If your schedules are similar, consider carpooling together.
3. Join a college club, student organization, campus committee, intramural team, or volunteer service group whose members may share the same personal or career interests as you.
4. Connect with a peer leader who has been trained to assist new students (e.g., peer tutor, peer mentor, or peer counselor) or with a peer who has more college experience than you.
5. Look for and connect with a motivated classmate in each of your classes and try working as a team to take notes, complete reading assignments, and study for exams. (Look especially to team up with a peer who may be in more than one class with you.)
6. Connect with faculty members in a field that you're considering as a major by visiting them during office hours, conversing briefly with them after class, or communicating with them via e-mail.
7. Connect with an academic support professional in your college's Learning Center for personalized academic assistance or tutoring related to any course in which you'd like to improve your performance.
8. Connect with an academic advisor to discuss and develop your educational plans.
9. Connect with a college librarian to get early assistance and a head start on any research project that you've been assigned.
10. Connect with a personal counselor or campus minister to discuss any college adjustment or personal life issues that you may be experiencing.

Peer interaction is especially important during the first term of college. At this stage of the college experience, new students have a strong need for belonging and social acceptance because many of them have just left the lifelong security of family and hometown friends. As a new student, it may be useful to view the early stages of your college experience through the lens of psychologist Abraham Maslow's hierarchy of human needs (see Figure 2.2). According to Maslow's hierarchy of needs, humans cannot reach their full potential and achieve peak performance until their more basic emotional and social needs have been met (e.g., their needs for personal safety, social acceptance, and self-esteem). Making early connections with your peers helps you meet these basic human needs, provides you with a base of social support to ease your integration into the college community, and prepares you to move up to higher levels of the need hierarchy (e.g., achieving educational excellence and fulfilling your potential).

Getting involved with campus organizations or activities is one way to connect you with other students. Also, try to interact with students who have spent more time at college than you. Sophomores can be valuable social resources for a new student. You're likely to find that they are willing to share their experiences with you because you have shown an interest in hearing what they have to say. You may be the first person who has ever asked them what their experiences have been like on your campus. You can learn from their experiences by asking them which courses and instructors they would recommend or what advisors they found to be most well informed and personable.

FIGURE 2.2

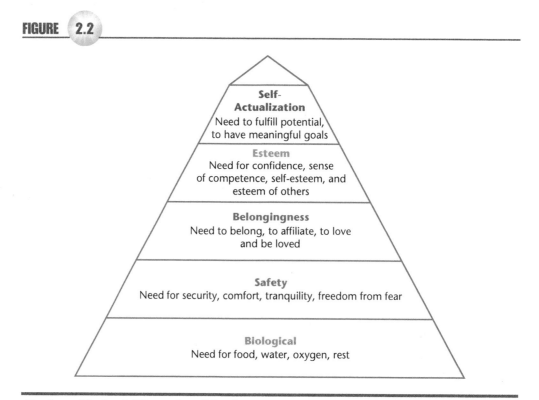

Abraham Maslow's Hierarchy of Needs

Remember

Your peers can be more than competitors or a source of negative peer pressure: they can also be collaborators, a source of positive social influence, and a resource for college success. Be on the lookout for classmates who are motivated to learn and willing to learn with you, and keep an eye out for advanced students who are willing to assist you. Start building your social support network by surrounding yourself with success-seeking and success-achieving students. They can be a stimulating source of positive peer power that can drive you to higher levels of academic performance and heighten your drive to complete college.

Think About It ———————————— *Journal Entry* 2.5

Think about the students in your classes this term. (1) Are there any students who might be good to connect with and form learning teams? (2) Do you have any classmates who are currently in more than one class with you and who might be good peer partners to team up with and work together on the courses you have in common?

Yes, Jordan (sits next to me)

Collaboration with Peers

Simply defined, collaboration is the process of two or more people working interdependently toward a common goal (as opposed to working independently or competitively). Collaboration involves true teamwork, in which teammates support one another's success and take equal responsibility for helping the team move toward its shared goal. Research on students from kindergarten through college shows that when students collaborate in teams, their academic performance and interpersonal skills improve dramatically (Cuseo, 1996).

To maximize the power of collaboration, use the following guidelines to make wise choices about teammates who will contribute positively to the quality and productivity of your learning team:

1. Observe your classmates with an eye toward identifying potentially good teammates. Look for fellow students who are motivated and who should contribute to your team's success, rather than those who you suspect may just be hitchhikers looking for a free ride.
2. Don't team up exclusively with peers who are similar to you in terms of their personal characteristics, backgrounds, and experiences. Instead, include teammates who differ from you in age; gender; ethnic, racial, cultural, or geographical background; learning style; and personality characteristics. Such variety brings different life experiences, styles of thinking, and learning strategies to your team, which enrich not only its diversity but its quality as well. If your team consists only of friends or classmates whose interests and lifestyles are similar to your own, this familiarity can interfere with your team's focus and performance because your common experiences can get you off track and on to topics that have nothing to do with the learning task (e.g., what you did last weekend or what you are planning to do next weekend).

"TEAM = Together Everyone Achieves More"
—Author unknown

"Surround yourself with only people who are going to lift you higher."
—Oprah Winfrey, actress and talk-show host

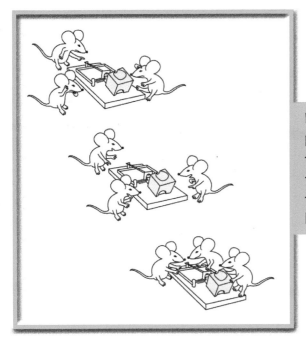

Research shows that when peers work collaboratively to reach a common goal, they learn more effectively and reach "higher levels" of thinking.

> **Remember**
>
> *Seek diversity; capitalize on the advantages of collaborating with peers with varied backgrounds and lifestyles. Simply stated, studies show that we learn more from people who are different from us than we do from people who are similar to us (Pascarella, 2001).*

Keep in mind that learning teams are not simply study groups formed the night before an exam. Effective learning teams collaborate more regularly and work on a wider variety of academic tasks than late-night study groups. In the following series of important academic tasks and situations, learning teams may be formed to improve your performance.

Note-Taking Teams

Immediately after class sessions end, take a couple of minutes to compare and share notes with other students. Since listening and note taking are demanding tasks, one student often picks up an important point that the others overlooked, and vice versa. By teaming up immediately after class to review your notes, your team has the opportunity to consult with your instructor about any missing or confusing information before the instructor leaves the classroom.

Author's Experience During my first term in college, I was having difficulty taking complete notes in my biology course because the instructor spoke rapidly and with an unfamiliar accent. I noticed another student (Alex) sitting in the front row who was trying to take notes the best he could, but he was experiencing the same difficulty. Following one particularly fast and complex lecture, we looked at each other and began to share our frustrations. We decided to do something about it by pairing up immediately after every class and compare our notes to identify points we missed or found confusing. First, we helped each other by comparing and sharing our notes in case one of us got something that the other missed. If there were points that we both missed or couldn't figure out, we went to the front of class together to consult with the instructor before he left the classroom. At the end of the course, Alex and I finished with the highest grades in the course.

— *Joe Cuseo*

Reading Teams

After completing your reading assignments, you can compare your highlighting and margin notes with classmates. Consult with one another and share what you thought were the most important points in the reading that should be studied for upcoming exams.

Writing Teams

Teammates can provide one another with feedback that can be used to revise and improve the quality of their individual writing. You can form writing teams with peers at any or all of the following stages in the writing process:

- **Topic selection and refinement.** To help generate a list of potential topics and subtopics
- **Prewriting.** To clarify your purpose and audience
- **First draft.** To improve your general style and tone
- **Final draft.** To proofread and correct mechanical errors before submitting your work

Library Research Teams

Many first-year students are unfamiliar with the process of conducting library research, and some experience "library anxiety" and try to avoid even stepping into the library, particularly if it's large and intimidating (Malvasi, Rudowsky, & Valencia, 2009). Forming library research teams is an effective way for you to develop a social support group that can make trips to the library less intimidating and transform library research from a "flying solo" experience into a collaborative experience.

> **Remember**
> It is ethical and acceptable for you to team up with others to search for and share resources. This is not cheating or plagiarizing, as long as your final product is completed individually and what you turn in to your instructor represents your own work.

Team-Instructor Conferences

Visiting course instructors outside of class with other classmates is an effective way to get additional assistance in preparing for exams and completing assignments for several reasons:

- You may feel more comfortable about seeing instructors on their turf if you are accompanied by peers, rather than entering this unfamiliar territory on your own. As the old expression goes, "There's safety in numbers."
- When you make an office visit as a team, the information shared by the instructor is heard by more than one person, so your teammates may pick up some useful information that you may have missed, misinterpreted, or forgotten, and you may do the same for them.
- You save instructors time by allowing them to help multiple students at the same time rather than requiring them to engage in repeat "performances" for students who visit individually at different times.
- You send a message to instructors that you're serious about the course and are a motivated student because you've taken the time—ahead of time—to connect with your peers and prepare for the office visit.

"Two heads are better than one, not because either is infallible, but because they are unlikely to go wrong in the same direction."

—C. S. Lewis, English novelist and essayist

Study Teams

Research clearly demonstrates that college students learn from peers as much as, or more than, they do from instructors and textbooks (Astin, 1993; Pascarella, 2005). When seniors at Harvard University were interviewed, nearly everyone who had been part of a study group considered this experience to be crucial to their academic progress and success (Light, 1990, 1992).

Research on study groups also indicates that they are effective only if each member has done required coursework in advance of the team meeting; for example, if each group member has done the required reading and other course assignments (Light, 2001). Thus, to fully capitalize and maximize the power of study teams, each member should study individually *before* studying in a group. Each member should come prepared with specific information or answers to share with teammates, as well as specific questions or points of confusion about which they hope to receive help from the team. This ensures that all team members are individually accountable and equally responsible for doing their own learning, as well as for contributing to the learning of their teammates.

After you receive the results of your course exams and assignments, you can collaborate with peers to review your results as a team. By comparing answers, you can better identify the sources of your mistakes. By observing the answers of teammates who may have received maximum credit on particular questions, you can get a clearer picture of where you went wrong and what you need to do better next time.

Teaming up after tests and assignments given early in the term is especially effective, because it enables you to get a better idea of what the instructor expects from students throughout the remainder of the course. What you learn from your peers can be used as early feedback to diagnose your mistakes, improve your next performance, and raise your grade while there's still plenty of time left in the course to do so.

Touching the Fourth (Home) Base of Community College Success: Personal Reflection and Self-Awareness

The final steps in the learning process, whether it be learning in the classroom or learning from experience, are to step back from the process, thoughtfully review it, and connect it to what you already know. Reflection may be defined as the flip side of active involvement; both processes are necessary for learning to be complete. Learning requires not only effortful action, but also thoughtful reflection. Active involvement gets and holds your focus of attention, which enables information to reach your brain, and personal reflection promotes consolidation, which "locks" that information into your brain's long-term memory (Bligh, 2000; Broadbent, 1970).

Brain research reveals that two different brain-wave patterns are associated with the mental states of involvement and reflection (Bradshaw, 1995; see Figure 2.3). The brain waves on the left reveal faster activity, indicating that the person is actively involved in the learning task and attending to it. The slower brain-wave pattern on the right indicates that the person is thinking deeply about information taken in, which will help consolidate or lock that information into long-term memory. Thus, effective learning combines active mental involvement (characterized by faster, shorter brain waves) with thoughtful reflection (characterized by slower, longer brain waves).

FIGURE   2.3

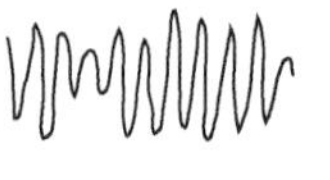

High-Amplitude Brain Waves Associated with a Mental State of *Active Involvement*.

High-Frequency Brain Waves Associated with a Mental State of *Reflective Thinking*.

© Kendall Hunt

Brain Wave Patterns

> "We learn to do neither by thinking nor by doing; we learn to do by thinking about what we are doing."
>
> —George Stoddard, former professor of psychology and education, University of Iowa

Personal reflection involves introspection—turning inward and inspecting yourself to gain deeper self-awareness of what you've done, what you're doing, or what you intend to do. Two forms of self-awareness are particularly important for success in college:

1. Self-assessment
2. Self-monitoring

Self-Assessment

Simply defined, self-assessment is the process of reflecting on and evaluating your personal characteristics, such as your personality traits, learning habits, and personal strengths or weaknesses. Self-assessment promotes self-awareness, which is the critical first step in the process of self-improvement, personal planning, and effective decision making. The following are important target areas for self-assessment and self-awareness because they reflect personal characteristics that play a pivotal role in promoting success in college and beyond:

- **Personal interests.** What you like to do or enjoy doing
- **Personal values.** What is important to you and what you care about doing
- **Personal abilities or aptitudes.** What you do well or have the potential to do well
- **Learning habits.** How you go about learning and the usual approaches, methods, or techniques you use to learn
- **Learning styles.** How you prefer to learn; that is, the way you like to:
    - Receive information—which learning format you prefer (e.g., reading, listening, or experiencing)
    - Perceive information—which sensory modality you prefer (e.g., vision, sound, or touch)
    - Process information—how you mentally deal with information once you have taken it in (e.g., think about it on your own or discuss it with others)
- **Personality traits.** Your temperament, emotional characteristics, and social tendencies (e.g., whether you lean toward being outgoing or reserved)
- **Academic self-concept.** Your personal beliefs about what kind of student you think you are and how you perceive yourself as a learner (e.g., your level of self-confidence and whether you believe success is within your control or depends on factors beyond your control)

Think About It — Journal Entry 2.6

1. How would you rate your academic self-confidence at this point in your college experience? (Circle one)

    very confident   (somewhat confident)   somewhat unconfident   very unconfident

2. Why did you make this choice?

    because I've been mostly successful in my classes.

Self-Monitoring

Research indicates that one key characteristic of successful learners is that they monitor or watch themselves and maintain self-awareness of the following:

- Whether they are using effective learning strategies. For example, they're aware of their level of attention or concentration in class.
- Whether they are comprehending what they are attempting to learn. For example, they're aware of whether they're understanding it at a deep level or merely memorizing it at a surface level.
- How to self-regulate or self-adjust their learning strategies to meet the different demands of different tasks or subjects. For example, they read technical material in a science textbook more slowly and stop to test their understanding more frequently than when they're reading a novel (Pintrich, 1995; Weinstein, 1994; Weinstein & Meyer, 1991).

Summary and Conclusion

Research reviewed in this chapter points to the conclusion that successful students are:

1. **Involved.** They invest time and effort in the college experience;
2. **Resourceful.** They capitalize on their surrounding resources;
3. **Interactive.** They interact and collaborate with others; and
4. **Reflective.** They are self-aware learners who assess and monitor their own performance.

Successful students are students who could honestly check almost every box in the following self-assessment checklist of success-promoting principles and practices.

A Checklist of Success-Promoting Principles and Practices

1. **Active Involvement**
   Inside the classroom, I:
   - **Get to class.** Treat it like a job; if you cut, your pay (grade) will be cut.
   - **Get involved in class.** Come prepared, listen actively, take notes, and participate.

   Outside the classroom, I:
   - **Read actively.** Take notes while you read to increase attention and retention.
   - **Double up.** Spend twice as much time on academic work outside the classroom than you spend in class—if you're a full-time student, that makes it a 40-hour academic workweek (with occasional "overtime").

2. **Use of Campus Resources**
   I capitalize on academic and student support services, such as the following:
   - Learning Center
   - Writing Center
   - Disability Services
   - College Library

- Academic Advisement
- Career Development Center
- Financial Aid Office
- Counseling Center
- Experiential Learning Resources

3. **Interpersonal Interaction and Collaboration**
   I interact with the following people:

   - **Peers.** Join student clubs and participate in campus organizations.
   - **Faculty members.** Connect with them immediately after class, in their offices, or via e-mail.
   - **Academic advisors.** See them for more than just a signature to register; find an advisor you can relate to and with whom you can develop an ongoing relationship.
   - **Mentors.** Try to find experienced people on campus who can serve as trusted guides and role models.

   I collaborate by doing the following:

   - **Form learning teams.** Join not only last-minute study groups but also teams that collaborate more regularly to work on such tasks as taking lecture notes, completing reading and writing assignments, conducting library research, and reviewing results of exams or course assignments.
   - **Participate in learning communities.** Enroll in two or more classes with the same students during the same term.

4. **Personal Reflection and Self-Awareness**
   I engage in:

   - **Self-assessment.** Reflect on and evaluate your personal traits, habits, strengths, and weaknesses.
   - **Self-monitoring.** Maintain self-awareness of how you're learning, what you're learning. and whether you're learning.

Think About It ———————————— *Journal Entry* 2.7

Before exiting this chapter, look back at the Checklist of Success-Promoting Principles and Practices and see how these ideas compare with those you recorded at the start of this chapter, when we asked you how you thought college would be different from high school and what it would take to be successful in college.

_____

_____

_____

_____

_____

(continued)

1. What ideas from your list and our checklist tend to match?

    _____

    _____

    _____

    _____

    _____

    _____

2. Were there any ideas on your list that were not on ours, or vice versa?

    _____

    _____

    _____

    _____

    _____

    _____

Learning More through the World Wide Web
Internet-Based Resources for Further Information on College Success

For additional information relating to the ideas discussed in this chapter, we recommend the following Web sites:

www.dartmouth.edu/~acskills/success/index.html

www.uni.edu/walsh/linda7.html

www.lifehack.org/article/lifehack/from-a-freshman-five-tips-for-success-in-college.html

2.1 Constructing a Master List of Campus Resources

1. Use each of the following sources to gain more in-depth knowledge about the specific support services available on your campus:

   - Information published in your college catalog and student handbook
   - Information posted on your college's Web site
   - Information gathered by speaking with professionals in different offices or centers on your campus

2. Using the preceding sources of information, construct a master list of all support services that are available to you on your campus. Your final product should be a list that includes the following:

   - The names of different support services your campus offers
   - The specific types of support each service provides
   - A short statement next to each specific support service listed, indicating whether you think you would benefit from this particular type of support
   - The name of a person whom you could contact for support from this service

Notes

- You can pair up with a classmate to work collaboratively on this assignment. Working together with a peer on any research task can reduce your anxiety, increase your energy, and generate synergy—which results in a final product that is superior to what could have been produced by one person working alone (independently).
- After you complete this assignment, save your master list of support services for future use. You might not have an immediate need for some of these services during your first term in college, but all of them are likely to be useful to you at some point in your college experience.

2.2 Support Services

Learning Center
Types of Support

Will I benefit?   Contact Person:

_____

Will I benefit?   Contact Person:

_____

Will I benefit?   Contact Person:

_____

Writing Center
Types of Support

Will I benefit?   Contact Person:

_____

Will I benefit?   Contact Person:

_____

Will I benefit?   Contact Person:

_____

Disability Services
Types of Support

Will I benefit?   Contact Person:

_____

Will I benefit?   Contact Person:

_____

Will I benefit?   Contact Person:

_____

College Library
Types of Support

Will I benefit?   Contact Person:

_____

Will I benefit?   Contact Person:

_____

Will I benefit?   Contact Person:

_____

Academic Advisement
Types of Services

Will I benefit?   Contact Person:

_____

Will I benefit?   Contact Person:

_____

Will I benefit?   Contact Person:

_____

Career Development Center
Types of Services

Will I benefit?   Contact Person:

_____

Will I benefit?   Contact Person:

_____

Will I benefit?   Contact Person:

_____

Financial Aid Office
Types of Services

Will I benefit?   Contact Person:

_____

Will I benefit?   Contact Person:

_____

Will I benefit?   Contact Person:

_____

Counseling Center
Types of Services

Will I benefit?   Contact Person:

_____

Will I benefit?   Contact Person:

_____

Will I benefit?   Contact Person:

_____

Experiential Learning Resources
Types of Services

Will I benefit?   Contact Person:

_____

Will I benefit?   Contact Person:

_____

Will I benefit?   Contact Person:

_____

Other
Types of Services

Will I benefit?   Contact Person:

_____

Will I benefit?   Contact Person:

_____

Will I benefit?   Contact Person:

_____

Alone and Disconnected: Feeling Like Calling It Quits

Josephine is a first-year student in her second week of college. She doesn't feel like she fits in with other students on her campus. She feels that by going to college she's taking time away from her family and longtime friends who are not in college, and she fears that her ties with them will be weakened or broken if she continues to spend so much time on school and schoolwork. Josephine is feeling so torn between college and her family and old friends that she's beginning to have second thoughts about whether she should have even begun college.

Discussion Questions

1. What might you say to Josephine that might persuade her to stay in college?

2. Could the college have done more during her first two weeks on campus to make Josephine (and other students) feel more connected with college and less disconnected from family?

3. Do you see anything that Josephine could do now to minimize the conflict or balance the tension she's experiencing between her commitment to college and her ties to family and friends?

Chapter 2 Reflection

WHAT do you believe is the most important principle of community college success?

I believe the most important Principle is being interactive, because working with others increases my learning.

WHY do you believe this is the most important one?

Because colaborating with others and participating in class increases my learning and retention

Explain HOW you will use this principle to assist you in being successful in college.

I will work with others and share notes after class and come prepared to class so I can participate in class discussions

Goal Setting, Motivation, and Character

3

| THOUGHT STARTER | *Journal Entry* 3.1 | LEARNING GOAL |

How would you define the word *successful*?

_____

_____

_____

_____

_____

_____

To develop meaningful goals to strive for, along with strategies for maintaining motivation and building character to achieve those goals.

What Does "Being Successful" Mean to You?

The word *success* means "to achieve a desired outcome"; it derives from the Latin root *successus,* which means "to follow or come after" (as in the word *succession*). Thus, by definition, success involves an order or sequence of actions that lead to a desired outcome. The process starts with identifying an end (goal) and then finding a means (sequence of steps) to reach that goal (achieving success). Goal setting is the first step in the process of becoming successful because it gives you something specific to strive for and ensures that you start off in the right direction. Studies consistently show that setting specific goals is a more effective self-motivational strategy than to simply tell yourself that you should "try hard" or "do your best" (Boekaerts, Pintrich, & Zeidner, 2000; Locke & Latham, 1990).

By setting goals, you show initiative—you work to gain control of your future and take charge of your life. By taking initiative, you demonstrate what psychologists call an internal locus of control—you believe that the locus (location or source) of control for events in your life is *internal*, and thus within you and your control, rather than *external*, or outside of you and beyond your control (controlled by such factors as luck, chance, or fate; Rotter, 1966).

Research reveals that individuals with a strong internal locus of control display the following characteristics:

1. Greater independence and self-direction (Van Overwalle, Mervielde, & De Schuyer, 1995)

"You've got to be careful if you don't know where you're going because you might not get there."
—Yogi Berra, Hall of Fame baseball player

"There is perhaps nothing worse than reaching the top of the ladder and discovering that you're on the wrong wall."
—Joseph Campbell, American professor and writer

"Success is getting what you want. Happiness is wanting what you get."
—Dale Carnegie, author of the bestselling book *How to Win Friends and Influence People* (1936) and founder of the Dale Carnegie Course, a worldwide program for business based on his teachings

"I'm a great believer in luck, and I find the harder I work the more I have of it."
—Thomas Jefferson, third president of the United States

2. More accurate self-assessment (Hashaw, Hammond, & Rogers, 1990; Lefcourt, 1982)
3. Higher levels of learning and achievement (Wilhite, 1990)
4. Better physical health (Maddi, 2002; Seligman, 1991)

> "What lies behind us and what lies in front of us are small matters compared to what lies within us."
>
> —Ralph Waldo Emerson, 19th-century American essayist and lecturer

An internal locus of control also contributes to the development of another positive trait, which psychologists call *self-efficacy*—the belief that you have the power to produce a positive effect on the outcomes of your life (Bandura, 1994). People with low self-efficacy tend to feel helpless, powerless, and passive; they allow things to happen *to* them rather than taking charge and making things happen *for* them. College students with a strong sense of self-efficacy believe they're in control of their educational success, regardless of their past or current circumstances.

If you have a strong sense of self-efficacy, you initiate action, put forth effort, and sustain that effort until you reach your goal. If you encounter setbacks or bad breaks along the way, you don't give up or give in: you persevere or push on (Bandura, 1986, 1997).

Students with a strong sense of academic self-efficacy have been found to:

1. Put great effort into their studies;
2. Use active-learning strategies;
3. Capitalize on campus resources; and
4. Persist in the face of obstacles (Multon, Brown, & Lent, 1991; Zimmerman, 1995).

Think About It ———————————— *Journal Entry* 3.2

> "Control your own destiny or someone else will."
>
> —Jack Welch, chemical engineer, author, and successful CEO of the General Electric Company

You are not required by law or by others to attend college; you've made the decision to continue your education. Do you believe you are in charge of your educational destiny?

_____

_____

_____

_____

Why or why not?

_____

_____

_____

_____

_____

_____

Students with self-efficacy also possess a strong sense of personal responsibility. As the breakdown of the word *responsible* implies, they are "response" "able"—i.e., they believe they are able to respond effectively to personal challenges, including educational challenges.

Students with self-efficacy do not have a false sense of entitlement. They don't feel they're entitled to, or owed, anything; they believe that success is earned and is theirs for the taking. For example, studies show that students who convert their college degrees into successful careers have two common characteristics: personal initiative and a positive attitude (Pope, 1990). They don't take a passive approach and assume good positions will fall into their laps, nor do they believe they are owed positions simply because they have college degrees or credentials. Instead, they become actively involved in the job-hunting process and use various job-search strategies (Brown & Krane, 2000).

"The price of greatness is responsibility."

—Winston Churchill, British prime minister during World War II and Nobel Prize winner in literature

"You miss 100 percent of the shots you never take."

—Wayne Gretzky, Hall-of-Fame hockey player, nicknamed "The Great One" and considered by many to be the greatest hockey player of all time

Think About It  Journal Entry 3.3

1. In what area or areas of your life do you feel that you've been able to exert the most control and achieve the most positive results?

_____

_____

_____

_____

2. In what area or areas of your life do you wish you had more control and were achieving better results?

_____

_____

_____

_____

3. What have you done in the area or areas of your life where you've taken charge and gained control that might be transferred or applied to the area or areas in which you need to gain more control?

_____

_____

_____

_____

Strategies for Effective Goal Setting

Motivation begins with goal setting. Studies show that people who neglect to set and pursue life goals are prone to feelings of "life boredom" and a belief that life is meaningless (Bargdill, 2000). Goals may be classified into three general categories: long-range, mid-range, and short-range, depending on the length of time it takes to reach them and the order in which they are to be achieved. Short-range goals need to be completed before a mid-range goal can be reached, and mid-range goals must be reached before a long-range goal can be achieved. For example, if your long-range goal is a successful career, you must complete the courses required for a degree (mid-range goal) that will allow your entry into a career; to reach your mid-range goal of a college degree, you need to successfully complete the courses you're taking this term (short-range goal).

This process is called *means-end analysis*, which involves working backward from your long-range goal (the end) and identifying the order and timing of the mid-range and short-range subgoals (the means) that need to be taken to reach your long-range goal (Brooks, 2009; Newell & Simon, 1959).

Setting Long-Range Goals

Setting effective long-range goals involves two processes: (1) self-awareness, or insight into who you are now, and (2) self-projection, or a vision of what you want to become in the future. When you engage in both of these processes, you're able to see a connection between your short- and your long-range goals.

Long-range goal setting enables you to take an approach to your future that is proactive—acting beforehand to anticipate and control your future life rather than putting it off and being forced to react to it without a plan. Research shows that people who neglect to set goals for themselves are more likely to experience boredom with life (Bargdill, 2000). Setting long-range goals and planning ahead also help reduce feelings of anxiety about the future because you've given it forethought, which gives you greater power to control it (i.e., it gives you a stronger sense of self-efficacy). As the old saying goes, "To be forewarned is to be forearmed."

Remember that setting long-range goals and developing long-range plans doesn't mean you can't adjust or modify them. Your goals can undergo change as you change, develop new skills, acquire new knowledge, and discover new interests or talents. Finding yourself and your path in life is one of the primary purposes of a college education. Don't think that the process of setting long-range goals means you will be locked into a premature plan and reduced options. Instead, it will give you something to reach for and some momentum to get you moving in the right direction.

"To fail to plan is to plan to fail."

—Robert Wubbolding, internationally known author, psychologist, and teacher

"You have brains in your head. You have feet in your shoes. You can steer yourself any direction you choose."

—Theodore Seuss Giesel, a.k.a. Dr. Seuss, famous author of children's books including *Oh, the Places You'll Go!*

Steps in the Goal-Setting Process

Effective goal setting involves a four-step sequence:

1. **Awareness of yourself.** Your personal interests, abilities and talents, and values;

2. **Awareness of your options.** The choices available to you;

3. **Awareness of the options that best fit you.** The goals most compatible with your personal abilities, interests, values, and needs;

4. **Awareness of the process.** The steps that you need to take to reach your chosen goal.

Discussed in the next sections are strategies for taking each of these steps in the goal-setting process.

Step 1. Self-Awareness

The goals you choose to pursue say a lot about who you are and what you want from life. Thus, self-awareness is a critical first step in the process of goal setting. You must know yourself before you can choose the goals you want to achieve. While this may seem obvious, self-awareness and self-discovery are often overlooked aspects of the goal-setting process. Deepening your self-awareness puts you in a better position to select and choose goals and to pursue a personal path that's true to who you are and what you want to become.

"Know thyself, and to thine own self be true."

—Plato, ancient Greek philosopher

© Kendall Hunt

Remember

Self-awareness is the first, most important step in the process of making any important life choice or decision.

No one is in a better position to know who you are, and what you want to be, than *you*. One effective way to get to know yourself more deeply is through self-questioning. You can begin to deepen your self-awareness by asking yourself questions that can stimulate your thinking about your inner qualities and priorities. Effective self-questioning can launch you on an inward quest or journey to self-discovery and self-insight, which is the critical first step to effective goal setting. For example, if your long-range goal is career success, you can launch your voyage toward achieving this goal by asking yourself thought-provoking questions relating to your personal:

"In order to succeed, you must know what you are doing, like what you are doing, and believe in what you are doing."

—Will Rogers, Native American humorist and actor

- **Interests.** What you like to do;
- **Abilities.** What you're good at doing; and
- **Values.** What you believe is worth doing.

The following questions are designed to sharpen your self-awareness with respect to your interests, abilities, and values. As you read each question, briefly note what thought or thoughts come to mind about yourself.

Know Thyself

Self-awareness is the first and most important step in the process of making effective choices or decisions.

Your Personal Interests

1. What tends to grab your attention and hold it for long periods?
2. What sorts of things are you naturally curious about or tend to intrigue you?
3. What do you enjoy and do as often as you possibly can?
4. What do you look forward to or get excited about?
5. What are your favorite hobbies or pastimes?
6. When you're with your friends, what do you like to talk about or spend time doing together?
7. What has been your most stimulating or enjoyable learning experience?
8. If you've had previous work or volunteer experience, what jobs or tasks did you find most enjoyable or stimulating?
9. When time seems to "fly by" for you, what are you usually doing?
10. What do you like to read about?
11. When you open a newspaper or log on to the Internet, what do you tend to read first?
12. When you find yourself daydreaming or fantasizing about your future life, what do you most find yourself doing?

Think About It ———————————— *Journal Entry* **3.4**

From your responses to the preceding questions, identify a long-range goal you could pursue that's compatible with your personal interests. In the space that follows, note the goal and the interests that are compatible with it.

_____

_____

_____

_____

_____

_____

Your Personal Abilities and Talents

1. What seems to come easily or naturally to you?
2. What would you say is your greatest talent or personal gift?
3. What do you excel at when you apply yourself and put forth your best effort?
4. What are your most advanced or well-developed skills?
5. What would you say has been the greatest accomplishment or achievement in your life thus far?
6. What about yourself are you most proud of, or what do you take the most pride in doing?
7. When others come to you for advice or assistance, what is it usually for?

"Never desert your line of talent. Be what nature intended you for and you will succeed."

—Sydney Smith, 18th-century English writer and defender of the oppressed

8. What would your best friend or friends say is your best quality, trait, or characteristic?
9. What things have you done that gave you a strong feeling of being successful?
10. If you've received awards or other forms of recognition, what have you received them for?
11. On what types of learning tasks or activities have you experienced the most success?
12. In what types of courses do you tend to earn the highest grades?

Think About It ——————————————— Journal Entry 3.5

From your responses to the preceding questions, identify a long-range goal you could pursue that's compatible with your personal abilities. In the space that follows, note the goal and the abilities that are compatible with it.

_____

_____

_____

_____

_____

_____

Your Personal Values

1. What matters most to you?
2. If you were to single out one thing you stand for or believe in, what would it be?
3. What would you say are your highest priorities in life?
4. What makes you feel good about what you're doing when you're doing it?
5. If there were one thing in the world you could change, improve, or make a difference in, what would it be?
6. When you have extra spending money, what do you usually spend it on?
7. When you have free time, what do you usually find yourself doing?
8. What does living a "good life" mean to you?
9. How would you define success? (What would it take for you to feel that you were successful?)
10. How do you define happiness? (What would it take for you to feel happy?)
11. Do you have any heroes or anyone you admire, look up to, or feel has set an example worth following? If yes, who and why?
12. Which of the following four personal qualities would you want to be known for? Rank them in order of priority to you (1 = highest, 4 = lowest).
    _____ Smart
    _____ Wealthy
    _____ Creative
    _____ Caring

"Do what you value; value what you do."

—Sidney Simon, *Values Clarification* and *In Search of Values* (1993)

Think About It ———————— *Journal Entry* **3.6**

From your responses to the preceding questions, identify a long-range goal you could pursue that's compatible with your personal values. In the space that follows, note the goal and the values that are compatible with it.

_____

_____

_____

_____

_____

_____

Step 2. Awareness of Your Options

The second critical step in the goal-setting process is to become aware of your long-range goal choices. For example, to effectively choose a career goal, you need to be aware of what career options are available to you and have a realistic understanding of the types of work done in these careers. To gain this knowledge, you'll need to capitalize on available resources, such as the following:

1. Reading books about different careers
2. Taking career development courses
3. Interviewing people in different career fields
4. Observing (shadowing) people working in different careers

One characteristic of effective goal setting is to create goals that are realistic. In the case of careers, getting firsthand experience in actual work settings (e.g., shadowing, internships, volunteer services, and part-time work) would give you a realistic view of what work is like in certain careers, as opposed to the idealized or fantasized way careers are portrayed on TV and in the movies.

Step 3. Awareness of the Options That Best Fit You

In college, you'll have many educational options and career goals from which to choose. To deepen your awareness of whether a field may be a good fit for you, take a course in that field to test out how well it matches your interests, values, talents, and learning style. Ideally, you want to select a field that most closely taps into, or builds on, your strongest skills and special talents. Choosing a field that's compatible with your strongest abilities should enable you to master the skills required by that field more deeply and efficiently. You're more likely to succeed or excel in a field that taps your talents, and the success you experience will, in turn, strengthen your self-esteem, self-confidence, and drive to continue with it. You've probably heard of the old proverb "If there's a will, there's a way" (i.e., when you're motivated, you're more

> "Students [may be] pushed into careers by their families, while others have picked one just to relieve their anxiety about not having a career choice. Still others may have picked popular or lucrative careers, knowing nothing of what they're really like or what it takes to prepare for them."
>
> —Lee Upcraft, Joni Finney, and Peter Garland, student development specialists

likely to succeed). However, it's also true that "If there's a way, there's a will" (i.e., when you know the way to do something well, you're more motivated to do it).

Think About It ———————————— *Journal Entry* **3.7**

Think about a career you're considering and answer the following questions:

1. Why are you considering this career? (What led or caused you to become interested in this choice?)

    _____

    _____

    _____

    _____

    _____

    _____

2. Would you say that your interest in this career is motivated primarily by intrinsic factors (i.e., factors "inside" of you, such as your personal abilities, interests, needs, and values)? Or, would you say that your interest in the career is motivated more heavily by extrinsic factors (i.e., factors "outside" of you, such as starting salary, pleasing parents, meeting family expectations, or societal expectations for your gender or ethnicity)? Explain.

    _____

    _____

    _____

    _____

    _____

    _____

Step 4. Awareness of the Process

The fourth and final step in an effective goal-setting process is becoming aware of the steps needed to reach your goal. For example, if you've set the goal of achieving a college degree in a particular major, you need to be aware of the course requirements that need to be completed for you to graduate in that major. Similarly, to set a career goal, you need to know what major or majors lead to that career, because some careers require a specific major but other careers may be entered through various majors.

Remember

The four-step process for effective goal setting applies to more than just educational goals. It's a strategic process that could and should be applied to any goal you set for yourself in life, at any stage of your life.

Snapshot Summary

3.1 The SMART Method of Goal Setting

A popular mnemonic device for remembering the key components of a well-designed goal is the acronym "SMART" (Doran, 1981; Mayer, 2003).

A SMART goal is one that is:

Specific: States exactly what the goal is and what will be done to achieve it.

Example: I'll achieve at least a "B" average this term by spending 25 hours per week on my course work outside of class and by using the effective learning strategies described in this book. (As opposed to the non-specific goal "I'm really going to work hard.")

Meaningful (and Measurable): The goal really matters to the individual, and progress toward reaching it can be steadily measured or tracked.

Example: I will achieve at least a "B" average this term because it will enable me to get into a field that I really want to pursue as a career, and I will measure my progress toward this goal by keeping track of the grades I'm earning in all my courses throughout the term.

Actionable: Identifies the concrete actions or behaviors that will be engaged in to reach the goal.

Example: I will achieve at least a "B" average this term by (1) attending all classes, (2) taking detailed notes in all my classes, (3) completing all reading assignments before

their due dates, and (4) avoiding cramming by studying in advance of all my major exams.

Realistic: The individual is capable of achieving or attaining the goal.

Example: Achieving a "B" average this term will be a realistic goal for me because my course load is manageable and I will not be working at my part-time job for more than 15 hours per week.

Timed: The goal is broken down into a timeline that includes short-range, mid-range, and long-range steps.

Example: To achieve at least a "B" average this term, first I'll acquire the information I need to learn by taking complete notes in class and on my assigned readings (short-range step). Second, I'll study the information I've acquired from my notes and readings in short study sessions held in advance of major exams (mid-range step). Third, I'll hold a final review session for all information previously studied on the day before my exams, and after exams I'll review my test results as feedback to determine what I did well and what I need to do better in order to maintain at least a "B" average (long-range step).

Note: The strategy for setting SMART goals is a transferable process that can be applied to goals in any aspect or dimension of your life, including health-related goals such as losing weight, social goals such as meeting new people, and fiscal goals such as saving money.

Strategies for Maintaining Motivation and Progress toward Your Goals

Reaching your goals requires will and energy; it also requires skill and strategy. Listed here are strategies for maintaining your motivation and commitment to reaching your goals.

1. **Visualize reaching your long-range goals.** Imagine vivid images of being successful, including not only what success looks like, but also what it feels like. For

example, if your goal is to achieve a college degree, imagine a crowd of cheering family, friends, and faculty at your graduation. Visualize how you'll be able to cherish and carry this proud memory with you for the rest of your life and how the benefits of a college degree will last a lifetime. Imagine yourself in the career that college enabled you to enter and your typical workday going something like this: You wake up in the morning and hop out of bed enthusiastically, looking forward to your day at work. When you're at work, time flies by, and before you know it, the day's over. When you return to bed that night and look back on your day, you feel good about what you did and how well you did it.

You can also use negative imagery to motivate yourself by imagining the worst-case scenario: failing to reach your goal and suffering the consequences. For example, vividly imagine yourself without any alternative other than a poor-paying, backbreaking job that you have to do to survive for the rest of your working life.

Author's Experience My father, who spent 50 years working in the coal mines of eastern Kentucky, always had a simple motivating statement for me to gain more education than he had. He would always say, "Son, I did not have the chance to go to school, so I have to write my name with an X and work in the coal mines. You have the opportunity to get an education and you do not have to break your back in those mines." What my father was telling me was that education would give me options in life that he did not have and that I should take advantage of those options by going to college. My dad's lack of education supplied me with drive and dedication to pursue education. My experience suggests that when you are developing your goals and motivating yourself to achieve them, it may be as important to know what you don't want as it is to know what you do want.

Aaron Thompson

2. **Put your goals in writing.** When you put your goals in writing, you remain aware of them and remember them. This can stimulate your motivation to put your plan into action by serving almost like a written contract that holds you accountable to following through on your commitment. Place your written goals where you see them regularly. Consider writing them on sticky notes and posting them in multiple places that you encounter on a daily basis (e.g., your laptop, refrigerator, and bathroom mirror). If you keep them constantly in sight, you'll keep them constantly in mind.

3. **Create a visual map of your goals.** Lay out your goals in the form of a flowchart to show the flow of steps you'll be taking from your short- through mid- to long-range goals. Visual diagrams can help you "see" where you want to go, enabling you to connect where you are now and where you want to be. Diagramming can be energizing because it gives you a sneak preview of the finish line and a map-like overview of how to get you there.

4. **Keep a record of your progress.** Research indicates that the act of monitoring and recording progress toward goals can increase motivation to continue pursuing them (Locke & Latham, 2005; Matsui, Okada, & Inoshita, 1983). The act of keeping records of your progress probably increases your motivation by giving you frequent feedback on your progress and positive reinforcement for staying on track and moving toward your target (long-range goal) (Bandura & Cervone, 1983; Schunk, 1995). For example, mark your accomplishments in red on your calendar, or keep a journal of the goals you've reached; your entries will keep you

motivated by supplying you with concrete evidence of your progress and commitment. You can also chart or graph your progress, which provides a powerful visual display of your upward trends and patterns. Keep the chart where you can see it on a daily basis so you can use it as an ongoing source of inspiration and motivation. You can add musical inspiration by playing a motivational song in your head to keep you going (e.g., "We Are the Champions" by Queen).

5. **Develop a "skeletal resume" of your goals.** Include your goals as separate sections or categories that will be progressively fleshed out as you complete them. Your to-be-completed resume can provide a framework or blueprint for organizing, building, and tracking progress toward your goals. It can also serve as a visual reminder of the things you plan to accomplish and eventually showcase to potential employers. Furthermore, every time you look at your growing resume, you're reminded of your past accomplishments, which can energize and motivate you to reach your future goals. As you fill in and build up your resume, you can literally see how much you've achieved, which boosts your self-confidence and motivation to continue achieving. (See Chapter 12, p. 367, for a sample skeletal resume.)

6. **Reward yourself for making steady progress toward your long-range goals.** Reward is already built into reaching your long-range goal because it represents the end of your trip, which lands you at your desired destination (e.g., in a successful career). However, short- and mid-range goals may not be desirable ends in themselves but rather the means to a desirable end (your long-range goal). Consequently, you need to intentionally reward yourself for landing on these smaller stepping stones on the way to your long-range goal. When you complete these short- and mid-range goals, record and reward your accomplishment (e.g., celebrate your successful completion of midterms or finals by treating yourself to something you enjoy).

   A habit of perseverance and persistence through all intermediate steps is needed to reach a long-range goal, and like any other habit, is more likely to continue if it's followed by a reward (positive reinforcement). Setting small goals, moving steadily toward them, and rewarding yourself for reaching them are components of a simple but powerful strategy. This strategy will help you maintain motivation over the extended period needed to reach a long-range goal.

7. **Capitalize on available campus resources that can help you stay on track and move toward your goal.** Research indicates that college success results from a combination of what students do for themselves (personal responsibility) and what they do to capitalize on resources that are available to them (resourcefulness; Pascarella & Terenzini, 1991, 2005). Successful college students are resourceful students: they seek out and take advantage of college resources to help them reach their goals.

   For example, a resourceful student who's having trouble deciding what field of study to pursue for a degree or credential will seek assistance from an academic advisor on campus. A resourceful student who's interested in a particular career but is unclear about the best educational path to take toward that career will use the Career Development Center as a resource.

8. **Use your social resources.** The power of social support groups for helping people achieve personal goals is well documented by research in various fields (Ewell, 1997; Moeller, 1999). You can use the power of people by surrounding yourself with peers who are committed to successfully achieving their educational goals and by avoiding "toxic" people who are likely to poison your plans or dampen your dreams.

"Life isn't a matter of milestones but of moments."

—Rose Fitzgerald Kennedy, philanthropist and mother of John F. and Robert F. Kennedy

"Willpower is the personal strength and discipline, rooted in strong motivation, to carry out your plans. 'Waypower' is the exertion of willpower that helps you find resources and support."

—Jerry Pattengale, historian, author, and advocate for first-year student success

"Develop an inner circle of close associations in which the mutual attraction is not sharing problems or needs. The mutual attraction should be values and goals."

—Denis Waitley, former mental trainer for U.S. Olympic athletes and author of *Seeds of Greatness* (XXXX)

For example, find a supportive and motivating friend and make a mutual pact to help each other reach your respective goals. This step could be taken to a more formal level by drawing up a "social contract" whereby you and your partner are "cowitnesses" or designated social-support agents whose role is to help each other stay on track and move toward long-range goals. Studies show that making a public commitment to a goal increases your commitment to it, probably because it becomes a matter of personal pride and integrity that's seen not only through your own eyes but also through the eyes of others (Hollenbeck, Williams, & Klein, 1989).

> "I make progress by having people around who are smarter than I am."
>
> —Henry Kaiser, successful industrialist, known as the father of American shipbuilding

Think About It — Journal Entry 3.8

1. What would you say is the biggest setback or obstacle you've overcome in your life thus far?

   I overcome d Vision disorder that affected my reading and writing

2. How did you overcome it? (What enabled you to get past it or prevented you from being blocked by it?)

   I had Vision therapy

9. **Convert setbacks into comebacks.** The type of thoughts you have after experiencing a setback can affect your emotional reaction to it and the action you take in response. For instance, what you think about a poor performance (e.g., a poor test grade) can affect your emotional reaction to that grade and what action, or lack of action, you take in response to it. You can react to the poor grade by knocking yourself down with self-putdowns ("I'm a loser") or by building yourself back up with positive pep talk ("I'm going to learn from my mistakes on this test and rebound with a stronger performance on the next one").

It's noteworthy that the root of the word *failure* is *fallere*, which means to "trip or fall," while the root word for *success* is *successus*, which means "to follow or come after." Thus, when we fail at something, it doesn't mean we've been defeated: it just means we've stumbled and fallen. Success can still be achieved after the fall by getting up, not giving up, and continuing to take the succession of steps need to successfully reach our goal.

If a poor past performance is seen not as a personal failure but as a learning opportunity, the setback may be turned into a comeback. Here are some notable people who turned early setbacks into successful comebacks:

- Louis Pasteur, famous bacteriologist, who failed his admission test to the University of Paris;
- Albert Einstein, Nobel Prize–winning physicist, who failed math in elementary school;
- Thomas Edison, prolific inventor, who was once expelled from school as "uneducable";
- Johnny Unitas, Hall-of-Fame football player, who was cut twice from professional football teams early in his career

In response to their early setbacks, these successful people didn't get bitter: they got better. Getting mad or sad about a setback will likely make you stressed or depressed and leave you focused on a past event that you can no longer control. Reacting rationally to a poor performance by focusing on how the results can be used as feedback to improve your future performance allows you to gain control of it and gives you the opportunity to convert the setback into a comeback.

This can be a challenging task because when you have an experience, your response to it passes through emotional areas of the brain before it reaches areas of the brain involved in rational thinking and reasoning (LeDoux, 1998). (See Figure 3.1.)

Thus, your brain reacts to events emotionally before it does rationally. If the experience triggers intense emotions (e.g., anger, anxiety, or sadness after receiving a bad test grade), your emotional reaction has the potential to "short-circuit"

FIGURE 3.1

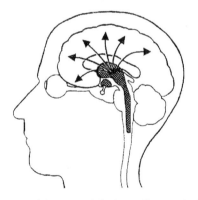

Information passes through the emotional center of the brain (lower, shaded area) before reaching the centers responsible for rational thinking (upper area). Thus, we need to counteract our tendency to respond emotionally and irrationally to personal setbacks by making a conscious attempt to respond rationally and reflectively.

The Brain's Human Attention System

or wipe out rational thinking. If you find yourself beginning to feel overwhelmed by negative emotions following a setback, you need to consciously and quickly block them with rational thoughts (e.g., thinking or saying to yourself, "Before I get carried away emotionally, let me think this through rationally"). This involves more than simply saying, "I have to think positively." Instead, you should develop a set of specific counterthinking strategies ready to use as soon as you begin to think negatively. Described here are thinking strategies that you can use to maintain motivation and minimize negative thinking in reaction to setbacks.

Remember

Don't let past mistakes bring you down emotionally or motivationally, but don't ignore or neglect them. Instead, inspect them, reflect on them, and correct them so that they don't happen again.

- **Develop self-awareness of your thinking patterns and habits.** Becoming aware of the nature of your thoughts is the first step to controlling them. Thinking often involves silent self-talk (i.e., talking silently to yourself). Thus, negative thinking often involves negative self-talk (e.g., "I'm a loser," "What's happening to me is just horrible," or "There's absolutely nothing I can do"). One of the best ways to become more aware of your self-talk, particularly negative self-talk, is to periodically write down your thoughts in a "thought journal" and review it with an eye for patterns of negative self-talk that you tend to use in certain situations (e.g., setbacks).

- **Substitute positive thoughts for negative thoughts.** Once you've become aware of your negative thoughts and the situations in which they occur, replace them with positive alternative thoughts. Let's say that one situation in which you experience negative thinking is during exams, especially when you see students turning in their tests well before you're finished. You think, "I must be doing terribly on this exam because others are getting through it so quickly. They must be smarter and better prepared than I am." You can stop this negative thinking by immediately substituting the following thought: "They're getting up and getting out because the test was difficult for them and they're giving up." Or, you can think to yourself, "They're rushing out because they're not taking the time to review their tests carefully before turning them in." The key to this thought-substitution strategy is to have specific, positive self-talk statements ready to use in situations where you tend to think negatively. Practice them so well that you think of them automatically and immediately. If those situations include personal setbacks or disappointing performances, your positive self-talk statements could include expressions such as "This isn't the end of the world," "Tomorrow's another day," or "I'll turn this setback into a comeback." By choosing and repeatedly using these positive self-talk statements, you train your mind to develop the habit of thinking in ways that are self-motivating rather than self-defeating.

> "The greatest weapon against stress is our ability to choose one thought over another."
>
> —William James, philosopher and one of the founders of American psychology

Whatever you do, don't let setbacks make you mad or sad, particularly at early stages in your college experience, because you're just beginning to learn what it takes to be successful in college. Look at mistakes in terms of what they can do *for* you, not *to* you. A bad performance can be turned into a good learning experience by using the results as an error detector for identifying sources or causes of your mistakes and as feedback for improving your future performance.

10. **Maintain positive expectations.** Just as your thoughts in reaction to something that's already taken place can affect your motivation, so can thoughts about what you *expect* to happen next. Your expectations of things to come can be either positive or negative. For example, before a test you could think, "I'm poised, confident, and ready to do it." Or you could think, "I know I'm going to fail this test; I just know it."

> "Whether you think you can or you can't, you're right."
>
> —Henry Ford, founder of Ford Motor Co. and one of the richest people of his generation

Expectations can lead to what sociologists and psychologists have called a self-fulfilling prophecy—a positive or negative expectation leads you to act in ways that are consistent with your expectation, which, in turn, make your expectation come true. For instance, if you expect you're going to fail an exam, you're less likely to put as much effort into studying for it. ("What's the use? I'm going to fail anyway.") During the test, your negative expectation is likely to reduce your test confidence and elevate your test anxiety: for example, if you experience difficulty with the first item on a test, you get anxious and begin to think you're going to have difficulty with all remaining items and flunk the entire exam. All of this negative thinking is likely to increase the probability that your expectation of doing poorly on the exam will become a reality.

In contrast, positive expectations can lead to a positive self-fulfilling prophecy: If you expect to do well on an exam, you're more likely to demonstrate higher levels of effort, confidence, and concentration, all of which combine to increase the likelihood that you'll earn a higher test grade. Research shows that learning and practicing positive self-talk increases a sense of hope—a belief in the ability to reach goals and the ability to actually reach them (Snyder, 1994).

Think About It ———————————————— *Journal Entry* 3.9

1. Would you consider yourself to be an optimist or a pessimist?

_____

2. In what situations are you more likely to think optimistically and pessimistically?

_____

_____

_____

_____

_____

Why?

_____

_____

_____

_____

_____

_____

_____

---

11. **Keep your eye on the prize.** Don't lose sight of the long-term consequences of your short-term choices and decisions. Long-range thinking is the key to reaching long-range goals. Unfortunately, however, humans are often more motivated by short-range thinking because it produces quicker results and more immediate gratification. It's more convenient and tempting to think in the short term ("I like it; I want it; I want it now.") Studies show that the later consequences occur, the less likely people are to consider those consequences when they make their decisions (Ainslie, 1975; Elster & Lowenstein, 1992; Lewin, 1935). For example, choosing to do what you feel like doing instead of working to meet a future deadline and choosing to buy something with a credit card instead of saving money for future use cause people to suffer the negative long-term consequences of procrastination and credit-card debt, respectively.

To be successful in the long run, you need to keep your focus on the big picture—your long-range goals and dreams that provide your motivation. At the same time, you need to focus on the details—the due dates, to-do lists, and day-to-day duties that require your perspiration.

Thus, setting an important life goal and steadily progressing toward that long-range goal require two focus points. One is a narrow-focus lens that allows you to view the details immediately in front of you. The other is a wide-focus lens that gives you a big-picture view of what's farther ahead of you (your long-range goal). Success involves seeing the connection between the small, short-term chores and challenges (e.g., completing an assignment that's due next week) and the large, long-range picture (e.g., college graduation and a successful future). Thus, you need to periodically shift from a wide-focus lens that gives you the bigger, more distant picture to a narrow-focus lens that shifts your attention to completing the smaller tasks immediately ahead of you and keeping on the path to your long-range goal: future success.

"A pessimist sees the difficulty in every opportunity; an optimist sees the opportunity in every difficulty."

—Winston Churchill, British prime minister during World War II and Nobel Prize winner in literature

"Many people take no care of their money till they come nearly to the end of it, and others do just the same with their time."

—Johann Wolfgang von Goethe, German poet, dramatist, and author of the epic *Faust*

Student
Perspective

"I want to make it big in life."

—College sophomore

"Whoever wants to reach a distant goal must take many small steps."

—Helmut Schmidt, former chancellor of West Germany

"If you do not find it within yourself, where will you go to get it?"

—Zen saying (Zen is a branch of Buddhism that emphasizes seeing deeply into the nature of things and ongoing self-awareness)

Author's Experience When I was an assistant coach for a youth soccer team, I noticed that many of the less successful players tended to make either one of two mistakes when they were trying to move with the ball. Some spent too much time looking down, focusing on the ball at their feet, trying to be sure that they did not lose control of it. By not lifting their heads and looking ahead periodically, they often missed open territory, open teammates, or an open goal. Other unsuccessful players made the opposite mistake: They spent too much time with their heads up, trying to see where they were headed. By not looking down at the ball immediately in front of them, they often lost control of the ball, moved ahead without it, or sometimes stumbled over it and fell flat on their faces. Successful soccer players were in the habit of shifting their focus between looking down to maintain control of the ball immediately in front of them and lifting their heads to see where they were headed.

The more I thought about how successful players alternated between handling the ball in front of them and viewing the goal farther ahead, the more it struck me that this was a metaphor for success in life. Successful people alternate between both of these perspectives so that they don't lose sight of how the short-range tasks in front of them connect with the long-range goal ahead of them.

— Joe Cuseo

> "We are what we repeatedly do. Excellence, then, is not an act, but a habit."
>
> —Aristotle, ancient Greek philosopher

> "Sow an act and you reap a habit; sow a habit and you reap a character; sow a character and you reap a destiny."
>
> —Frances E. Willard, 19th-century American educator and women's rights activist

> "As gold which he cannot spend will make no man rich, so knowledge which he cannot apply will make no man wise."
>
> —Dr. Samuel Johnson, famous English literary figure and original author of the *Dictionary of the English Language* (1747)

> "Mere knowledge is not power; it is only possibility. Action is power; and its highest manifestation is when it is directed by knowledge."
>
> —Francis Bacon, English philosopher, lawyer, and champion of modern science

> "You can lead a horse to water, but you can't make him drink."
>
> —Proverb

> "Education is not the filling of a pail, but the lighting of a fire."
>
> —William Butler Yeats, Irish poet and playwright

● **Remember**

Keep your future dreams and current tasks in clear focus. Integrating these two perspectives will produce an image that can provide you with the inspiration to complete your college education and the determination to complete your day-to-day tasks.

Motivation: Moving toward Your Long-Range Goals

The word *motivation* derives from the Latin *movere*, meaning "to move." Success comes to those who exert effort to move toward their goals. Knowledge of all kinds of success-promoting strategies, such as those discussed in this text, provides only the potential for success; turning this potential into reality requires motivation, which converts knowledge into action. If you have all the knowledge, strategies, and skills for being successful but don't have the will to succeed, there's no way you will succeed. Studies show that without a strong personal commitment to attain a goal, it will not be reached, no matter how well designed the goal and the plan to reach it are (Locke & Latham, 1990).

Motivation consists of three elements that may be summarized as the "three Ds" of motivation:

1. Drive
2. Discipline
3. Determination

Drive

Drive is the force within you that supplies you with the energy needed to overcome inertia and initiate action. Much like shifting into the drive gear is necessary to move your car forward, it takes personal drive to move forward and toward your goals.

People with drive aren't just dreamers: they're dreamers and doers. They take action to convert their dreams into reality, and they hustle—they go all out and give it their all, all of the time, to achieve their goals. College students with drive approach college with passion and enthusiasm. They don't hold back and work halfheartedly: they give 100 percent and put their whole heart and soul into the experience.

"Success comes to those who hustle."

—Abraham Lincoln, 16th American president and author of the Emancipation Proclamation, which set the stage for the abolition of slavery in the United States

Think About It — ————————————— Journal Entry 3.10

1. Think about something that you do with drive, effort, and intensity. What thoughts, attitudes, and behaviors do you display when you do it?

_____

_____

_____

_____

_____

_____

2. Do you see ways in which you could apply the same approach to your college experience?

_____

_____

_____

_____

_____

_____

_____

Discipline

Discipline includes such positive qualities as commitment, devotion, and dedication. These personal qualities enable you to keep going over an extended period. Successful people think big, but start small—they take all the small steps and diligently do all the little things that need to be done, which in the long run, add up to a big accomplishment: the achievement of their long-range goal.

People who are self-disciplined accept the day-to-day sweat, toil, and perspiration needed to attain their long-term aspirations. They're willing to tolerate short-term strain or pain for long-term gain. They have the self-control and self-restraint needed to resist the impulse for instant gratification or the temptation to do what they feel like doing instead of what they need to do. They're willing to sacrifice their immediate needs and desires in the short run to do what is necessary to put them where they want to be in the long run.

"I long to accomplish some great and noble task, but it is my chief duty to accomplish small tasks as if they were great and noble."

—Helen Keller, seeing- and hearing-impaired author and activist for the rights of women and the handicapped

Student
Perspective

"Why is it so hard when I *have* to do something and so easy when I *want* to do something?"

—First-year student

Remember

Sacrifices that are made for a short time can bring benefits that last a lifetime.

"Self-discipline is the ability to make yourself do the thing you have to do, when it ought to be done, whether you like it or not."

—Thomas Henry Huxley, 19th-century English biologist

Sometimes you've got to do what you have to do in order to get to do what you want to do.

The ability to postpone immediate wants or needs is a key characteristic of self-discipline.

Studies show that individuals with dedication—who are deeply committed to what they do—are more likely to report that they are healthy and happy (Maddi, 2002; Myers, 1993).

Author's Experience   When I entered college in the mid-1970s, I was a first-generation student from an extremely impoverished background. Not only did I have to work to pay for part of my education, but I also needed to assist my family financially. I stocked grocery store shelves at night during the week and waited tables at a local country club on the weekends. Managing my life, time, school, and work required full-time effort. However, I always understood that my purpose was to graduate from college and all of my other efforts supported that goal. Thus, I went to class and arrived on time even when I did not feel like going to class. One of my greatest successes in life was to keep my mind and body focused on the ultimate prize: getting a college education. That success has paid off many times over.

Aaron Thompson

Determination

"If you are going through hell, keep going."

—Winston Churchill, British prime minister during World War II and Nobel Prize winner in literature

People who are determined pursue their goals with a relentless tenacity. They have the fortitude to persist in the face of frustration and the resiliency to bounce back after setbacks. When the going gets tough, they keep going. If they encounter something on the road to their goal that's hard to do, they work harder and longer to do it. They don't give up or give in: they dig deeper and give more.

People with determination are also more likely to seek out challenges. Research indicates that people who continue to pursue opportunities for personal growth and self-development throughout life are more likely to report feeling happy and healthy (Maddi, 2002; Myers, 1993). Rather than remaining stagnant and simply doing what's safe, secure, or easy, they stay hungry and display an ongoing commitment to personal growth and development; they keep striving and driving to be the best they can possibly be in all aspects of life.

"Success is peace of mind which is a direct result of self-satisfaction in knowing you made the effort to become the best that you are capable of becoming."

—John Wooden, college basketball coach and creator of the Pyramid of Success (XXXX)

Remember

On the highway to success, you can't be a passive passenger; you're the driver and at the wheel. Your goal setting will direct you there, and your motivation will drive you there.

Summary and Conclusion

Goal setting only becomes meaningful if you have motivation to reach the goals you set. Motivation may be said to consist of three Ds: drive, dedication, and determination. Drive is the internal force that gives you the energy to overcome inertia and initiate action. Discipline consists of positive personal qualities such as commitment, devotion, and dedication that enable you to sustain your effort over time. Determination enables you to relentlessly pursue your goals, persist in the face of frustration, and bounce back after any setback.

Reaching your goals requires all three Ds; it also involves the use of effective self-motivational strategies, such as:

- Visualizing reaching your long-range goals;
- Putting goals in writing;
- Creating a visual map of your goals;
- Keeping a record of your progress;
- Developing a skeletal resume;
- Rewarding yourself for progress toward long-range goals;
- Capitalizing on available campus and social resources;
- Converting setbacks into comebacks by using positive self-talk, maintaining positive expectations, and avoiding negative self-fulfilling prophecies; and
- Keeping your eye on the long-term consequences of your short-term choices and decisions.

Studies of highly successful people, whether they are scientists, musicians, writers, chess masters, or basketball stars, consistently show that achieving high levels of skill and success requires practice (Levitin, 2006). This is true even of people whose success is thought to be to be due to natural gifts or talents. For example, during the Beatles' first four years as a band and before they burst into musical stardom, they performed live an estimated 1,200 times, and many of these performances lasted five or more hours a night. They performed (practiced) for more hours during those first four years than most bands perform during their entire career. Similarly, before Bill Gates became a computer software giant and creator of Microsoft, he logged almost 1,600 hours of computer time during one seven-month period alone, averaging eight hours a day, seven days a week (Gladwell, 2008).

Reaching long-range goals means making small steps; they aren't achieved in one quick, quantum leap. If you are patient and persistent and consistently practice effective strategies, their positive effects will accumulate gradually and eventually have a significant impact on your success in college and beyond.

Remember

Success isn't a short-range goal; it's not a sprint but a long-distance run that takes patience and perseverance to complete. What matters most is not how fast you start but where you finish.

Learning More through the World Wide Web

Internet-Based Resources for Further Information on Goal Setting

For additional information related to the ideas discussed in this chapter, we recommend the following Web sites:

www.siue.edu/SPIN/activity.html

www.selfmotivationstrategies.com

3.1 Prioritizing Important Life Goals

Consider the following life goals. Rank them in the order of their priority for you (1 = highest, 5 = lowest):

_____ Emotional well-being

_____ Spiritual growth

_____ Physical health

_____ Social relationships

_____ Rewarding career

Self-Assessment Questions

1. What was the primary reason behind your choices of first- and last-ranked goals?
2. Have you established any short- or mid-range goals for reaching your highest-ranked choice? If yes, what are they? If no, what could they be?

3.2 Setting Goals for Reducing the Gap between the Ideal Scenario and the Current Reality

Think of an aspect of your life with a gap between what you hoped it would be (the ideal) and what it is (the reality).

On the lines that follow, identify goals you could purse that would reduce this gap:

Long-range goal: _____

Mid-range goal: _____

Short-range goal: _____

(For information on long-, mid-, and short-range goals, see p. 52.) Use the form below to identify more strategies for reaching each of these three goals. Consider the following areas for each goal:

- Actions to be taken:
- Available resources:
- Possible roadblocks:
- Potential solutions to roadblocks:

Long-range goal: _____

- Actions to be taken:
- Available resources:
- Possible roadblocks:
- Potential solutions to roadblocks:

Mid-range goal: _____

- Actions to be taken:
- Available resources:
- Possible roadblocks:
- Potential solutions to roadblocks:

Short-range goal: _____

- Actions to be taken:
- Available resources:
- Possible roadblocks:
- Potential solutions to roadblocks:

3.3 Converting Setbacks into Comebacks: Transforming Pessimism into Optimism

In *Hamlet,* Shakespeare wrote, "There is nothing good or bad, but thinking makes it so." His point was that experiences have the potential to be positive or negative, depending on how people interpret them and react to them.

Listed here is a series of statements representing negative interpretations and reactions to a situation or experience:

1. "I'm just not good at this."

2. "There's nothing I can do about it."

3. "Things will never be the same."

4. "Nothing is going to change."

5. "This always happens to me."

6. "This is unbearable."

7. "Everybody is going to think I'm a loser."

8. "I'm trapped, and there's no way out."

For each of the preceding statements, replace the negative statement with a statement that represents a more positive interpretation or reaction.

(For help in constructing these positive statements, see the discussion of thought-substitution strategies on p. 63.)

Goals and Motivation

Lorraine has decided to go to her local community college to become an RN. She knows that nurses make good money and it is easy to get a job in the profession right now. All she really cares about is having a good job and making money. She did not realize the classes would be difficult and she has a hard time getting through them since she really is not that interested in them. She started her clinicals and HATED what she was being asked to do. She was not prepared for all the bodily fluids she would see in one day. Lorraine decides nursing is not for her and is angry that no one told her she would hate it this much! She has to find a different major now that will still make a lot of money, but she is angry that she wasted more than a year of her life as well as the money she has spent on her education.

Discussion Questions

1. Why do you think Lorraine is really unhappy with the events that have unfolded during the past year?

2. What could Lorraine have done differently to avoid this situation?

3. What goals would you suggest Lorraine set for herself?

Lorraine is clearly motivated by money; is that what is going to make her happy? Why or why not?

Chapter 3 Reflection

What is the one thing that motivates you the most in college?

the end result

HOW and WHY does this motivate you?

because I know what the reward is

What is the one obstacle that gets in the way of your success?

lack of enjoyment

How can you use your motivation to overcome your obstacle(s)?

I can take courses that apply to my professional goals

Managing Time and Preventing Procrastination

4

THOUGHT STARTER | *Journal Entry* **4.1**

LEARNING GOAL

To help you appreciate the significance of managing time and supply you with a powerful set of time-management strategies that can be used to promote your success in college and beyond.

Complete the following sentence with the first thought that comes to your mind.

For me, time is . . .

_____

_____

_____

_____

The Importance of Time Management

For many first-year students, the beginning of college means the beginning of more independent living and self-management. Even if you've lived on your own for some time, managing time is an important skill to possess because you're likely juggling multiple responsibilities, including school, family, and work. Studies show that most first-year community college students are attending classes while working either part-time or full-time (American Association of Community Colleges, 2009). In college, the academic calendar and your class schedule will differ radically from those during high school. You will have less "seat time" in class each week and more "free time" outside of class, which you will have the freedom to self-manage; it will not be closely monitored by school authorities or family members, and you will be expected to do more academic work on your own outside of class. Personal time-management skills grow in importance when a person's time is less structured or controlled by others, leaving the individual with more decision-making power about how personal time will be spent. Thus, it is no surprise that research shows the ability to manage time effectively as playing a crucial role in college success (Erickson, Peters, & Strommer, 2006).

Simply stated, college students who have difficulty managing their time have difficulty managing college. In one study, sophomores who had an outstanding first year in college (both academically and socially) were compared with another group of sophomores who struggled during their freshman year. Interviews conducted with these students revealed one key difference between the two groups: The sophomores who experienced a successful first year repeatedly brought up the topic of time during the interviews. The successful students said they had to think carefully about how they spent their time and budget their time because it was a scarce resource. In contrast, the sophomores who experienced difficulty in their first year of

Student Perspective

"The major difference [between high school and college] is time. You have so much free time on your hands that you don't know what to do for most of the time."

—First-year college student (Erickson & Strommer, 1991)

Student Perspective

"I cannot stress enough that you need to intelligently budget your time."

—Words written by a first-year student in a letter of advice to students who are about to begin college

college hardly talked about the topic of time during their interviews, even when they were specifically asked about it (Light, 2001).

Studies also indicate that managing time plays a pivotal role in the lives of working adults. Setting priorities and balancing multiple responsibilities (work, family, and school) that compete for limited time and energy can be a juggling act and a source of stress for people of all ages (Harriott & Ferrari, 1996).

For these reasons, time management should be viewed not only as a college-success strategy but also as a life-management and life-success skill. Studies show that people who manage their time well report being more in control of their lives and happier (Myers, 1993). In short, when you gain greater control of your time, you become more satisfied with your life.

Author's Experience   I started the process of earning my doctorate a little later in life than other students. I was a married father with a preschool daughter (Sara). Since my wife left for work early in the morning, it was always my duty to get up and get my daughter's day going in the right direction. In addition, I had to do the same for me—which was often harder than doing it for my daughter. Three days of my week were spent on campus in class or in the library. (We did not have quick access to research on computers then as you do now.) The other two days of the workweek and the weekend were spent on household chores, family time, and studying. I knew that if I was going to have any chance of finishing my Ph.D. in a reasonable amount of time and have a decent family life, I had to adopt an effective schedule for managing my time. Each day of the week, I held to a very strict routine. I got up in the morning, drank coffee while reading the paper, took a shower, got my daughter ready for school, and took her to school. Once I returned home, I put a load of laundry in the washer, studied, wrote, and spent time concentrating on what I needed to do to be successful from 8:30 a.m. to 12:00 p.m. every day. At lunch, I had a pastrami and cheese sandwich and a soft drink while rewarding myself by watching *Perry Mason* reruns until 1:00 p.m. I then continued to study until it was time to pick up my daughter from school. Each night I spent time with my wife and daughter and prepared for the next day. I lived a life that had a preset schedule. By following this schedule, I was able to successfully complete my doctorate in a decent amount of time while giving my family the time they needed. (By the way, I still watch *Perry Mason* reruns.)

— *Aaron Thompson*

Strategies for Managing Time

Effective time management involves three key mental processes:

1. **Analysis.** Breaking down time into specific segments and work into smaller tasks;
2. **Itemizing.** Identifying all key tasks that need to be done and by what dates; and
3. **Prioritizing.** Organizing and attacking tasks in order of their importance.

The following steps can help you apply these skills to find more time in your schedule and use this time more productively.

1. **Break down your time and become more aware of how it's spent.** Have you ever asked yourself, "Where did all the time go?" or told yourself, "I just can't seem to find the time"? One way to find out where your time went is by taking a time inventory (Webber, 1991). To do this, you conduct a time analysis by breaking down and tracking your time, recording what you do and when you do it. By mapping out how you spend time, you become more aware of how much total time you have available to you and how its component parts are used up, including patches of wasted time in which you get little or nothing accomplished. You don't have to do this time analysis for more than a week or two. This should be long enough to give you some sense of where your time is going and allow you to start developing strategies for using your time more effectively and efficiently.

Think About It

Journal Entry **4.2**

1. What is your greatest time waster?

_____

_____

_____

_____

_____

_____

"Dost thou love life? Then do not squander time, for that is the stuff life is made of."

—Benjamin Franklin, 18th-century inventor, newspaper writer, and signer of the *Declaration of Independence*

2. Is there anything you can do right now to stop or eliminate it?

_____

_____

_____

_____

_____

_____

_____

2. **Identify which key tasks you need to accomplish and when you need to accomplish them.** We make lists to be sure we don't forget items we need from the grocery store or people we want to be sure are invited to a party. We can use the same list-making strategy for work tasks so that we don't forget to do them or forget to do them on time. Studies of effective people show that they are list makers and they write out lists not only for grocery items and wedding invitations, but also for things they want to accomplish each day (Covey, 1990).

You can itemize your tasks by listing them in one of the following time-management tools:

© Gary Woodward, 2013. Under license from Shutterstock, Inc.

- **Personal digital assistant (PDA) or cell phone.** You can use these to do a lot more than check social networking sites and send and receive text messages. Use the calendar tools in these devices to record due dates and set up the alert functions to remind you of these deadlines. Many PDAs and smartphones will also allow you to set up task or "to-do" lists and to set priorities for each item you enter.
- **Small, portable planner.** List all your major assignments and exams for the term, along with their due dates. If you pull all work tasks from different courses into one place, it is easier to keep track of what you have to do and when you have to do it.

Using a personal planner is an effective way to itemize your academic commitments.

● **Large, stable calendar.** Record in the calendar's date boxes your major assignments for the academic term and when they are due. Place the calendar in a position or location where it's in full view and you can't help but see it every day (e.g., on your bedroom or refrigerator door). If you regularly and literally "look" at the things you have to do, you're less likely to "overlook" them, forget about them, or subconsciously push them out of your mind.

| Think About It |  Journal Entry | 4.3 |

1. Do you have a calendar for the current academic term that you carry with you?

_____

_____

2. If yes, why? If no, what do you use instead?

_____

_____

_____

_____

_____

_____

3. How does that work for you?

_____

_____

_____

_____

_____

_____

Author's Experience
My mom was the person who ensured I got up for school on time. Once I got to school, the bell would ring to let me know to move on to the next class. When I returned home, I had to do my homework and chores. My daily and weekly schedules were dictated by others.

When I entered college, my mom quickly realized that I needed to develop my own system for being organized, focused, and productive without her assistance. Since I came from a modest background, I had to work my way through college. Juggling schedules became an art and science for me. I knew the things that I could not miss, such as work and school, and the things I could miss—TV and girls. (OK, TV, but not girls.)

After college, I spent 10 years in business—a world where I was measured by being on time and a productive "bottom line." It was during this time that I discovered a scheduling book. When I became a professor, I had other mechanisms to make sure I did what I needed to do when I needed to do it. This was largely based on when my classes were offered. Other time was dedicated to working out and spending time with my family. Now, as an administrator, I have an assistant who keeps my schedule for me. She tells me where I am going, how long I should be there, and what I need to accomplish while I am there. Unless you take your parents with you or have the luxury of a personal assistant, it's important to determine which activities are required and to allow time in your schedule for fun. Use a planner!

—Aaron Thompson

3. **Rank your tasks in order of their importance.** Once you've itemized your work by listing all tasks you need to do, prioritize them—determine the order in which you will do them. Prioritizing basically involves ranking your tasks in terms of their importance, with the highest-ranked tasks appearing at the top of your list to ensure that they are tackled first. How do you determine which tasks are most important and should be ranked highest? Two key criteria or standards of judgment can be used to help determine which tasks should be your priorities:

- **Urgency.** Tasks that are closest to their deadline or due date should receive high priority. For example, finishing an assignment that's due tomorrow should receive higher priority than starting an assignment that's due next month.
- **Gravity.** Tasks that carry the heaviest weight (count the most) should receive highest priority. For example, if an assignment worth 100 points and another worth 10 points are due at the same time, working on the 100-point task should receive higher priority. You want to be sure you invest your work time on work tasks that matter most. Just like investing money, you want to invest your time on tasks that yield the greatest dividends or payoff.

One strategy for prioritizing your tasks is to divide them into A, B, and C lists (Lakein, 1973). The A list is for *essential* tasks—what you *must* do now. The B list is for *important* tasks—what you *should* do soon. Finally, the C list is for *optional* tasks—what you *could* or *might* do later if there is time remaining after you've completed the tasks on the A and B lists. Organizing your tasks in this fashion can help you decide how to divide your labor in a way that ensures you put first things first. What you don't want to do is waste time on unimportant things and deceive yourself into thinking that you're keeping busy and getting things done when actually you're doing things that just take your time (and mind) away from the more important things.

At first glance, itemizing and prioritizing may appear to be rather boring chores. However, if you look at these mental tasks carefully, they require many higher-level thinking skills, such as:

1. **Analysis.** Breaking down time into its component elements or segments and breaking down work into specific tasks;

2. **Evaluation.** Critically evaluating the relative importance or value of tasks; and
3. **Synthesis.** Organizing individual tasks into classes or categories based on their level of priority.

Thus, developing self-awareness about how you spend time is more than a menial clerical task: when done with thoughtful reflection, it's an exercise in higher-level thinking. It's also a good exercise in values clarification, because what people choose to spend their time on is a more accurate indicator of what they truly value than what they *say* they value.

Develop a Time-Management Plan

"Time = Life. Therefore waste your time and waste your life, or master your time and master your life."

—Alan Lakein, international expert on time management and author of the bestselling book *How to Get Control of Your Time and Your Life* (1973)

Humans are creatures of habit. Regular routines help us organize and gain control of our lives. Doing things by design, rather than leaving them to chance or accident, is the first step toward making things happen for us rather than allowing them to happen to us by chance or accident. By developing an intentional plan for how you're going to spend your time, you're developing a plan to gain greater control of your life.

Don't buy into the myth that you don't have time to plan because it takes too much time that could be spent on getting started and getting things done. Time-management experts estimate that the amount of time you spend planning your work reduces your total work time by a factor of three (Lakein, 1973). In other words, for every one unit of time you spend planning, you save three units of work time. Thus, five minutes of planning time will typically save you 15 minutes of total work time, and 10 minutes of planning time will save you 30 minutes of work time. This saving of work time probably occurs because you develop a clearer game plan or plan of attack for identifying what needs to be done and the best order in which to get it done. A clearer sense of direction reduces the number of mistakes you may make due to false starts—starting the work but then having to restart it because you started off in the wrong direction. If you have no plan of attack, you're more likely to go off track and in the wrong direction; when you discover this at some point after you've started, you're then forced to retreat and start over.

As the old proverb goes, "A stitch in time saves nine." Planning your time represents the "stitch" (in time) that saves you nine additional stitches (units of time). Like successful chess players, successful time managers plan ahead and anticipate their next moves.

Elements of a Comprehensive Time-Management Plan

Once you've accepted the notion that taking the time to plan your time saves you time in the long run, you're ready to design a time-management plan. The following are the key elements of a comprehensive, well-designed plan for managing time:

1. **A good time-management plan should have several time frames.** Your academic time-management plan should include:
   - A *long-range* plan for the entire academic term that identifies deadline dates for reports and papers that are due toward the end of the term;
   - A *mid-range* plan for the upcoming month and week; and
   - A *short-range* plan for the following day.

The preceding time frames may be integrated into a total time-management plan for the term by taking the following steps:

a.   Identify deadline dates of all assignments, or the time when each of them must be completed (your long-range plan).

b.   Work backward from these final deadlines to identify dates when you plan to begin taking action on these assignments (your short-range plan).

c.   Identify intermediate dates when you plan to finish particular parts or pieces of the total assignment (your mid-range plan).

This three-stage plan should help you make steady progress throughout the term on college assignments that are due later in the term. At the same time, it will reduce your risk of procrastinating and running out of time.

Here's how you can put this three-stage plan into action this term. Develop a long-range plan for the academic *term*.

- Review the *course syllabus (course outline)* for each class you are enrolled in this term, and highlight all major exams, tests, quizzes, assignments, and papers and the dates on which they are due.

Remember

College professors are more likely than high school teachers to expect you to rely on your course syllabus to keep track of what you have to do and when you have to do it. Your instructors may not remind you about upcoming papers, tests, quizzes, assignments, etc.

- Obtain a *large calendar* for the academic term (available at your campus book-store or Learning Center) and record all your exams, assignments, and so on, for all your courses in the calendar boxes that represent their due dates. To fit this information within the calendar boxes, use creative abbreviations to represent different tasks, such as E for exam and TP for term paper (not toilet paper). When you're done, you'll have a centralized chart or map of deadline dates and a potential master plan for the entire term.

- Activate the calendar and task list functions on your PDA or cell phone. Enter your schedule, important dates, and deadlines, and set alert reminders. Since you carry your PDA or cell phone with you regularly, you will always have this information at your fingertips.

- **Plan your** *week*.

    a.   Make a map of your *weekly schedule* that includes times during the week when you are in class, when you typically eat and sleep, and if you are employed, when you work.

    b.   If you are a full-time college student, find *at least 25 total hours per week* when you can do academic work outside the classroom. (These 25 hours can be pieced together in any way you like, including time between daytime classes and work commitments, evening time, and weekend time.) When adding these 25 hours to the time you spend in class each week, you will end up with a 40-hour workweek, similar to any full-time job. If you are a part-time student, you should plan on spending at least two hours on academic work outside of class for every hour that you're in class.

    c.   Make good use of your *free time between classes* by working on assignments and studying in advance for upcoming exams. See Do It Now! 4.1 for a summary of how you can make good use of your out-of-class time to improve your academic performance and course grades.

Student *Perspective*

"The amount of free time you have in college is much more than in high school. Always have a weekly study schedule to go by. Otherwise, time slips away and you will not be able to account for it."

—First-year college student (Rhoads, 2005)

- **Plan your *day*.**
  a. Make a *daily to-do list*.

  Remember

  If you write it out, you're less likely to block it out and forget about it.

  b. Attack daily tasks in *priority order*.

  Remember

  "First things first." Plan your work by placing the most important and most urgent tasks at the top of your list, and work your plan by attacking tasks in the order in which you have listed them.

- Carry a *small calendar, planner, or appointment book* with you at all times. This will enable you to record appointments that you may make on the run during the day and will allow you to jot down creative ideas or memories of things you need to do, which sometimes pop into your mind at the most unexpected times.
- Carry *portable work* with you during the day—that is, work you can take with you and do in any place at any time. This will enable you to take advantage of "dead time" during the day. For example, carry material with you that you can read while sitting and waiting for appointments or transportation, allowing you to resurrect this dead time and convert it to "live" work time.
- Wear a *watch* or carry a cell phone that can accurately and instantly tell you what time it is and what date it is. You can't even begin to manage time if you don't know what time it is, and you can't plan a schedule if you don't know what date it is. Set the time on your watch or cell phone slightly ahead of the actual time; this will help ensure that you arrive to class, work, or meetings on time.

"In high school we were given a homework assignment every day. Now we have a large task assigned to be done at a certain time. No one tells [us] when to start or what to do each day."

—First-year college student (Rhoads, 2005)

Student *Perspective*

"I was constantly missing important meetings during my first few weeks because I did not keep track of the dates and times. I thought I'd be told again when the time was closer, just as had been done in high school. Something I should have done to address that would have been to keep a well-organized planner for reference."

—Advice to new students from a college sophomore (Walsh, 2005)

Think About It ——————————— *Journal Entry* 4.4

1. Do you make a to-do list of things you need to get done each day?

   never   seldom   often   almost always

2. If you selected "never" or "seldom," why don't you?

   _____

   _____

   _____

   _____

   _____

   _____

4.1   DO IT **NOW**

Making Productive Use of Free Time Outside the Classroom

Unlike in high school, homework in college often does not involve turning things in to your instructor daily or weekly. The academic work you do outside the classroom may not even be collected and graded. Instead, it is done for your own benefit to help prepare yourself for upcoming exams and major assignments (e.g., term papers or research reports). Rather than formally assigning work to you as homework, your professors expect that you will do this work on your own and without supervision. Listed below are strategies for working independently and in advance of college exams and assignments. These strategies will increase the quality of your time management in college and the quality of your academic performance.

Working Independently in Advance of Exams

Use the following strategies to use out-of-class time wisely to prepare for exams:

- **Complete reading assignments** relating to lecture topics before the topic is discussed in class. This will make lectures easier to understand and will prepare you to participate intelligently in class (e.g., ask meaningful questions of your instructor and make informed comments during class discussions).
- **Review your class notes** between class periods so that you can construct a mental bridge from one class to the next and make each upcoming lecture easier to follow. When reviewing your notes before the next class, rewrite any class notes that may be sloppily written the first time. If you find notes related to the same point all over the place, reorganize them by combining them into one set of notes. Lastly, if you find any information gaps or confusing points in your notes, seek out the course instructor or a trusted classmate to clear them up before the next class takes place.
- **Review information** you highlighted in your reading assignments to improve your retention of the information. If certain points are confusing to you, discuss

them with your course instructor during office hours or with a fellow classmate outside of class.
- **Integrate key ideas** in your class notes with information that you have highlighted in your assigned reading that relates to the same major point or general category. In other words, put related information from your lecture notes and your reading in the same place (e.g., on the same index card).
- **Use a part-to-whole study method** whereby you study material from your class notes and assigned reading in small pieces during short, separate study sessions that take place well in advance of the exam; then make your last study session before the exam a longer review session during which you restudy all the small parts together as a whole. It's a myth that studying in advance is a waste of time because you'll forget it all anyway by test time. As you'll see in Chapter 6, information studied in advance of an exam remains in your brain and is still there when you later review it. Even if you cannot recall the previously studied information when you first start reviewing it, you will relearn it faster than you did the first time, thus proving that some memory of it was retained from your earlier study sessions.

Work Independently Well in Advance of Due Dates for Term Papers and Research Reports

Work on large, long-range assignments by breaking them into the following smaller, short-term tasks:

- Search for and select a topic.
- Locate sources of information on the topic.
- Organize the information obtained from these sources into categories.
- Develop an outline of the report's major points and the order or sequence in which you plan to discuss them.
- Construct a first draft of the paper (and, if necessary, a second draft).
- Write a final draft of the paper.
- Proofread the final draft of your paper for minor mechanical mistakes, such as spelling and grammatical errors, before submitting it to your instructor.

2. **A good time-management plan should include reserve time to take care of the unexpected.** You should always hope for the best but should always be prepared for the worst. Your time-management plan should include a buffer zone or safety net, building in extra time that you can use to accommodate unforeseen developments or unexpected emergencies. Just as you should plan to save money in your bank for unexpected extra costs (e.g., emergency medical expenses), you should plan to save time in your schedule for unexpected events that cost you time (e.g., dealing with unscheduled tasks or taking longer than expected to complete already-planned tasks).

3. **A good time-management plan should capitalize on your biological rhythms.** When you plan your daily schedule, be aware of your natural peak periods and down times. Studies show that individuals differ in terms of the time of day when their bodies naturally tire and prefer to sleep or become energized and prefer to wake up. Some people are "early birds" who prefer to go to sleep early and wake up early; others are "night owls" who prefer to stay up late at night and get up late in the morning (Natale & Ciogna, 1996). (Teenagers are more likely to fall into the category of night owls.) Individuals also vary with respect to the times of day when they are at their highest and lowest levels of energy. Naturally, early birds are more likely to be morning people whose peak energy period occurs before noon; night owls are likely to be more productive in the late afternoon and evening. Also, most people experience a post-lunch dip in energy in the early afternoon (Monk, 2005).

   Be aware of your most productive hours of the day and schedule your highest-priority work and most challenging tasks for when you tend to work at peak performance levels. For example, schedule out-of-class academic work so that you're tackling academic tasks that require intense thinking (e.g., technical writing or complex problem solving) when you are most productive; schedule lighter work (e.g., light reading or routine tasks) at the times when your energy level tends to be lower. Also, keep your natural peak and down times in mind when you schedule your courses. Try to arrange your class schedule in such a way that you experience your most challenging courses at the times of the day when your body (brain) is most ready and able to accept that challenge.

4. **A good time-management plan should include a balance of work and recreation.** Don't only plan work time: plan time to relax, refuel, and recharge. Your overall plan shouldn't turn you into an obsessive-compulsive workaholic. Instead, it should represent a balanced blend of work and play, which includes activities that promote your mental and physical wellness, such as relaxation, recreation, and reflection. You could also arrange your schedule of work and play as a self-motivation strategy by using your play time to reward your work time.

Remember

A good time-management plan should help you stress less, learn more, and earn higher grades while leaving you time for other important aspects of your life. A good plan not only enables you to get your work done on time, but also enables you to attain and maintain balance in your life.

A good time-management plan includes a balanced blend of time planned for both work and recreation.

© Kendall Hunt

Author's Experience My mom is a schoolteacher, and when my sister and I were growing up she had a strict policy: when we came home from school we could have a snack, but after that we were not allowed to do anything else until our homework was finished. I remember that on days when it was really nice outside, I would beg and plead (and sometimes even argue) with my mom about going outside to play. She always won, and often I had wasted so much time arguing that I completely missed out on the opportunity to play at all. At the time I thought my mom was really mean. As I grew older (in high school and college), though, it became easy to put my homework first. My mom had taught me the importance of prioritizing and completing important things (like homework) before things that were not as important.

Julie McLaughlin

Think About It ———————————————————— *Journal Entry* 4.5

1. What activities do you engage in for fun or recreation?

_____

_____

_____

2. What do you do to relax or relieve stress?

_____

_____

_____

3. Brainstorm a list of activities you could do to relieve stress:

_____

_____

5. **A good time-management plan should have some flexibility.** Some people are immediately turned off by the idea of developing a schedule and planning their time because they feel it overstructures their lives and limits their freedom. It's only natural for you to prize your personal freedom and resist anything that appears to restrict your freedom in any way. A good plan preserves your freedom by helping you get done what must be done, reserving free time for you to do what you want and like to do.

6. **A good time-management plan shouldn't enslave you to a rigid work schedule.** It should be flexible enough to allow you to occasionally bend it without having to break it. Just as work commitments and family responsibilities can crop up unexpectedly, so, too, can opportunities for fun and enjoyable activities. Your plan should allow you the freedom to modify your schedule so that you can take advantage of these enjoyable opportunities and experiences. However, you should plan to make up the work time you lost. In other words, you can borrow or trade work time for play time, but don't "steal" it; you should plan to pay back the work time you borrowed by substituting it for a play period that existed in your original schedule.

Remember

When you create a personal time-management plan, remember that it is your plan—you own it and you run it. It shouldn't run you.

Converting Your Time-Management Plan into an Action Plan

Once you've planned the work, the next step is to work the plan. A good action plan is one that gives you a preview of what you intend to accomplish and an opportunity to review what you actually accomplished. You can begin to implement an action plan by constructing a daily to-do list, bringing that list with you as the day begins, and checking off items on the list as you get them done. At the end of the day, review your list and identify what was completed and what still needs to be done. The uncompleted tasks should become high priorities for the next day.

At the end of the day, if you find yourself with many unchecked items still remaining on your daily to-do list, this could mean that you're are spreading yourself too thin by trying to do too many things in a day. You may need to be more realistic about the number of things you can reasonably expect to accomplish per day by shortening your daily to-do list.

Being unable to complete many of your intended daily tasks may also mean that you need to modify your time-management plan by adding work time or subtracting activities that are drawing time and attention away from your work (e.g., taking cell-phone calls during your planned work times).

Think About It ——————————— *Journal Entry* **4.6**

1. By the end of a typical day, how often do you find that you accomplished most of the important tasks you hoped to accomplish?

    never   seldom   often   almost always

2. Why?

_____

_____

_____

_____

_____

_____

Dealing with Procrastination

Procrastination Defined

The word *procrastination* derives from two roots: *pro* (meaning "forward") plus *crastinus* (meaning "tomorrow"). As these roots suggest, procrastinators don't abide by the proverb "Why put off to tomorrow what can be done today?" Their philosophy is just the opposite: "Why do today what can be put off until tomorrow?" Adopting this philosophy promotes a perpetual pattern of postponing what needs to be done until the last possible moment, which results in rushing frantically to get it done (and compromising its quality), getting it only partially done, or not finishing it.

Research shows that 80 to 95 percent of college students procrastinate (Steel, 2007) and almost 50 percent report that they procrastinate consistently (Onwuegbuzie, 2000). Furthermore, the percentage of people reporting that they procrastinate is on the rise (Kachgal, Hansen, & Nutter, 2001).

Procrastination is such a serious issue for college students that some colleges and universities have opened "procrastination centers" to provide help exclusively for students who are experiencing problems with procrastination (Burka & Yuen, 1983).

Student
Perspective

"I believe the most important aspect of college life is time management. DO NOT procrastinate because, although this is the easy thing to do at first, it will catch up with you and make your life miserable."

—Advice from a first-year student to new college students

A procrastinator's idea of planning ahead and working in advance often boils down to this scenario.

Author's Experience During my early years in college, I was quite a procrastinator. During my sophomore year, I waited to do a major history paper until the night before it was due. Back then, I had a word processor that was little more than a typewriter; it allowed you to save your work to a floppy disk before printing. I finished writing my paper around 3:00 a.m. and hit "print," but about halfway through the printing I ran out of paper. I woke up my roommate to ask if she had paper, but she didn't. So, at 3:00 a.m. I was forced to get out of my pajamas, get into my street clothes, get into my car, and drive around town to find someplace open at three in the morning that sold typing paper. By the time I found a place, got back home, printed the paper, and washed up, it was time to go to class. I could barely stay awake in any of my classes that day, and when I got my history paper back, the grade wasn't exactly what I was hoping for. I never forgot that incident. My procrastination on that paper caused me to lose sleep the night before it was due, lose attention in all my other classes on the day it was due, and lose points on the paper that I managed to do. Thereafter, I was determined not to let procrastination get the best of me.

Julie McLaughlin

Procrastination is by no means limited to college students. It is a widespread problem that afflicts people of all ages and occupations (Harriott & Ferrari, 1996). This is why you'll find many books on the subject of time management in the self-help section of any popular bookstore. It's also why you see so many people at the post office on April 15 every year, mailing their tax returns at the last possible moment ("Haven't Filed Yet," 2003).

Myths That Promote Procrastination

Before there can be any hope of putting a stop to procrastination, procrastinators need to let go of two popular myths (misconceptions) about time and performance.

Myth 1. "I work better under pressure" (e.g., on the day or night before something is due). Procrastinators often confuse desperation with motivation. Their belief that they work better under pressure is often just a rationalization to justify or deny the truth, which is that they *only* work when they're under pressure—that is, when they're running out of time and are under the gun to get it done just before the deadline.

It's true that some people will only start to work and will work really fast when they're under pressure, but that does not mean they're working more *effectively* and producing work of better *quality.* Because they're playing "beat the clock," procrastinators' focus is no longer on doing the job *well* but on doing the job *fast* so that it gets done before they run out of time. This typically results in a product that turns out to be incomplete or inferior to what could have been produced if the work process began earlier.

Confusing rapidity with quality is a sin. It's an indisputable fact that it takes more time to do higher-quality work, particularly if that job requires higher-level thinking skills such as thinking critically and creatively (Ericsson & Charness, 1994). Academic work in college often requires deep learning and complex thinking, which require time for reflection. Deep thoughts and creative ideas take time to formulate, incubate, and eventually "hatch," which is not likely to happen under time pressure (Amabile, Hadley, & Kramer, 2002). Working under pressure on tasks that require higher-level thinking would be similar to trying to complete a long, challenging test within a short time frame. What happens is people have less time to think, to attend to fine details, to double-check their work, and to fine-tune their final product. Research indicates that most procrastinators admit that the work they produce is of poorer quality because they procrastinate (Steel, Brothen, & Wambach, 2001; Wesley, 1994) and that they experience considerable anxiety and guilt about their procrastination habit (Tice & Baumeister, 1997).

Myth 2. "Studying in advance is a waste of time because you will forget it all by test time." This misconception is commonly used to justify procrastinating with respect to preparing for upcoming exams. As will be discussed in Chapter 6, studying that is distributed (spread out) over time is more effective than massed (crammed) studying. Furthermore, last-minute studying that takes place the night before exams often results in lost sleep time due to the need to pull late-nighters or all-nighters. This fly-by-night strategy interferes with retention of information that has been studied and elevates test anxiety because of lost dream (a.k.a. rapid eye movement, or REM) sleep, which enables the brain to store memories and cope with stress (Hobson, 1988; Voelker, 2004). Research indicates that procrastinators experience higher rates of stress-related physical disorders, such as insomnia, stomach problems, colds, and flu (McCance & Pychyl, 2003).

Working under time pressure adds to performance pressure because procrastinators are left with no margin of error to correct mistakes, no time to seek help on their work, and no chance to handle random catastrophes that may arise at the last minute (e.g., an attack of the flu or a family emergency).

"Haste makes waste."

—Benjamin Franklin, 18th-century inventor, newspaper writer, and signer of the *Declaration of Independence*

Think About It ———————————————— *Journal Entry* **4.7**

Have you ever put off work for so long that getting it done turned into an emergency situation?

Explain:

_____

_____

_____

_____

_____

_____

Psychological Causes of Procrastination

Sometimes, procrastination has deeper psychological roots. People may procrastinate for reasons related not directly to poor time-management habits but more to emotional issues involving self-esteem or self-image. For instance, studies show that procrastination is sometimes used as a psychological strategy to protect one's self-esteem, which is referred to as self-handicapping. This strategy may be used by some procrastinators (consciously or unconsciously) to give themselves a "handicap" or disadvantage. Thus, if their performance turns out to be less than spectacular, they can conclude (rationalize) that it was because they were performing under a handicap—lack of time (Smith, Snyder, & Handelsman, 1982).

For example, if the grade they receive on a test or paper turns out to be low, they can still "save face" (self-esteem) by concluding that it was because they waited until the last minute and didn't put much time or effort into it. In other words, they had the ability or intelligence to earn a good grade; they just didn't try very hard. Better yet, if they happened to luck out and get a good grade despite doing it at the last minute, then the grade just shows how intelligent they are! Thus, self-handicapping creates a fail-safe scenario that's guaranteed to protect the procrastinator's self-image. If the work performance or product is less than excellent, it can be blamed on external factors (e.g., lack of time); if it happens to earn them a high grade, they can attribute the result to their extraordinary ability, which enabled them to do so well despite doing it all at the last minute.

In addition to self-handicapping, other psychological factors have been found to contribute to procrastination, including the following:

- **Fear of failure.** Feeling that it's better to postpone the job, or not do it, than to fail at it (Burka & Yuen, 1983; Soloman & Rothblum, 1984).
- **Perfectionism.** Having unrealistically high personal standards or expectations, which leads to the belief that it's better to postpone work or not do it than to risk doing it less than perfectly (Flett, Blankstein, Hewitt, & Koledin, 1992; Kachgal et al., 2001).

"We didn't lose the game; we just ran out of time."

—Vince Lombardi, legendary football coach

"Procrastinators would rather be seen as lacking in effort than lacking in ability."

—Joseph Ferrari, professor of psychology and procrastination researcher

"Striving for excellence motivates you; striving for perfection is demoralizing."

—Harriet Braiker, psychologist and bestselling author

- **Fear of success.** Fearing that doing well will show others that the procrastinator has the ability to achieve success and others will expect the procrastinator to maintain those high standards by doing "repeat performances" (Beck, Koons, & Milgram, 2000; Ellis & Kraun, 1977).
- **Indecisiveness.** Having difficulty making decisions, including decisions about what to do or how to begin doing it (Anderson, 2003; Steel, 2003).
- **Thrill seeking.** Enjoying the adrenaline rush triggered by rushing to get things done just before a deadline (Szalavitz, 2003).

If these or any other issues are involved, their underlying psychological causes must be dealt with before procrastination can be overcome. Because they have deeper roots, it may take some time and professional assistance to uproot them. A good place to get such assistance is the Personal Counseling Office. Personal counselors on college campuses are professional psychologists who are trained to deal with psychological issues that can contribute to procrastination.

Think About It ———————————— *Journal Entry* **4.8**

1. How often do you procrastinate?

        rarely   occasionally   frequently   consistently

2. When you do procrastinate, what is the usual reason?

_____

_____

_____

_____

_____

_____

Self-Help Strategies for Beating the Procrastination Habit

Once inaccurate beliefs or emotional issues underlying procrastination have been identified and dealt with, the next step is to move from gaining self-insight to taking direct action on the procrastination habit itself. Listed here are our top strategies for minimizing or eliminating the procrastination habit.

1. **Continually practice effective time-management strategies.** If effective time-management practices, such as those previously cited in this chapter, are implemented consistently, they can turn into a habit. Studies show that when people repeatedly practice effective time-management strategies, they gradually become part of their routine and develop into habits. For example, when procrastinators repeatedly practice effective time-management strategies with respect to tasks that they procrastinate on, their procrastination tendencies begin to fade and are gradually replaced by good time-management habits (Ainslie, 1992; Baumeister, Heatherton, & Tice, 1994).

For many procrastinators, getting started is often their biggest obstacle.

"Just do it!"

—Commercial slogan of a popular athletic equipment company, named after the Greek goddess of victory: Nike

Student
Perspective

"Did you ever dread doing something, then it turned out to take only about 20 minutes to do?"

—Conversation overheard in a coffee shop between two college students

"There is nothing to fear but fear itself."

—Franklin D. Roosevelt, 32nd president of the United States and the only American to win four presidential elections

2. **Make the start of work as inviting or appealing as possible.** Getting started can be a key stumbling block for many procrastinators. They experience what's called "start-up stress" when they're about to begin a task they expect will be unpleasant, difficult, or boring (Burka & Yuen, 1983). If you have trouble starting your work, one way to give yourself a jump-start is to arrange your work tasks in an order that allows you to start on tasks that you're likely to find most interesting or most likely to experience success with. Once you overcome the initial inertia and get going, you can ride the momentum you've created to attack the tasks that you find less appealing and more daunting.

You're also likely to discover that the dreaded work wasn't as difficult, boring, or time-consuming as it appeared to be. When you sense that you're making some progress toward getting work done, your anxiety begins to decline. As with many experiences in life that are dreaded and avoided, the anticipation of the event turns out to be worse than the event itself. Research on students who hadn't started a project until it was about to be due indicates that these students experience anxiety and guilt about delaying their work, but once they begin working, these negative emotions decline and are replaced by more positive feelings (McCance & Pychyl, 2003).

3. **Make the work manageable.** Work becomes less overwhelming and less stressful when it's handled in small chunks or pieces. You can conquer procrastination for large tasks by using a "divide and conquer" strategy: divide the large task into smaller, more manageable units, and then attack and complete them one at a time.

Don't underestimate the power of short work sessions. They can be more effective than longer sessions because it's easier to maintain momentum and concentration for shorter periods. If you're working on a large project or preparing for a major exam, dividing your work into short sessions will enable you to take quick jabs and poke small holes in it, reducing its overall size with each successive punch. This approach will also give you the sense of satisfaction that comes with knowing that you're making steady progress toward completing a big task—continually chipping away at it in short strokes and gradually taking away the pressure associated with having to go for a big knockout punch right before the final bell (deadline).

Author's Experience The two biggest projects I've had to complete in my life were writing my doctoral thesis and writing this textbook! The strategy that enabled me to keep going until I completed both of these large tasks was to make up short-term deadlines for myself (e.g., complete 5–10 pages each week). I psyched myself into thinking that these were real "drop-dead" deadlines and that if I didn't meet them and complete these small, shorter-term tasks, I was going to drop the ball and fail to get the whole job done. I think these self-imposed deadlines worked for me because they gave me short, more manageable tasks to work on that allowed me to make steady progress toward my larger, long-term task. It was as if I took a huge, hard-to-digest meal and broke it up into small, bite-sized pieces that I could easily swallow and gradually digest over time, as opposed to trying to consume a large meal right before bedtime (the final deadline).

Joe Cuseo

4. **Organization matters.** Research indicates that disorganization is a factor that contributes to procrastination (Steel, 2003). How well we organize our workplace and manage our work materials can reduce our risk of procrastination. Having the right materials in the right place at the right time can make it easier to get to our work and get going on our work. Once we've made a decision to get the job done, we don't want to waste time looking for the tools we need to begin doing it. For procrastinators, this time delay may be just the amount of time they need to change their minds and not start their work.

One simple yet effective way to organize your college work materials is by developing your own file system. You can begin to create an effective file system by filing (storing) materials from different courses in different colored folders or notebooks. This will allow you to keep all materials related to the same course in the same place and give you direct and immediate access to the materials you need as soon as you need them. Such a system helps you get organized, reduces stress associated with having things all over the place, and reduces the risk of procrastination by reducing the time it takes for you to start working.

5. **Location matters.** *Where* you work can influence when or whether you work. Research demonstrates that distraction is a factor that can contribute to procrastination (Steel, 2003). Thus, it may be possible for you to minimize procrastination by working in an environment whose location and arrangement prevent distraction and promote concentration.

Distractions tend to come in two major forms: social distractions (e.g., people nearby who are not working) and media distractions (e.g., cell phones, e-mails, text messages, iPods, Internet, and TV). Research indicates that the number of hours per week that college students spend watching TV is *negatively* associated with academic success: more TV leads to lower college grade point averages, less likelihood of graduating college with honors, and lower levels of personal development (Astin, 1993).

Remember

Select a workplace and arrange your workspace to minimize distraction from people and media. Try to remove everything from your work site that's not directly relevant to your work.

Think About It ———————————————————— *Journal Entry* **4.9**

List your two most common sources of distraction while working. Next to each distraction, identify a strategy that you might use to reduce or eliminate it.

Source of Distraction   Strategy for Reducing This Distraction

1. _____

_____

2. _____

_____

Lastly, keep in mind that you can arrange your work environment in a way that not only disables distraction, but also enables concentration. You can enable or empower your concentration by working in an environment that allows you easy access to work support materials (e.g., class notes, textbooks, and a dictionary) and social support (e.g., working with a group of motivated students who will encourage you to get focused, stay on task, and keep on track to complete your work tasks).

6. **Arrange the order or sequence of your work tasks to intercept procrastination when you're most likely to experience it.** While procrastination often involves difficulty starting work, it can also involve difficulty continuing and completing work (Lay & Silverman, 1996). As previously mentioned, if you have trouble starting work, it might be best to first do tasks that you find most interesting or easiest. However, if you have difficulty maintaining or sustaining your work until it's finished, you might try to schedule work tasks that you find easier and more interesting *in the middle or toward the end* of your planned work time. If you're performing tasks of greater interest and ease at a point in your work when you typically lose interest or energy, you may be able to sustain your interest and energy long enough to continue working until you complete them, which means that you'll have completed your entire list of tasks. Also, doing your most enjoyable and easiest tasks later can provide an incentive or reward for completing your less enjoyable tasks first.

7. **If you're close to completing a task, don't stop until you complete it.** It's often harder to restart a task than it is to finish a task that you've already started, because once you've overcome the initial inertia associated with getting started, you can ride the momentum that you've already created. Furthermore, finishing a task can give you a sense of closure—the feeling of personal accomplishment and self-satisfaction that comes from knowing that you "closed the deal." Placing a checkmark next to a completed task and seeing that it's one less thing you have to do can motivate you to continue working on the remaining tasks on your list.

Summary and Conclusion

Mastering the skill of managing time is critical for success in college and in life beyond college. Time is a valuable personal resource; the better you use it, the greater control you have over your life. On the other hand, if you ignore or abuse this resource, you run the risk of reducing the quality of your work and the quality of your life. Once you let go of the pervasive and pernicious procrastination-promoting myth that you work better under pressure (e.g., on the day or night before something is due), you can begin planning how to manage your time and control your future.

Managing time involves three key processes:

1. Analysis of how we spend time, which will allow us to become more consciously aware of our time-spending habits and enable us to know where all our time actually goes.
2. Development of a plan that connects our short-range, mid-range, and long-range tasks (i.e., for the next day, the next week, and the end of the term).
3. Evaluation of our priorities to ensure that we put most of our time into what's most important or matters the most.

These are the three keys to effective time management; they are also likely to be the keys to managing any personal resource, such as your money or your relationships.

Learning More through the World Wide Web

Internet-Based Resources for Further Information on Time Management

For additional information related to the ideas discussed in this chapter, we recommend the following Web sites:

www.time-management-guide.com/procrastination.html

www.studygs.net/timman.htm

www.essortment.com/lifestyle/timemanagement_sjmu.htm

(This site includes time-management strategies designed specifically for adult or non-traditional-aged students.)

4.1 Who's in Charge?

You have a paper due tomorrow for your 10:00 a.m. class. You stay up late writing the paper, and then your friends call and ask you to go out. The paper is finished, and you decide you can print it off when you get to school tomorrow. You have a great time with your friends and oversleep, waking at 9:45 a.m. You go straight to the computer lab and experience difficulties printing off your paper. You find a lab technician to help you, but it takes him 40 minutes to retrieve the paper. You run into class (45 minutes late) and give the paper to your instructor, who informs you that she will take the paper for late credit because the class policy states that any papers handed in after the beginning of class are considered late.

1. Who is primarily responsible for this paper being late? Why?

2. How could the situation have been avoided or handled differently?

4.2 Term at a Glance

Review the syllabus (course outline) for each course you're enrolled in this term, and complete the following information for each:

Term _____, Year _____

Course ↓	Professor ↓	Exams ↓	Projects & Papers ↓	Other Assignments ↓	Attendance Policy ↓	Late & Makeup Assignment Policy ↓

1. Is the overall workload what you expected? Are you surprised by the amount of work required in any particular course or courses?

2. At this point in the term, what do you see as your most challenging or demanding course or courses? Why?

3. Do you think you can handle the total workload required for the full set of courses you're enrolled in this term?

4. What adjustments or changes could you make to your personal schedule that would make it easier to accommodate your academic workload this term?

4.3 Your Week at a Glance

On the blank grid that follows, map out your typical week for this term. Start by recording what you usually do on these days, including when you have class, when you work, and when you relax or recreate. You can use abbreviations or write tasks out in full if you have enough room in the box (J = job, R&R = rest/relaxation, etc.). List the abbreviations you create at the bottom of the page so that your instructor can follow them.

If you're a *full-time* student, find *25 hours* in your week that you can devote to homework (HW). These 25 hours could be found between classes, during the day, in the evenings, or on the weekends. If you can find 25 hours per week for homework, in addition to your class schedule, you'll have a 40-hour schoolwork week, which research has shown to result in good grades and success in college.

If you're a *part-time* student, find *two hours* you can devote to homework *for every hour* that you're in class (e.g., if you're in class nine hours per week, find 18 hours of homework time).

	Sunday	Monday	Tuesday	Wednesday	Thursday	Friday	Saturday
7:00 a.m.							
8:00 a.m.							
9:00 a.m.							
10:00 a.m.							
11:00 a.m.							
12:00 p.m.							
1:00 p.m.							
2:00 p.m.							
3:00 p.m.							
4:00 p.m.							
5:00 p.m.							
6:00 p.m.							
7:00 p.m.							
8:00 p.m.							
9:00 p.m.							
10:00 p.m.							
11:00 p.m.							

4.4 Personal Time Inventory

1. Go to the following Web site:

    www.ulc.psu.edu/studyskills/time_management.html#monitoring_your_time

2. Complete the time management exercise at this site. The exercise asks you to estimate the number of hours per day or week that you spend doing various activities (e.g., sleeping, employment, and commuting). As you enter the amounts of time you engage in these activities, the total number of remaining hours available in the week for academic work will be automatically computed.

3. After completing your entries, answer the following questions:
    *   How many hours per week do you have available for academic work?
    *   Do you have two hours available for academic work outside of class for each hour you spend in class?
    *   What time wasters do you detect that might be easily eliminated or reduced to create more time for academic work outside of class?

4.5 Ranking Priorities

Look at the tasks below and decide if they are A, B, or C priorities:

_____ Going for a run

_____ Writing a paper that is due tomorrow

_____ Paying your electric bill that is due next week

_____ Checking out what your friends are doing on Facebook

_____ Getting your haircut

_____ Making an appointment with your academic advisor to register for classes

_____ Playing your favorite video game

_____ Making it to your doctor's appointment

_____ Helping your sister plan her wedding

_____ Picking up your child's prescription from the pharmacy

_____ Studying for your final exams

_____ Calling your cousin to catch up on family gossip

_____ Making reservations for your vacation

_____ Going to see the hot new movie that has come out

_____ Getting your oil changed in your car

_____ Getting your car washed

Procrastination: The Vicious Cycle

Delilah has a major paper due at the end of the term. It's now past midterm and she still hasn't started to work on her paper. She tells herself, "I should have started sooner."

However, Delilah continues to postpone starting her work on the paper and begins to feel anxious and guilty about it. To relieve her growing anxiety and guilt, she starts doing other tasks instead, such as cleaning her room and returning e-mails. This makes Delilah feel a little better because these tasks keep her busy, take her mind off the term paper, and give her the feeling that at least she's getting something accomplished. Time continues to pass; the deadline for the paper is growing dangerously close. Delilah now finds herself in the position of having lots of work to do and little time in which to do it.

Source: Burka & Yuen (1983)

Discussion Questions

1. What do you predict Delilah will do at this point?

2. Why did you make the above prediction?

3. What grade do you think Delilah will receive on her paper?

4. What do you think Delilah will do on the next term paper she's assigned?

5. Other than starting sooner, what recommendations would you have for Delilah (and other procrastinators like her) to break this cycle of procrastination and prevent it from happening repeatedly?

Chapter 4 Reflection

Looking back on suggestions from this chapter, what are three things you can do to start managing your time better?

1.

2.

3.

Explain how you are going to make this happen.

Higher-Level Thinking

Moving beyond Basic Knowledge to Critical and Creative Thinking

THOUGHT STARTER | *Journal Entry* **5.1**

LEARNING GOAL

To increase awareness of what it means to think at a higher level and how higher-level thinking can be used to achieve excellence in college and beyond.

To me, critical thinking means . . .

(At a later point in this chapter, we'll discuss critical thinking and ask you to flash back to the response you made here.)

_____

_____

_____

_____

Think About It —————— *Journal Entry* **5.2**

To me, thinking is . . .

_____

_____

_____

_____

_____

_____

_____

Student
Perspective

"To me, thinking at a higher level means deep thought. It is when you have to put your time and effort into whatever you are thinking or writing."

—First-year college student

What Is Higher-Level Thinking?

The term *higher-level thinking* (or *higher-order thinking*) refers to a more advanced level of thought than that used for learning basic skills and acquiring factual knowledge. Higher-level thinking involves reflecting on the knowledge you've acquired and taking additional mental action on it, such as evaluating its validity, integrating it with something else you've learned, or creating new ideas.

From *Thriving in the Community College & Beyond*, Second Edition by Joseph B. Cuseo, Aaron Thompson, Julie A. McLaughlin, and Steady H. Moono. Copyright © 2013 by Kendall Hunt Publishing Company. Reprinted by permission.

Contestants performing on TV quiz shows such as *Jeopardy!* or *Who Wants to Be a Millionaire?* are responding with factual knowledge to questions that ask for information about who, what, when, and where. If these contestants were to be tested for higher-level thinking, they would be answering more challenging questions about why, how, and what if.

Remember

The focus of higher-level thinking is not just to answer questions but also to question answers.

© Rafael Ramirez Lee, 2013. Under license from Shutterstock, Inc.

As its name implies, higher-level thinking involves raising the bar and jacking up your thinking to levels that go beyond merely remembering, reproducing, or regurgitating factual information. "Education is what's left over after you've forgotten all the facts" is an old saying that carries a lot of truth. Studies show that students' memory of facts learned in college often fades with time (Pascarella & Terenzini, 1991, 2005). Memory for factual information has a short lifespan; the ability to think at a higher level is a durable, lifelong learning skill that lasts a lifetime.

Compared to high school classes, college courses focus less on memorizing information and more on thinking about issues, concepts, and principles (Conley, 2005). Remembering information in college may get a grade of "C," demonstrating comprehension of that information may get you a "B," and going beyond comprehension to demonstrate higher-level thinking will earn you an "A." In national surveys of college professors teaching freshman-through senior-level courses in various fields, more than 95 percent of them report that the most important goal of a college education is to develop students' ability to think critically (Gardiner, 2005; Milton, 1982). Similarly, college professors teaching introductory courses to freshmen and sophomores indicate that the primary educational purpose of their courses is to develop students' critical thinking skills (Higher Education Institute, 2009; Stark et al., 1990).

Simply stated, college professors are often more concerned with teaching you *how* to think than with teaching you *what* to think (i.e., what facts to remember).

Student Perspective

"To me, thinking at a higher level means to think and analyze something beyond the obvious and find the deeper meaning."

—First-year college student

Remember

Your college professors will often expect you to do more than just retain or reproduce information: they'll ask you to demonstrate higher levels of thinking with respect to what you've learned, such as analyze it, evaluate it, apply it, or connect it with other concepts that you've learned.

Student Perspective

"To me, thinking at a higher level means going beyond understanding something on a superficial and general level; it requires a deep and profound thought process."

—First-year college student

This is not to say that acquiring knowledge and basic comprehension are unimportant. They are important because they supply you with the raw material needed to manufacture higher-level thinking. Deep learning and a broad base of knowledge provide the stepping stones you need to climb to higher levels of thinking.

This is not to say that basic knowledge and comprehension are unimportant. Rather, they provide the foundational steps necessary for you to climb to higher levels of thinking, as illustrated in Figure 5.1.

FIGURE 5.1

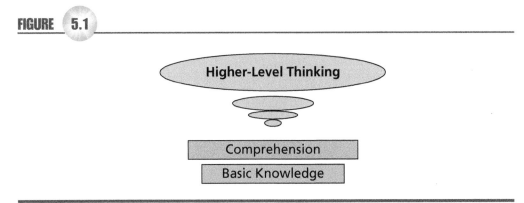

The Relationship between Knowledge, Comprehension, and Higher-Level Thinking

Defining and Describing the Major Forms of Higher-Level Thinking

When your college professors ask you to "think critically," they're usually asking you to use one or more of the eight forms of thinking listed in Snapshot Summary 5.1. As you read the description of each form of thinking, note whether or not you've heard of it before.

Snapshot Summary

5.1   Major Forms of Higher-Level Thinking

1. **Application (applied thinking).** Putting knowledge into practice to solve problems and resolve issues;
2. **Analysis (analytical thinking).** Breaking down information to identify its key parts and underlying elements;
3. **Synthesis.** Building up ideas by integrating them into a larger whole or more comprehensive system;
4. **Multidimensional thinking.** Taking multiple perspectives (i.e., viewing issues from different vantage points);
5. **Inferential reasoning.** Making arguments or judgments by inferring (stepping to) a conclusion that's supported by empirical (observable) evidence or logical consistency;
6. **Balanced thinking.** Carefully considering arguments for and against a particular position or viewpoint;
7. **Critical thinking.** Evaluating (judging the quality of) arguments, conclusions, and ideas;
8. **Creative thinking.** Generating ideas that are unique, original, or distinctively different.

Application (Applied Thinking)

When you learn something deeply, you transform information into knowledge; when you translate knowledge into action, you're engaging in a higher-level thinking process known as *application*. Applied thinking moves you beyond simply knowing something to actually doing something with the knowledge you possess: you use the knowledge you've acquired to solve a problem or resolve an issue. For example, if you use knowledge you've acquired in a human relations course (or from Chapter 10 of this text) to resolve an interpersonal conflict, you're engaging in application. Similarly, when you use knowledge acquired in a math course to solve a problem that you haven't seen before, you're using applied thinking. Application is a powerful form of higher-level thinking because it allows you to transfer your knowledge to new situations or contexts and put it into practice.

Look back at the eight forms of thinking described in Snapshot Summary 5.1. Which of these forms of thinking had you heard of before? Did you use any of these forms of thinking on high school exams or assignments? Explain.

_____

_____

_____

_____

_____

_____

    Always be on the lookout for ways to apply the knowledge you acquire to your personal life experiences and current events or issues. When you use your knowledge for the practical purpose of doing something good, such as bettering yourself or others, you not only demonstrate application; you also demonstrate *wisdom* (Staudinger, 2008).

Analysis (Analytical Thinking)

The mental process of analysis is similar to the physical process of peeling an onion. When you analyze something, you take it apart or break it down and pick out its key parts, main points, or underlying elements. For example, if you were to analyze a textbook chapter, you would go beyond reading just to cover the content: you would read it to uncover the author's main ideas and distinguish them from background information and incidental details.

    In an art course, you would use analysis to identify the components or elements of a painting or sculpture (e.g., its structure, texture, tone, and form). In the natural and social sciences, you would use analysis to identify underlying reasons or causes for natural (physical) phenomena and social events, which is commonly referred to as "causal analysis." For instance, causal analysis of the September 11, 2001, attack on the United States would involve identifying the factors that led to the attack or the underlying reasons for why the attack took place.

Synthesis

A form of higher-level thinking that's basically the opposite of analysis is *synthesis*. When you analyze, you break information into its parts; when you synthesize, you build it up by taking separate parts or pieces of information and connecting them to form an integrated whole (like piecing together parts of a puzzle). You engage in synthesis when you connect ideas presented in different courses: for instance, when you integrate ethical concepts learned in a philosophy course with marketing concepts learned in a business course to produce a set of ethical guidelines for marketing and advertising products.

| Think About It | *Journal Entry* 5.4 |

A TV commercial for a particular brand of liquor (which shall remain nameless) once showed a young man getting out of his car in front of a house where a party is going on. The driver gets out of his car, takes out a knife, slashes his tires, and goes inside to join the party. Using the higher-level thinking skill of analysis, what would you say are the underlying or embedded messages in this commercial?

_____

_____

_____

_____

_____

_____

Synthesis involves more than a summary. It goes beyond just condensing information to a higher level of thinking that involves finding and forming meaningful connections across separate pieces of information and weaving them together to form a cohesive picture. When you're synthesizing, you're thinking conceptually by converting isolated facts and separated bits of information and integrating them into a *concept*—a larger system or network of related ideas.

Although synthesis and analysis are virtually opposite thought processes, they complement each other. When you analyze, you disassemble information into its key parts. When you synthesize, you reassemble information into a whole. For instance, when writing this book, we analyzed published material in many fields (e.g., psychology, history, philosophy, and biology) and identified information from parts of these fields that were most relevant to promoting the success of beginning college students. We then synthesized or reassembled these parts to create a new whole—the textbook you're now reading.

Multidimensional Thinking

When you engage in multidimensional thinking, you view yourself and the world around you from different angles or vantage points. In particular, a multidimensional thinker is able to think from four key perspectives and determine how each of them influences, and is influenced by, the issue under discussion.

1. **Person (self).** How does this issue affect me as an individual? (The perspective of person.)
2. **Place.** What impact does this issue have on people living in different countries? (The perspective of place.)

3. **Time.** How will future generations of people be affected by this issue? (The perspective of time.)
4. **Culture.** How is this issue likely to be interpreted or experienced by groups of people who share different social customs and traditions? (The perspective of culture.)

Each of these four general perspectives has specific elements embedded within it. The four major perspectives, along with the key elements that comprise each of them, are listed and described in Snapshot Summary 5.2.

Snapshot Summary

5.2   Perspectives Associated with Multidimensional Thinking

Perspective 1: PERSON (Perspectives on different dimensions of oneself.)

Key Components

- **Intellectual (cognitive):** Knowledge, style of thinking, and self-concept
- **Emotional:** Feelings, emotional adjustment, and mental health
- **Social:** Interpersonal relationships and social interactions
- **Ethical:** Values and moral convictions
- **Physical:** Health and wellness
- **Spiritual:** Beliefs about the meaning or purpose of life and the hereafter
- **Vocational (occupational):** Means of making a living and earning an income

Perspective 2: PLACE (Perspectives beyond the self that include progressively wider social and spatial distance.)

Key Components

- **Family:** Parents, children, and other relatives
- **Community:** Local communities and neighborhoods
- **Society:** Societal institutions (e.g., schools, churches, and hospitals) and groups within society (e.g., social groups differing in age, gender, race, or socioeconomic status)
- **Nation:** One's own country or place of citizenship
- **International:** Citizens of different nations and territories
- **Global:** Planet earth (e.g., its life forms and natural resources)
- **Universe:** The galaxy that includes earth, other planets, and celestial bodies

Perspective 3: TIME (Chronological perspective.)

Key Components

- **Historical:** The past
- **Contemporary:** The present
- **Futuristic:** The future

Perspective 4: CULTURE (Perspective of particular groups of people who share the same social heritage and traditions.)

Key Components

- **Linguistic (language):** How group members communicate via spoken and written words and through nonverbal communication (body language)
- **Political:** How the group organizes societal authority and uses it to govern itself, make collective decisions, and maintain social order
- **Economic:** How the material wants and needs of the group are met through allocation of limited resources, and how wealth is distributed among its members
- **Geographical:** How the group's physical location influences the nature of social interactions and the way its members adapt to and use their environment
- **Aesthetic:** How the group appreciates and expresses artistic beauty and creativity through the arts (e.g., visual art, music, theater, literature, and dance)
- **Scientific:** How the group views, understands, and investigates natural phenomena through research (e.g., scientific tests and experiments)
- **Ecological:** How the group views its relationship to the surrounding biological world (e.g., other living creatures) and the physical environment
- **Anthropological:** How the group's culture originated, evolved, and developed over time
- **Sociological:** How the group's society is structured and organized into social subgroups and social institutions
- **Psychological:** How group members tend to think, feel, and interact with each other, and how their attitudes, opinions, or beliefs have been acquired
- **Philosophical:** The group's ideas or views on the nature of truth, goodness, wisdom, beauty, and the meaning or purpose of life
- **Theological:** Group members' ideas and beliefs about a transcendent, supreme being, and how they express their shared faith in a supreme being

Important human issues don't exist in isolation but as parts of complex, interconnected systems that involve interplay of multiple factors and perspectives. For example, global warming is a current issue that involves the earth's atmosphere gradually thickening and trapping more heat due to a collection of greenhouse gases, which are being produced primarily by the burning of fossil fuels. It's theorized that this increase in manmade pollution is causing temperatures to rise (and sometimes fall) around the world and is contributing to natural disasters, such as droughts, wildfires, and dust storms (Joint Science Academies Statement, 2005; National Resources Defense Council, 2012). Understanding and addressing this issue involves interrelationships among a variety of perspectives, as depicted in Figure 5.2.

FIGURE 5.2

Person	Global warming involves us on an individual level because our personal efforts at energy conservation in our homes and our willingness to purchase energy-efficient products can play a major role in solving this problem.
Place	Global warming is an international issue that extends beyond the boundaries of one's own country to all countries in the world, and its solution will require worldwide collaboration.
Time	If the current trend toward higher global temperatures caused by global warming continues, it could seriously threaten the lives of future generations of people who inhabit our planet.
Culture	The problem of global warming has been caused by industries in technologically advanced cultures, yet the problem of rising global temperatures is likely to have its most negative impact on less technologically advanced cultures that lack the resources to respond to it (Joint Science Academies Statement, 2005). To prevent this from happening, technologically advanced cultures will need to use their advanced technology to devise alternative methods for generating energy that don't release heat-trapping gases into the atmosphere.

Understanding Global Warming from Four Key Perspectives

Addressing the issue of global warming also involves different components of our culture, including: (1) ecology: understanding the delicate interplay between humans and their natural environment, (2) science: need for research and development of alternative sources of energy, (3) economics: managing the cost incurred by industries to change their existing sources of energy, (4) politics: devising incentives or laws to encourage changes in industries' use of energy sources, and (5) international relations: collaboration between our nation and other nations that are currently contributing to this worldwide problem and that play pivotal roles in its future solution.

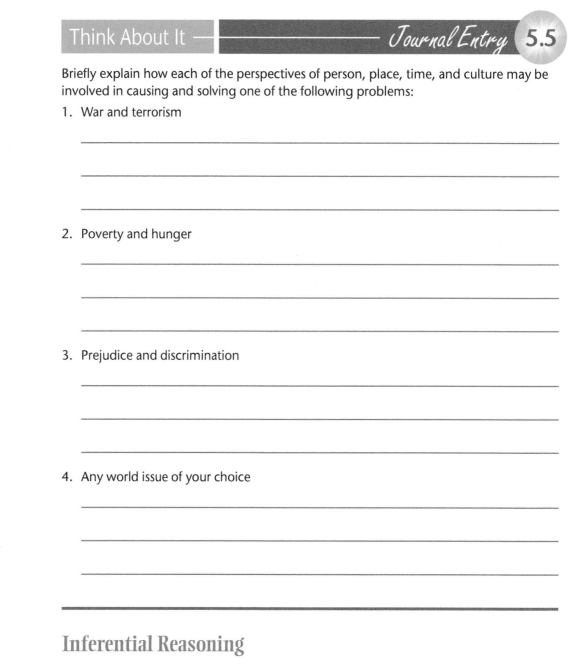

Briefly explain how each of the perspectives of person, place, time, and culture may be involved in causing and solving one of the following problems:

1. War and terrorism

   _____

   _____

   _____

2. Poverty and hunger

   _____

   _____

   _____

3. Prejudice and discrimination

   _____

   _____

   _____

4. Any world issue of your choice

   _____

   _____

   _____

Inferential Reasoning

When people make arguments or arrive at conclusions, they do so by starting with a premise (a statement or an observation) and use it to infer (step to) a conclusion. The following sentence starters demonstrate the process of inferential reasoning:

> *"Because this is true, it follows that . . ."*

> *"Based on this evidence, I can conclude that . . ."*

Inferential reasoning is the primary thought process humans use to reach conclusions about themselves and the world around them. This is also the form of thinking that you will use to make arguments and reach conclusions about ideas presented in your college courses. You'll often be required to take positions and draw conclusions by supporting them with solid evidence and sound reasoning. In a sense, you'll be asked to take on the role of a courtroom lawyer trying to prove a case by supplying supporting arguments and evidence (exhibit A, exhibit B, etc.).

The following are two major ways in which you use inferential reasoning to support your points or arguments:

1. **Citing empirical (observable) evidence.** Supporting your point with specific examples, personal experiences, facts, figures, statistical data, scientific research findings, expert testimonies, supporting quotes, or statements from leading authorities in the field.

2. **Using principles of logical consistency.** Showing that your conclusion follows or flows logically from an established premise or proposition. The following are examples that demonstrate logical consistency:

   - The constitution guarantees all U.S. citizens the right to vote (established premise);
   - U.S. citizens include women and people of color; therefore,
   - Granting women and people of color the right to vote was/is logically consistent (and constitutional).

Both empirical evidence and logical consistency can be used to support the same argument. For instance, advocates for lowering the legal drinking age to 18 have argued that: (1) in other countries where drinking is allowed at age 18, statistics show that they have fewer binge-drinking and drunk-driving problems than the United States (empirical evidence), and (2) 18-year-olds in the United States are considered to be legal adults with respect to such rights and responsibilities as voting, serving on juries, joining the military, and being held responsible for committing crimes; therefore, 18-year-olds should have the right to drink.

Think About It ——————————————— *Journal Entry* 5.6

Can you think of any arguments *against* lowering the drinking age to 18 that are based on empirical (observable) evidence or logical consistency?

_____

_____

_____

_____

_____

_____

_____

Unfortunately, errors can be made in the inferential reasoning process, often referred to as *logical fallacies*. Some of the more common logical fallacies are summarized in Snapshot Summary 5.3.

Snapshot Summary

5.3 Logical Fallacies: Inferential-Reasoning Errors

Critical thinking is a higher-level thinking skill that allows you to evaluate and detect errors in your own reasoning and in the reasoning of others. Some of the more common reasoning errors are summarized here. **As you read the following list of logical errors, make a brief note in the margin of any example of these errors that you have observed or experienced.**

- **Dogmatism.** Stubbornly clinging to a personally held viewpoint that's unsupported by evidence and remaining closed-minded (non-receptive) to other viewpoints that are better supported by evidence. (For instance, those who believe that America's form of capitalism is the only economic system that can work in a successful democracy, while refusing to acknowledge that there are other successful democratic countries with different types of capitalistic economies.)

- **Selective perception.** Seeing only examples and instances that support a position while overlooking or ignoring those that contradict it (e.g., those who believe in astrology who only notice and point out people whose personalities happen to fit their astrological signs, while overlooking those who don't).

"Belief can be produced in practically unlimited quantity and intensity, without observation or reasoning, and even in defiance of both by the simple desire to believe."

—George Bernard Shaw, Irish playwright and 1925 Nobel Prize winner for literature

- **Double standard.** Having two sets of standards for judgment: a higher standard for judging others and a lower standard for judging oneself. This is the classic "do as I say, not as I do" hypocrisy (e.g., critically evaluating and challenging the opinions of others but not our own).

- **Wishful thinking.** Thinking that something is true not on the basis of logic or evidence, but because the person wants it to be true. (For instance, a teenage girl who believes she will not become pregnant, even though she and her boyfriend always have sex without using any form of contraception.)

- **Hasty generalization.** Reaching a conclusion prematurely on the basis of a limited number of instances or experiences (e.g., concluding that people belonging to a group are all or nearly all "that way" on the basis of personal experiences with only one or two individuals).

- **Jumping to a conclusion.** Making a leap of logic to reach a conclusion that's based on only one reason or factor while ignoring other possible reasons and contributing factors (e.g., immediately concluding that "I must be a real loser" after being rejected for a date or a job).

- **Glittering generality.** Making a positive general statement without supplying details or evidence to back it up (e.g., writing a letter of recommendation describing someone as a "wonderful person" with a "great personality" but not providing any reasons or evidence to support these claims).

- **Straw man argument.** Distorting an opponent's argument position and then attacking it (e.g., attacking an opposing political candidate for supporting censorship and restricting civil liberties when the opponent supported only a ban on violent pornography).

- *Ad hominem* **argument.** Aiming an argument at the person rather than the person's argument (e.g., telling a younger person, "You're too young and inexperienced to know what you're talking about," or telling an older person, "You're too old-fashioned to understand this issue"). Literally translated, the term *ad hominem* means "to the man."

- **Red herring.** Bringing up an irrelevant issue that disguises or distracts attention from the real issue being discussed or debated (e.g., responding to criticism of former President Richard Nixon's involvement in the Watergate scandal by arguing, "He was a good president who accomplished many good things while he was in office"). The term *red herring* derives from an old practice of dragging a herring—a strong-smelling fish—across a trail to distract the scent of pursuing dogs. (In the example, Nixon's effectiveness as a president is an irrelevant issue or a red herring; the real issue being discussed is Nixon's behavior in the Watergate scandal.)

- **Smoke screen.** Intentionally disguising or covering up true reasons or motives with reasons that confuse or mislead others (e.g., opposing gun control legislation by arguing that it is a violation of the constitutional right to bear arms without revealing that the opponent of the legislation is receiving financial support from gun manufacturing companies).

- **Slippery slope.** Using fear tactics by arguing that not accepting a position will result in a "domino effect"—one bad thing happening after another, like a series of falling dominoes (e.g., "If someone experiments with marijuana, it will automatically lead to loss of motivation, harder drugs, and withdrawal from college").

- **Rhetorical deception.** Using deceptive language to conclude that something is true without providing reasons or evidence (e.g., glibly making statements such as: "Clearly this is . . ." "It is obvious that . . ." or "Any reasonable person can see . . ." without explaining why it's so clear, obvious, or reasonable).

- **Circular reasoning (a.k.a. "begging the question").** Drawing a conclusion that's merely a rewording or restatement of one's position without any supporting reasons or evidence, leaving the original question still unanswered and the issue still unsolved. This form of reasoning basically draws conclusion logically by claiming "it's true because it's true" (e.g., "Stem cell research shouldn't be legal because it shouldn't be done").
- **Appealing to authority or prestige.** Believing that if an authority figure or celebrity says it's true, then it must be true or should be done (e.g., buying product X simply because a famous actor or athlete uses it, or believing that if someone in authority, such as the U.S. president, says something should be done, then it must be the right or best thing to do).
- **Appealing to tradition or familiarity.** Concluding that if something has always been thought to be true or has always been done in a certain way, then it must be true or the best way to do it (e.g., "This is the way it's always been done, so it must be right").
- **Appealing to popularity or the majority (a.k.a. jumping on the bandwagon).** Believing that if it's popular or held by the majority of people, it must be true (e.g., "So many people believe in psychics, it has to be true; they can't all be wrong").
- **Appealing to emotion.** Believing in something based on the emotional intensity experienced when the claim is made, rather than the quality of reasoning or evidence used to support the claim (e.g., "If I feel strongly about something, it must be true"). The expressions "always trust your feelings" and "just listen to your heart" may not always lead to the most accurate conclusions and the best decisions, because they can be driven more by emotion than by reason.

Balanced Thinking

Balanced thinking involves seeking out and carefully considering evidence for and against a particular position. The process of supporting a position with evidence is technically referred to as *adduction*; when you adduce, you offer reasons *for* a position. The process of arguing against a position by presenting contradictory evidence or reasons is called *refutation*; when you refute, you provide a rebuttal by supplying evidence *against* a particular position. The opposing position's stronger arguments are acknowledged, and its weaker ones are refuted (Fairbairn & Winch, 1996).

Balanced thinking involves both adduction and refutation. The goal of a balanced thinker is not to stack up evidence for one position or the other, but to be an impartial investigator who looks at supporting and opposing evidence for both sides of an issue and attempts to reach a conclusion that's not biased or one-sided. Thus, the first step in the process of seeking truth should not be to immediately jump in and take an either-or (for or against) stance on a debatable issue. Instead, your first step should be to look at arguments for and against each position, acknowledge the strengths and weaknesses of both sides of the argument, and identify what additional information may still be needed to make a fair judgment or reach a reasonable conclusion.

Balanced thinking requires more than just adding up the number of arguments for and against a position; it also involves weighing the strength of those arguments because arguments can vary in terms of their level of importance and degree of support. When evaluating arguments, ask yourself, "How sure am I about the conclusion made by this argument?" Determine whether the evidence is:

1. **Definitive.** So strong or compelling that a definite conclusion should be reached;
2. **Suggestive.** Strong enough to suggest that a tentative conclusion may be reached; or
3. **Inconclusive.** Too weak to reach any conclusion.

"The more you know, the less sure you are."

—Voltaire, French historian, philosopher, and advocate for civil liberty

> ## Remember
>
> *A characteristic of balanced thinking is being mindful of the weight (degree of importance) you assign to different arguments and articulating how their weight has been factored into your final conclusion (e.g., in a written report or class presentation).*

In some cases, after reviewing both supporting and contradictory evidence for opposing positions, balanced thinking may lead you to suspend judgment and to withhold making a firm decision that favors one position over the other. A balanced thinker may occasionally reach the following conclusions: "Right now, I can't be sure; the evidence doesn't strongly favor one position over the other" or "More information is needed before I can make a final judgment or reach a firm conclusion." This isn't being wishy-washy: it's a legitimate conclusion to draw, as long as it is an informed conclusion that's supported with sound reasons and solid evidence. In fact, it's better to hold an undecided but informed viewpoint based on balanced thinking than to hold a definite opinion that's uninformed, biased, or based on emotion, such as the opinions offered loudly and obnoxiously by people on radio and TV talk shows.

"Too often we enjoy the comfort of opinion without the discomfort of thought."

—John F. Kennedy, 35th U.S. president

Think About It ———————— *Journal Entry* 5.7

Consider the following positions:

1. Course requirements should be eliminated; college students should be allowed to choose the classes they want to take for their degrees.

2. Course grades should be eliminated; college students should take classes on a pass-fail basis.

Using balanced thinking, identify one or more arguments *for* and *against* each of these positions.

_____

_____

_____

_____

_____

_____

> ## Remember
>
> *When you combine balanced thinking with multidimensional thinking, you become a more complex and comprehensive thinker who is capable of viewing any issue from opposing sides and different angles.*

Critical Thinking

Critical thinking is a form of higher-level thinking that involves *evaluation or judgment*. The evaluation can be either positive or negative: for example, a movie critic can give a good (thumbs up) or bad (thumbs down) review of a film. However, critical thinking involves much more than simply stating, "I liked it," or "I didn't like it." Specific reasons or evidence must be supplied to support the critique; failure to do so makes the criticism unfounded—i.e., it has no foundation or basis of support.

Think About It ———	——— *Journal Entry* **5.8**

Flash back to the journal entry at the start of this chapter. How does your response to the incomplete sentence compare with the definition of critical thinking we just provided?

_____

_____

_____

_____

_____

If you wrote that critical thinking means "being critical" or negatively criticizing something or somebody, don't feel bad. Many students think that critical thinking has this negative meaning or connotation.

Critical thinking is used to evaluate many things besides films, art, or music: it's also used to judge the quality of ideas, beliefs, choices, and decisions, whether they be your own or those of others. It's also a skill that's highly valued by professors teaching students at all stages in the college experience and all subjects in the college curriculum (Higher Education Institute, 2009; Stark et al., 1990). By working on developing these skills now, you'll significantly improve your academic performance throughout your college experience. You can start developing the mental habit of critical thinking by regularly asking yourself the following questions as criteria for evaluating any idea or argument:

1. **Validity (truthfulness).** Is it true or accurate?
2. **Morality (ethics).** Is it fair or just?
3. **Beauty (aesthetics).** Is it beautiful or artistic?
4. **Practicality (usefulness).** Can it be put to use for practical purposes?
5. **Priority (order of importance or effectiveness).** Is it the best option or alternative?

Since thinking skills are valued by professors who are teaching students at all stages of the college experience and in all subjects in the curriculum, developing these skills should be time well spent and should improve your academic performance significantly.

Creative Thinking

When you think creatively, you generate something new or different, whether that may be a novel idea, strategy, or work product. Creative thinking leads you to ask the question, "Why not?" (e.g., "Why not do it a different way?"). It could be said that when you think critically, you look "inside the box" and evaluate the quality of its content. When you think creatively, you look "outside the box" to imagine other packages containing different content.

Any time you combine two existing ideas to generate a new idea, you're engaging in creative thinking. Creative thinking can be viewed as an extension or higher form of synthesis, whereby parts of separate ideas are combined or integrated to create a final product that turns out to be different (and better) than what previously existed (Anderson & Krathwohl, 2001). Even in the arts, what's created isn't totally original or unique. Instead, artistic creativity typically involves a combination or rearrangement of previously existing elements to generate a new "whole"—a final product that is distinctive or noticeably different. For instance, hard rock was created by combining elements of blues and rock and roll, and folk rock took form when Bob Dylan combined musical elements of acoustic blues and amplified rock (Shelton et al., 2003). Robert Kearns (subject of the film *Flash of Genius*) combined preexisting mechanical parts to create the intermittent windshield wiper (Seabrook, 2008).

Creative and critical thinking are two of the most important forms of higher-level thinking, and they work well together. We use creative thinking to ask new questions and generate new ideas; we use critical thinking to evaluate or critique the ideas we create (Paul & Elder, 2004). A creative idea must not only be different or original: it must also be effective (Sternberg, 2001; Runco, 2004). If critical thinking reveals that the quality of what we've created is poor, we then shift back to creative thinking to generate something new and improved. Or, we may start by using critical thinking to evaluate an old idea or approach and come to the judgment that it's not very good. This unfavorable evaluation naturally leads to and turns on the creative thinking process, which tries to come up with a new idea or different approach that's better than the old one.

Brainstorming is a problem-solving process that effectively illustrates how creative and critical thinking complement each other. The steps or stages involved in the process of brainstorming are summarized in Do It Now! 5.1. As the brainstorming process suggests, creativity doesn't just happen suddenly or effortlessly, like the so-called stroke of genius: instead, it takes considerable mental effort (Paul & Elder, 2004; De Bono, 2007). Although creative thinking initially involves some spontaneous and intuitive leaps, it also involves careful reflection and evaluation of whether any of those leaps actually land you on a good idea.

"The principal mark of genius is not perfection but originality, the opening of new frontiers."
—Arthur Koestler, Hungarian novelist and philosopher

"The blues are the roots. Everything else are the fruits."
—Willie Dixon, blues songwriter; commenting on how all forms of contemporary American music contain elements of blues music, which originated among African American slaves

"Creativity is allowing oneself to make mistakes; art is knowing which ones to keep."
—Scott Adams, creator of the *Dilbert* comic strip and author of *The Dilbert Principle*

"Creativity isn't 'crazytivity'."
—Edward De Bono, internationally known authority on creative thinking

5.1 | DO IT **NOW**

The Process of Brainstorming

1. List as many ideas as you can, generating them rapidly without stopping to evaluate their validity or practicality. Studies show that worrying about whether an idea is correct often blocks creativity (Basadur, Runco, & Vega, 2000). So, at this stage of the process, just let your imagination run wild; don't worry about whether the idea you generate is impractical, unrealistic, or outrageous.
2. Use the ideas on your list as a springboard to trigger additional ideas, or combine them to create new ideas.
3. After you run out of ideas, review and critically evaluate the list of ideas you've generated and eliminate those that you think are least effective.
4. From the remaining list of ideas, choose the best idea or best combination of ideas.

Note: The first two steps in the brainstorming process involve *divergent thinking*—a form of creative thinking that allows you to go off in different directions and generate diverse ideas. In contrast, the last two steps in the process involve *convergent thinking*—a form of critical thinking in which you converge (focus in) and narrow down the ideas, evaluating each of them for their effectiveness.

Author's Experience   Several years ago, I was working with a friend to come up with ideas for a grant proposal. We started out by sitting at his kitchen table, exchanging ideas while sipping coffee; then we both got up and began to pace back and forth, walking all around the room while bouncing different ideas off each other. Whenever a new idea was thrown out, one of us would jot it down (whoever was pacing closer to the kitchen table at the moment).

After we ran out of ideas, we shifted gears, slowed down, and sat down at the table again to critique each of the ideas we'd just generated during our "binge-thinking" episode. After some debate, we finally settled on an idea that we judged to be the best of all the ideas we produced, and we used this idea for the grant proposal.

Although I wasn't fully aware of it at the time, the stimulating thought process we were using was called brainstorming because it involved both of its key stages: we first engaged in creative thinking during our fast-paced walking and idea-production stage, and followed that with critical thinking during our slower-paced sitting and idea-evaluation stage.

Joe Cuseo

> "Imagination should give wings to our thoughts, but imagination must be checked and documented by the factual results of the experiment."
>
> —Louis Pasteur, French microbiologist, chemist, and inventor of pasteurization (a method for preventing milk and wine from going sour)

Lastly, keep in mind that creative thinking is not restricted to the arts: it can occur in all subject areas, even in fields that seek precision and definite answers. For example, in math, creative thinking may involve using new approaches or strategies for arriving at a correct solution to a problem. In science, creative thinking takes place when a scientist first uses imaginative thinking to create a hypothesis or logical hunch ("What might happen if . . . ?"), then conducts an experiment to test whether that hypothesis proves to be true.

Strategies for Developing Higher-Level Thinking Skills and Using Them to Improve Academic Performance

Thus far, this chapter has been devoted primarily to helping you get a clear idea of what higher-level thinking is and what its major forms are. The remainder of this chapter focuses on helping you develop habits of higher-level thinking and applying (or how to apply) these habits to improve your performance in the first year of college and beyond.

1. **Cross-reference and connect any ideas you acquire in class with related ideas you acquire from your assigned reading.** When you discover information in your reading that relates to something you've learned about in class (or vice versa), make a note of it in the margin of your textbook or your class notebook. By integrating knowledge you've obtained from these two major sources, you're using synthesis—a higher-level thinking skill that you can then demonstrate on course exams and assignments to improve your course grades.

2. **When listening to lectures and completing reading assignments, pay attention not only to the content being covered, but also to the thought process that accompanies the content.** Periodically ask yourself what forms of higher-level thinking your instructors are using during major segments of a class presentation and what your textbook authors are using in different sections of a chapter. The more conscious you are of the types of higher-level thinking skills you're being exposed to, the more likely you are to acquire those thinking skills and demonstrate them on exams and assignments.

3. **Periodically pause to reflect on your own thinking process.** When working on your courses, ask yourself what type of thinking you're doing (e.g., analysis, synthesis, or evaluation) during the work process. When you think about your own thinking, you're engaging in a mental process known as *metacognition*—that is, you're aware of how you're thinking while you're thinking (Flavell, 1985; Hartman, 2001). Metacognition is a mental habit that's associated with higher-level thinking and improved problem-solving skills (Halpern, 2003; Resnick, 1986).

> "To think is to talk to oneself."
>
> —Immanuel Kant, German philosopher

Asking yourself higher-level thinking questions during lectures should prevent you from asking questions like this one.

4. **Develop habits of higher-level thinking by asking yourself higher-level thinking questions.** One simple but powerful way to think about your thinking is through self-questioning. Since questions have the power to activate and elevate your thinking, and since thinking often involves talking silently to yourself, if you make an intentional attempt to ask yourself good questions, you can train your mind to think at a higher level. A good question can serve as a launching pad that propels you to higher levels of thinking in your quest to answer it. The higher the level of thinking called for by the questions you regularly ask yourself, the higher the level of thinking you will display in class discussions, on college exams, and in written assignments.

> "If you do not ask the right questions, you do not get the right answers."
>
> —Edward Hodnett, British poet

Using Self-Questioning Strategies to Promote Your Critical and Creative Thinking

As we mentioned in Chapter 2, effective learners are effective self-monitors—they watch themselves while learning and monitor whether they are really understanding what they're attempting to learn (Weinstein & Underwood, 1985). Similarly, effective thinkers engage in a slightly different form of self-monitoring known as metacognition—they think about how they are thinking (Flavell, 1985).

Happy Hour, 4–6 PM
All Drinks—$2

Followed by Reflection Hour:
"What is Happiness?"
All Thoughts—Priceless

Pub & Grub

© Kendall Hunt

Asking yourself a good question can stimulate your higher-level thinking about almost any experience, whether it takes place inside or outside the classroom.

Think About It ——————— *Journal Entry* 5.9

Critically evaluate the common practice of bars selling alcoholic drinks at reduced prices that's depicted in the preceding cartoon by answering the following questions:

1. What are the assumptions or implications of calling this practice "happy hour"?

_____

_____

_____

_____

2. What are arguments for and against this practice?

_____

_____

_____

_____

Since questions have the power to activate and elevate your thinking, you can capitalize on their power by intentionally asking yourself good questions.

In Do It Now! 5.2, you'll find numerous questions that have been intentionally designed to promote higher-level thinking. The questions are constructed in a way that will allow you to easily fill in the blank and apply the type of thinking called for by the question to ideas or issues being discussed in any course you may take. Considerable research indicates that students can learn to use questions such as these to improve their higher-level thinking ability in various subject areas (King, 1990, 1995, 2002).

As you read each set of trigger questions, place a checkmark next to one question in the set that could be applied to a concept or issue being covered in a course you're taking this term.

5.2   DO IT NOW!

Self-Questioning Strategies for Triggering Different Forms of Higher-Level Thinking

Application (applied thinking). Putting knowledge into practice to solve problems and resolve issues.

Trigger Questions
- How can this idea be used to _____?
- How could this concept be implemented to _____?
- How can this theory be put into practice to _____?
- What could be done to prevent or reduce _____?

Analysis (analytical thinking). Breaking down information into its essential elements or parts.

Trigger Questions
- What are the main ideas contained in _____?
- What are the important aspects of _____?
- What are the issues raised by _____?
- What are the major purposes of _____?
- What assumptions or biases lie hidden within _____?
- What are the reasons behind _____?

Synthesis. Integrating separate pieces of information to form a more complete product or pattern.

Trigger Questions
- How can this idea be joined or connected with _____ to create a more complete or comprehensive understanding of _____?
- How could these different _____ be grouped together into a more general class or category?
- How could these separate _____ be reorganized or rearranged to produce a more comprehensive understanding of the big picture?

Multidimensional thinking. Thinking that involves viewing yourself and the world around you from different angles or vantage points.

Trigger Questions
- How would _____ affect different dimensions of myself (emotional, physical, etc.)?
- What broader impact would _____ have on the social and physical world around me?
- How might people living in different times (e.g., past and future) view _____?
- How would people from different cultural backgrounds interpret or react to _____?
- Have I taken into consideration all the major factors that could influence _____ or be influenced by _____?

Inferential reasoning. Making an argument or judgment by inferring (stepping to) a conclusion that's supported by empirical (observable) evidence or logical consistency.

Trigger Questions Seeking Empirical Evidence
- What examples support the argument that _____?
- What research evidence is there for _____?
- What statistical data document that this _____ is true?

Trigger Questions Seeking Logical Consistency
- Since _____ is true, why shouldn't _____ also be true?
- If people believe in _____, shouldn't they practice _____?
- To make the statement that _____, wouldn't it have to be assumed that _____?

Balanced thinking. Carefully considering reasons for and against a particular position or viewpoint.

Trigger Questions

- Have I considered both sides of _____?
- What are the strengths (advantages) and weaknesses (disadvantages) of _____?
- What evidence supports and contradicts _____?
- What are arguments for and counterarguments against _____?

Trigger Questions for Adduction (arguing for a particular idea or position by supplying supporting evidence)

- What proof is there for _____?
- What are logical arguments for _____?
- What research evidence supports _____?

Trigger Questions for Refutation (arguing against a particular idea or position by supplying contradictory evidence)

- What proof is there against _____?
- What logical arguments indicate that _____ is false?
- What research evidence contradicts _____?
- What counterarguments would provide an effective rebuttal to _____?

Critical thinking. Making well-informed evaluations or judgments.

Trigger Questions for Evaluating Validity (truthfulness)

- Is _____ true or accurate?
- Is there sufficient evidence to support the conclusion that _____?
- Is the reasoning behind _____ strong or weak?

Trigger Questions for Evaluating Morality (ethics)

- Is _____ fair?
- Is _____ just?
- Is this action consistent with the professed or stated values of _____?

Trigger Questions for Evaluating Beauty (aesthetics)

- What is the artistic merit of _____?
- Does _____ have any aesthetic value?
- Does _____ contribute to the beauty of _____?

Trigger Questions for Evaluating Practicality (usefulness)

- Will _____ work?
- How can _____ be put to good use?
- What practical benefit would result from _____?

Trigger Questions for Evaluating Priority (order of importance or effectiveness)

- Which one of these _____ is the most important?
- Is this _____ the best option or choice available?
- How should these _____ be ranked from first to last (best to worst) in terms of their effectiveness?

Creative thinking. Generating ideas that are unique, original, or distinctively different.

Trigger Questions

- What could be invented to _____?
- Imagine what would happen if _____?
- What might be a different way to _____?
- How would this change if _____?
- What would be an ingenious way to _____?

Note: Save these higher-level thinking questions so that you can use them when completing different academic tasks required by your courses (e.g., preparing for exams, writing papers or reports, and participating in class discussions or study-group sessions). Try to get into the habit of periodically stepping back to reflect on your thinking process. Ask yourself what type of thinking you are doing (such as analysis, synthesis, or evaluation) and record your personal reflections in writing. You could even keep a "thinking log" or "thinking journal" to increase self-awareness of the thinking strategies you develop across time, or how your thinking strategies may vary across different courses and academic fields. This strategy will not only help you acquire higher-level thinking skills, but will also help you describe the thinking skills you have acquired during job interviews and in letters of application for career positions.

5. **To stimulate creative thinking, use the following strategies:**

- **Be flexible.** Think about ideas and objects in unusual or unconventional ways. The power of flexible and unconventional thinking is well illustrated in the movie *Apollo 13*, which is based on the real story of an astronaut saving his life by creatively using duct tape as an air filter. The inventor of the printing press (Johannes Gutenberg) made his groundbreaking discovery while watching a machine being used to crush grapes at a wine harvest. He thought that the same type of machine could be used to press letters onto paper (Dorfman, Shames, & Kihlstrom, 1996).

- **Be experimental.** Play with ideas, trying them out to see whether they'll work and work better than the status quo. Studies show that creative people tend to be mental risk-takers who experiment with ideas and techniques (Sternberg, 2001). Consciously resist the temptation to settle for the security of familiarity. Doing things the way they've always been done doesn't mean you're doing them the best way possible. It may mean that it's just the most habitual (and mindless) way to do them. When people cling rigidly or stubbornly to what's conventional or traditional, what they're doing is clinging to the comfort or security of what's most familiar and predictable, which blocks originality, ingenuity, and openness to change.

- **Get mobile.** Get up and move around. Studies show that when we stand up, the brain gets approximately 10 percent more oxygen than it does when we're sitting down (Sousa, 2006). Since oxygen provides fuel for the brain, our ability to think creatively is stimulated when we think on our feet and move around, rather than sitting on our butts for extended periods of time.

- **Get it down.** Carry a pen and a small notepad or packet of sticky notes (or a portable electronic recording device) with you at all times to record creative ideas, because these ideas often come to mind at the most unexpected times. The process of creative ideas suddenly popping into your mind is sometimes referred to as *incubation*—just like incubated eggs can hatch at any time, ideas can suddenly hatch and pop into consciousness after you've sat on them for a while. Unfortunately, however, just as an idea can suddenly come into mind, it can just as suddenly slip out of mind when you start thinking about something else. You can prevent this from happening by having the right equipment on hand to record your creative ideas as soon as you have them.

- **Get diverse.** Seek ideas from diverse social and informational sources. Bouncing your ideas off of different people and getting their ideas about your idea is a good way to generate energy, synergy, and serendipity (accidental discoveries). Studies show that creative people venture well beyond the boundaries of their particular areas of training or specialization (Baer, 1993; Kaufman & Baer, 2002). They have wide-ranging interests and knowledge, which they draw upon and combine to generate new ideas (Riquelme, 2002). Be on the lookout to combine the knowledge and skills you acquire from different subject areas and different people to create bridges to new ideas.

- **Take a break.** When working on a problem that you can't seem to solve, stop working on it for a while and come back to it later. Creative solutions often come to mind after you stop thinking about the problem. When you're trying so hard and working so intensely on a problem or challenging task, your attention may become mentally set or rigidly fixed on one aspect of it (German & Barrett, 2005; Maier, 1970). Taking your mind off of it and returning to it at a later point allows the problem to incubate in your mind at a lower level of consciousness and stress. This can sometimes give birth to a sudden solution. Furthermore, when you come back to the task later, your focus of attention is likely to shift to a different feature or aspect of the problem. This new focus may enable you to view the problem from a different angle or vantage point, which can lead to a breakthrough idea that was blocked by your previous perspective (Anderson, 2000).

"I make progress by having people around who are smarter than I am—and listening to them. And I assume that everyone is smarter about something than I am."

—Henry Kaiser, successful industrialist, known as the father of American shipbuilding

"*Eureka!*" (Literally translated, "I have found it!")

—Attributed to Archimedes, ancient Greek mathematician and inventor, when he suddenly discovered (while sitting in a bathtub) how to measure the purity of gold

- **Reorganize the problem.** When you're stuck on a problem, try rearranging its parts or pieces. Rearrangement can transform the problem into a different pattern that provides you with a new perspective. The new perspective may position you to suddenly see a solution that was previously overlooked, much like changing the order of letters in a word jumble can suddenly enable you to see the hidden, scrambled word. By changing the wording of any problem you're working on, or by recording ideas on index cards (or sticky notes) and laying them out in different orders and arrangements, you may suddenly see a solution.

- If you're having trouble solving problems that involve a sequence of steps (e.g., math problems), try reversing the sequence and start by working from the end or middle. The new sequence changes your approach to the problem by forcing you to come at it from a different direction, which can sometimes provide you with an alternative path to its solution.

- **Be persistent.** Studies show that creativity takes time, dedication, and hard work (Ericsson, 2006; Ericsson & Charness, 1994). Creative thoughts often do not emerge in one sudden stroke of genius, but evolve gradually after repeated reflection and persistent effort.

> "Creativity consists largely of re-arranging what we know in order to find out what we do not know."
>
> —George Keller, prolific American architect and originator of the Union Station design for elevated train stations

> "Genius is 1% inspiration and 99% perspiration."
>
> —Thomas Edison, scientist and creator of more than 1,000 inventions, including the light bulb, phonograph, and motion picture camera

Think About It — Journal Entry 5.10

Look back at the forms of thinking described in Do It Now! 5.2. Identify one question listed under each set of trigger questions and fill in the blank with an idea or issue being covered in a course you're taking this term.

_____

_____

_____

_____

_____

_____

_____

Think About It ———————————————— *Journal Entry* **5.11**

The popularity of sticky notes is no doubt due to their versatility—you can post them on almost anything, remove them from where they were stuck (without a mess), and re-stick them somewhere else.

Think creatively for a minute. In what ways could college students use sticky notes to help complete the academic tasks they face in college? Think of as many ways as possible.

_____

_____

_____

_____

_____

_____

Summary and Conclusion

Since higher-level thinking is the number one educational goal of college professors, developing this skill is crucial for achieving academic excellence. In addition to improving academic performance in college, developing higher-level thinking skills has three other critical benefits.

1. **Higher-level thinking is essential in today's "information age" in which new information is being generated at faster rates than at any other time in human history.** The majority of new workers in the information age will no longer work with their hands but will instead work with their heads (Miller, 2003), and, as discussed in Chapter 12, employers will value college graduates who have inquiring minds and possess higher-level thinking skills (Harvey, Moon, Geall, & Bower, 1997; Peter D. Hart Research Associates, 2006).

2. **Higher-level thinking skills are vital for citizens in a democracy.** Authoritarian political systems, such as dictatorships and fascist regimes, suppress critical thought and demand submissive obedience to authority. In contrast, citizens living in a democracy are expected to control their political destiny by choosing (electing) their political leaders; thus, judging and choosing wisely are crucial civic responsibilities in a democratic nation. Citizens living and voting in a democracy must use higher-level reasoning skills, such as balanced and critical thinking, to make wise political choices.

3. **Higher-level thinking is an important safeguard against prejudice, discrimination, and hostility.** Racial, ethnic, and national prejudices often stem from narrow, self-centered, or group-centered thinking (Paul & Elder, 2002). Prejudice often results from oversimplified, dualistic thinking that can lead individuals to categorize other people into either "in" groups (us) or "out" groups (them). This type of dualistic thinking can lead, in turn, to ethnocentrism—the tendency to view one's own racial or ethnic group as the superior "in" group and see other

groups as inferior "out" groups. Development of higher-level thinking skills, such as taking multiple perspectives and using balanced thinking, counteracts the type of dualistic, ethnocentric thinking that leads to prejudice, discrimination, and hate crimes.

Learning More through the World Wide Web

Internet-Based Resources for Further Information on Higher-Level Thinking

For additional information related to the ideas discussed in this chapter, we recommend the following Web sites:

Critical Thinking:

www.criticalthinking.org

Creative Thinking:

www.amcreativityassoc.org

Higher-Level Thinking Skills:

www.wcu.edu/ceap/houghton/Learner/think/thinkhigherorder.html

Chapter 5 Exercises

5.1 Self-Assessment of Higher-Level Thinking Characteristics

Listed here are four general characteristics of higher-level thinkers accompanied by a set of traits related to each characteristic. When you read the traits listed beneath each of the general characteristics, place a checkmark next to any trait that you think is true of you.

Characteristics of a Higher-Level Thinker

1. **Tolerant and Accepting**
   - Keep emotions under control when someone criticizes their viewpoint
   - Do not tune out ideas that conflict with their own
   - Feel comfortable with disagreement
   - Are receptive to hearing different points of view

2. **Inquisitive and Open-Minded**
   - Are eager to continue learning new things from different people and different experiences
   - Have an inquiring mind that's genuinely curious, inquisitive, and ready to explore new ideas
   - Find differences of opinion and opposing viewpoints interesting and stimulating
   - Attempt to understand why people hold different viewpoints and try to find common ground between them

3. **Reflective and Tentative**
   - Suspend judgment until all the evidence is in, rather than making snap judgments before knowing the whole story
   - Acknowledge the complexity, ambiguity, and uncertainty associated with certain issues, and are willing to perhaps say, "I need to give this more thought," or "I need more evidence before I can draw a conclusion"
   - Take time to think things through before drawing conclusions, making choices, and reaching decisions
   - Periodically reexamine personal viewpoints to see whether they should be maintained or changed as a result of new experiences and evidence

4. **Honest and Courageous**
   - Give fair consideration to ideas that others may instantly disapprove of or find distasteful
   - Are willing to express personal viewpoints that may not conform to those of the majority
   - Are willing to change old opinions or beliefs when they are contradicted by new evidence
   - Are willing to acknowledge the limitations or weaknesses of their attitudes and beliefs

Look back at the list and count the number of checkmarks you placed in each of the four general areas:

1. Tolerant and Accepting = _____
2. Inquisitive and Open-Minded = _____
3. Reflective and Tentative = _____
4. Honest and Courageous = _____

For which characteristic did you have: (a) the *most* checkmarks, (b) the *least* checkmarks?

What do you think accounts for this difference?

Trick or Treat: Confusing or Challenging Test?

Students in Professor Plato's philosophy course just got their first exam back and they're going over the test together in class. Some students are angry because they feel that Professor Plato deliberately included "trick questions" to confuse them. Professor Plato responds by saying that his test questions were not designed to trick the class but to "challenge them to think."

Discussion Questions

1. Why do you think that some students thought that Professor Plato was trying to trick or confuse them?

2. What do you think the professor meant when he told his students that his test questions were designed to "challenge them to think"?

3. On future tests, what might the students do to reduce the likelihood that they will feel tricked again?

4. On future tests, what might Professor Plato do to reduce the likelihood that students will complain about being asked "trick questions"?

Chapter 5 Reflection

How can you use critical thinking to be a more successful student? Explain. List three action steps you can do to make this happen.

How can you use critical thinking to improve your personal life? Explain.

How can you use creative thinking to be a more successful student? Explain. List three action steps you can do to make this happen.

How can you use creative thinking to improve your personal life? Explain.

Learning Style

LEARNING GOAL

To increase awareness of your own learning style and identify strategies that match your learning style.

Read to answer these key questions:

1. What is my learning style?

_____

_____

_____

_____

2. What is the best learning environment for me?

_____

_____

_____

_____

3. What are some specific learning strategies that match my learning style?

_____

_____

_____

_____

4. How is learning style connected to personality type?

_____

_____

_____

_____

5. What are some specific learning strategies that are based on personality type?

    _____

    _____

    _____

    _____

6. How can I understand and adapt to my professor's personality type (or "psych out" the professor)?

    _____

    _____

    _____

    _____

7. How can I create my success?

    _____

    _____

    _____

    _____

"Learning is a treasure that will follow its owner anywhere."
Chinese Proverb

Knowing about your learning style can help you to choose effective strategies for learning in school and on the job. Knowing about your preferred learning environment can help you increase productivity. Discovering your multiple intelligences will help you to gain an appreciation of your gifts and talents that can be used to develop your self-confidence and choose the career that is right for you.

What Is Learning Style?

Just as each individual has a unique personality, each individual has a unique learning style. It is important to remember that there are no good or bad learning styles. Learning style is simply your preferred way of learning. It is how you like to learn and how you learn best. By understanding your learning style, you can maximize your potential by choosing the learning techniques that work best for you. This chapter explores the many factors that determine how you learn best. Each individual also has a preferred learning environment. Knowing about your preferred learning environment and learning style helps you be more productive, increase achievement, be more creative, improve problem solving, make good decisions, and learn effectively. Personality type also influences how we learn. Knowing about how you learn best helps to reduce frustration and increase your confidence in learning.

Gary Price[1] developed the Productivity Environmental Preference Survey (PEPS) which is included in the textbook. He identified sixteen different elements of learning style and environmental factors that influence productivity and satisfaction in school and on the job. As you read the description of each of these elements, think about your preferences and place a checkmark next to them.

1. **Visual.** Some students learn through reading, observing, or seeing things.
   - Those who prefer visual learning benefit from pictures and reading.
   - Those who are not visual learners may dislike reading. If auditory learning is preferred, attend the lecture first to hear the lecturer talk about the subject and then do the reading. It is important to do the reading because not all the material is covered in the lecture.
2. **Design.** Some students study best in a more formal environment or less formal environment.
   - If you prefer a formal environment, sit in a straight chair and use a desk.
   - If you prefer an informal environment, sit on the sofa or a soft chair or on some pillows on the floor.
3. **Persistence.** Some students may finish what they start, whereas others have many things going on at once and may not finish what they started. Persistence may indicate whether or not you procrastinate in finishing tasks.
   - If you are persistent, you generally finish what you start.
   - If you lack persistence, you may get bored or easily distracted. You may find it easier to break tasks into small steps and work steadily toward completing assignments on time. Think about your college and career goals to increase motivation and persistence.
4. **Motivation.** Some students are self-motivated to learn, and others lack motivation.
   - If you are self-motivated, you usually like school and enjoy learning on your own.
   - If you lack motivation, think about your reasons for attending college and review the material in the motivation chapter in this book.
5. **Time of day.** Some students are most awake and learn easier early in the day while others are most awake and learn better in the afternoon or evening.
   - If you are most alert in the morning, schedule your classes and learning for earlier in the day and your routine tasks for later in the day when you are tired.
   - If you are most alert in the late afternoon or evening, schedule your classes and learning during that time.
6. **Light.** Some students prefer bright light for studying and others find bright light uncomfortable or irritating. Having the right light can help you to be more productive.
   - If you prefer bright light, study near a window with light shining over your shoulder or invest in a good study lamp.
   - If you prefer dim lights, sit away from direct sunlight or use a shaded light.
7. **Intake.** Some students like to eat or drink something while studying while others find eating or drinking to be distracting.
   - If you prefer intake while learning, drink water and have nutritious snacks such a fruits and vegetables.
   - Some students do not need intake to study.

8. **Tactile.** Some students prefer to touch the material or use a "hands-on" approach to learning while others do not need to touch what they are learning.
   - Students who prefer tactile learning like manipulative and three-dimensional materials. They learn from working with models and writing. Taking notes is one of the best tactile learning strategies.
   - Students who are not tactile learners can focus on visual or auditory strategies for learning.

9. **Kinesthetic.** Kinesthetic learning is related to tactile learning. Some students learn best by movement and experiencing what they are learning while other students do not use movement to learn.
   - Students who prefer kinesthetic learning enjoy field trips, drama, and becoming physically involved with learning. For example, they can learn fractions by slicing an apple into parts. It is important to be actively involved in learning.
   - Students who are not kinesthetic learners will use another preferred method of learning such as auditory or visual learning.

10. **Structure.** Some students prefer more or less structure. This preference may also be related to your personality type (judging or perceptive).
    - Students who prefer more structure want the teacher to give details and directions about how to complete the assignment.
    - Students who prefer less structure want the teacher to give assignments in which the students can choose the topic and organize the material on their own.

11. **Authority.** Some students are more or less independent learners.
    - Some students prefer to have the professor or a tutor to guide learning. In the college environment, students may prefer traditional face-to-face classes.
    - Others prefer to work on their own. In the college environment, students may prefer online classes or independent study.

12. **Mobility.** Some students like to move around frequently while studying while others can sit still for longer periods of time.
    - If you prefer mobility, you may find it difficult to sit still for a long time. Take a break every 15–20 minutes to move around. When choosing an occupation, consider one that requires you to move around.
    - If you don't need to move around while studying, a desk and chair are sufficient to help you concentrate on learning.

13. **Sound.** Some students need a quiet environment for study while others find it distracting if it is too quiet.
    - If you prefer quiet, use the library or find another quiet place. If you cannot find a quiet place, sound-blocking earphones or earplugs may be helpful.
    - If you study better with sound, play soft music or study in open areas. Use headphones for your music if you are studying with those who prefer quiet.

14. **Temperature.** Some students perform better in cool temperatures and others prefer warmer temperatures.
    - If you prefer a warm environment, remember to bring your sweater or jacket. Sit near a window or other source of heat.
    - If you prefer a cooler environment, study in a well-ventilated environment or even outside in the shade.

15. **Auditory.** Some students learn through listening and talking while others find it distracting.
    - Those who prefer auditory learning find it easier to learn through lectures, audio materials, discussion, and oral directions.
    - Those who do not prefer auditory learning may find their mind wandering during lectures and become confused by oral directions. It is helpful to read the material before the lecture and take notes during the lecture. Review the notes periodically to remember the material.

16. **Alone or with peers.** Some students prefer to study alone and others prefer to study in groups. This may be related to your personality type (introvert, extravert).
- You may find other people distracting and prefer to study alone. Find a private area to study.
- You may enjoy working in a group because talking with others helps you to learn.

Think About It ——————————— Journal Entry 6.2

1. Review the 16 elements of learning style and environment in this chapter and in the PEPS learning style assessment included with this textbook. Write a paragraph about your ideal learning environment.

_____

_____

_____

_____

_____

_____

2. What are your strongest learning preferences?

_____

_____

_____

_____

_____

3. What environment makes you most productive?

_____

_____

_____

_____

_____

Learning Techniques

It is important to connect specific learning strategies to your preferred learning style. Even if you have definite preferences, you can experiment with other styles to improve your learning. If you become frustrated with a learning task, first try a familiar technique that you have used successfully in the past. If that does not work, experiment with different ways of learning. If one technique does not work, try another. It is powerful to combine techniques. For example, it is a good idea to make pictures of what you want to remember (visual), recite the ideas you want to remember (auditory), and take notes (tactile).

The following are specific techniques for each type of learner. Underline or highlight techniques that are useful to you.

Auditory Learning Techniques

You like to learn by listening. You are good at listening to lectures, audio materials, and learning through discussions. You generally understand, comprehend, and remember oral instructions. Here are some auditory learning strategies that you might find useful.

- Before reading, skim through the textbook and look at the major headings. As you are reading, ask questions or say out loud what you think will be important to remember.
- Since you learn by listening, you may not think you need to take notes on college lectures. However, note taking is needed for review and long-term recall. Focus on writing down the key ideas in your notes and leave spaces to fill in the details. Immediately after the lecture, review your lecture notes to add details you heard in the lecture. To review your notes, read them aloud.
- To prepare for exams, rehearse or say information verbally. For example, while studying math, say the equations out loud.
- Use auditory tools for learning such as lectures, videos, discussions, and recordings.
- Work in a quiet area to avoid distractions.
- Make it a priority to attend lectures and participate in discussion sessions. Sit near the front of the classroom so that you can hear clearly. Ask questions in class.
- Discuss what you are learning with other students. Discuss what you are learning with a friend or form a study group where you can discuss what you are learning.
- Participate actively in class discussions.
- Use memory devices, rhymes, poems, rhythms, or music to remember what you are studying. For example, turn facts into a rap song or a musical jingle to aid in recall.
- Memorize key concepts by repeating them aloud.
- Read the textbook and any directions for assignments or tests out loud if possible. Hear the words or directions in your mind if you cannot read them aloud.
- When learning new or difficult material, begin with auditory learning techniques and then reinforce the learning with visual, kinesthetic, and tactile learning strategies according to your preferences.

Visual Learning Techniques

You learn best by reading, observing, and seeing things. You remember what you read and see.

- Use color to highlight the important points in the text while reading. Review the important points by looking at the highlighted passages again.
- Take notes and use underlining and highlighting in different colors to highlight the important points. Include flow charts, graphs, and pictures in your notes. Make summary sheets or mind maps to summarize or review your notes.
- Use pictures, diagrams, flow charts, maps, graphs, time lines, video, and mult-media to aid in learning and prepare for exams. Use flash cards to remember important details and facts.
- Sit in front of the class so you can carefully observe the professor. Copy what is written on the board.
- Organize your work area to avoid visual distractions.
- Create visual reminders to keep on track. Make lists on note pads or use sticky notes as reminders.
- Make a visual image of what you are learning. For example, while reading history, picture in your mind's eye what it would be like to live in that historical period.
- Before answering an essay question, picture the answer in your mind, create a mind map, or write a quick outline.
- Use outlines or mind maps to review for exams.
- When learning new or difficult material, begin with visual learning strategies and then reinforce your learning with audio, kinesthetic, and tactile learning strategies.
- Practice remembering what you hear for those situations where you cannot get the material or instructions in writing. Using mnemonic memory devices may be helpful in remembering what you hear.

Tactile Learning Techniques

You need to be involved in your learning by doing things with your hands and your sense of touch. You prefer to touch the material as you learn and you need "hands-on" kinds of activities, which will help you learn by doing.

- Try to select educational courses that allow you to "do" things. For example, take courses that involve science experiments, writing, practicing math problems, etc.
- As you are reading, mark or highlight the key ideas and review them to enhance recall. Writing a journal or making a summary sheet of key ideas will help you to remember what you have read.
- Attend lectures and take notes. The physical act of writing will help you to remember the important points in the lecture.
- To prepare for exams, use a mind map, outline or drawing to help you to remember.
- Use real objects to help you to learn. For example, in a physics class, if you are studying levers, create a simple lever and observe how it functions. If you are studying geography, use a globe or map to aid in studying.
- Keep your desk clear of distracting objects.
- Use flash cards to review for exams.

- When learning new or difficult material, begin with tactile learning strategies and then reinforce your learning with visual, auditory, and kinesthetic learning strategies according to your preferences.

Kinesthetic Learning Techniques

You learn better when you are able to move around while learning. You prefer to be active and it is important for you to be actively involved to remember. Here are some learning strategies for kinesthetic learners:

- Quickly skim through material before reading it in detail. As you are reading, think about how the material applies to your personal life. Underline the key ideas and review them to enhance recall.
- Writing a journal or make a summary sheet of key ideas to help you to remember what you have read.
- Take notes on lectures. You are more likely to remember what you have written down.
- To prepare for exams, use flashcards to learn detailed information and review them while walking around.
- Move while studying. For example, read while using your exercise bike or stair stepper.
- Use kinesthetic learning experiences such as drama, building, designing, visiting, interviewing, and going on field trips.
- Actively participate in discussions to increase motivation and recall.
- Use all of your senses (sight, touch, taste, smell, and hearing) to help you to remember. For example, when studying Spanish, picture yourself speaking the language, use flash cards you can touch to remember the vocabulary, imagine the smell of Mexican food, say the words out loud, and listen to recordings of the language.
- Actively participate in classroom exercises to involve yourself in learning and motivate yourself to learn.
- Avoid long classes if possible. For example, choose a class that meets one hour on Mondays, Wednesdays, and Fridays instead of three hours on Monday.
- If you have a choice on how to do your assignments, do a skit or create a video.
- Look for courses or majors with hands-on activities, labs, or field trips.
- Take frequent breaks and study in different locations.
- Use a study group to teach the material to someone else.
- Use bright colors to highlight reading material.
- If you find it helpful, listen to music while you are studying.
- Chew gum to stay alert while studying.
- To prepare for exams, write practice answers and essays. Break the material to be reviewed into small parts and review frequently.
- When learning new and difficult material, begin with kinesthetic learning strategies and then reinforce your learning with visual, tactile, and auditory techniques according to your preferences.

If you are having difficulties learning some new material in college, list some strategies that you might try:

1. _____

2. _____

3. _____

4. _____

Developing Your E-Learning Style

There are many opportunities for learning online, including online courses, professional development, or learning for your personal life. Students who are independent learners or introverts who enjoy individual learning in a quiet place may prefer online learning. Students who prefer having a professor to guide learning with immediate feedback and extraverts who are energized by social interaction may prefer traditional classroom education. Because of work, family, and time constraints, online learning might be a convenient way to access education. No matter what your learning style, you are likely to be in situations where you may want to take advantage of online learning. If you have never taken an online course, be aware of some of the myths of online learning. One of the most popular myths is than online courses are easier than traditional courses. Online courses cover the same content and are just as rigorous as traditional face-to-face courses. It is likely that your online course will require more writing; instead of responding verbally in discussions, you will have to write your answer. Online courses generally require the same amount of time as traditional courses. However, you will save time in commuting to class and have the added convenience of working on your class at any time or place where you can access the Internet.

© 2014, Naypong. Used under license with Shutterstock, Inc.

Here are some suggestions for a successful e-learning experience.

- The most important factor in online learning is to **log in regularly** and complete the work in a systematic way. Set goals for what you need to accomplish each week and do the work a step at a time. Get in the habit of regularly doing your online study, just as you would attend a traditional course each week.
- It is important to **carefully read the instructions** for the assignments and **ask for help** if you need it. Your online professor will not know when you need help.
- Begin your online work by getting familiar with the requirements and components of the course. Generally online courses have reading material, quizzes, discussion boards, chat rooms, assignments, and multimedia presentations. Make sure that you **understand all the resources, components, and requirements** of the course.
- **Have a backup plan** if your computer crashes or your Internet connection is interrupted. Colleges generally have computer labs where you can do your work if you have technical problems at home.
- Remember to **participate** in the online discussions or chats. It is usually part of your grade and a good way to learn from other students and apply what you have learned. The advantage of online communication is that you have time to think about your responses.
- **Check your grades** online to make sure you are completing all the requirements. Celebrate your success as you complete your online studies. Online learning becomes easier with experience.

Personality and Learning Preferences

Learning preferences are also connected to personality type. As a review, personality has four dimensions:

1. Extraversion or Introversion
2. Sensing or Intuition
3. Thinking or Feeling
4. Judging or Perceiving

What is your personality type? To review, read the following brief descriptions and think about your preferences:

Extraverts focus their energy on the world outside themselves. They enjoy interaction with others and get to know a lot of different people. They enjoy and are usually good at communication. They are energized by social interaction and prefer being active. These types are often described as talkative and social.

Introverts focus their energy on the world inside of themselves. They enjoy spending time alone and think about the world in order to understand it. Introverts like more limited social contacts, preferring smaller groups or one-on-one relationships. These types are often described as quiet or reserved.

Sensing persons prefer to use the senses to take in information (what they see, hear, taste, touch, smell). They focus on "what is" and trust information that is concrete and observable. They learn through experience.

Intuitive persons rely on instincts and focus on "what could be." While we all use our five senses to perceive the world, the intuitive person is interested in relationships, possibilities, meanings, and implications. They value inspiration and trust their "sixth sense" or hunches. We all use our senses and intuition in our daily lives, but we usually have a preference for one mode or another.

Thinking individuals make decisions based on logic. They are objective and analytical. They look at all the evidence and reach an impersonal conclusion. They are concerned with what they think is right.

Feeling individuals make decisions based on what is important to them and matches their personal values. They are concerned about what they feel is right.

Judging types like to live in a structured, orderly, and planned way. They are happy when their lives are structured and matters are settled. They like to have control over their lives. Judging does not mean to judge others. Think of this type as orderly and organized.

Perceptive types like to live in a spontaneous and flexible way. They are happy when their lives are open to possibilities. They try to understand life rather than control it. Think of this type as spontaneous and flexible.

Learning Strategies for Different Personality Types

Based on the above descriptions of learning preferences, the following learning strategies are suggested along with some cautions for each type. As you read these descriptions, think about those suggestions and cautions that apply to you.

Extravert

1. Since extraverts learn best when talking, discuss what you have learned with others. Form a study group.
2. Extraverts like variety and action. Take frequent breaks and do something active during your break such as walking around.
3. *Caution!* You may become so distracted by activity and socialization that your studying does not get done.

Introvert

1. Since introverts like quiet for concentration, find a quiet place to study by yourself.
2. Plan to study for longer periods of time and in a way that minimizes interruptions. Turn off the phone or study in the library.
3. *Caution!* You may miss out on sharing ideas and the fun social life of college.

Sensing

1. Sensing types are good at mastering facts and details.
2. Think about practical applications in order to motivate yourself to learn. Ask, "How can I use this information?"
3. *Caution!* You may miss the big picture or general outline by focusing too much on the facts and details. Make a general outline to see the relationship and meaning of the facts.

Intuitive

1. Intuitive types are good at learning concepts and theories.
2. As you are reading, ask yourself, "What is the main point?"
3. *Caution!* Because this type focuses on general concepts and theories, they are likely to miss details and facts. To learn details, organize them into broad categories that have meaning for you.

Thinking

1. Thinking types are good at logic.
2. As you are reading, ask yourself, "What do I think of these ideas?" Discuss or debate your ideas with others.
3. Allow time to think and reflect on your studies.
4. If possible, pick instructors whom you respect and who are intellectually challenging.
5. *Caution!* Others may be offended by your logic and love of debate. Learn to respect the ideas of others.

Feeling

1. Feeling types need a comfortable environment in order to concentrate.
2. For motivation, search for personal meaning in your studies. Ask how the material affects you or others. Look for a supportive environment or study group.
3. Help others to learn.
4. When possible, choose classes that relate to your personal interests.
5. If possible, select instructors who get to know the students and establish a positive learning environment.
6. *Caution!* You may neglect studying because of time spent helping others or may find it difficult to pay attention to material that is not personally meaningful.

Judging

1. Judging types are orderly and organized. Find ways to organize the material to learn it easier.
2. If possible, select instructors who present material in an organized way.
3. Set goals and use a schedule to motivate yourself. This type is naturally good at time management.
4. Use a daily planner, calendar, or to-do list.
5. *Caution!* Being too structured and controlled may limit your creativity and cause conflict with others who are different. Judging types are sometimes overachievers who get stressed easily.

Perceptive

1. Perceptive students are good at looking at all the possibilities and keeping options open.
2. Allow enough time to be thorough and complete your work.
3. Keep learning fun and interesting.
4. Study in groups that have some perceptive types and some judging types. In this way, you can explore possibilities, have fun, and be organized.
5. *Caution!* Work on managing your time to meet deadlines. Be careful not to overextend yourself by working on too many projects at once.

| Think About It | *Journal Entry* **6.3** |

Write a paragraph about your personality type and how it affects your learning style. Begin your paragraph by listing the four letters of your personality type. Tell how these personal characteristics affect your learning style. Include at least four learning strategies that match your personality type. For example:

My personality type is ISFJ. Being an introvert, I like quiet for concentration and prefer to study quietly in the library. I am also a sensing type . . .

_____

_____

_____

_____

Understanding Your Professor's Personality

Different personality types have different expectations of teachers.

- Extraverts want faculty who encourage class discussion.
- Introverts want faculty who give clear lectures.
- Sensing types want faculty who give clear assignments.
- Intuitive types want faculty who encourage independent thinking.
- Thinking types want faculty who make logical presentations.
- Feeling types want faculty who establish personal rapport with students.
- Judging types want faculty to be organized.
- Perceptive types want faculty to be entertaining and inspiring.

What can you do if your personality and the professor's personality are different? This is often the case. In a study reported by *Consulting Psychologist Press,* college faculty were twice as likely as students to be introverted intuitive types interested in abstractions and learning for its own sake.[3] College students are twice as likely as faculty to be extraverted sensing types who are interested in practical learning. There are three times more sensing and perceptive students than faculty. Faculty tend to be intuitive and judging types. Students expect faculty to be practical, fun, and flexible. Faculty tend to be theoretical and organized. In summary:

College faculty tend to be	College students tend to be
Introverted	Extraverted
Intuitive	Sensing
Judging	Perceptive

Of course, the above is not always true, but there is a good probability that you will have college professors who are very different from you. First, try to understand the professor's personality. This has been called "psyching out the professor." You can usually tell the professor's personality type on the first day of class by examining class materials and observing his or her manner of presentation. If you understand the professor's personality type, you will know what to expect. Next, try to appreciate what the professor has to offer. You may need to adapt your style to fit. If you are a perceptive type, be careful to meet the due dates of your assignments. Experiment with different study techniques so that you can learn the material presented.

"The wisest mind has something yet to learn."
George Santayana

"Tell me and I forget. Teach me and I remember. Involve me and I learn."
Benjamin Franklin

© 2014, Alexander Raths. Used under license with Shutterstock, Inc.

Think About It ———————————————————— *Journal Entry* 6.4

How can you use your knowledge of personality type to understand your professor's teaching style and expectations? What should you do if your personality does not match the professor's personality? For example, if your professor is a judging type and you are a perceptive type, how can you adapt to be successful in this course?

_____

_____

_____

_____

_____

_____

_____

6.1

DO IT **NOW** !

Learning Style

Test what you have learned by selecting the correct answers to the following questions.

Working Independently in Advance of Exams

Use the following strategies to use out-of-class time wisely to prepare for exams:

1. The best environment for learning
   a. matches your learning style.
   b. is a straight chair and a desk.
   c. includes music in the background.

2. Kinesthetic types learn best by
   a. listening to lectures.
   b. reading the textbook.
   c. taking notes and reviewing them.

3. If you become frustrated in learning, it is best to
   a. keep trying.
   b. take a long break.
   c. take a short break and then apply your preferred learning style.

4. Introverts would probably prefer
   a. studying quietly in the library.
   b. participating in a study group.
   c. learning through classroom discussions.

5. When working on a term paper, perceptive types would probably prefer
   a. organizing the project and completing it quickly.
   b. making a plan and finishing early.
   c. looking at all the possibilities and keeping their options open.

How did you do on the quiz? Check your answers:
1. a, 2. c, 3. c, 4. a, 5. c

KEYS TO SUCCESS

Create Your Success

We are responsible for what happens in our lives. We make decisions and choices that create the future. Our behavior leads to success or failure. Too often we believe that we are victims of circumstance. When looking at our lives, we often look for others to blame for how our lives are going:

- My grandparents did it to me. I inherited these genes.
- My parents did it to me. My childhood experiences shaped who I am.
- My teacher did it to me. He gave me a poor grade.
- My boss did it to me. She gave me a poor evaluation.
- The government did it to me. All my money goes to taxes.
- Society did it to me. I have no opportunity.

These factors are powerful influences in our lives, but we are still left with choices. Concentration camp survivor Viktor Frankl wrote a book, *Man's Search for Meaning*, in which he describes his experiences and how he survived his ordeal. His parents, brother, and wife died in the camps. He suffered starvation and torture. Through all of his sufferings and imprisonment, he still maintained that he was a free man because he could make choices.

We who lived in concentration camps can remember the men who walked through the huts comforting others, giving away their last piece of bread. They may have been few in number, but they offer sufficient proof that everything can be taken from a man but one thing: the last of the human freedoms—to choose one's attitude in any given set of circumstances, to choose one's own way. . . . Fundamentally, therefore, any man can, even under such circumstances, decide what shall become of him—mentally and spiritually. He may retain his human dignity even in a concentration camp.[7]

Viktor Frankl could not choose his circumstances at that time, but he did choose his attitude. He decided how he would respond to the situation. He realized that he still had the freedom to make choices. He used his memory and imagination to exercise his freedom. When times were the most difficult, he would imagine that he was in the classroom lecturing to his students about psychology. He eventually did get out of the concentration camp and became a famous psychiatrist.

Hopefully none of you will ever have to experience the circumstances faced by Viktor Frankl, but we all face challenging situations. It is empowering to think that our behavior is more a function of our decisions than of our circumstances. It is not productive to look around and find someone to blame for your problems. Psychologist Abraham Maslow says that instead of blaming, we should see how we can make the best of the situation.

One can spend a lifetime assigning blame, finding a cause, "out there" for all the troubles that exist. Contrast this with the responsible attitude of confronting the situation, bad or good, and instead of asking, "What caused the trouble? Who was to blame?" asking, "How can I handle the present situation to make the best of it?"[8]

Author Stephen Covey suggests that we look at the word responsibility as "response-ability."[9] It is the ability to choose responses and make decisions about the future. When you are dealing with a problem, it is useful to ask yourself what decisions you made that led to the problem. How did you create the situation? If you created the problem, you can create a solution.

At times, you may ask, "How did I create this?" and find that the answer is that you did not create the situation. We certainly do not create earthquakes or hurricanes, for example. But we do create or at least contribute to many of the things that happen to us. Even if you did not create your circumstances, you can create your reaction to the situation. In the case of an earthquake, you can decide to panic or find the best course of action at the moment.

Stephen Covey believes that we can use our resourcefulness and initiative in dealing with most problems. When his children were growing up and they asked him how to solve a certain problem, he would say, "Use your R and I!" He meant resourcefulness and initiative. He notes that adults can use this R and I to get good jobs.

But the people who end up with the good jobs are the proactive ones who are solutions to problems, not problems themselves, who seize the initiative to do whatever is necessary, consistent with correct principles, to get the job done.[10]

Use your resourcefulness and initiative to create the future that you want.

© 2014, Anson0618. Used under license with Shutterstock, Inc.

JOURNAL ENTRIES

Learning Style and Intelligence

Go to http://www.collegesuccess1.com/JournalEntries.htm for Word files of the Journal Entries

Success over the Internet

Visit the *College Success* Website at http://www.collegesuccess1.com/

The *College Success Website* is continually updated with new topics and links to the material presented in this chapter. Topics include:

- Learning style assessments
- Learning style and memory
- Learning style and personality type

Contact your instructor if you have any problems in accessing the *College Success Website.*

Notes

1. Gary E. Price, "Productivity Environmental Preference Survey," Price Systems, Inc., Box 1818, Lawrence, KS 66044-8818.

2. Modified and reproduced by special permission of the Publisher, Consulting Psychologist Press, Inc., Palo Alto, CA 94303, from *Introduction to Type in College* by John K. Ditiberio and Allen L. Hammer. Copyright 1993 by Consulting Psychologist Press, Inc. All rights reserved. Further reproduction is prohibited without the Publisher's written consent.

3. John K. Ditiberio and Allen L. Hammer, *Introduction to Type in College* (Palo Alto, CA: Consulting Psychologist Press, 1993), 7.

4. Howard Gardner, *Intelligence Reframed: Multiple Intelligences for the Twenty-First Century* (Boulder, CO: Basic Books, 1999).

5. Thomas Armstrong, *Multiple Intelligences in the Classroom* (Alexandria, VA: Association for Curriculum Development, 1994).

6. "Emotional Intelligence in Career Planning," https://www1.cfnc.org/, accessed August 2013.

7. Viktor Frankl, *Man's Search for Meaning* (New York: Pocket Books, 1963), 104–5.

8. Quoted in Rob Gilbert, ed., *Bits and Pieces*, November 4, 1999.

9. Stephen Covey, *The Seven Habits of Highly Effective People* (New York: Simon and Schuster, 1989), 71.

10. Ibid., 75.

Learning Style Quiz

Name _____ Date _____

Read the following questions and circle the letter of the best answer for each in your opinion. There are no right or wrong answers in this quiz. Just circle what you usually prefer.

1. When learning how to use my computer, I prefer to
   a. read the manual first.
   b. have someone explain how to do it first.
   c. just start using the computer and get help if I need it.

2. When getting directions to a new location, it is easier to
   a. look at a map.
   b. have someone tell me how to get there.
   c. follow someone or have him or her take me there.

3. To remember a phone number, I
   a. look at the number and dial it several times.
   b. repeat it silently or out loud to myself several times.
   c. remember the number by the pattern pressed on the keypad, the tones of each number, or writing it down.

4. For relaxation, I prefer to
   a. read a book or magazine.
   b. listen to or play music.
   c. go for a walk or do something physical.

5. I am better at
   a. reading.
   b. talking.
   c. physical activities.

6. In school, I learn best by
   a. reading.
   b. listening.
   c. hands-on activities.

7. I tend to be a
   a. thinker.
   b. talker.
   c. doer.

8. When I study for a test, it works best when I
   a. read and picture the information in my head.
   b. read and say the ideas out loud or silently.
   c. highlight, write notes, and outline.

9. It is easier for me to remember
   a. faces.
   b. names.
   c. events.

10. On a Saturday, I would prefer to
    a. see a movie.
    b. go to a concert.
    c. participate in athletics or be outside.

11. In a college class, it is most important to have
    a. a good textbook with pictures, graphs, and diagrams.
    b. a good teacher who gives interesting lectures.
    c. hands-on activities.

12. It is easier for me to study by
    a. reading and reviewing the material.
    b. discussing the subject with others.
    c. writing notes or outlines.

13. When I get lost, I prefer to
    a. look at the map.
    b. call or ask for directions.
    c. drive around the area until I recognize familiar landmarks.

14. When cooking, I often
    a. look for new recipes.
    b. talk to others to get new ideas.
    c. just put things together and it generally comes out okay.

15. When assembling a new toy or piece of furniture, I usually
    a. read the instructions first.
    b. talk myself through each step.
    c. start putting it together and read the directions if I get stuck.

16. When solving a problem, it is more useful to
    a. read a bestselling book on the topic.
    b. talk over the options with a trusted friend.
    c. do something about it.

17. Which statement do you like the best?
    a. A picture is worth a thousand words.
    b. Talk to me and I can understand.
    c. Just do it.

18. When I was a child, my mother said I
    a. spent a lot of time reading, taking photos, or drawing.
    b. had lots of friends and was always talking to someone on the phone.
    c. was always taking things apart to see how they worked.

Score your quiz:

Number of A answers	_____	Visual Learner
Number of B answers	_____	Auditory Learner
Number of C answers	_____	Kinesthetic/Tactile Learner

What did you discover as a result of taking this quiz?

Learning Style Applications

Name _____ Date _____

How would you use the knowledge of your learning style to deal with the following college situations? Your instructor may use this exercise for a group activity and class discussion.

1. You have just been assigned a 10-page term paper.

2. You have to study for a challenging math test.

3. You have to write up a lab report for a biology class. It includes drawings of a frog you have dissected.

4. You are taking a required course for your major and it is taught by only one professor. You dislike this professor.

5. You are taking a business class and have been assigned a group project to design a small business. It is worth 50 percent of your grade.

6. You have signed up for an economics course and find it difficult to stay awake during the lecture.

7. You signed up for a philosophy course to meet a humanities requirement. The vocabulary in this course is unfamiliar.

8. As part of the final exam, you have to prepare a five-minute presentation for your art history class.

Improving Memory and Reading

7

LEARNING GOAL

To comprehend memory processes and acquire memory strategies to support learning and reading.

Read to answer these key questions:

1. How does the memory work?

_____

_____

_____

_____

2. Why do we forget?

_____

_____

_____

_____

3. How can I remember what I study?

_____

_____

_____

_____

4. What are some memory tricks?

_____

_____

_____

_____

5. How can I apply memory techniques to reading?

    _____

    _____

    _____

    _____

    _____

6. What is a reading system for college texts?

    _____

    _____

    _____

    _____

7. What are some ways to improve reading speed and comprehension?

    _____

    _____

    _____

    _____

8. Why is positive thinking a key to remembering and reading?

    _____

    _____

    _____

    _____

    _____

Learning how to improve your memory and remember what you read will be a great asset in college, on the job, and in life in general. This chapter describes how memory works and provides some practical techniques for improving your memory. Once you understand how memory works, you can apply these techniques to remembering what you read. Positive thinking will help you be successful in remembering and reading effectively.

Improving Your Memory

How Does the Memory Work?

Understanding how the memory works provides the framework for effective study techniques. There are three stages of memory: **sensory register, short-term memory,** and **long-term memory.** Understanding these stages of memory will help you learn how to store information in your long-term memory, which lasts a lifetime.

- **Sensory register.** The first stage of memory is called sensory register. It is the initial moment of perception. This stage of memory lasts less than a second and is used to record sensory experience (what you see, hear, taste, touch, or do). It is like a quickly fading snapshot of what your senses perceive. The purpose of the sensory register is to allow the brain to process information and to focus on relevant information. To remember information for more than a second, it must be transferred to short-term memory.

- **Short-term memory (STM).** Paying attention to the information you have perceived in the sensory register transfers the information to STM. STM is temporary and limited, lasting only about half a minute. The information must be rehearsed or renewed for longer storage. STM records what we see, hear, feel, taste, or touch. Information is best stored in STM through recitation or mentally talking to ourselves. If the information is not repeated, it is very quickly lost. For example, when you meet a person for the first time, the person's name is often quickly forgotten because it is only stored in short-term memory. The purpose of STM is to ponder the significance of the stimuli we have received, detect patterns, and decide if the information is important enough to remember.

  Grouping together or chunking bits of information can increase the limited capacity of STM. George Miller of Harvard University found that the optimum number of chunks or bits of information that we can hold in STM is five to nine.[1] For example, we remember telephone numbers of seven digits by using a hyphen to separate the numbers into two more easily remembered chunks. We divide our Social Security numbers into three chunks for easier recall.

  According to George Miller's research, we often use the "Magical Number Seven" technique to remember material. It is much easier to remember material that is grouped in chunks of seven or less. You can find many examples of groups of seven used to enhance memory. There are seven days of the week and seven numbers in your driver's license and license plate. There are also seven dwarfs, seven deadly sins, and seven wonders of the world!

- **Long-term memory (LTM).** Long-term memory has a large capacity and is used to store information more permanently. You will want to use your LTM to store important information that you want to be able to recall at a later date. Most psychologists agree that once information is in LTM, it is there forever. Although the information is available, the problem becomes how to access it. Think of LTM as a library in which many available books are stored. If the books in the library are randomly stored, retrieval of information becomes extremely difficult. If the books are properly stored and indexed, we can find them more easily.

How are long-term memories formed? Short-term memories become long-term through repetition or meaningful association. Creating long-term memories takes some purposeful action. We are motivated to take some purposeful action to remember if the information has some survival value. When we touch a hot stove, this memory moves from sensory register to short-term memory and then is stored in long-term memory to avoid injury in the future. In an academic setting, we must convince ourselves of the survival value of what we are learning. Is the information needed to pass a test, to be successful in a career, or for personal reasons? If so, it is easier to take the action required to store information in long-term memory. Emotions such as fear, anger, or joy are also involved in the storing of memories. In the hot stove example, fear elevates the importance of the memory and helps us to store it in long-term memory. In the educational setting, an interest or joy in learning helps to store information in long-term memory.

In summary, when you are trying to store information in your memory, the first step is receiving information through the five senses to store in the sensory register, similar to entering data in a computer through the use of a keyboard. This takes less than a second. The next step involves paying attention to the sensory stimulus in order to transfer it to STM for the purpose of seeing patterns and judging significance or importance. Information only stays in STM for 30 seconds or less unless rehearsed or repeated. If you decide that the information is likely to be on a test and you need to remember it, you must organize the material in a meaningful way or repeat it to store the information in LTM. Information must be stored in LTM in order for you to remember it permanently. Effective techniques for storing information in LTM will be presented later in this chapter.

FIGURE 7.1

How Does the Memory Work?

Sensory Register	Initial moment of perception	Lasts less than a second
STM Short Term Memory	Temporary and limited	Lasts less than 30 seconds
LTM Long Term Memory	Permanent storage of information	Lasts forever, although you may lose access through disuse

Short-Term Memory and Long-Term Memory

Why Do We Forget?

Is it true that we never forget? Material that is stored in the sensory register is forgotten in less than one second. Material stored in STM is forgotten in 30 seconds unless rehearsed or repeated. We do not forget material stored in LTM, but we can lose access to the information, similar to when a book is filed incorrectly in the library. The book is in the library, but we cannot find it.

© 2014, Edyta Pawlowska. Used under license with Shutterstock, Inc.

Examining the following lists of items frequently forgotten or remembered can give us insight into why forgetting or losing access occurs.

We frequently forget these things:

- Unpleasant experiences
- Names of people, places, or things
- Numbers and dates
- What we have barely learned
- Material we do not fully understand
- What we try to remember when embarrassed, frustrated, tired, or ill
- Material we have learned by cramming
- Ideas or theories that conflict with our beliefs

We tend to remember these things:

- Pleasant experiences
- Material that is important to us
- What we have put an effort into learning
- What we have reviewed or thought about often
- Material that is interesting to us
- Muscular skills such as riding a bike
- What we had an important reason to remember
- Items we discuss with others
- Material that we understand
- Frequently used information

Theories of Forgetting

An understanding of theories of forgetting is also helpful in developing techniques for effective study and learning. There are many theories about why we forget or lose access to information stored in LTM.

1. **I forgot.** If you forget a name, number, or fact, you might just say, "I forgot." The information was stored in STM and never made it to LTM. Have you ever been introduced to a person and really not listened to his or her name? You didn't forget it. You never learned it.
2. **The mental blur.** If you are studying and don't understand the material, you will not remember it.
3. **The decay theory.** If you do not use information, you lose access to it, just as weeds grow over a path that is seldom used.
4. **Interference theory.** New memories interfere with old memories, and old memories interfere with new memories. Interference is especially likely when the memories are similar. For example, when I meet my students in the hallway, it is difficult to remember which class they are in because I have several similar classes.
5. **Reactive interference.** We tend not to remember ideas or subjects that we dislike.
6. **Reconstruction theory.** What we remember becomes distorted over time. Our personal biases affect what we remember.
7. **Motivated forgetting.** We choose to remember pleasant experiences and to forget unpleasant experiences.

Minimizing Forgetting

> "Just as iron rusts from disuse, even so does inaction spoil the intellect."
>
> Leonardo da Vinci

Herman Ebbinghaus (1850–1909), a German psychologist and pioneer in research on forgetting, described a curve of forgetting.[2] He invented nonsense syllables such as WUX, CAZ, BIJ, and ZOL. He chose these nonsense syllables so that there would be no meaning, associations, or organizations that could affect the memory of the words. He would learn these lists of words and measure forgetting over time. The following is a chart of time and forgetting of nonsense syllables.

Time	Percent Forgotten
After 20 minutes	47
After 1 day	62
After 2 days	69
After 15 days	75
After 31 days	78

We can draw three interesting conclusions from examining these figures. First, **most of the forgetting occurs within the first 20 minutes**. Immediate review, or at least review during the first 20 minutes, would prevent most of the forgetting. Second, forgetting slows down over time. The third conclusion is that forgetting is significant after 31 days. Fortunately, we do not need to memorize nonsense syllables. We can use meaning, associations, organization, and proper review to minimize forgetting.

Review is important in transferring information from short-term to long-term memory. You can also minimize forgetting over time through the proper use

Memorization Tips
- Meaningful organization
- Visualization
- Recitation
- Develop an interest
- See the big picture first
- Intend to remember
- Learn small amounts frequently
- Basic background
- Relax

7.1   DO IT **NOW**

Improving Your Memory

Test what you have learned by circling the letters of the correct answers to the following questions.

1. Information is stored permanently in the
   a. sensory register.
   b. short-term memory (STM).
   c. long-term memory (LTM).

2. You never forget.
   a. False.
   b. True.
   c. This is true only if the information is stored properly in long-term memory.

3. According to Ebbinghaus, the greatest rate of forgetting occurs
   a. within the first 20 minutes.
   b. within the first day.
   c. within the first 15 days.

4. If you do not review information stored in long-term memory, you will
   a. still remember it because it is in long-term memory.
   b. probably lose access to the information.
   c. lose the information forever.

5. The best way to review is
   a. in a 45-minute study session.
   b. in a 20-minute study session.
   c. in three- to five-minute study sessions spaced out over time.

How did you do on the quiz? Check your answers: 1. c, 2. c, 3. a, 4. b, 5. c

---

of review.[3] Let's assume that you spend 45 minutes studying and learning something new. The optimum schedule for review would look like this:

After 10 minutes	Review for 5 minutes
After 1 day	Review for 5 minutes
After 1 week	Review for 3 minutes
After 1 month	Review for 3 minutes
After 6 months	Review for 3 minutes

By spending about 20 minutes in review time, you can remember 90 to 100 percent of the material. The short periods of review are much easier to accomplish than spending larger periods of review. Make good use of your time by having material for review immediately available. When you have three to five minutes available, review some material that you have learned previously. You will be improving access to material stored in long-term memory, and you will be able to easily recall the information for an exam or for future use in your career.

How Can I Remember What I Study?

Based on the above theories of memory and forgetting, here are some practical suggestions for storing information in LTM. Information stored in LTM can be retrieved for tests in college and for success in your career and personal life.

"Today I will do what others won't, so I can accomplish what others can't."

Jerry Rice

Meaningful Organization

There is no better method of memory improvement than imposing your own form of personal organization on the material you are trying to remember. Psychologists have even suggested that your intelligence quotient (IQ) may be related to how well

ACTIVITY

Magical Number Seven

Remember George Miller's Magical Number Seven Theory? It is more efficient to limit the number of categories to seven or less, although you can have subcategories. Examine the following list of words.

goat	horse	cow
carrot	cat	lettuce
banana	tomato	pig
celery	orange	peas
cherry	apple	strawberry

Look at the list for one minute. Then look away from the list and write down all the words you can recall. Record the number of words you remembered: _____

Note that the following lists are divided into categories: animals, crops, and tropical fruits.

animals	crops	tropical fruits
lion	wheat	banana
giraffe	beans	kiwi
kangaroo	corn	mango
coyote	hay	guava
bear	oats	orange

Look at the above list for one minute. Then look away from the list and write down the words you recall. Record the number of words you remembered: _____

You probably remembered more from the second list because the list is organized into categories. Notice that there are only five words in each category. Remember that it is easier to remember lists with seven items or less. If these words have some meaning for you, it is easier to remember them. A farmer from the Midwest would probably have an easier time remembering the crops. A person from Hawaii would probably remember the list of tropical fruits. We also tend to remember unusual items and the first and last items on the list. If you need to memorize a list, pay more attention to the mundane items and the items in the middle of the list.

you have organized material you learned in the past. When learning new material, cluster facts and ideas into categories that are meaningful to you.

Visualization

Another very powerful memorization technique is visualization. The right side of the brain specializes in visual pictures and the left side in verbal functions. If you focus on the words only, you are using only half of your brain. If you can focus on the words and accompany them with pictures, you are using your brain in the most efficient way. Advertisers use pictures as powerful influences to motivate you to purchase their products. You can use the same power of visualization to enhance your studying. While you are studying history, picture what life would be like in that time period. In engineering, make pictures in your mind or on paper to illustrate scientific principles. Challenge yourself to see the pictures along with the words. Add movement to your pictures, as in a video. During a test, relax and recall the pictures.

Recitation

Although scientists are still researching and learning how the memory works and how information is stored, we do know that recitation, rehearsal, and reviewing the ideas are powerful techniques for learning. Memories exist in the brain in the form of a chemical neural trace. Some researchers think that it takes about four or five seconds for this neural trace to be established in LTM. It is through recitation that we keep the ideas in our mind long enough to store them in LTM. Often students say they cannot remember the material that they have just read. The reason for this problem is not a lack of intelligence, but rather a simple lack of rehearsal. If information obtained through reading is stored in STM, it is very quickly forgotten. Say aloud or to yourself the material you want to remember. This process takes about five seconds.

Applying the recitation technique can help you remember names. When you are introduced to someone, first pay attention to make sure that you have heard the name correctly. Ask the person to repeat their name if necessary. Repeat the name out loud or in your mind. Say something like, "Glad to meet you, *Lydia*." Say the name silently to yourself five times to establish the neural trace. If possible, make a visual connection with the name. If the person's name is Frank, you might picture a hot dog, for example. Thinking about the name or reviewing it will help to access the name in the future.

Remember that most of the forgetting occurs in the first 20 minutes after learning something. Reviewing the material within 20 minutes is the fastest and most effective way to remember it. You will also need to review the information you have stored in LTM periodically so it is more accessible. This periodic review can be done effectively in three to five minutes.

Develop an Interest

We tend to remember what interests us. People often have phenomenal memories when it comes to sports, automobiles, music, stamp collecting, or anything they consider fun or pursue as a hobby. Find something interesting in your college studies. If you are not interested in what you are studying, look for something interesting or even pretend that you are interested. Reward yourself for studying by doing something enjoyable.

Attitude has a significant impact on memory. Approaching your studies with a positive attitude will help you to find something interesting and make it easier to

"Knowledge is power, but enthusiasm pulls the switch."
Ivern Ball

"The secret of a good memory is attention, and attention to a subject depends on interest in it. We rarely forget what makes a deep impression on our mind."
Tyron Edwards

© 2014, Zurijeta. Used under license with Shutterstock, Inc.

remember. In addition, the more you learn about a topic, the more interesting it becomes. Often we judge a subject as boring because we know nothing about it.

Another way to make something interesting is to look for personal meaning. How can I use this information in my future career? Does the information relate to my personal experience in some way? How can I use this information? What is the importance of this information? And finally, is this information likely to be on the test?

See the Big Picture First

Imagine looking at a painting one inch at a time. It would be difficult to understand or appreciate a painting in this way. College students often approach reading a textbook in the same way. They focus on the small details without first getting an idea of the main points. By focusing on the details without looking at the main points, it is easy to get lost.

The first step in reading is to skim the chapter headings to form a mental outline of what you will be learning. Then read for detail. Think of the mind as a file cabinet or a computer. Major topics are like folders in which we file detailed information. When we need to find or access the information, we think of the major topic and look in the folder to find the details. If we put all of our papers into the file drawer without organization, it is difficult to find the information we need. Highlight or underline key ideas to focus on the main points and organize what you are learning.

Be selective and focus on key ideas to increase learning efficiency. Herman Ebbinghaus studied the length of time needed to remember series of six nonsense syllables and 12 nonsense syllables.[4] We might assume that it would take twice as long to remember 12 syllables as it would six syllables. Ebbinghaus found that it took 15 times longer to memorize 12 syllables. The Magic Number Seven Theory seems to apply to the number of items that can be memorized efficiently.

Does this mean that we should try to remember only seven or less ideas in studying a textbook chapter? No—it is most efficient to identify seven or fewer key ideas and then cluster less important ideas under major headings. In this way, you can remember the key ideas in the chapter you are studying. The critical thinking required by this process also helps in remembering ideas and information.

Intend to Remember

Tell yourself that you are going to remember. If you think you won't remember, you won't remember. This step also relates to positive thinking and self-confidence and will take some practice to apply. Once you have told yourself to remember, apply some of the above techniques such as organizing, visualizing, and reciting. If you intend to remember, you will pay attention, make an effort to understand, and use memory techniques to strengthen your memory.

One practical technique that involves intent to remember is the memory jogger. This involves doing something unusual to jog or trigger your memory. If you want to be sure to remember your books, place your car keys on the books. Since you cannot go anywhere without your keys, you will find them and remember the books too. Another application is putting your watch on your right hand to remember to do something. When you look at your left hand and notice that the watch is not there, the surprise will jog your memory for the item you wish to recall. You can be creative with this technique and come up with your own memory joggers.

Distribute the Practice

Learning small amounts of material and reviewing frequently are more effective than a marathon study session. One research study showed that a task that took 30 minutes to learn in one day could be learned in 22 minutes if spread over two days. This is almost a 30 percent increase in efficiency.[5]

If you have a list of vocabulary words or formulas to learn, break the material into small parts and frequently review each part for a short period of time. Consider putting these facts or figures on index cards to carry with you in your purse or pocket. Use small amounts of time to quickly review the cards. This technique works well because it prevents fatigue and helps to keep motivation high. One exception to the distributed practice rule is creative work such as writing a paper or doing an art project, where a longer time period is needed for creative inspiration and immediate follow-through.

A learning technique for distributed practice is summed up in the acronym **SAFMEDS**, which stands for Say All Fast for one Minute Each Day and Shuffle.[6] With this technique, you can easily and quickly learn 100 or more facts. To use this technique, prepare flash cards that contain the material to be learned (vocabulary, foreign language words, numbers, dates, places, names, formulas). For example, if you are learning Spanish, place the Spanish word on one side of the card and the English word on the other side. Just writing out the flash cards is an aid to learning and is often sufficient for learning the material. Once the cards are prepared, *say* the Spanish word and see if you can remember what it means in English. Look at the back of the card to see if your answer is correct. Do this with *all* of the cards as *fast* as you can for *one minute each day*. Then *shuffle* the cards and repeat the process the next day.

It is important that you do this activity quickly. Don't worry if you do not know the answer. Just flip each card over, quickly look at the answer, and put the cards that you missed into a separate pile. At the end of the minute, count the number of cards you answered correctly. You can learn even faster if you take the stack of cards you missed and practice them quickly one more time. Shuffling the cards helps you to remember the actual meanings of the words, instead of just the order in which they appear. In the case of the Spanish cards, turn the cards over and say each English word to see if you can remember the equivalent word in Spanish. Each day, the number of correct answers will increase, and you will have a concrete measure of your learning. Consider this activity as a fun and fast-moving game to challenge yourself.

Create a Basic Background

You remember information by connecting it to things you already know. The more you know, the easier it is to make connections that make remembering easier. You will even find that it is easier to remember material toward the end of a college class because you have established a basic background at the beginning of the semester. With this in mind, freshman-level courses will be the most difficult in college because they form the basic background for your college education. College does become easier as you establish this basic background and practice effective study techniques.

You can enhance your basic background by reading a variety of books. Making reading a habit also enhances vocabulary, writing, and spelling. College provides many opportunities for expanding your reading horizons and areas of basic knowledge.

Relax While Studying

The brain works much better when it is relaxed. As you become more confident in your study techniques, you can become more relaxed. Here are some suggestions to help you relax during study time.

- Use distributed practice to take away some of the pressure of learning; take breaks between periods of learning. Give yourself time to absorb the material.
- Plan ahead so that you do not have to cram. Waiting until the last minute to study produces anxiety that is counterproductive.
- If you are anxious, try a physical activity or relaxation exercise before study sessions. For example, imagine a warm, relaxing light beginning at the feet and moving slowly up the body to the top of the head. Feel each part of the body relax as the light makes contact with it. You will find other relaxation techniques in Chapter 12.
- If you are feeling frustrated, it is often a good idea to stop and come back to your studies later. You may gain insight into your studies while you are more relaxed and doing something else. You can often benefit from a fresh perspective.

Think About It ———————————————— *Journal Entry* **7.2**

Review the memory techniques explained in this chapter: meaningful organization, visualization, recitation, develop an interest, see the big picture, intend to remember, distribute the practice, create a basic background, and relax while studying. List and briefly explain at least three techniques you are willing to try, and give examples of how you would use each of the three memory techniques you select.

_____

_____

_____

_____

Using Mnemonics and Other Memory Tricks

Memory tricks can be used to enhance your memory. These memory tricks include acrostics, acronyms, peg systems, and loci systems. These systems are called *mnemonics*, from the Greek word *mneme* which means "to remember."

Mnemonic devices are very effective. A research study by Gerald R. Miller found that students who used mnemonic devices improved their test scores by up to 77 percent.[7] Mnemonics are effective because they help to organize material. They have been used throughout history, in part as a way to entertain people with amazing memory feats.

Mnemonics are best used for memorizing facts. They are not helpful for understanding or thinking critically about the information. Be sure to memorize your mnemonics carefully and review them right before exam time. Forgetting the mnemonic or a part of it can cause major problems.

Acrostics

Acrostics are creative rhymes, songs, poems, or sentences that help us to remember. Maybe you previously learned some of these in school.

- Continents: Eat an Aspirin after a Nighttime Snack (Europe, Antarctica, Asia, Africa, Australia, North America, South America)
- Directions of the compass: Never Eat Sour Watermelons (North, East, South, West)
- Geological ages: Practically Every Old Man Plays Poker Regularly (Paleocene, Eocene, Oligocene, Miocene, Pliocene, Pleistocene, Recent)
- Guitar Strings: Eat All Dead Gophers Before Easter (E, A, D, G, B, E)
- Oceans: I Am a Person (Indian, Arctic, Atlantic, Pacific)
- Metric system in order: King Henry Drinks Much Dark Chocolate Milk (Kilometer, hectometer, decameter, meter, decimeter, centimeter, millimeter
- Notes on the treble clef in music: Every Good Boy Does Fine (E, G, B, D, F)
- Classification in biology: Kings Play Cards on Fairly Good Soft Velvet (Kingdom, Phylum, Class, Order, Family, Genus, Species, Variety)

Memorization Tricks
• Acrostics
• Acronyms
• Peg systems
• Loci systems
• Visual clues
• Say it aloud
• Have a routine
• Write it down

An effective way to invent your own acrostics is to first identify key ideas you need to remember, underline these key words or write them down as a list, and think of a word that starts with the first letter of each idea you want to remember. Rearrange the words if necessary to form a sentence. The more unusual the sentence, the easier it is to remember.

In addition to acrostics, there are many other creative memory aids:

- Days in each month: Thirty days hath September, April, June, and November. All the rest have 31, except February which has 28 until leap year gives it 29.
- Spelling rules: *i* before *e* except after *c*, or when sounding like *a* as in neighbor and weigh.
- Numbers: Can I remember the reciprocal? To remember the reciprocal of pi, count the letters in each word of the question above. The reciprocal of pi = .3 1 8 3 10

Mnemonics become more powerful when used with visualization. For example, if you are trying to remember the planets, use a mnemonic and then visualize Saturn as a hulahoop dancer to remember that it has rings. Jupiter could be a king with a number of maids to represent its moons.

Acronyms

Acronyms are commonly used as shortcuts in our language. The military is especially fond of using acronyms. For example, NASA is the acronym for the National Aeronautics and Space Administration. You can invent your own acronyms as a memory trick. Here are some common ones that students have used:

- The colors of the spectrum: Roy G. Biv (red, orange, yellow, green, blue, indigo, violet)
- The Great Lakes: HOMES (Huron, Ontario, Michigan, Erie, Superior)
- The stages of cell division in biology: IPMAT (interphase, prophase, metaphase, and telophase)

To make your own acronym, list the items you wish to remember. Use the first letter of each word to make a new word. The word you make can be an actual word or an invented word.

Peg Systems

Peg systems start with numbers, typically 1 to 100. Each number is associated with an object. The object chosen to represent each number can be based on rhyme or on a logical association. The objects are memorized and used with a mental picture to recall a list. There are entertainers who can have the audience call out a list of 100 objects and then repeat all of the objects through use of a peg system. Here is an example of a commonly used peg system based on rhyme:

One	Bun	Six	Sticks
Two	Shoe	Seven	Heaven
Three	Tree	Eight	Gate
Four	Door	Nine	Wine
Five	Hive	Ten	Hen

For example, if I want to remember a grocery list consisting of milk, eggs, carrots, and butter, I would make associations between the peg and the item I want to remember. The more unusual the association is, the better. I would start by making a visual connection between *bun*, my peg word, and *milk*, the first item on the list. I could picture dipping a bun into a glass of milk for a snack. Next I would make a connection between *shoe* and *eggs*. I could picture eggs being broken into my shoe as a joke. Next I would picture a *tree* with orange *carrots* hanging from it and then a *door* with *butter* dripping from the doorknob. The technique works because of the organization provided by the pegs and the power of visualization.

There are many variations of the peg system. One variation is using the letters of the alphabet instead of numbers. Another variation is to visualize objects and put them in a stack, one on top of the other, until you have a great tottering tower, like a totem pole telling a story. Still another variation is to use your body or your car as a peg system. Using our example of the grocery list above, visualize balancing the milk on your head, carrying eggs in your hands, having carrots tied around your waist and smearing butter on your feet. Remember that the more unusual the pictures, the easier they are to remember.

Loci Systems

Loci or location systems use a series of familiar places to aid the memory. The Roman orators often used this system to remember the outline of a speech. For example, the speaker might connect the entry of a house with the introduction, the living room with the first main point, and each part of the speech with a different room. Again, this technique works through organization and visualization.

Another example of using a loci system to remember a speech or dramatic production is to imagine a long hallway. Mentally draw a picture of each topic or section you need to remember, and then hang each picture on the wall. As you are giving your speech or acting out your part in the play, visualize walking down the hallway and looking at the pictures on the wall to remind yourself of the next topic. For multiple topics, you can place signs over several hallway entrances labeling the contents of each hallway.

Visual Clues

Visual clues are helpful memory devices. To remember your books, place them in front of the door so you will see them on your way to school. To remember to take your finished homework to school, put it in your car when you are done. To remember to fill a prescription, put the empty bottle on the front seat of your car. Tie a bright ribbon on your backpack to remind you to attend a meeting with your study group. When parking your car in the mall, look around and notice landmarks such as nearby stores or row numbers. When you enter a large department store, notice the items that are near the door you entered. Are you worried that you left the iron on? Tie a ribbon around the handle of the iron each time you turn it off or unplug it. To find out if you have all the items you need to go skiing, visualize yourself on the ski slope wearing all those items.

Say It Aloud

Some people are auditory learners and can remember items by repeating them out loud. For example, if you want to remember where you hid your diamond ring; say it out loud a few times. Then reinforce the memory by making a visual picture of where you have hidden the ring. You can also use your auditory memory by making a rhyme or song to remember something. Commercials use this technique all the time to try to get you to remember a product and purchase it.

Have a Routine

Do you have a difficult time trying to remember where you left your keys, wallet, or purse? Having a routine can greatly simplify your life and help you to remember. As you enter your house, hang your keys on a hook each time. Decide where you will place your wallet or purse and put it in the same place each time. When I leave for work, I have a mental checklist with four items: keys, purse, glasses, and cell phone.

Write It Down

One of the easiest and most effective memory techniques is to simply write something down. Make a grocery list or to-do list, send yourself an email, or tape a note to your bathroom mirror or the dashboard of your car.

Remembering Names

Many people have difficulty remembering names of other people in social or business situations. The reason we have difficulty in remembering names is that we do not take the time to store the name properly in our memories. When we first meet someone, we are often distracted or thinking about ourselves. We are trying to remember our own names or wondering what impression we are making on the other person.

To remember a name, first make sure you have heard the name correctly. If you have not heard the name, there is no way you can remember it. Ask the person to repeat his or her name or check to see if you have heard it correctly. Immediately use the name. For example, say "It is nice to meet you, *Nancy*." If you can mentally repeat the name about five times, you have a good chance of remembering it. You can improve the chances of remembering the name if you can make an association. For example, you might think, "She looks like my daughter's friend Nancy." Some people remember names by making a rhyme such as "fancy Nancy."

Review the memory tricks explained in this chapter: acrostics, acronyms, peg systems, loci systems, visual clues, say it aloud, have a routine, write it down, and remembering names. List and briefly explain at least three memory tricks you are willing to try, and give examples of how you would use each of the three memory tricks you select.

_____

_____

_____

_____

_____

_____

Optimize Your Brain Power

The mind can be strengthened and remain healthy throughout life. Scientists have studied a group of nuns from Mankato, Minnesota, who have lived long lives and suffer less from dementia and brain diseases than the general population. These

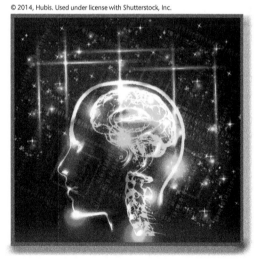

nuns have lived a long time because they do not drink to excess or smoke. They have kept their minds healthy into old age by staying mentally active. They keep active by discussing current events, playing cards, practicing math problems, and doing crossword puzzles. Arnold Scheibel, head of the UCLA Brain Institute, gives the following suggestions for strengthening your mind.

- Do jigsaw and crossword puzzles.
- Play a musical instrument.
- Fix something. The mental challenge stimulates the brain.
- Participate in the arts. Draw or paint something.
- Dance. Exercise and rhythm are good for the brain.
- Do aerobic exercise. This promotes blood flow to the brain.
- Meet and interact with interesting people.
- Read challenging books.
- Take a college class.[8]

Doing these kinds of activities can actually stimulate the development of neurons and nerve connections in the brain so that the brain functions more efficiently. The good news is that you can do this at any age.

Besides doing mental exercises to strengthen your brain, you can take other actions to keep your brain healthy. Here are some ideas:

1. **Do aerobic exercise.** Exercise improves the flow of oxygen to the brain. The brain needs oxygen to function. Researchers have just found that the human brain can grow new nerve cells by putting subjects on a three-month aerobic workout regimen. It was interesting to note that these new nerve cells could be

generated at any age and are important in reversing the aging process and delaying the onset of Alzheimer's disease or other cognitive disorders.[9] For optimum health and learning, it is important to exercise the body as well as the mind.

2. **Get enough rest.** Nobel laureate Francis Crick, who studies the brain at the Salk Institute, proposes that the purpose of sleep is to allow the brain to "take out the trash." Sleep provides time for the brain to review the events of the day and to store what is needed and discard what is not worth remembering. During sleep, the brain sorts memories and stores significant ones in long-term memory. Studies have shown that when humans and lab animals are taught a new task and deprived of sleep, they do not perform the task the next day as well as non-sleep-deprived subjects.[10]

3. **Eat a balanced, low-fat diet.** The brain needs nutrients, vitamins, and minerals to be healthy. Low-fat diets have been shown to improve mental performance.[11]

4. **Eat proteins and carbohydrates.** Proteins are the building blocks of neurotransmitters that increase mental activity. Carbohydrates provide energy and are the building blocks of neurotransmitters that have a calming effect.[12]

5. **Drink caffeine in moderation.** Caffeine can make you feel stressed, making it difficult to think.

6. **Don't abuse drugs or alcohol.** These substances kill brain cells and change brain chemistry.

7. **Use safety gear.** Wear a seat belt when driving and a helmet when biking or skating to reduce head injuries.

Think About It — Journal Entry 7.4

What is your plan for keeping your brain healthy throughout life? Include some of these ideas: diet, exercise, music, art, games, fixing something, challenging your brain, social contacts, and continued learning.

_____

_____

_____

_____

_____

_____

Improving Your Reading

Myths about Reading

Effective reading techniques are crucial to college success. The level and quantity of reading expected in college may be greatly increased over what you have experienced in the past. The following are some myths about reading that cause problems for many college students.

1. **"If I read a chapter, I should remember what I read."** Many students say that they read the chapter, but "it goes in one ear and out the other." After such a frustrating experience, students often conclude that they cannot read well or are not intelligent enough to succeed in college. If you just read the chapter, you have stored it in short-term memory, which lasts about 30 seconds. Reading a chapter takes a lot of effort. You want to make sure the effort you have invested pays off by storing the material in long-term memory. You can then retrieve the information in the future, as well as pass exams. Material is stored in long-term memory through rehearsal or review. Without review, you will not remember.

2. **"I do not need to read if I go to class."** The role of the college professor is to supplement material in the text and increase student understanding of the material. Some professors do not even cover topics contained in the text and consider it the student's responsibility to learn textbook material. If you do not read the text, you may miss out on important material that is not presented during class. Reading the text also helps you understand the material that the professor presents.

3. **"Practice makes perfect."** Students think that if they keep reading the way they are reading, their reading will get better. The truth is that "perfect practice makes perfect." If you are reading in a way that enhances memory, you will get better and better. Success in college reading may mean learning some new reading habits. You will learn about effective reading habits in this chapter.

4. **"Learn the facts that will be on the test."** Focusing on details without looking at the big picture can slow down learning and lead to frustration. If you start with the big picture or outline, then it is easier to learn the details.

A Study System for Reading a College Text: SQ4R

There are many systems for reading a college textbook. All successful systems involve ways to store information in long-term memory: recognizing major points, organizing material to be learned, reviewing, intending to remember, and critical thinking about reading. The crucial step in transferring information to long-term memory is rehearsal, reviewing, or reciting. You need to keep information in your mind for five to 5 seconds in order for it to be stored in long-term memory. The **SQ4R system (Survey, Question, Read, Recite, Review, Reflect)** is a simple and effective way to store information in long-term memory. This system was derived from an information-processing theory developed by Francis P. Robinson in 1941

FIGURE 7.2

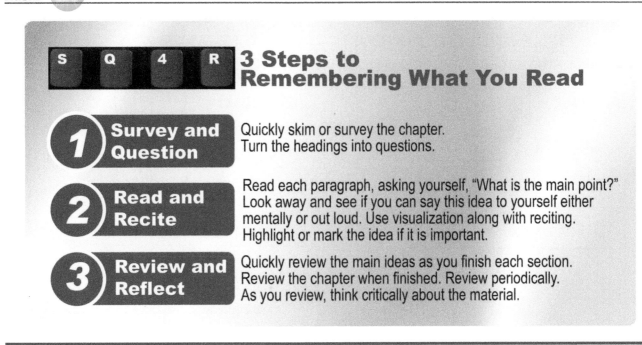

3 Steps to
Remembering What You Read

1 Survey and Question
Quickly skim or survey the chapter.
Turn the headings into questions.

2 Read and Recite
Read each paragraph, asking yourself, "What is the main point?"
Look away and see if you can say this idea to yourself either
mentally or out loud. Use visualization along with reciting.
Highlight or mark the idea if it is important.

3 Review and Reflect
Quickly review the main ideas as you finish each section.
Review the chapter when finished. Review periodically.
As you review, think critically about the material.

The SQ4R System for reading a college textbook

for use by military personnel attending college during World War II. Since that time, the system has been used by many colleges to teach students effective study skills. The system can be broken down into three steps.

Step 1: Survey and Question. The first step is to survey and question the chapter before you begin reading. Read the title and first paragraph or introduction to the chapter and then look quickly through the chapter, letting your eyes glide across bold headings, diagrams, illustrations, and photos. Read the last paragraph or summary of the chapter. This process should take five minutes or less for a typical chapter in a college textbook.

While you are surveying the chapter, ask yourself questions. Take each major heading in the chapter and turn it into a question. For example, in this section of the book you might ask: What is a system for reading a college text? Why do I need a system? What is SQ4R? What is the first step of SQ4R? You can also ask some general questions as you survey the chapter: What is the main point? What will I learn? Do I know something about this? Can I find something that interests me? How can I use this? Does this relate to something said in class? What does this mean? Is this a possible test question? Asking questions will help you to become an active reader and to find some personal meaning in the content that will help you remember it. If you at least survey and question the relevant textbook material before you go to class, you will have the advantage of being familiar with some of the key ideas to be discussed.

There are several benefits to taking this first step:

- This is the first step in rehearsal for storage of information into long-term memory.
- The quick survey is a warmup for the brain, similar to an athlete's warmup before exercise.

- A survey step is also good practice for improving your reading speed.
- Reading to answer questions increases comprehension, sparks interest, and has the added bonus of keeping you awake while reading.

> "The important thing is to not stop questioning."
>
> Albert Einstein

If you want to be able to read faster, improve your reading comprehension, and increase retention of your reading material, practice the survey and question step before you begin your detailed reading.

Step 2: Read and recite. The second step in reading a text is to read and recite. Read each paragraph and look for the most important point or topic sentence. If the point is important, highlight or underline it. You might use different colors to organize the ideas. You can also make a notation or outline in the margin of the text if the point is especially significant, meaningful, useful, or likely to appear on an exam. A picture, diagram, or chart drawn in the margin is a great way to use visualization to improve retention of the material. If you are reading online, take notes on the important points or use cut and paste to collect the main ideas in a separate document.

Next, look away and see if you can say the main point to yourself either silently or out loud. Reciting is even more powerful if you combine it with visualization. Make a video in your head to illustrate what you are learning. Include color, movement, and sound if possible. Reciting is crucial to long-term memory storage. It will also keep you awake. Beginning college students will find this step a challenge, but practice makes it a habit that becomes easier and easier.

If you read a paragraph or section and do not understand the main point, try these techniques:

1. **Notice any vocabulary or technical terms that are unfamiliar.** Look up these words in a dictionary or in the glossary at the back of the book. Use index cards; write the words on one side and the definition on the other side. Use the SAFMEDS technique (Say All Fast in one Minute Each Day Shuffle) discussed earlier in this chapter. You are likely to see these vocabulary words on quizzes and exams.
2. **Read the paragraph again.** Until you get into the habit of searching for the main point, you may need to reread a paragraph until you understand. If this does not work, reread the paragraphs before and after the one you do not understand.

3. **Write a question in the margin and ask your instructor or tutor to explain.** College instructors have office hours set aside to assist students with questions, and faculty are generally favorably impressed with students who care enough to ask questions. Most colleges offer tutoring free of charge.

4. **If you are really frustrated, put your reading away and come back to it later.** You may be able to relax and gain some insight about the material.

5. **Make sure you have the proper background for the course.** Take the introductory course first.

6. **Assess your reading skills.** Colleges offer reading assessments, and counselors can help you understand your skill level and suggest appropriate courses. Most colleges offer reading courses that can help you to be successful in college.

7. **If you have always had a problem with reading, you may have a learning disability.** A person with a learning disability is of average or higher-than-average intelligence, but has a problem that interferes with learning. Most colleges offer assessment that can help you understand your learning disability and tutoring that is designed to help you to compensate for the disability.

Step 3: Review and reflect. The last step in reading is to review and reflect. After each section, quickly review what you have highlighted or underlined. Again, ask questions. How can I use this information? How does it relate to what I already know? What is most important? What is likely to be on the exam? Is it true? Learn to think critically about the material you have learned.

When you finish the chapter, quickly (in a couple of minutes) look over the highlights again. This last step, review and reflect, is another opportunity for rehearsal. At this point, you have stored the information in long-term memory and want to make sure that you can access the information again in the future. Think of this last step as a creative step in which you put the pieces together, gain an understanding, and begin to think of how you can apply your new knowledge to your personal life. This is the true reward of studying.

Review is faster, easier, and more effective if done immediately. As discussed previously in this chapter, most forgetting occurs in the first 20 minutes after exposure to new information. If you wait 24 hours to review, you will probably have forgotten 80 percent of the material and will have to spend a longer time in review. Review periodically to make sure that you can access the material easily in the future, and review again right before the test.

As you read about the above steps, you may think that this process takes a lot of time. Remember that it is not how much you read, but how you read that is important. In reality, the SQ4R technique is a time-saver in that you do not have to reread all the material before the test. You just need to quickly review information that is stored in long-term memory. Rereading can be purely mechanical and consume your time with little payoff. Rather than rereading, spend your time reciting the important points. With proper review, you can remember 80 to 90 percent of the material.

In his book *Accelerated Learning*, Colin Rose states that you can retain 88 percent of the material you study using the following review schedule.[13] He also notes that the rate of retention using this schedule is four times better than the expected curve of forgetting.

1. Review immediately within 30 seconds.
2. Review after a few minutes.

FIGURE 7.3

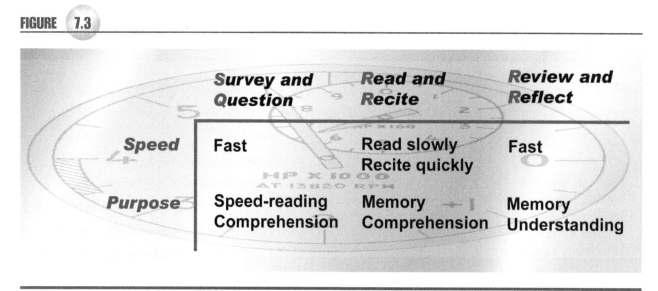

	Survey and Question	Read and Recite	Review and Reflect
Speed	Fast	Read slowly Recite quickly	Fast
Purpose	Speed-reading Comprehension	Memory Comprehension	Memory Understanding

This chart summarizes the speed and purpose of each SQ4R step

3. Review after one hour.
4. Review a day later after an overnight rest.
5. Review after a week.
6. Review after one month.

Suggestions for review schedules vary, but the key point is that review is most effective when it is done in short sessions spaced out over time.

Online Reading Strategies

To read efficiently, you will need some reading strategies for the vast amount of online material you will use in college and in everyday life. First, determine your purpose for reading. If you are reading for entertainment, to interact with others, or to find needed information, quickly scan the material to see if it meets your needs. Look for bulleted lists, menu bars, highlighted words, and headers; read only what suits your purpose. Avoid getting lost on your search by using browser tools such as favorites/bookmarks or the history, which is a list of the pages you have visited before. Use multiple browser windows to compare or synthesize information. To avoid eyestrain while reading online, be sure to take breaks and look away from the screen. It is important to get up and stretch periodically.

If you are study reading for an online course, first scan the material for key words. Then carefully read each section and summarize what you have learned. If you cannot do this, reread the section. If you are an auditory learner, you can repeat to yourself what you have learned, either silently or aloud. If you are a kinesthetic learner who learns by the hands-on approach, take notes on the important points. You can save time by opening a separate document in a new window and cutting and pasting the important points into your notes. Be sure to include the source of the material, so that you can use it in writing papers or find the material again. As in reading print material, use some techniques to assure good comprehension: as you read each section, visualize what you are reading, ask questions, and think critically about the material.

Think About It ——————————————— *Journal Entry* 7.5

Describe a system for college reading. Include these ideas: survey, question, read, recite, review, and reflect.

_____

_____

_____

_____

_____

_____

Guidelines for Marking Your Textbook

Marking your textbook can help you pick out what is important, save time, and review the material. It is a great way to reinforce your memory and help you access the material you have learned. In high school, you were given the command, "Thou shalt not mark in thy book!" College is different. You have paid for the book and need to use it as a tool. Even if you plan to sell your book, you can still mark it up. Here are some guidelines for marking your book:

- Underline or mark the key ideas in your text. You don't have to underline complete sentences; just underline enough to make sense when you review your markings. This technique works especially well for kinesthetics or tactile learners. If reading online, use the highlighter tool to mark the main points and then cut and paste the main points into a separate document.
- Aim for marking or highlighting about 20 percent of the most important material. If you mark too much of your reading, it will be difficult to review the main points.
- Read each paragraph first. Ask yourself, "What is the main point?" Highlight or mark the main point if it is important. Not every paragraph has a main point that needs to be marked.
- Use other marks to help you organize what you have read. Write in numbers or letters and use different colors to help you organize ideas.
- Most college texts have wide margins. Use these margins to write down questions, outlines, or key points to remember.
- Learn to be brief, fast, and neat in your marking or highlighting.
- If you are tempted to mark too much, use the double system of first underlining with a pencil as much as you want and then using a highlighter to pick out the most important 20 percent of the material in the chapter.

- Use different kinds of marks and symbols, such as the following:
  - Single or double underlines
  - Brackets around an important paragraph
  - Numbers or letters to organize points
  - Circles or squares to make important words stand out
  - An asterisk or star in the margin for a very important idea
  - A question mark next to something you do not understand
  - "DEF" in the margin to point out a definition
  - Use your imagination to come up with your own symbols
- Learn to recognize organizing patterns in your reading. These patterns will help you to pick out and mark the important ideas.
  - **The listing pattern.** Identify and mark the items in the list. Use numbers and letters to identify the parts of a list.
  - **The sequence pattern.** This pattern presents a list in a certain order. Note the items in the list and the order by using numbers or letters.
  - **The definition pattern.** Circle the word being defined. Underline the definition.
  - **The comparison/contrast pattern.** This pattern explains similarities or differences. Underline or mark these.
  - **The cause/effect pattern.** This pattern describes the reasons things happen. Underline or mark the cause and the effect.
- Quickly review the important points after you have marked each section. Quickly review again when you have finished the chapter. If you review within 20 minutes, the review will be faster and easier.

Reading for Speed and Comprehension

In *How to Read for Speed and Comprehension,* Gordon Wainwright suggests using different gears, or speeds, when reading for different purposes.[14] Understanding these four gears can be helpful for college students.

1. **Studying.** In this gear, the maximum reading speed is about 200 words per minute. It is used for material that is difficult or unfamiliar, such as a college textbook. For this material, a high quality of retention is required. It involves the steps described in SQ4R.
2. **Slow reading.** In this gear, reading speed ranges from 150 to 300 wpm. It is used for material that is fairly difficult when a good quality of retention is desired.
3. **Rapid reading.** In rapid reading, speeds range from 300 to 800 wpm. It is used for average or easy material. Use this gear for review of familiar material.
4. **Skimming.** Skimming is a type of very fast reading, done at 800 to 1000 wpm. With practice, it is possible to skim at 2000 to 3000 wpm. Using this technique, the eyes glide quickly down the page looking for specific information. Not every group of words or line is read. The eyes focus quickly on key ideas, bold headings, and titles. The purpose is to get a quick overview of the important ideas in the material.

Different reading speeds are used for different purposes. In college reading, it is more important to have good comprehension and retention than speed. However, we all live busy lives, and many college students today try to combine study, work, family, and social life. Learning to read faster is important to survival. You can learn to read faster by practicing skimming as a first step in reading. The next step is to slow down, look for the major points, and rehearse them so that they are stored in long-term memory. Using the SQ4R study technique described above will guide you through the process so that you can remember what you read.

7.2

DO IT NOW

Improving Reading

Test what you have learned by circling the letters of the correct answers to the following questions.

1. If you have read the chapter and can't remember what you have read,
   a. read the chapter again.
   b. remember to select important points and review them.
   c. skim over the text to get a general idea of what you will be reading.

2. When you start reading a new textbook,
   a. begin with chapter one.
   b. focus on the details you will need to remember.
   c. skim over the text to get a general idea of what you will be reading.

3. The first step in reading a chapter in a college textbook is to
   a. survey and question.
   b. read and recite.
   c. review and reflect.

4. As you are reading each paragraph in a college textbook, it is most important to
   a. read quickly.
   b. identify the main point and recite it.
   c. focus on the details first.

5. When marking a college textbook, it is recommended to mark about
   a. 50%.
   b. 30%.
   c. 20%.

How did you do on the quiz? Check your answers: 1. b, 2. c, 3. a, 4. b, 5. c

What to Do If Your Reading Goes in One Ear and Out the Other

1. **Silence your inner critic.**
   If you have always told yourself that you are a poor reader or hate reading, these thoughts make it difficult to read. Think positively and tell yourself that with some effort, you can read and understand. Focus on what you can do, rather than what you can't do.
2. Look for the key ideas and underline them.
3. **Try visualization.**
   Make a mental picture or video with the material you are reading.
4. **Look for personal meaning.**
   Can you relate the material to your life in any way?
5. Do a quick scan of the material to find some major points and then reread the material closely.
6. Try talking to the text as you read it. Ask questions. Why is this important? Do you know anything about this? Do you agree or disagree?

Do you think it is a good or bad idea? Can you use this information in the future? Can you find something interesting in the text? Challenge the material and think critically about it. Make humorous remarks. Imagine yourself in the situation. What would it be like and what would you do? You can write your comments in the text or do this silently in your head.

© 2014, wavebreakmedia. Used under license with Shutterstock, Inc.

Improving Reading Concentration

Hank Aaron said that what separates the superstar from the average ballplayer is that the superstar concentrates just a little longer. Athletes are very aware of the power of concentration in improving athletic performance. Coaches remind athletes to focus on the ball and to develop good powers of concentration and visualization. Being able to concentrate on your reading helps you to study more efficiently.

It is important to have a regular place for studying that has all the needed materials. You will need a table or desk with space for a computer, space for writing, and a comfortable chair. Keep a good supply of writing materials, computer supplies, and reference materials. To minimize fatigue and eyestrain, good lighting is essential. It is best to have an overhead light and a lamp. Place the lamp to your left if you are right-handed. In this way, you will not be writing in a shadow. Do the reverse if you are left-handed. If you have space, use two lamps with one placed on each side. Eliminate glare by using a lampshade. Study lamps often come with a deflector on the bottom of the lampshade that further eliminates glare. Lighter colors on your desk and wall also help to eliminate glare and fatigue.

In setting up your regular place for studying, keep in mind your environmental preferences as identified by your PEPS learning style inventory. Consider these factors:

- Do you need a quiet environment to focus on your studies?
- Do you prefer bright or dim light?
- Do you prefer a warm or cool environment?
- Do you prefer learning by yourself or with others?
- Do you study best in the morning or the afternoon?

Having and using a well-equipped and comfortable study place reduces external distractions. Internal distractions are many and varied and may be more difficult to manage. Internal distractions include being hungry, tired, or ill. It is a good idea to eat and be well rested before reading any course material. If you are ill, rest and get well. Study when you feel better. Many internal distractions are mental, such as personal problems, worrying about grades, lack of interest or motivation, frustration, or just daydreaming.

Here are some ideas for dealing with internal mental distractions while reading.

1. **Become an active reader.** Read to answer questions. Search for the main idea. Recite or re-say the main idea in your mind. Reflect and think critically about the material you are reading. Mark or highlight the text. Visualize what you are reading.
2. **Remind yourself of your purpose for reading.** Think of your future college and career goals.
3. **Give yourself permission to daydream.** If you like to daydream, give yourself permission to daydream as a break from your studies. Come back to your studies with a more relaxed attitude.
4. **Plan to deal with worry.** Worry is not a very good motivator and it interferes with memory. Take some positive action to deal with problems that cause you to worry. If you are worried about your grades, what can you do right now to improve your chances of making better grades? See a college counselor if worrying about personal problems interferes with studying.
5. **Break the task into small parts.** If the task seems overwhelming, break it into small parts and do the first part. If you have 400 pages to read in 10 days, read

Improving Reading Concentration

1. Become an active reader
2. Remember your purpose
3. Use daydreaming to relax
5. Plan to deal with worry
6. Break tasks into small parts

40 pages each day. Make a schedule that allows time to read each day until you have accomplished your goal. Use distributed practice in your studies. Study for a short time each day rather than holding a marathon study session before the test.

Reading Strategies for Different Subjects

While the SQ4R technique is a good general strategy for reading textbook material, there are steps that you will need to add depending on the subject area you are studying.

Math

1. Make sure you have the proper prerequisites or background courses before you begin your math class.
2. When skimming a math book, keep in mind that many of the topics will be unfamiliar to you. You should be able to understand the first few pages and build your knowledge from there. If all the concepts are familiar to you, you may be taking a class that you do not need.
3. It is not enough to read and understand mathematical concepts. Make sure that you add practice to your study system when studying math. Practice gives you the self-confidence to relax when working with math.
4. It is helpful to read over your math book before you go to class so that you will know what areas need special attention.
5. Focus on understanding the math problems and concepts rather than on memorizing problems.
6. Do not get behind in your math studies. You need to understand the first step before you can go on to the next.
7. Ask for help as soon as you have difficulties.

Science

1. In science classes, the scientific method is used to describe the world. The scientific method relies on questioning, observing, hypothesizing, researching, and analyzing. You will learn about theories and scientific principles. Highlight or mark theories, names of scientists, definitions, concepts, and procedures.
2. Understand the scientific principles and use flash cards to remember details and formulas.
3. Study the charts, diagrams, tables, and graphs. Draw your own pictures and graphs to get a visual picture of the material.
4. Use lab time as an opportunity to practice the theories and principles that you have learned.

Social and Behavioral Sciences

1. Social and behavioral scientists focus on principles of behavior, theories, and research. Notice that there are different theories that explain the same phenomena. Highlight, underline, and summarize these theories in your own words.
2. When looking at the research, ask yourself what the point of the research was, who conducted the research, when the research was completed, what data was collected, and what conclusions were drawn.
3. Think of practical applications of theories.
4. Use flash cards to remember details.

Literature Courses

When taking a course in literature, you will be asked to understand, appreciate, interpret, evaluate, and write about the literature.

1. Underline the names of characters and write plot summaries.

2. Write notes about your evaluation of literary works.

3. Make flash cards to remember literary terms.

4. Write down important quotes or note page numbers on a separate piece of paper so that you don't have to go back and find them later when you are writing about a work.

Foreign Language Courses

Foreign language courses require memorization and practice.

1. Distribute the practice. Practice a small amount each day. It is not possible to learn everything at once.

2. Complete the exercises as a way to practice and remember.

3. Study out loud.

4. Practice speaking the language with others.

5. Use flash cards to remember vocabulary.

6. Make charts to practice verb conjugations.

7. Ask for help if you do not understand.

8. Learn to think in the foreign language. Translating from English causes confusion because the structures of languages are different.

"Whatever the mind of man can conceive and believe, it can achieve."

Napoleon Hill

KEYS TO SUCCESS

Positive Thinking

You can improve your memory and your reading (as well as your life) by using positive thinking. Positive thinking involves two aspects: thinking about yourself and thinking about the world around you. When you think positively about yourself, you develop confidence in your abilities and become more capable of whatever you are attempting to do. When you think positively about the world around you, you look for possibilities and find interest in what you are doing.

Golfer Arnold Palmer has won many trophies, but places high value on a plaque on his wall with a poem by C.W. Longenecker:

If you think you are beaten, you are.
If you think you dare not, you don't.
If you like to win but think you can't,

It's almost certain that you won't.
Life's battles don't always go
To the stronger woman or man,
But sooner or later, those who win
Are those who think they can.[15]

Success in athletics, school, or any other endeavor begins with positive thinking. To remember anything, you first have to believe that you can remember. Trust in your abilities. Then apply memory techniques to help you to remember. If you think that you cannot remember, you will not even try. To be a good reader, you need to think that you can become a good reader and then work toward learning, applying, and practicing good reading techniques.

The second part of positive thinking involves thinking about the world around you. If you can convince yourself that the world and your college studies are full of interesting possibilities, you can start on a journey of adventure to discover new ideas. It is easier to remember and to read if you can find the subject interesting. If the topic is interesting, you will learn more about it. The more you learn about a topic, the more interesting it becomes, and you are well on your way in your journey of discovery. If you tell yourself that the task is boring, you will struggle and find the task difficult. You will also find it difficult to continue.

You can improve your reading through positive thinking. Read with the intent to remember and use reading techniques that work for you. We remember what interests us, and having a positive attitude helps us to find something interesting. To find something interesting, look for personal meaning. How can I use this information? Does it relate to something I know? Will this information be useful in my future career? Why is this information important? Write down your personal goals and remind yourself of your purpose for attending college. You are not just completing an assignment: you are on a path to discovery.

To be successful in college and to remember what you read, start with the belief that you can be successful. Anticipate that the journey will be interesting and full of possibilities. Enjoy the journey!

© 2014, Anson0618. Used under license with Shutterstock, Inc.

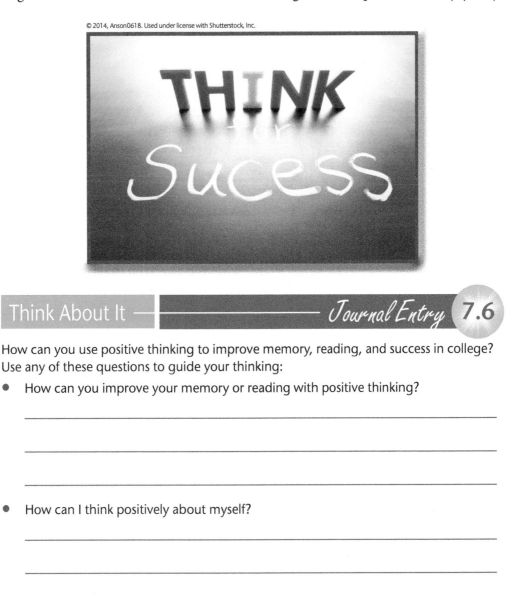

Think About It ——————————————— *Journal Entry* 7.6

How can you use positive thinking to improve memory, reading, and success in college? Use any of these questions to guide your thinking:

- How can you improve your memory or reading with positive thinking?

_____

_____

_____

- How can I think positively about myself?

_____

_____

_____

- How can I think positively about my college experience?

  _____

  _____

  _____

- What is the connection between belief and success?

  _____

  _____

  _____

- How can positive thinking make college more fun?

  _____

  _____

  _____

JOURNAL ENTRIES

Improving Memory and Reading

Go to http://www.collegesuccess1.com/JournalEntries.htm for Word files of the Journal Entries

Success over the Internet

Visit the *College Success* Website at http://www.collegesuccess1.com/

The *College Success Website* is continually updated with new topics and links to the material presented in this chapter. Topics include:

- Memory techniques
- Reading strategies
- How to concentrate
- How to highlight a textbook
- Speed reading
- How to study science
- Study groups
- Examples of mnemonics

Contact your instructor if you have any problems in accessing the *College Success Website.*

Notes

1. G. A. Miller, "The Magical Number Seven, Plus or Minus Two: Some Limits on Our Capacity for Processing Information," *Psychological Review* 63 (March 1956): 81–97.
2. Colin Rose, *Accelerated Learning* (New York: Dell Publishing, 1985), 33–36.
3. Ibid., 50–51.
4. Walter Pauk, *How to Study in College* (Boston: Houghton Mifflin, 1989), 96–97.
5. Rose, *Accelerated Learning*, 34.
6. Adapted from Paul Chance, *Learning and Behavior* (Pacific Grove, CA: Brooks/Cole, 1979), 301.
7. Pauk, *How to Study in College*, 108.
8. Daniel Golden, "Building a Better Brain," *Life Magazine*, July 1994, 63–70.
9. Mary Carmichael, "Stronger, Faster, Smarter," *Newsweek*, March 26, 2007, 38–46.
10. Scott LaFee, "A Chronic Lack of Sleep Can Lead to the Big Sleep," *San Diego Union Tribune*, October 8, 1997.
11. Randy Blaun, "How to Eat Smart," *Psychology Today*, May/June 1996, 35.
12. Ibid.
13. Rose, *Accelerated Learning*, 51.
14. Gordon R. Wainwright, *How to Read for Speed and Comprehension* (NJ: Prentice-Hall, 1977), 100–101.
15. Rob Gilbert, ed., *Bits and Pieces* (Fairfield, NJ: The Economics Press, 1998), Vol. R, No. 40, p. 12.

Scenarios

Name _____ Date _____

Review the main ideas on improving memory and reading. Based on these ideas, how would you be successful in the following situations? You may want to do this as a group activity in your class.

1. You just read the assigned chapter in economics and cannot remember what you read. It went in one ear and out the other.

2. In your anatomy and physiology class, you are required to remember the scientific names for 100 different muscles in the body.

3. You signed up for a philosophy class because it meets general education requirements. You are not interested in the class at all.

4. You have a midterm in your literature class and have to read 400 pages in one month.

5. You must take American history to graduate from college. You think that history is boring.

6. You have been introduced to an important business contact and would like to remember his/her name.

7. You are enrolled in an algebra class. You continually remind yourself that you have never been good at math. You don't think that you will pass this class.

8. You have noticed that your grandmother is becoming very forgetful. You want to do whatever is possible to keep your mind healthy as you age.

Memory Test

Name _____ Date _____

Part 1. Your professor will read a list of 15 items. Do not write them down. After listening to this list, see how many you can remember and write them here.

1.   6.   11.

2.   7.   12.

3.   8.   13.

4.   9.   14.

5.   10.   15.

After your professor has given you the answers, write the number of words you remembered: _____

Part 2. Your professor will discuss memory techniques that you can use to improve your test scores and then will read another list. Again, do not write the words down, but try to apply the recommended techniques. Write as many words as you can remember.

1.   6.   11.

2.   7.   12.

3.   8.   13.

4.   9.   14.

5.   10.   15.

How many words did you remember this time? _____

Practice with Mnemonics

Name _____   Date _____

Join with a group of students in your class to invent some acrostics and acronyms.

Acrostics

Acrostics are creative rhymes, songs, poems, or sentences that help us to remember. To write an acrostic, think of a word that starts with the same letter as each idea you want to remember. Sometimes you can rearrange the words if necessary to form a sentence. At other times, it is necessary to keep the words in order. The more unusual the sentence, the easier it is to remember.

> **Example:** Classification in biology: Kings Play Cards on Fairly Good Soft Velvet (Kingdom, Phylum, Class, Order, Family, Genus, Species, Variety)

Create an acrostic for the planets in the solar system. Keep the words in the same order as the planets from closest to the sun to farthest from the sun.

> Mercury, Venus, Earth, Mars, Jupiter, Saturn, Uranus, Neptune, Pluto

_____

_____

_____

Acronyms

To make your own acronym, list the items you wish to remember. Use the first letter of each word to make a new word. The new word you invented can be an actual word or an invented word.

> **Example:** The Great Lakes: HOMES (Huron, Ontario, Michigan, Erie, and Superior)

The following are the excretory organs of the body. Make an acronym to remember them. Rearrange the words if necessary.

> intestines, liver, lungs, kidneys, skin

_____

_____

_____

Write down any acrostics or acronyms that you know. Share them with your group.

Check Your Textbook Reading Skills

Name _____   Date _____

As you read each of the following statements, mark your response using this key:

1 I seldom or never do this.

2 I occasionally do this, depending on the class.

3 I almost always or always do this.

_____ 1. Before I read the chapter, I quickly skim through it to get main ideas.

_____ 2. As I skim through the chapter, I form questions based on the bold printed section headings.

_____ 3. I read with a positive attitude and look for something interesting.

_____ 4. I read the introductory and summary paragraphs in the chapter before I begin reading.

_____ 5. As I read each paragraph, I look for the main idea.

_____ 6. I recite the main idea so I can remember it.

_____ 7. I underline, highlight, or take notes on the main ideas.

_____ 8. I write notes or outlines in the margin of the text.

_____ 9. After reading each section, I do a quick review.

_____ 10. I quickly review the chapter immediately after reading it.

_____ 11. During or after reading, I reflect on how the material is useful or meaningful to me.

_____ 12. I read or at least skim the assigned chapter before I come to class.

_____ 13. I have planned reading time in my weekly schedule.

_____ 14. I generally think positively about my reading assignments.

_____ Total points

Check your score.
42–36 You have excellent college reading skills.
35–30 You have good skills, but can improve.
29–24 Some changes are needed.
23–14 Major changes are needed.

Becoming an Efficient College Reader

Name _____ Date _____

1. Based on your responses to the reading skills checklist on the previous page, list some of your good reading habits.

2. Based on this same checklist, what are some areas you need to improve?

3. Review the material on SQ4R and reading for speed and comprehension. Write five intention statements about how you plan to improve your reading. I intend to . . .

4. Review the material on how to concentrate while reading. List some ideas that you can use.

Surveying and Questioning a Chapter

Name _____   Date _____

Using the *next chapter* assigned in this class or any other class, answer these questions. Again, challenge yourself to do this activity quickly. Can you finish the exercise in five to seven minutes? Notice your beginning and end times.

1. What is the title of the chapter? Write the title in the form of a question. For example, the title of this chapter is "Improving Memory and Reading." A good question would be, "How can I improve my memory and reading?"

2. Briefly list one key idea mentioned in the introduction or first paragraph.

3. Write five questions you asked yourself while surveying this chapter. Read the bold section headings in the chapter and turn them into questions. For example, one heading in this chapter is "Myths about Reading." This heading might prompt you to ask, "What are some myths about reading? Do I believe in some of these myths?"

4. List three topics that interest you.

5. Briefly write one key idea from the last paragraph or chapter summary.

6. How long did it take you to do this exercise? Write your time here.

7. What did you think of this exercise on surveying and questioning a chapter?

Taking Notes, Writing, and Speaking

Read to answer these key questions:

1. Why is it important to take notes?

_____

_____

_____

_____

2. What are some good listening techniques?

_____

_____

_____

_____

3. What are some tips for taking good lecture notes?

_____

_____

_____

_____

4. What are some note-taking systems?

_____

_____

_____

_____

5. What is the best way to review my notes for the test?

_____

_____

_____

_____

6. What is power writing?

_____

_____

_____

_____

7. How can I make a good speech?

_____

_____

_____

_____

Knowing how to listen and take good notes can make your college life easier and may help you in your future career as well. Professionals in many occupations take notes as a way of recording key ideas for later use. Whether you become a journalist, attorney, architect, engineer, or other professional, listening and taking good notes can help you to get ahead in your career.

Good writing and speaking skills are important to your success in college and in your career. In college, you will be asked to write term papers and complete other writing assignments. The writing skills you learn in college will be used later in jobs involving high responsibility and good pay; on the job, you will write reports, memos, and proposals. In college, you will probably take a speech class and give oral reports in other classes; on the job, you will present your ideas orally to your colleagues and business associates.

Why Take Notes?

The most important reason for taking notes is to remember important material for tests or for future use in your career. If you just attend class without taking notes, you will forget most of the material by the next day.

How does taking notes enhance memory?

- In college, the lecture is a way of supplementing the written material in the textbook. Without good notes, an important part of the course is missing. Note taking provides material to rehearse or recite, so that it can be stored in long-term memory.
- When you take notes and impose your own organization on them, the notes become more personally meaningful. If they are meaningful, they are easier to remember.
- Taking notes helps you to make new connections. New material is remembered by connecting it to what you already know.
- For kinesthetic and tactile learners, the physical act of writing the material is helpful in learning and remembering it.
- For visual learners, notes provide a visual map of the material to be learned.
- For auditory learners, taking notes is a way to listen carefully and record information to be stored in the memory.
- Note taking helps students to concentrate, maintain focus, and stay awake.
- Attending the lectures and taking notes helps you to understand what the professor thinks is important and to know what to study for the exam.

The College Lecture

You will experience many different types of lectures while in college. At larger universities, many of the beginning-level courses are taught in large lecture halls with 300 people or more. More advanced courses tend to have fewer students. In large lecture situations, it is not always possible or appropriate to ask questions. Under these circumstances, the large lecture is often supplemented by smaller discussion sessions where you can ask questions and review the lecture material. Although attendance may not be checked, it is important to attend both the lectures and the discussion sessions.

"Education is not a problem. It is an opportunity."
Lyndon B. Johnson

A formal college lecture is divided into four parts. Understanding these parts will help you to be a good listener and take good notes.

1. **Introduction.** The professor uses the introduction to set the stage and to introduce the topic of the lecture. Often an overview or outline of the lecture is presented. Use the introduction as a way to begin thinking about the organization of your notes and the key ideas you will need to write down.
2. **Thesis.** The thesis is the key idea in the lecture. In a one-hour lecture, there is usually one thesis statement. Listen carefully for the thesis statement and write it down in your notes. Review the thesis statement and related ideas for the exam.

3. **Body.** The body of the lecture usually consists of five or six main ideas with discussion and clarification of each idea. As a note taker, your job is to identify the main ideas, write them in your notes, and put in enough of the explanation or examples to understand the key ideas.

4. **Conclusion.** In the conclusion, the professor summarizes the key points of the lecture and sometimes asks for questions. Use the conclusion as an opportunity to check your understanding of the lecture and to ask questions to clarify the key points.

How to Be a Good Listener

Effective note taking begins with good listening. What is good listening? Sometimes students confuse listening with hearing. Hearing is done with the ears. Listening is a more active process done with the ears and the brain engaged. Good listening requires attention and concentration. Practice these ideas for good listening:

- **Be physically ready.** It is difficult to listen to a lecture if you are tired, hungry, or ill. Get enough sleep so that you can stay awake. Eat a balanced diet without too much caffeine or sugar. Take care of your health and participate in an exercise program so that you feel your best.

- **Prepare a mental framework.** Look at the course syllabus to become familiar with the topic of the lecture. Use your textbook to read, or at least survey, the material to be covered in the lecture. If you are familiar with the key concepts from the textbook, you will be able to understand the lecture and know what to write down in your notes. If the material is in your book, there is no need to write it down in your notes.

    The more complex the topic, the more important it is for you to read the text first. If you go to the lecture and have no idea what is being discussed, you may be overwhelmed and find it difficult to take notes on material that is totally new to you. Remember that it is easier to remember material if you can connect it to material you already know.

- **Find a good place to sit.** Arrive early to get a good seat. The best seats in the classroom are in the front and center of the room. If you were buying concert tickets, these would be the best and most expensive seats. Find a seat that will help you to hear and focus on the speaker. You may need to find a seat away from your friends to avoid distractions.

- **Have a positive mental attitude.** Convince yourself that the speaker has something important to say and be open to new ideas. This may require you to focus on your goals and to look past some distractions. Maybe the lecturer doesn't have the best speaking voice or you don't like his or her appearance. Focus on what you can learn from the professor rather than outward appearances.

- **Listen actively to identify the main points.** As you are listening to the lecture, ask yourself, "What is the main idea?" In your own words, write the main points down in your notes. Do not try to write down everything the professor says. This will be impossible and unnecessary. Imagine that your mind is a filter and you are actively sorting through the material to find the key ideas and write them down in your notes. Try to identify the key points that will be on the test and write them in your notes.

- **Stay awake and engaged in learning.** The best way to stay awake and focused is to listen actively and take notes. Have a mental debate with the professor. Listen for the main points and the logical connection between ideas. The physical act of writing the notes will help to keep you awake.

Tips for Good Note Taking

Here are some suggestions for taking good notes:

1. Attend all of the lectures. Because many professors do not take attendance, students are often tempted to miss class. If you do not attend the lectures, however, you will not know what the professor thinks is important and what to study for the test. There will be important points covered in the lectures that are not in the book.

2. Have the proper materials. A three-ring notebook and notebook paper are recommended. Organize notes chronologically and include any handouts given in class. You can have a small notebook for each class or a single large notebook with dividers for each class. Just take the notebook paper to class and later file it in your notebook at home. Use your laptop as an alternative to a paper notebook.

3. Begin your notes by writing the date of the lecture, so you can keep your notes in order.

4. Write notes on the front side only of each piece of paper. This will allow you to spread the pages out and see the big picture or pattern in the lectures when you are reviewing.

5. Write notes neatly and legibly so you can read and review them easily.

6. Do not waste time recopying or typing your notes. Your time would be better spent reviewing your notes.

7. As a general rule, do not rely on a tape recorder for taking notes. With a tape recorder, you will have to listen to the lecture again on tape. For a semester course, this would be about 45 hours of tape! It is much faster to review carefully written notes.

8. Copy down everything written on the board and the main points from Power-Point or other visual presentations. If it is important enough for the professor to write on the board, it is important enough to be on the test.

9. Use key words and phrases in your notes. Leave out unimportant words and don't worry about grammar.

10. Use abbreviations as long as you can read them. Entire sentences or paragraphs are not necessary and you may not have time to write them.

11. Don't loan your whole notebook to someone else because you may not get it back. If you want to share your notes, make copies.

© 2014, Monkey Business Images. Used under license with Shutterstock, Inc.

12. If the professor talks too fast, listen carefully for the key ideas and write them down. Leave spaces in your notes to fill in later. You may be able to find the information in the text or get the information from another student.

13. Explore new uses of technology for note taking. Students are taking notes and sharing them on Facebook and GradeGuru, for example.

Think About It ───────────────── *Journal Entry* **8.1**

Write one paragraph giving advice to a new student about taking notes in college. Use any of these questions to guide your thinking:

● Why is note taking necessary in college?

_____

_____

_____

_____

_____

● How can you be a good listener?

_____

_____

_____

_____

_____

● What are some tips for taking good notes?

_____

_____

_____

_____

_____

● What are some ideas that don't work?

_____

_____

_____

_____

_____

Note-Taking Systems

There are several systems for taking notes. How you take notes will depend on your learning style and the lecturer's speaking style. Experiment with these systems and use what works best for you.

Note-Taking Systems

- Cornell format
- Outline method
- Mind map

The Cornell Format

The Cornell format is an efficient method of taking notes and reviewing them. It appeals to students who are logical, orderly, and organized and have lectures that fit into this pattern. The Cornell format is especially helpful for thinking about key points as you review your notes.

FIGURE 8.1

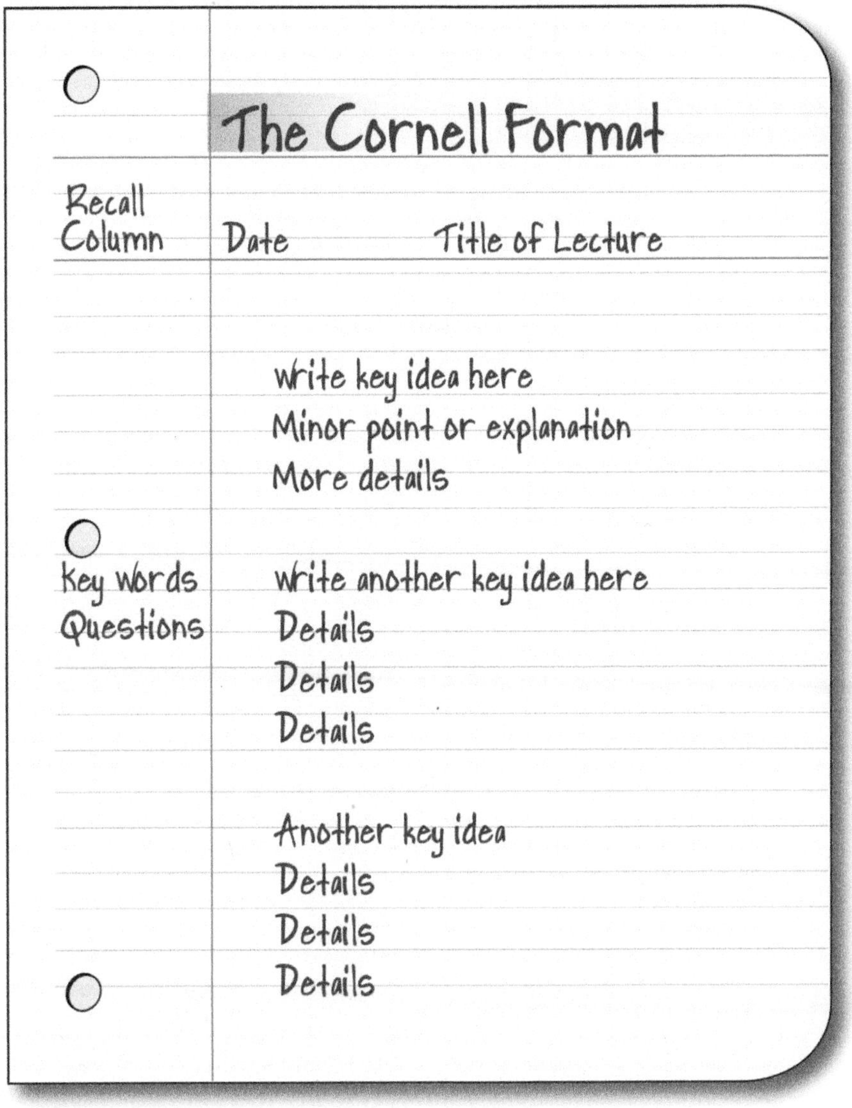

The Cornell Format

Recall Column	Date Title of Lecture
	Write key idea here
	Minor point or explanation
	More details
Key words	Write another key idea here
Questions	Details
	Details
	Details
	Another key idea
	Details
	Details
	Details

The Cornell format is an efficient way of organizing notes and reviewing them

Step 1: Prepare. To use the Cornell format, you will need a three-ring notebook with looseleaf paper. Draw or fold a vertical line 2½ inches from the left side of the paper. This is the recall column that can be used to write key ideas when reviewing. Use the remaining section of the paper for your notes. Write the date and title of the lecture at the top of the page.

Step 2: Take notes. Use the large area to the right of the recall column to take notes. Listen for key ideas and write them just to the right of the recall column line, as in the diagram above. Indent your notes for minor points and illustrative details. Then skip a space and write the next key idea. Don't worry about using numbers or letters as in an outline format. Just use the indentations and spacing to highlight and separate key ideas. Use short phrases, key words, and abbreviations. Complete sentences are not necessary, but write legibly so you can read your notes later.

Step 3: Use the recall column for review. Read over your notes and write down key words or ideas from the lecture in the recall column. Ask yourself, "What is this about?" Cover up the notes on the right-hand side and recite the key ideas of the lecture. Another variation is to write questions in the margin. Find the key ideas and then write possible exam questions in the recall column. Cover your notes and see if you can answer the questions.

The Outline Method

If the lecture is well organized, some students just take notes in outline format. Sometimes lecturers will show their outline as they speak.

- Use Roman numerals to label main topics. Then use capital letters for main ideas and Arabic numerals for related details or examples.
- You can make a free-form outline using just indentation to separate main ideas and supporting details.
- Leave spaces to fill in material later.
- Use a highlighter to review your notes as soon as possible after the lecture.

The Mind Map

A mind map shows the relationship between ideas in a visual way. It is much easier to remember items that are organized and linked together in a personally meaningful way. As a result, recall and review is quicker and more effective. Mind maps have appeal to visual learners and those who do not want to be limited by a set structure, as in the outline formats. They can also be used for lectures that are not highly structured. Here are some suggestions for using the mind-mapping technique:

- Turn your paper sideways to give you more space. Use standard-size notebook paper or consider larger sheets if possible.
- Write the main idea in the center of the page and circle it.
- Arrange ideas so that more important ideas are closer to the center and less important ideas are farther out.
- Show the relationship of the minor points to the main ideas using lines, circles, boxes, charts, and other visual devices. Here is where you can use your creativity and imagination to make a visual picture of the key ideas in the lecture.

FIGURE  8.2

The Outline Method

Date   Title of Lecture

    I. Key Idea
       A. Important Idea
          Detail or example
          Detail
          Detail
       B. Important Idea
          Detail
          Detail

(Leave Space here)

    II. Key Idea
       A. Important Idea
          Detail or example
          Detail
          Detail

If a lecture is well organized, the outline format of taking notes works well

- Use symbols and drawings.
- Use different colors to separate main ideas.
- When the lecturer moves to another main idea, start a new mind map.
- When you are done with the lecture, quickly review your mind maps. Add any written material that will be helpful in understanding the map later.
- A mind map can also be used as:
  - a review tool for remembering and relating the key ideas in the textbook;
  - a preparation tool for essay exams in which remembering main ideas and relationships is important; and
  - the first step in organizing ideas for a term paper.

FIGURE 8.3

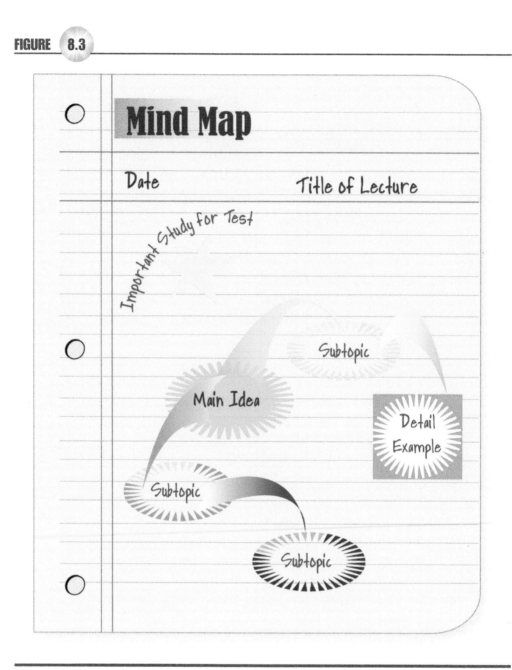

The mind map format of taking notes shows the relationship between ideas in a visual way

Improving Note-Taking Efficiency

Improve note-taking efficiency by listening for key words that signal the main ideas and supporting details. Learn to write faster by using telegraphic sentences, abbreviations, and symbols.

Telegraphic Sentences

Telegraphic sentences are short, abbreviated sentences used in note taking. They are very similar to the text messages sent on a cell phone. There are four rules for telegraphic sentences:

1. Write key words only.

2.   Omit unnecessary words (*a, an, the*).
3.   Ignore rules of grammar.
4.   Use abbreviations and symbols.

Here is an example of a small part of a lecture followed by a student's telegraphic notes:

Heavy drinking of alcoholic beverages causes students to miss class and to fall behind in schoolwork. College students who are considered binge drinkers are at risk for many alcohol-related problems. Binge drinking is simply drinking too much alcohol at one time. Binge drinking is defined by researchers as drinking five or more drinks in a row for men or four or more drinks in a row for women. Researchers estimate that two out of five college students (40 percent) are binge drinkers.

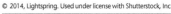
© 2014, Lightspring. Used under license with Shutterstock, Inc.

Binge drinking—too much alcohol at one time
    Men = 5 in row
    Women = 4
    2 out of 5 (40%) college students binge

Signal Words

Signal words are clues to understanding the structure and content of a lecture. Recognizing signal words can help you identify key ideas and organize them in your notes. The table on the following page lists some common signal words and their meaning.

Abbreviations

If you have time, write out words in their entirety for ease of reading. If you are short on time, use any abbreviation as long as you can read it. Here are some ideas:
1.   Use the first syllable of the word.

democracy	dem
education	ed
politics	pol
different	diff
moderate	mod
characteristic	char
develop	dev

2.   Use just enough of the word so that you can recognize it.

republican	repub
prescription	prescrip
introduction	intro
intelligence	intell
association	assoc

3.   Abbreviate or write out the word the first time, then use an acronym. For example, for the United States Department of Agriculture, abbreviate it as "US Dept of Ag" and then write it as USDA in subsequent references. Other examples:

short-term memory	STM
as soon as possible	ASAP

4.   Omit vowels.

background	bkgrnd
problem	prblm
government	gvt

Signal Words

Type	Examples	Meaning
Main idea words	And most important A major development The basic concept is Remember that The main idea is We will focus on The key is	Introduce the key points that need to be written in your notes.
Example words	To illustrate For example For instance	Clarify and illustrate the main ideas in the lecture. Write these examples in your notes after the main idea. If multiple examples are given, write down the ones you have time for or the ones that you understand the best.
Addition words	In addition Also Furthermore	Add more important information. Write these points down in your notes.
Enumeration words	The five steps First, second, third Next	Signal a list. Write down the list in your notes and number the items.
Time words	Before, after Formerly Subsequently Prior Meanwhile	Signal the order of events. Write down the events in the correct order in your notes.
Cause and effect words	Therefore As a result If . . ., then	Signal important concepts that might be on the exam. When you hear these words, label them "cause" and "effect" in your notes and review these ideas for the exam.
Definition words	In other words It simply means That is In essence	Provide the meanings of words or simplify complex ideas. Write these definitions or clarifications in your notes.
Swivel words	However Nevertheless Yes, but Still	Provide exceptions, qualifications, or further clarification. Write down qualifying comments in your notes.
Compare and contrast words	Similarly Likewise In contrast	Present similarities or differences. Write these similarities and differences in your notes and label them.
Summary words	In conclusion To sum up In a nutshell	Restate the important ideas of the lecture. Write the summaries in your notes.
Test words	This is important. Remember this. You'll see this again. You might want to study this for the test.	Provide a clue that the material will be on the test. Write these down in your notes and mark them in a way that stands out. Put a star or asterisk next to these items or highlight them. Each professor has his or her own test clue words.

5. Use g in place of ing.
    checking   ckg
    decreasing   decrg
6. Write your notes in text message format.

Symbols

Use common symbols or invent your own to speed up the note-taking process.

Common Symbols Used in Note Taking

Symbol	Meaning	Symbol	Meaning
&	and	B4	before
w	with	BC	because
wo	without	esp	especially
wi	within	diff	difference
<	less than	min	minimum
>	more than	gov	government
@	at	ex	example
/	per	↑	increasing
2	to, two, too	↓	decreasing
∴	therefore	=	equal
vs	versus, against	≠	not equal

How to Review Your Notes

Immediate review. Review your notes as soon as possible after the lecture. The most effective review is done immediately or at least within 20 minutes. If you wait until the next day to review, you may already have forgotten much of the information. During the immediate review, fill in any missing or incomplete information. Say the important points to yourself. This begins the process of rehearsal for storing the information in long-term memory.

© 2014, Terence. Used under license with Shutterstock, Inc.

There are various methods for review depending on your note-taking system:

*   For the Cornell format, use the recall column to write in key words or questions. Cover your notes and see if you can recall the main ideas. Place checkmarks by the items you have mastered. Don't worry about mastering all the key points from the beginning. With each review, it will be easier to remember the information.
*   For the outline format, use a highlighter to mark the key ideas as you repeat them silently to yourself.
*   For mind maps, look over the information and think about the key ideas and their relationships. Fill in additional information or clarification. Highlight important points or relationships with color.

Intermediate review. Set up some time each week for short reviews of your notes and the key points in your textbook from previous weeks. Quickly look over the notes and recite the key points in your mind. These intermediate reviews will help you to master the material and avoid test anxiety.

Test review. Complete a major review as part of your test preparation strategy. As you look through your notes, turn the key ideas into possible test questions and answer them.

> "You have to get your education. Then nobody can control your destiny."
>
> Charles Barkley

Final review. The final review occurs after you have received the results of your test. Ask yourself these questions:

- What percentage of the test questions came from the lecture notes?
- Were you prepared for the exam? If so, congratulate yourself on a job well done. If not, how can you improve next time?
- Were your notes adequate? If not, what needs to be added or changed?

8.1   DO IT NOW !

Learning and Note Taking

Test what you have learned by selecting the correct answers to the following questions.

Working Independently in Advance of Exams

Use the following strategies to use out-of-class time wisely to prepare for exams:

1. When taking notes on a college lecture, it is most important to
   a. write down everything you hear.
   b. write down the main ideas and enough explanation to understand them.
   c. write down names, dates, places, and numbers.

2. To be a good listener,
   a. read or skim over the material before you attend the lecture.
   b. attend the lecture first and then read the text.
   c. remember that listening is more important than note taking.

3. To stay awake during the lecture,
   a. drink lots of coffee.
   b. sit near your friends so you can make some comments on the lecture.
   c. listen actively by taking notes.

4. Since attendance is not always checked in college classes,
   a. it is not necessary to attend class if you read the textbook.
   b. it is acceptable to miss lectures as long as you show up for the exams.
   c. it is up to you to attend every class.

5. The best time to review your notes is
   a. as soon as possible after the lecture.
   b. within 24 hours.
   c. within one week.

How did you do on the quiz? Check your answers: 1. b, 2. a, 3. c, 4. c, 5. a

Think About It ———————————— *Journal Entry* 8.3

> "The highest reward for a person's toil is not what they get for it, but what they become by it."
>
> John Ruskin

Write five intention statements about improving your note-taking skills. Consider your note-taking system, how to take notes more efficiently, and the best way to review your notes. I intend to . . .

_____

_____

_____

_____

Power Writing

Effective writing will help you in school, on the job, and in your personal life. Good writing will help you to create quality term papers. The writing skills that you learn in college will be used later in jobs involving high responsibility and good pay. You can become an excellent writer by learning about the steps in POWER writing: prepare, organize, write, edit, and revise.

Power Writing
• Prepare
• Organize
• Write
• Edit
• Revise

Prepare

Plan your time. The first step in writing is to plan your time so that the project can be completed by the due date. Picture this scene: It is the day that the term paper is due. A few students proudly hand in their term papers and are ready to celebrate their accomplishments. Many of the students in the class are absent, and some will never return to the class. Some of the students look as though they haven't slept the night before. They look stressed and weary. At the front of the class is a line of students wanting to talk with the instructor. The instructor has heard it all before:

- I had my paper all completed and my printer jammed.
- My hard drive crashed and I lost my paper.
- I was driving to school and my paper flew off my motorcycle.
- I had the flu.
- My children were sick.
- I had to take my dog to the vet.
- My dog ate my paper.
- My car broke down and I could not get to the library.
- My grandmother died and I had to go to the funeral.
- My roommate accidentally took my backpack to school.
- I spilled salad dressing on my paper, so I put it in the microwave to dry it out and the writing disappeared!

"The most valuable of all education is the ability to make yourself do the thing you have to do, when it has to be done, whether you like it or not."
Aldous Huxley

To avoid being in this uncomfortable and stressful situation, plan ahead. Plan to complete your project at least one week ahead of time so that you can deal with life's emergencies. Life does not always go as planned. You or your children may get sick, or your dog may do strange things to your homework. Your computer may malfunction, leading you to believe it senses stress and malfunctions just to frustrate you even more.

Prepare
• Plan your time
• Find space and time
• Choose general topic
• Gather information
• Write thesis statement

© 2014, Benjamin Howell. Used under license with Shutterstock, Inc.

To avoid stress and do your best work, start with the date that the project is due and then think about the steps needed to finish. Write these dates on your calendar or on your list of things to do. Consider all these components:

Project due date:

To do	By when?
1. Brainstorm ideas.	_____
2. Choose a topic.	_____
3. Gather information.	_____
4. Write a thesis statement.	_____
5. Write an outline.	_____
6. Write the introduction.	_____
7. Write the first draft.	_____
8. Prepare the bibliography.	_____
9. Edit.	_____
10. Revise.	_____
11. Print and assemble.	_____

Find a space and time. Find a space where you can work. Gather the materials that you will need to write. Generally, writing is best done in longer blocks of time. Determine when you will work on your paper and write the time on your schedule. Start right away to avoid panic later.

Choose a general topic. This task will be easy if your topic is already clearly defined by your instructor or your boss at work. Make sure that you have a clear idea of what is required, such as length, format, purpose, and method of citing references and topic. Many times the choice of a topic is left to you. Begin by doing some brainstorming. Think about topics that interest you. Write them down. You may want to focus your attention on brainstorming ideas for five or 10 minutes, and then put the project aside and come back to it later. Once you have started the process of thinking about the ideas, your mind will continue to work and you may have some creative inspiration. If inspiration does not come, repeat the brainstorming process.

Gather information. Go to your college library and use the Internet to gather your information. As you begin, you can see what is available, what is interesting to you, and what the current thinking is on your topic. Note the major topics of interest that might be useful to you. Once you have found some interesting material, you will feel motivated to continue your project. As you find information relevant to your topic, make sure to write down the sources of your information to use in your bibliography. The bibliography contains information about where you found your material. Write down the author, the title of the publication, the publisher, and the place and date of publication. For Internet resources, list the address of the website and the date accessed.

Write the thesis statement. The thesis statement is the key idea in your paper. It provides a direction for you to follow. It is the first step in organizing your work. To write a thesis statement, review the material you have gathered and then ask these questions:

- What is the most important idea?
- What question would I like to ask about it?
- What is my answer?

For example, if I decide to write a paper for my health class on the harmful effects of smoking, I would look at current references on the topic. I might become interested

in how the tobacco companies misled the public on the dangers of smoking. I would think about my thesis statement and answer the questions stated above.

- **What is the most important idea?** Smoking is harmful to your health.
- **What question would I like to ask about it?** Did the tobacco companies mislead the public about the health hazards of smoking?
- **What is my answer?** The tobacco companies misled the public about the hazards of smoking in order to protect their business interests.
- **My thesis statement:** Tobacco companies knew that smoking was hazardous to health, but to protect their business interests, they deliberately misled the public.

The thesis statement helps to narrow the topic and provide direction for the paper. I can now focus on reference material related to my topic: research on health effects of smoking, congressional testimony relating to regulation of the tobacco industry, and how advertising influences people to smoke.

Organize

At this point you have many ideas about what to include in your paper, and you have a central focus, your thesis statement. Start to organize your paper by listing the topics that are related to your thesis statement. Here is a list of topics related to my thesis statement about smoking:

Organize
- List related topics
- Arrange in logical order
- Have an organizational structure

- Tobacco companies' awareness that nicotine is addictive
- Minimizing health hazards in tobacco advertisements
- How advertisements encourage people to smoke
- Money earned by the tobacco industry
- Health problems caused by smoking
- Statistics on numbers of people who have health problems or die from smoking
- Regulation of the tobacco industry
- Advertisements aimed at children

Think about the topics and arrange them in logical order. Use an outline, a mind map, a flowchart, or a drawing to think about how you will organize the important topics. Keep in mind that you will need an introduction, a body, and a conclusion. Having an organizational structure will make it easier for you to write because you will not need to wonder what comes next.

Write

Write the First Sentence

Begin with the main idea.

Write the Introduction

This is the road map for the rest of the paper. The introduction includes your thesis statement and establishes the foundation of the paper. It introduces topics that will be discussed in the body of the paper. The introduction should include some interesting points that provide a "hook" to motivate the audience to read your paper. For example, for a paper on the hazards of smoking, you might begin with statistics on how many people suffer from smoking-related illnesses and premature death. Note the large profits earned by the tobacco industry. Then introduce other topics: deception, advertisements, and regulation. The introduction provides a guide or outline of what will follow in the paper.

Write the Body of the Paper

The body of the paper is divided into paragraphs that discuss the topics that you have introduced. As you write each paragraph, include the main idea and then explain it and give examples. Here are some good tips for writing:

1. Good writing reflects clear thinking. Think about what you want to say and write about it so the reader can understand your point of view.
2. Use clear and concise language. Avoid using too many words or scholarly-sounding words that might get in the way of understanding.
3. Don't assume that the audience knows what you are writing about. Provide complete information.
4. Provide examples, stories, and quotes to support your main points. Include your own ideas and experiences.
5. Beware of plagiarism. Plagiarism is copying the work of others without giving them credit. It is illegal and can cause you to receive a failing grade on your project or even get you into legal trouble. Faculty regularly uses software programs that identify plagiarized material in student papers. You can avoid plagiarism by using quotation marks around an author's words and providing a reference indicating where you found the material. Another way to avoid plagiarism is by carefully reading your source material while using critical thinking to evaluate it. Then look away from the source and write about the ideas in your own words, including your critical thinking about the subject. Don't forget to include a reference for the source material in your bibliography.

Write the Conclusion

The conclusion summarizes the topics in the paper and presents your point of view. It makes reference to the introduction and answers the question posed in your thesis statement. It often makes the reader think about the significance of your point and the implications for the future. Make your conclusion interesting and powerful.

Include References

No college paper is complete without references. References may be given in footnotes, endnotes, a list of works cited, or a bibliography. You can use your computer to insert these references. There are various styles for citing references depending on your subject area. There are computer programs that put your information into the correct style. Ask your instructor which style to use for your particular class or project. Three frequently used styles for citing references are APA, Chicago, and MLA.

1. The American Psychological Association (APA) style is used in psychology and other behavioral sciences. Consult the *Publication Manual of the American Psychological Association*, 6th ed. (Washington, DC: American Psychological Association, 2010). You can find this source online at www.apastyle.org.

2. Chicago style is used by many professional writers in a variety of fields. Consult the *Chicago Manual of Style*, 16th ed. (Chicago: University of Chicago Press, 2010). You can find this source online at www.chicagomanualofstyle.org/home.html.

3. The Modern Language Association (MLA) style is used in English, classical languages, and the humanities. Consult the *MLA Handbook for Writers of Research Papers*, 7th ed. (New York: Modern Language Association, 2009). This source is available online at www.mla.org/style.

Each of these styles uses a different format for listing sources, but all include the same information. Make sure you write down this information as you collect your reference material. If you forget this step, it is very time-consuming and difficult to find later.

- Author's name
- Title of the book or article
- Journal name
- Publisher
- City where book was published
- Publication date
- Page number (and volume and issue numbers, if available)

Here are some examples of citations in the APA style:

- **Book.** Include author, date of publication, title, city of publication, and publisher.
  Fralick, M. (2014). *College and career success* (6th ed.). Dubuque, IA: Kendall Hunt.

- **Journal article.** Include author, date, title, name of journal, volume and issue numbers, pages.
  Fralick, M. (1993). College success: A study of positive and negative attrition. *Community College Review, 20*(5), 29–36.

- **Website.** Include author, date listed or updated, document title or name of website, URL or website address, and date accessed. Include as many of the above items as possible. Methods of citing information from the Internet are still evolving.
  Fralick, M. (2014, October). Note taking. Retrieved October 2013 from College Success 1 at www.collegesuccess1.com/

Save Your Work

As soon as you have written the first paragraph, save it on your computer. If your computer is not backed up by a remote server such as iCloud or Carbonite, save another copy on a flash drive. When you are finished, print your work and save a paper copy. Then, if your hard drive crashes, you will still have your work at another location. If your file becomes corrupted, you will still have the paper copy. Following these procedures can save you a lot of headaches. Any writer can tell you stories of lost work because of computer problems, lightning storms, power outages, and other unpredictable events.

Put It Away for a While

The last step in writing the first draft is easy. Put it away for a while and come back to it later. In this way, you can relax and gain some perspective on your work. You will be able to take a more objective look at your work to begin the process of editing and revising.

Writer's Block

Many people who are anxious about writing experience "writer's block." You have writer's block if you find yourself staring at that blank piece of paper or computer screen not knowing how to begin or what to write. Here are some tips for avoiding writer's block.

- **Write freely.** Just write anything about your topic that comes to mind. Don't worry about organization or perfection at this point. Don't censure your ideas. You can always go back to organize and edit later. Free-writing helps you to overcome one of the main causes of writer's block: you think it has to be perfect from the beginning. This expectation of perfection causes anxiety. You freeze up and become unable to write. Perhaps you have past memories of writing where the teacher made many corrections on your paper. Maybe you lack confidence in your writing skills. The only way you will become a better writer is to keep writing and perfecting your writing skills, so to start the writing process, just write what comes to mind. Don't worry how great it is. You can fix it later. Just begin.

- **Use brainstorming if you get stuck.** For five minutes, focus your attention on the topic and write whatever comes to mind. You don't even need to write full sentences; just jot down ideas. If you are really stuck, try working on a different topic or take a break and come back to it later.

- **Realize that it is only the first draft.** It is not the finished product and it does not have to be perfect. Just write some ideas on paper; you can revise them later.

- **Read through your reference materials.** The ideas you find can get your mind working. Also, reading can make you a better writer.

- **Break the assignment up into small parts.** If you find writing difficult, write for five minutes at a time. Do this consistently and you can get used to writing and can complete your paper.

- **Find a good place for writing.** If you are an introvert, look for a quiet place for concentration. If you are an extrovert, go to a restaurant or coffee shop and start your writing.
- **Beware of procrastination.** The more you put off writing, the more anxious you will become and the more difficult the task will be. Make a schedule and stick to it.

Edit and Revise

The editing and revising stage allows you to take a critical look at what you have written. It takes some courage to do this step. Once people see their ideas in writing, they become attached to them. With careful editing and revising, you can turn in your best work and be proud of your accomplishments. Here are some tips for editing and revising:

1. **Read your paper as if you were the audience.** Pretend that you are the instructor or another person reading your paper. Does every sentence make sense? Did you say what you meant to say? Read what you have written, and the result will be a more effective paper.
2. **Read paragraph by paragraph.** Does each paragraph have a main idea and supporting details? Do the paragraphs fit logically together? Use the cut-and-paste feature on your computer to move sentences and paragraphs around if needed.
3. **Check your grammar and spelling.** Use the spell check and grammar check on your computer. These tools are helpful, but they are not thorough enough. The spell check will pick up only misspelled words. It will skip words that are spelled correctly but not the intended word—for example, if you use "of" instead of "on" or "their" instead of "there." To find such errors, you need to read your paper after doing a spell check.
4. **Check for language that is biased in terms of gender, disability, or ethnic group.** Use words that are gender neutral. If a book or paper uses only the pronoun "he" or "she," half of the population is left out. You can often avoid sexist language by using the plural forms of nouns:

(singular)   The successful student knows *his* values and sets goals for the future.

(plural)   Successful students know *their* values and set goals for the future.

After all, we are trying to make the world a better place, with opportunity for all. Here are some examples of biased language and better alternatives.

Biased Language	Better Alternatives
policeman	police officer
chairman	chair
fireman	firefighter
postman	mail carrier
mankind	humanity
manmade	handcrafted
housewife	homemaker
crippled and disabled persons	persons with disabilities

5. **Have someone else read your paper.** Ask your reader to check for clarity and meaning. After you have read your paper many times, you do not really see it anymore. If you need assistance in writing, colleges offer tutoring or writing labs where you can get help with editing and revising.

Tips for Editing and Revising

1. Read your paper objectively
2. Read paragraph by paragraph
3. Check grammar and spelling
4. Check for biased language
5. Have someone else read your paper
6. Review the introduction and conclusion
7. Prepare final copy
8. Prepare title page

6. **Review your introduction and conclusion.** They should be clear, interesting, and concise. The introduction and conclusion are the most powerful parts of your paper.

7. **Prepare the final copy.** Check your instructor's instructions on the format required. If there are no instructions, use the following format:
   - Use double-spacing.
   - Use 10- or 12-point font.
   - Use one-inch margins on all sides.
   - Use a three-inch top margin on the first page.
   - Single-space footnotes and endnotes.
   - Number your pages.

8. **Prepare the title page.** Center the title of your paper and place it one third of the page from the top. On the bottom third of the page, center your name, the professor's name, the name of the class, and the date.

Final Steps

Make sure you follow instructions about using a folder or cover for your paper. Generally professors dislike bulky folders or notebooks because they are difficult to carry. Imagine your professor trying to carry 50 notebooks to his or her office! Unless asked to do so, do not use plastic page protectors. Professors like to write comments on papers, and it is extremely difficult to write on papers with page protectors.

Turning your paper in on time is very important. Some professors do not accept late papers. Others subtract points if your paper is late. Put your paper in the car or someplace where you will have to see it before you go to class. **Then reward yourself for a job well done!**

Think About It ———————————————— *Journal Entry* **8.4**

Write five intention statements about improving your writing. While thinking about your statements, consider the steps of POWER writing: prepare, organize, write, edit, and revise. Do you need to work on problems such as writer's block or getting your writing done on time? I intend to . . .

1. Stay organized
2. break project into pieces
3. Revise several times
4. take break to gain perspective

Effective Public Speaking

You may need to take a speech class in order to graduate from college, and many of your classes will require oral presentations. Being a good speaker can contribute to your success on the job as well. A study done at Stanford University showed that one of the top predictors of success in professional positions was the ability to be a

good public speaker.[1] You will need to present information to your boss, your colleagues, and your customers or clients.

Learn to Relax

Whenever I tell students that they will need to take a speech class or make an oral presentation, I see a look of panic on their faces. Good preparation can help you to feel confident about your oral presentation. Professional speaker Lilly Walters believes that you can deal with 75 percent of your anxiety by being well prepared.[2] You can deal with the remaining 25 percent by using some relaxation techniques.

- If you are anxious, admit to yourself that you are anxious. If it is appropriate, as in a beginning speech class, you can even admit to the audience that you are anxious. Once you have admitted that you are anxious, visualize yourself confidently making the speech.
- You do not have to be perfect; it is okay to make mistakes. Making mistakes just shows you are human like the rest of us.
- If you are anxious before your speech, take three to five deep breaths. Breathe in slowly and hold your breath for five seconds, and then breathe out slowly. Focus your mind on your breathing rather than your speech.
- Use positive self-talk to help you to relax. Instead of saying to yourself, "I will look like a fool up there giving the speech," tell yourself, "I can do this" or "It will be okay."
- Once you start speaking, anxiety will generally decline.
- With experience, you will gain confidence in your speaking ability and will be able to relax more easily.

Preparing and Delivering Your Speech

Write the Beginning of the Speech

The beginning includes a statement of your objective and what your speech will be about. It should prepare the audience for what comes next. You can begin your speech with a personal experience, a quote, a news article, or a joke. Jokes can be effective, but they are risky. Try out your joke with your friends to make sure that it is funny. Do not tell jokes that put down other people or groups.

Write the Main Body of the Speech

The main body of the speech consists of four or five main points. Just as in your term paper, state your main points and then provide details, examples, or stories that illustrate them. As you present the main points of your speech, consider your audience. Your speech will be different depending on whether it is made to a group of high school students, your college classmates, or a group of professionals. You can add interest to your speech by using props, pictures, charts, PowerPoint, music, or video clips. College students today are increasingly using PowerPoint software to make classroom presentations. If you are planning to enter a professional career, learning how to make PowerPoint presentations will be an asset.

Write the Conclusion

In your conclusion, summarize and review the key points of your speech. The conclusion is like the icing on a cake. It should be strong, persuasive, and interesting. Invest some time in your ending statement. It can be a call to action, a recommendation for the future, a quote, or a story.

Practice Your Speech

Practice your speech until you feel comfortable with it. Prepare a memory system or notes to help you deliver your speech. You will want to make eye contact with your audience, which is difficult if you are trying to read your speech. A memory system useful for delivering speeches is the loci system. Visualize a house, for example: the entryway is the introduction, and each room represents a main point in the speech. Visualize walking into each room and what you will say in each room. Each room can have items that remind you of what you are going to say. At the conclusion, you say good-bye at the door. Another technique is to prepare brief notes or outlines on index cards or sheets of paper. When you are practicing your speech, time it to see how long it is. Keep your speech within the time allowed. Most people tend to speak longer than necessary.

Review the Setup

If you are using props, make sure that you have them ready. If you are using equipment, make sure it is available and in working condition. Make arrangements in advance for the equipment you need and, if possible, check to see that it is running properly right before your presentation.

Deliver the Speech

Wear clothes that make you feel comfortable, but not out of place. Remember to smile and make eye contact with members of the audience. Take a few deep breaths if you are nervous. You will probably be less nervous once you begin. If you make a mistake, keep your sense of humor. I recall the famous chef Julia Child doing a live television production on how to cook a turkey. As she took the turkey out of the oven, it slipped and landed on the floor right in front of the television cameras. She calmly picked it up and said, "And remember that you are the only one that really knows what goes on in the kitchen." It was one of the shows that made her famous.

8.2

DO IT NOW!

Writing and Speaking

Test what you have learned by selecting the correct answers to the following questions.

1. To make sure to get your paper done on time,
   a. have someone remind you of the deadline.
   b. write the due date on your calendar and the date for completion of each step.
   c. write your paper just before the due date to increase motivation.

2. The thesis statement is the
   a. most important sentence in each paragraph.
   b. key idea in the paper.
   c. summary of the paper.

3. If you have writer's block, it is helpful to
   a. delay writing your paper until you feel relaxed.
   b. make sure that your writing is perfect from the beginning.
   c. begin with brainstorming or free writing.

4. No college paper is complete without
   a. the references.
   b. a professional-looking cover.
   c. printing on quality paper.

5. You can deal with most of your anxiety about public speaking by
   a. striving for perfection.
   b. visualizing your anxiety.
   c. being well prepared.

How did you do on the quiz? Check your answers:
1. b, 2. b, 3. c, 4. a, 5. c

Think About It ——————— *Journal Entry* **8.5**

Write one paragraph giving advice to a new college student on how to make a speech. Use any of these questions to guide your thinking:

- What are some ways to deal with anxiety about public speaking?

  - prepare
  - Practice
  - dont worry about what people think

- How can you make your speech interesting?

  - Gestures
  - Acting
  - Inflection on different words

- What are some steps in preparing a speech?
  - think of a topic
  - write a draft
  - edit
  - write final draft and practice
  - present

- What are some ideas that don't work?
  - not writing a speech
  - not practicing

KEYS TO SUCCESS

Be Selective

Psychologist and philosopher William James said, "The essence of genius is knowing what to overlook."[3] This saying has a variety of meanings. In reading, note taking, marking a college textbook, and writing, it is important to be able to pick out the main points first and then identify the supporting details. Imagine you are trying to put together a jigsaw puzzle. You bought the puzzle at a garage sale and all the pieces are there, but the lid to the box with the picture of the puzzle is missing. It will be very difficult, if not impossible, to put this puzzle together. Reading, note taking, marking, and writing are very much like putting a puzzle together. First you will need an understanding of the main ideas (the big picture) and then you can focus on the details.

How can you get the overall picture? When reading, you can get the overall picture by skimming the text. As you skim the text, you get a general outline of what the chapter contains and what you will learn. In note taking, actively listen for the main ideas and write them down in your notes. In marking your text, try to pick out about 20 percent of the most important material and underline or highlight it. In writing, think about what is most important, write your thesis statement, and then provide the supporting details. To select what is most important, be courageous, think, and analyze.

Does this mean that you should forget about the details? No, you will need to know some details too. The supporting details help you to understand and assess the value of the main idea. They help you to understand the relationship between ideas. Being selective means getting the general idea first, and then the details will make sense to you and you will be able to remember them. The main ideas are like scaffolding or a net that holds the details in some kind of framework so you can remember them. If you focus on the details first, you will have no framework or point of reference for remembering them.

Experiment with the idea of being selective in your personal life. If your schedule is impossibly busy, be selective and choose to do the most important or most valuable activities. This takes some thinking and courage too. If your desk drawer is stuffed with odds and ends and you can never find what you are looking for, take everything out and only put back what you need. Recycle, give away, or throw away surplus items around the house. You can take steps toward being a genius by being selective and taking steps to simplify and organize your life and your work.

Think About It — Journal Entry 8.6

How can being selective help you achieve success in college and in life? Use any of these questions to guide your thinking:

- How can being selective help you to be a better note taker, writer, or speaker?

_____

_____

_____

_____

_____

- How can being selective help you to manage your time and your life?

_____

_____

_____

_____

_____

- What is the meaning of this quote by William James: "The essence of genius is knowing what to overlook?"

_____

_____

_____

_____

_____

JOURNAL ENTRIES

Taking Notes, Writing, and Speaking

Go to http://www.collegesuccess1.com/JournalEntries.htm for Word files of the Journal Entries

Success over the Internet

Visit the College Success Website at http://www.collegesuccess1.com/

The *College Success Website* is continually updated with new topics and links to the material presented in this chapter. Topics include:

- Note taking
- Mind maps
- Memory and note taking
- Telegraphic sentences
- Signal words
- Listening to lectures
- Grammar and style
- Quotes to use in speeches and papers
- The virtual public speaking assistant
- Researching, organizing, and delivering a speech
- Best speeches in history

Contact your instructor if you have any problems accessing the *College Success Website.*

Notes

1. T. Allesandra and P. Hunsaker, *Communicating at Work* (New York: Fireside, 1993), 169.
2. Lilly Walters, *Secrets of Successful Speakers: How You Can Motivate, Captivate, and Persuade* (New York: McGraw-Hill, 1993), 203.
3. Quoted in Rob Gilbert, ed., *Bits and Pieces,* August 12, 1999, 15.

Note-Taking Checklist

Name _____ Date _____

Place a checkmark next to the note-taking skills you have now.

_____ I attend every (or almost every) lecture in all my classes.

_____ I check the syllabus to find out what is being covered before I go to class.

_____ I read or at least skim through the reading assignment before attending the lecture.

_____ I attend lectures with a positive attitude about learning as much as possible.

_____ I am well rested so that I can focus on the lecture.

_____ I eat a light, nutritious meal before going to class.

_____ I sit in a location where I can see and hear easily.

_____ I have a laptop or a three-ring binder, looseleaf paper, and a pen for taking notes.

_____ I avoid external distractions (friends, sitting by the door).

_____ I am alert and able to concentrate on the lecture.

_____ I have a system for taking notes that works for me.

_____ I am able to determine the key ideas of the lecture and write them down in my notes.

_____ I can identify signal words that help to understand key points and organize my notes.

_____ I can write quickly using telegraphic sentences, abbreviations, and symbols.

_____ If I don't understand something in the lecture, I ask a question and get help.

_____ I write down everything written on the board or on visual materials used in the class.

_____ I review my notes immediately after class.

_____ I have intermediate review sessions to review previous notes.

_____ I use my notes to predict questions for the exam.

_____ I have clear and complete notes that help me to prepare adequately for exams.

Evaluate Your Note-Taking Skills

Name _____ Date _____

Use the note-taking checklist on the previous page to answer these questions.

1. Look at the items that you checked. What are your strengths in note taking?

2. What are some areas that you need to improve?

3. Write at least three intention statements about improving your listening and note-taking skills.

Assess Your College Writing Skills

Name _____ Date _____

Read the following statements and rate how true they are for you at the present time. Use the following scale:

5 · Definitely true
4 Mostly true
3 Somewhat true
2 Seldom true
1 Never true

_____ I am generally confident in my writing skills.

_____ I have a system for reminding myself of due dates for writing projects.

_____ I start writing projects early so that I am not stressed by finishing them at the last minute.

_____ I have the proper materials and a space to write comfortably.

_____ I know how to use the library and the Internet to gather information for a term paper.

_____ I can write a thesis statement for a term paper.

_____ I know how to organize a term paper.

_____ I know how to write the introduction, body, and conclusion of a paper.

_____ I can cite references in the appropriate style for my subject.

_____ I know where to find information about citing material in APA, MLA, or Chicago style.

_____ I know what plagiarism is and know how to avoid it.

_____ I can deal with "writer's block" and get started on my writing project.

_____ I know how to edit and revise a paper.

_____ I know where I can get help with my writing.

_____ **Total**

60–70	You have excellent writing skills, but can always learn new ideas.
50–59	You have good writing skills, but there is room for improvement.
Below 50	You need to improve writing skills. The skills presented in this chapter will help. Consider taking a writing class early in your college studies.

Thinking about Writing

Name _____ Date _____

List 10 suggestions from this chapter that could help you improve your writing skills.

1.

2.

3.

4.

5.

6.

7.

8.

9.

10.

Learning Style Quiz

Name _____ Date _____

John is a new college student who needs help with college success skills. Using what you have learned in this chapter, give John some advice on how to take notes in class. This exercise can be done individually or as a group exercise in class.

John is a new college student who has just graduated from high school. He is not sure what he wants to do with his life, but his parents want him to go to college. He misses the first class in Psychology 101 because he thinks nothing important happens on the first day. On the second day of class, John walks into class and finds some friends from high school. He takes a seat near them and starts a lively conversation. He has no books, paper, or pencil.

The lecture is on the biological foundations of behavior. The topic is new for John and he is unfamiliar with the terms and concepts used in the lecture. He notices that the professor is wearing a tie that he must have purchased in 1970 and has an irritating habit of scratching his head. In addition, he is boring and speaks in a dull and monotonous way. John finds it difficult to concentrate. He becomes sleepy and starts to doze off during the lecture. At the end of the lecture, John realizes that he is going to have problems with psychology. For the next class, John brings a tape recorder and records the class. Again he finds it difficult to stay awake during the lecture. He works late at night and has scheduled this class for 8:00 in the morning.

What are the five most important suggestions you could make to help John take notes and be successful in this class?

1.

2.

3.

4.

5.

Test-Taking Skills and Strategies

What to Do before, during, and after Exams

LEARNING GOAL

To strengthen your performance on college exams and professional tests.

1. On which of the following types of activities do you tend to perform best? (Circle one.) On which do you perform worst? (Circle one.)

   Taking multiple-choice tests

   Taking essay tests

   Writing papers

   Making oral presentations

2. What do you think accounts for the fact that you perform better on one than the other?

   _____

   _____

   _____

   _____

   _____

   _____

   _____

Test-Taking Strategies

Academic learning in college involves three stages: acquiring information from lectures and readings, studying that information and storing it in your brain as knowledge, and demonstrating that knowledge on exams. What follows is a series of strategies related to stage three of this process: test taking. The strategies are divided into three categories:

- Strategies to use in advance of the test,
- Strategies to use during the test, and
- Strategies to use after test results are returned.

Pre-Test Strategies: What to Do in Advance of the Test

Your ability to remember what you've studied depends not only on how much and how well you studied, but also on how you will be tested (Stein, 1978). You may be able to remember what you've studied if you are tested in one format (e.g., multiple-choice questions), but may not remember the material as well if the test is in a different format (e.g., essay questions). You need to be aware of the type of test you'll be taking and adjust your study strategies accordingly.

College test questions fall into two major categories: (1) recognition questions, and (2) recall questions. Each of these types of questions requires a different type of memory and a different study strategy.

1. **Recognition test questions.** Recognition questions ask you to select or choose the correct answer from choices that are provided for you. Falling into this category are multiple-choice, true-false, and matching questions. These test questions don't require you to supply or produce the correct answer on your own; instead, you're asked to recognize or pick out the correct answer, similar to identifying the correct criminal in a lineup of suspects.
2. **Recall test questions.** Recall questions require you to retrieve information you've studied and reproduce it on your own at test time. As the word *recall* implies, you have to call back to mind the information you need and supply it yourself, rather than selecting it or picking it out from information that's supplied for you. Recall test questions include essay, fill-in-the-blank, and short-answer questions, which require a written response.

Since recognition test questions ask you to recognize or identify the correct answer from among answers that are provided for you, repeatedly reading over your class and textbook notes to identify important concepts may be an effective study strategy for multiple-choice and true-false test questions. Doing so matches the type of mental activity you'll be asked to perform on the exam—read over and identify correct answers.

On the other hand, recall test questions, such as essay questions, require you to retrieve information and generate answers on your own. Studying for essay tests by looking over your class notes and highlighted reading will not prepare you to recall information because it does not simulate what you'll be doing on the test itself. However, when you study for essay tests, if you retrieve information without looking at it and write out your answers to questions, you ensure that your practice (study) sessions match your performance (test) situation because you are rehearsing what you'll be expected to do on the test—write essays.

Two strategies that are particularly effective for practicing the type of memory retrieval you will need to perform on essay tests are recitation and creation of retrieval cues. Each of these strategies is described below.

Recitation

Recitation involves saying the information you need to recall without looking at it. Research indicates that memory for information is significantly strengthened when students study by trying to generate that information on their own, rather than simply looking it over or rereading it (Roediger & Karpicke, 2006). Reciting strengthens recall memory in three ways:

1. Recitation forces you to actively retrieve information, which is what you will have to do on the test, instead of passively reviewing information that's in front of you and in full view, which is not what you will do on the test.

2. Recitation gives you clear feedback on whether you can recall the information you're studying. If you can't retrieve and recite it without looking at it, you know for sure that you won't be able to recall it at test time and that you need to study it further. One way to provide yourself with this feedback is to put the question on one side of an index card and the answer on the flip side. If you find yourself flipping over the index card to look at the answer in order to remember it, you clearly cannot retrieve the information on your own and need to study it further.

3. Recitation encourages you to use your own words; this gives you feedback on whether you can paraphrase the information. If you can paraphrase it (rephrase it in your own words), it's a good indication you really understand it, and if you really understand it, you're more likely to recall it at test time.

Recitation can be done silently, by speaking aloud, or by writing out what you're saying. We recommend speaking aloud or writing out what you're reciting because these strategies involve physical action, which keeps you actively involved in the learning process.

Creation of Retrieval Cues

Suppose you're trying to remember the name of a person you know but just cannot recall it. If a friend gives you a clue (e.g., the first letter of the person's name or a name that rhymes with it), it's likely to suddenly trigger your memory of that person's name. What your friend did was provide you with a retrieval cue. A *retrieval cue* is a type of memory reminder (like a string tied around your finger) that brings back to your mind what you've temporarily forgotten. Since human memories are stored as parts in an interconnected network, if you're able to recall one piece or segment of the network (the retrieval cue), it can trigger recall of the other pieces of information linked to it in the same organizational network (Willingham, 2001).

Think About It ——————————————— *Journal Entry* **9.2**

1. Think of material in a course you're taking this term that could be easily grouped into categories to help you remember that material. What is the course?

   _____

2. What categories could you use to organize information that's been covered in the course?

   _____

   _____

   _____

   _____

   _____

Studies show that students who can't remember previously studied information are better able to recall that information if they are given a retrieval cue. In one study, students studied a long list of items that included different animals (e.g., giraffe, coyote, and turkey). When given a blank sheet of paper to write down the names of those animals, they weren't able to recall all of them. However, when the word *animals* was written on top of the answer sheet to provide a retrieval cue, the students were often able to recall many animals they couldn't name without the retrieval cue (Tulving, 1983). Research findings such as these suggest that category names can serve as powerful retrieval cues. If you take information that you need to recall on an essay test and organize it into categories, you can use these category names as retrieval cues at test time.

Another strategy for creating retrieval cues is to come up with your own catchwords or catchphrases that you can use to "catch" or batch together all related ideas you're trying to remember. For instance, an acronym can serve as a catchword, with each letter acting as a retrieval cue for a batch of related ideas. Suppose you're studying for an essay test in abnormal psychology that will include questions testing your knowledge of different forms of mental illness. You could create the acronym SCOT as a retrieval cue to help you remember to include each of the following elements of mental illness in your essay answers: symptoms (S), causes (C), outcomes (O), and therapies (T). See Do It Now! 9.1 for ideas on how to create your own memory retrieval cues.

9.1 DO IT NOW!

Key Questions to Guide Creation of Your Own Retrieval Cues

1. Can you relate or associate what you're trying to remember with something you already know, or can you create a short meaningful story out of it? (Meaningful Association)
2. Can you remember it by visualizing an image of it, or by visually associating the pieces of information you want to recall with familiar places or sites? (Visualization)
3. Can you represent each piece of information you're trying to recall as a letter and string the letters together to form a single word or short phrase? (Acronym)
4. Can you rhyme what you're trying to remember with a word or expression you know well, or can you create a little poem, jingle, or melody out of it that contains the information? (Rhythm and Rhyme)

Remember

On multiple-choice questions, you're given a list of answers and you pick out the right one. On essay questions, you have a blank sheet of paper and you have to dig out the answer on your own, which means you have to recite (rehearse) your answers before the test and use memory retrieval cues during the test to dig up the information you need to remember.

Strategies to Use Immediately before a Test

1. **Before the exam, try to take a brisk walk.** Physical activity increases mental alertness by increasing oxygen flow to the brain; it will also decrease tension by increasing the brain's production of emotionally "mellowing" brain chemicals (e.g., serotonin and endorphins).

2. **Come fully armed with all the test-taking tools you need.** In addition to the required supplies (e.g., No. 2 pencil, pen, blue book, Scantron, calculator, etc.), bring backup equipment in case you experience equipment failure (e.g., an extra pen in case your first one runs out of ink or extra pencils in case your original one breaks).

3. **Try to get to the classroom a few minutes early.** Arriving at the test ahead of time gives you a chance to review any formulas and equations you may have struggled to remember and any memory retrieval cues you've created (e.g., acronyms). You want to be sure that you have this information in your working memory when you receive the exam so that you can get it down on paper before you forget it. Arriving early also allows you to take a few minutes to get into a relaxed pre-test state of mind by thinking positive thoughts, taking slow, deep breaths, and stretching your muscles. Also, avoid last-second discussions with unprepared classmates about the test just before the test is to be handed out; their hurried and harried questions can often cause confusion and elevate your level of test anxiety.

4. **Sit in the same seat that you normally occupy in class.** Research indicates that memory is improved when information is recalled in the same place where it was originally received or reviewed (Sprenger, 1999). Thus, taking the test in the same seat you normally occupy during lectures should improve your test performance because it puts you in the same place where you originally heard much of the information that is going to appear on the test. Studies show that when students take a test in the same environment that they studied in, they tend to remember more of that information at test time than do students who study in one place and take the test in a different place (Smith, Glenberg, & Bjork, 1978). While it is unlikely that you'll be able to do all your studying in the same room that you will take your test in, it may be possible to do your final review in your classroom or in an empty classroom with similar features. This could strengthen your memory for the information you studied because the features of the room may become associated with the information, and seeing these features again at test time may help trigger memory of it (Tulving, 1983).

Student
Perspective

"Avoid flipping through notes (cramming) immediately before a test. Instead, do some breathing exercises and think about something other than the test."

—Advice to first-year students from a college sophomore (Walsh, 2005)

A classic and intriguing study supporting this hypothesis was conducted on a group of deep-sea divers who learned a list of words on a beach or underwater and were later tested for their memory of the words. Half of the divers who learned the words on the beach remained there to take the test while the other half were tested underwater; and half of the group who studied the words underwater took the test there while the other half took the test on the beach. The results showed that the divers who took the test in the same place where they learned recalled 40 percent more than the divers who did their learning and testing in different places (Godden & Baddeley, 1975). This finding strongly suggests that the retrieval of information is improved if it takes place in the same place where learning occurs.

Other studies have shown that if students are exposed to a distinctive or unique aroma while they are studying (e.g., the smell of chocolate) and are exposed to that same smell again during a later memory test, they display better memory for the information they studied than do students who didn't study and take the test with the same aroma present (Schab, 1990). Perhaps one practical application of this finding is to wear a distinctive-smelling cologne or perfume while studying and use it again on the day of the test. This might improve your memory for the information you studied by matching the scent of your study environment with the scent of your test environment. Although this strategy may seem silly, keep in mind that the area of the human brain where smell is perceived has connections with the brain's memory pathways (Jensen, 1998). This may account for why people commonly report that certain smells can trigger memories of past experiences (e.g., the smell of a summer breeze triggering memories of summer games played during childhood). Thus, don't underestimate the sense of smell's potential for promoting memory.

9.2   DO IT NOW!

Nutritional Strategies for Strengthening Your Academic Performance

There is evidence that the following nutritional strategies can improve mental performance on days when our knowledge is tested:

1. **Eat breakfast on the day of the exam.** Numerous studies show that students who eat a nutritious breakfast on the day they are tested are more likely to achieve higher test scores than students who do not. Breakfast on the day of an exam should include grains, such as whole-wheat toast, whole-grain cereal, oatmeal, or bran, because those foods contain complex carbo-hydrates that will deliver a steady stream of energy to the body throughout the day; this should help sustain your test-taking endurance or stamina. Also, these complex carbohydrates should help your brain generate a steady stream of serotonin, which may reduce your level of nervousness or tension on test days.

   > "No man can be wise on an empty stomach."
   >
   > —George Eliot, 19th-century English novelist

2. **Make the meal you eat before an exam a light meal.** You don't want to take tests while feeling hungry, but the meal you consume nearest test time should not be a large one. We tend to get sleepy after consuming a large meal because it elevates our blood sugar to such a high level that large amounts of insulin are released into the bloodstream in order to reduce our blood sugar level. This draws blood sugar away from the brain, which results in a feeling of mental fatigue.

3. **If you feel you need an energy boost immediately before an exam, eat a piece of fruit rather than a candy bar.** Candy bars are processed sweets that can offer a short burst of energy provided by synthetic sugar. Unfortunately, this short-term rise in blood sugar and quick jolt of energy are typically accompanied by increased bodily tension followed by a sudden drop in energy and a feeling of sluggishness (Haas, 1994). The key is to find a food that can produce a state of elevated energy without elevating tension (Thayer, 1996) and maintains that state of energy at an even level. The best nutritional option for producing a sustained, steady state of energy is the natural sugar contained in a piece of fruit, not processed sugar that's artificially slipped into a candy bar.

4. **Avoid consuming caffeine before an exam.** Even though caffeine is a stimulant that increases alertness, it also qualifies as a legal drug that can significantly increase bodily tension and nervousness; these are feelings you don't want to experience during a test, particularly if you're prone to test anxiety. Also, caffeine is a diuretic, which means it will increase your urge to urinate. This is a distracting urge you certainly want to avoid during an exam when you're confined to a classroom for an extended period of time, sitting on your butt (and bladder).

Consuming large doses of caffeine or other stimulants before exams may increase your alertness, but may also increase your level of stress and test anxiety.

Strategies to Use during a Test

1. **Read the directions completely and look over the entire test.** It is important to read the instructions and understand what is being asked of you on the test. You should also look over the test in its entirety so you know what type of questions are being asked, how many questions there are, and approximately how much time you will need to complete the test.

2. **As soon as you receive a copy of the test, write down key information you need to remember.** In particular, write down any hard-to-remember terms, formulas, and equations and any memory retrieval cues you may have created as soon as you start the exam to ensure that you don't forget this information once you begin getting involved with answering specific test questions.

3. **Answer the easier test questions first.** As soon as you receive the test, before launching into answering the first question listed, check out the layout of the test. Note the questions that are worth the most points and the questions that you know well. You can do this by first surveying the test and putting a checkmark next to questions whose answers you're unsure of; come back to these questions later after you've answered the questions you're sure of, to ensure all their points are added into your final test score.

Think About It ———————————— *Journal Entry* **9.3**

1. During tests, if I experience memory block, I usually . . .

_____

_____

_____

2. I am most likely to experience memory block in the following subject areas:

_____

_____

_____

---

4. **Prevent "memory block" from setting in.** If you tend to experience memory block for information that you know is stored in your brain, use the following strategies:

   - Mentally put yourself back in the environment or situation where you studied the information. Recreate the steps in which you learned the information that you've temporarily forgotten by mentally picturing the place where you first heard or saw it and where you studied it, including sights, sounds, smells, and time of day. This memory-improvement strategy is referred to as *guided retrieval*, and research supports its effectiveness for recalling information, including information recalled by eyewitnesses to a crime (Glenberg, 1997; Glenberg, Bradley, Kraus, & Renzaglia, 1983).

- Think of any idea or piece of information that may be related to the information you can't remember. Studies show that when students experience temporary forgetting, they're more likely to suddenly recall that information if they first recall a piece or portion of information that relates to it in some way (Reed, 1996). This related piece of information can trigger your memory for the forgotten information because related pieces of information are typically stored within the same neural network of cells in the brain.

- Take your mind off the question and turn to another question. This may allow your subconscious to focus on the forgotten information, which may trigger your conscious memory of it. Also, you may find some information included in the other questions that can help you remember an answer to a previous test question.

- Before turning in your test, carefully review and double-check your answers. This is the critical last step in the process of effective test taking. Sometimes the rush and anxiety of taking a test can cause test takers to overlook details, misread instructions, unintentionally skip questions, or make absentminded mistakes. When you're done, take time to look over your answers to be sure you didn't make any mindless mistakes. Avoid the temptation to immediately cut out because you're pooped out, or to take off on an ego trip by being among the first and fastest students in class to finish the test. Instead, take the full amount of test time available to you. When you think about the amount of time and effort you put into preparing for the exam, it's foolish not to take a little more time on the exam itself.

Strategies to Answer Multiple-Choice Questions

Multiple-choice questions are commonly used on college tests, on certification or licensing exams to practice in particular professions (e.g., nursing and teaching), and on admissions tests for graduate school (e.g., master's and doctoral degree programs) or professional school (e.g., law school and medical school). Since you're likely to encounter multiple-choice tests frequently in college and beyond, this section of the text is devoted to a detailed discussion of strategies for answering such test questions. These strategies are also applicable to true-false tests, which are really multiple-choice tests that involve two choices (true or false).

| Think About It ——————————— Journal Entry 9.4 |

1. How would you rate your general level of test anxiety during most exams? (Circle one.)

                 high   moderate   low

    Explain.

    _____

    _____

    _____

    _____

    _____

2. What types of tests or subjects tend to produce the most test stress or test anxiety for you?

_____

_____

_____

Why?

_____

_____

_____

_____

_____

_____

_____

1. **Read the question and think of the answer in your head before looking at the answers.** If you do this and your answer is one of the options, there is a good chance that it is the correct answer.
2. **Read all choices listed and use a process-of-elimination approach.** You can find an answer by eliminating choices that are clearly wrong and continue to do so until you're left with one answer that is the most accurate option. Keep in mind that the correct answer is often the one that has the highest probability or likelihood of being true; it doesn't have to be absolutely true—just truer than the other choices listed.
3. **Use *test-wise* strategies when you don't know the correct answer.** Your first strategy on any multiple-choice question should be to choose an answer based on your knowledge of the material, rather than trying to outsmart the test or the test maker by guessing the correct answer based on how the question is worded. However, if you've relied on your knowledge and used the process-of-elimination strategy to eliminate clearly wrong choices but you're still left with two or more answers that appear to be correct, then you should turn to being *test wise*, which refers to your ability to use the characteristics of the test question itself (such as its wording or format) to increase your chances of selecting the correct answer (Flippo & Caverly, 2009). Listed here are three test-wise strategies for multiple-choice questions whose answers you don't know or can't remember:
   - **Pick an answer that contains qualifying words.** Look for words such as *usually, probably, likely, sometimes, perhaps,* or *may.* Knowledge often doesn't come neatly wrapped in the form of absolute truths, so choices that are stated as broad generalizations are more likely to be false. For example, answers containing words such as *always, never, only, must,* and *completely* are more likely to be false than true.
   - **Pick the longest answer.** True statements often require more words to make them true.

A *process-of-elimination* approach is an effective test-taking strategy to use when answering difficult multiple-choice questions.

- Pick a middle answer rather than the first or last answer. For example, on a question with four choices, if you've narrowed down the correct answer to a "b" or "c" versus an "a" or "d" choice, go with the "b" or "c" choice. Studies show that instructors have a tendency to place correct answers as middle choices rather than as the first or last choice (Linn & Gronlund, 1995), perhaps because they think the correct answer will be too obvious or stand out if it's listed at the beginning or end.

4. **Check to be sure that your answers are aligned with the right questions.** When looking over your test before turning it in, search carefully for questions you may have skipped and intended to go back to later. Sometimes you may skip a test question on a multiple-choice test and forget to skip the number of that question on the answer form, which will throw off all your other answers by one space or line. On a computer-scored test, this means that you may get multiple items marked wrong because your answers are misaligned, resulting in a "domino effect" of wrong answers, which can do major damage to your test score. As a damage-prevention measure, check all of your answers to be sure there are no blank lines or spaces on your answer sheet to set off this damaging domino effect.

5. **Don't feel that you must remain locked in to your first answer.** When checking your answers on multiple-choice and true-false tests, don't be afraid to change an answer after you've given it more thought. There have been numerous studies on the topic of changing answers on multiple-choice and true-false tests dating back to 1928 (Kuhn, 1988). These studies consistently show that most changed test answers go from being incorrect to correct, resulting in improved test scores (Bauer, Kopp, & Fischer, 2007; Benjamin, Cavell, & Shallenberger, 1984; Prinsell, Ramsey, & Ramsey, 1994). In one study of more than 1,500 students' midterm exams in an introductory psychology course, it was found that students who changed answers went from incorrect to correct 75 percent of the time (Kruger, Wirtz, & Miller, 2005). These findings probably reflect the fact that students often catch mistakes when they read the question again or when they find some information later in the test that causes them to reconsider their first answer.

Don't buy into the common belief that your first answer is always your best answer. If you have good reason to think a change should be made, don't be afraid to make it. The only exception to this general rule is when you find yourself changing many of your original answers; this is an indication that you were not well prepared for the exam and are just doing a lot of random second-guessing.

Think About It —————————————————— *Journal Entry* 9.5

1. On exams, do you ever change your original answers?

    _____

2. If you do change answers, what's the usual reason you make changes?

    _____

    _____

    _____

    _____

    _____

    _____

Strategies for Answering Essay Questions

Along with multiple-choice questions, essay questions are among the most commonly used forms of questions on college exams. Listed below are strategies that will help you achieve peak levels of performance on essay questions.

1. **Focus on main ideas first.** Before you begin answering the question by writing full sentences, make a brief outline or list of bullet points to represent the main ideas you will include in your answers. Outlines are effective for several reasons:

    *   **An outline helps you remember the major points.** It prevents you from becoming so wrapped up in the details of constructing sentences and choosing words for your answers that you lose the big picture and forget the most important points you need to make.
    *   **An outline improves your answer's organization.** In addition to reminding you of the points you intend to make, an outline gives you a plan for sequencing your ideas in an order that ensures they flow smoothly. One factor that instructors consider when awarding points for an answer to an essay question is how well that answer is organized. An outline makes your answer's organization clearer by calling your attention to its major categories and subcategories.
    *   **Having an advanced idea of what you will write reduces your test anxiety.** An outline takes care of the answer's organization beforehand so you don't have the added stress of worrying about how to organize your answer at the same time you're writing and explaining your answer.

- **An outline can add points to an incomplete answer's score.** If you run out of test time before writing out your full answer to an essay question, an outline allows your instructor to see what you planned to include in your written answer. Your outline itself is likely to earn you points because it demonstrates your knowledge of the major points called for by the question. In contrast, if you skip an outline and just start writing answers to test questions one at a time, you run the risk of not getting to questions you know well before your time is up; you'll then have nothing on your test to show what you know about those unfinished questions.

Exhibit 1

Identical twins

Parents/family tree

Adoption
6/6

No freewill

No afterlife

6/6

1. There are several different studies that scientists conduct, but one study that they conduct is to find out how genetics can influence human behavior in <u>identical twins</u>. Since they are identical, they will most likely end up very similar in behavior because of their identical genetic makeup. Although environment has some impact, genetics are still a huge factor and they will, more likely than not, behave similarly. Another type of study is with <u>parents and their family trees</u>. Looking at a subject's family tree will explain why a certain person is bipolar or depressed. It is most likely caused by a gene in the family tree, even if it was last seen decades ago. Lastly, another study is with adopted children. If an <u>adopted child</u> acts a certain way that is unique to that child, and researchers find the parents' family tree, they will most likely see similar behavior in the parents and siblings as well.

2. The monistic view of the mind-brain relationship is so strongly opposed and criticized because there is a belief or assumption that <u>free will</u> is taken away from people. For example, if a person commits a horrendous crime, it can be argued "monistically" that the chemicals in the brain were the reason, and that a person cannot think for themselves to act otherwise. This view limits responsibility.

   Another reason that this view is opposed is because it has been said that <u>there is no afterlife</u>. If the mind and brain are one and the same, and there is <u>NO</u> difference, then once the brain is dead and is no longer functioning, so is the mind. Thus, it cannot continue to live beyond what we know today as life. <u>And</u> this goes against many religions, which is why this reason, in particular, is heavily opposed.

Written answers to two short essay questions given by a college sophomore, which demonstrate effective use of bulleted lists or short outlines (in the side margin) to ensure recall of most important points.

2. **Get directly to the point on each essay question.** Avoid elaborate introductions that take up your test time (and your instructor's grading time) but don't earn you any points. For example, an answer that begins with the statement "This is an interesting question that we had a great discussion on in class . . ." is pointless because it will not add points to your test score. The time available to you on essay tests is often limited, so you can't afford flowery introductions that waste valuable test time and don't contribute anything to the overall test score.

   One effective way to get directly to the point on essay questions is to include part of the question in the first sentence of your answer. For example, suppose the test question asks you to "Argue for or against capital punishment by explaining how it will or will not reduce the nation's murder rate." Your first sentence could be "Capital punishment will not reduce the murder rate for the following reasons . . ." Thus, your first sentence becomes your thesis statement, which immediately points you directly to the major points you're going to make in your answer and earns immediate points for your answer.

3. **Answer all essay questions with as much detail as possible.** Don't assume that your instructor already knows what you're talking about or will be bored by details. Instead, take the approach that you're writing to someone who knows little or nothing about the subject—as if you're an expert teacher and the reader is a clueless student.

Remember

As a rule, it's better to over explain than under explain your answers to essay questions.

4. **Support your points with evidence—facts, statistics, quotes, or examples.** When taking essay tests, take on the role of a lawyer making a case by presenting concrete evidence (exhibit A, exhibit B, etc.). Since timed essay tests can often press you for time, be sure to prioritize and cite your most powerful points and persuasive evidence. If you have time later, you can return to add other points worth mentioning.

Do It Now! 9.3 contains thinking verbs that you're likely to see in college writing assignments and the types of mental action typically called for by each of these verbs. As you read the following list, make a short note after each mental action, indicating whether or not you've been asked to use such thinking on any assignments you completed before college.

9.3   **DO IT NOW!**

Ten Mental-Action Verbs Commonly Found in Essay-Test Questions

1. **Analyze.** Break the topic down into its key parts and evaluate the parts in terms of their accuracy, strengths, and weaknesses.
2. **Compare.** Identify the similarities and differences between major ideas.
3. **Contrast.** Identify the differences between ideas, particularly sharp differences and opposing viewpoints.
4. **Describe.** Provide details (e.g., who, what, where, and when).
5. **Discuss.** Analyze (break apart) and evaluate the parts (e.g., strengths and weaknesses).
6. **Document.** Support your judgment and conclusions with references or information sources.
7. **Explain.** Provide reasons that answer the questions "Why?" and "How?"
8. **Illustrate.** Supply concrete examples or specific instances.
9. **Interpret.** Draw your own conclusion about something, and explain why you came to that conclusion.
10. **Support.** Back up your ideas with research findings, factual evidence, or logical arguments.

"I keep six honest serving men. They taught me all I knew. Their names are what and why and how and when and where and who."

—Rudyard Kipling, "The Elephant's Child," *Just So Stories*

Think About It ———————— Journal Entry 9.6

1. Which of the mental actions in the list in Do It Now! 9.3 were most often required on your high school writing assignments?

_____

_____

_____

2. Which were least often (or never) required?

_____

_____

_____

5. **Leave space between your answers to essay questions.** This strategy will enable you to easily add information to your original answers if you have time or if you recall something later in the test that you forgot initially.

6. **Proofread your essay for spelling and grammar.** Before turning in your test, proofread what you've written and correct any obvious spelling or grammatical errors you find. Eliminating them is likely to improve your test score. Even if your instructor doesn't explicitly state that grammar and spelling will count in determining your grade, these mechanical mistakes are still likely to influence your professor's overall evaluation of your written work.

7. **Neatness counts.** Many years of research indicates that neatly written essays tend to be scored higher than sloppy ones, even if the answers are essentially the same (Huck & Bounds, 1972; Klein & Hart, 1968; Hughes et al., 1983; Pai et al., 2010). These findings are understandable when you consider that grading essay answers is a time-consuming task that requires your instructor to plod through multiple styles of handwriting whose readability may range from crystal-clear to cryptic. Make an earnest attempt to write as clearly as possible, and if you finish the test with time to spare, clean up your work by rewriting any sloppily written words or sentences.

Think About It ———————— Journal Entry 9.7

Rate yourself in terms of how frequently you use these test-taking strategies according to the following scale:

    4 = always   3 = sometimes   2 = rarely   1 = never

1. I take tests in the same seat that I usually sit in
   to take class notes.   4   3   2   1

2. I answer easier test questions first.   4   3   2   1

3. I use a process-of-elimination approach on multiple-choice tests to eliminate choices until I find one that is correct or appears to be the most accurate option.   4   3   2   1

4. On essay questions, I outline or map out my ideas before I begin to write the answer.   4   3   2   1

5. I look for information included on the test that may help me answer difficult questions or that may help me remember information I've forgotten.   4   3   2   1

6. I leave extra space between my answers to essay questions in case I want to come back and add more information later.   4   3   2   1

7. I carefully review my work, double-checking for errors and skipped questions before turning in my tests.   4   3   2   1

How can you improve in the areas you scored the lowest?

_____

_____

_____

_____

_____

_____

Strategies for Online Tests

More instructors are using technology to enhance their courses. It is very possible that you could have to take an online test even when you are not taking an online course. When taking a test online, you should always read the instructions carefully. Below are some things you should consider when taking online tests.

1. **Online tests are often timed.** Because you are taking these tests outside of class, you are able to use your notes and books. For this reason, many instructors will place a time limit on the test. If you do not complete the test in time, it will shut off when your time is up and you won't be able to do the rest of the test. Be sure to study for online timed tests. You will not have enough time to look up all of the answers, and if you don't study, you won't do well.

2. **Backtracking might be prohibited.** Sometimes you have to answer a question before you can move on to the next question, and once you move on, you cannot go back and change an answer. If this is a timed test, be sure to use your time wisely and don't spend too much time on any one question.

When taking online tests, be sure you are using a reliable computer and you are free from anything that could take your focus away from the test (i.e., cell phone, children, etc.). If something does go wrong during the test, be sure to contact your instructor immediately.

Post-Test Strategies: What to Do after Receiving Test Results

1. **Use your test results as feedback to improve your future performance.** Your test score is not just an end result: it can be used as a means to an end—a higher score on your next test performances and a higher course grade. When you get tests back, examine them carefully and be sure to note any written comments your instructor may have made. If your test results are disappointing, don't get bitter, get better. Use the results as feedback to diagnose where you went wrong so that you can avoid making the same mistakes again. If your test results were positive, see where you went right so you can do it right again.
2. **Seek additional feedback.** In addition to using your own test results as a source of feedback, ask for feedback from others whose judgment you trust and value. Three social resources you can use to obtain feedback on how to improve your performance are your instructors, professionals in your Learning or Academic Support Center, and your peers.

Make appointments with your instructors to visit them during office hours and get their feedback on how you might be able to improve your test performance. You'll likely find it easier to see your instructors after a test than before it, because most students don't realize that it's just as valuable to seek feedback from instructors following an exam as it is to get last-minute help before an exam.

Tutors and other learning support professionals on your campus can be excellent sources of feedback about what adjustments to make in your study habits or test-taking strategies to improve your future performance. Also, be alert and open to receiving feedback from trusted peers. While feedback from experienced professionals is valuable, don't overlook your peers as another source of information on how to improve your performance. You can review your test with other students in class, particularly with students who did exceptionally well. Their tests can provide you with models of what type of work your instructor expects on exams. You might also consider asking successful students what they did to be successful—for example, what they did to prepare for the test and what they did during the test.

Whatever you do, don't let a bad test grade get you mad, sad, or down, particularly if it occurs early in the course when you're still learning the rules of the game. Look at mistakes in terms of what they can do *for* you, rather than to you. A poor test performance can be turned into a valuable learning experience by using test results as a source of feedback and as an error detector to pinpoint the source of your mistakes. Look back at your mistakes so you can move forward and progress toward future success.

> "When you make a mistake, there are only three things you should do about it: admit it; learn from it; and don't repeat it."
>
> —Paul "Bear" Bryant, legendary college football coach

> "Failure is not fatal, but failure to change might be."
>
> —John Wooden, legendary college basketball coach

Remember

Your past mistakes should be neither ignored nor neglected: they should be detected and corrected so that you don't replay them on future tests.

Snapshot Summary

9.1 Key Features of Performance-Enhancing Feedback

When asking for feedback from others on your academic performance, seek feedback that is likely to improve your future performance. Effective performance-enhancing feedback has the following features:

- Performance-enhancing feedback is *specific*. It precisely identifies what you should do to improve your performance and how you should go about doing it. For example, after a test, seek feedback from your instructors that provides you with more than just information about what your grade is or why you lost points: seek specific information about what you could do to improve your performance next time.

- Performance-enhancing feedback is *prompt*. It comes soon after completing a task, because this is the time when you are most motivated to receive it and most likely to retain it. For example, as soon as possible after completing tests or assignments, review your performance with classmates or your professor.

- Performance-enhancing feedback is *proactive*. It comes early in the learning process when you still have plenty of time to use it to improve your performance. For example, seek feedback from instructors early in the term, so you have more time to use that feedback to improve your course performance and course grade.

Remember

Just as you learn before tests by preparing for your performance, you can learn after tests by reviewing your performance.

Strategies for Pinpointing the Source of Lost Points on Exams

On test questions where you lost points, identify the stage in the learning process where the breakdown occurred by asking yourself the following questions:

1. **Did you have the information you needed to answer the question correctly?** If you didn't have the information, what was the source of the missing information? Was it information presented in class that didn't get into your notes? If so, look at our strategies for improving listening and note-taking habits (see p. 130). If the missing information was contained in your assigned reading, check whether you're using effective reading strategies (see p. 135).

2. **Did you have the information but not study it because you didn't think it was important?** If you didn't realize the information would be on the test, review the study strategies for finding and focusing on the most important information in class lectures and reading assignments (see p. 132).

3. **Did you study it, but not retain it?** Not remembering information you studied may mean one of three things:
   - You didn't store the information adequately in your brain, so your memory trace wasn't strong enough to recall. This suggests that more study time needs to be spent on recitation or rehearsal (see p. 162).
   - You may have tried to cram in too much information in too little time just before the exam and may have not given your brain time enough to "digest" (consolidate) it and store it in long-term memory. The solution would be to distribute your study time more evenly in advance of the next exam and take advantage of the part-to-whole study method (see p. 146).
   - You put in enough study time and you didn't cram, but you didn't study effectively or strategically. For example, you may have studied for essay questions by just reading over your class notes and reading highlights rather than

rehearsing and reciting them. The solution would be to adjust your study strategy so that it better matches or aligns with the type of test you're taking (see p. 162).

4. **Did you study the material but not really understand it or learn it deeply?** This suggests you may need to self-monitor your comprehension more carefully while studying to track whether you truly understand the material at a deeper level (see p. 154).

5. **Did you know the information but find yourself unable to retrieve it during the exam?** If you had the information on the "tip of your tongue" during the exam, this indicates that you did retain it and it was stored (saved) in your brain, but you couldn't get at it and get it out (retrieve it) when you needed it. This error may be corrected by making better use of memory retrieval cues (see p. 163).

6. **Did you know the answer but just make a careless test-taking mistake?** If your mistake was careless, the solution may be simply to take more time to review your test once you've completed it and check for absentminded errors before turning it in (see p. 170). Or, your careless errors may be the result of test anxiety that's interfering with your ability to concentrate during exams.

Strategies for Reducing Test Anxiety

1. **Understand what test anxiety is and what it's not.** Don't confuse anxiety with stress. Stress is a physical reaction that prepares your body for action by arousing and energizing it; this heightened arousal and energy can be used productively to strengthen your performance. In fact, if you're totally stress-free during an exam, it may mean that you're too "laid back" and couldn't care less about how well you're doing. Stress is something that cannot and should not be completely eliminated when you're trying to reach peak levels of performance, whether academic or athletic. Instead of trying to block out stress altogether, your goal should be to control it, contain it, and maintain it at a level that maximizes the quality of your performance. The key is to keep stress at a moderate level, thereby capitalizing on its capacity to help you get psyched up or pumped up, but preventing it from reaching such a high level that you become psyched out or stressed out.

    If you experience the following symptoms during tests, your stress level may be high enough to be accurately called test anxiety:

    - You feel physical symptoms of tension during the test, such as pounding heartbeat, rapid pulse, muscle tension, sweating, or an upset stomach.
    - Negative thoughts and feelings rush through your head—for example, fear of failure or self-defeating putdowns such as "I always mess up on exams."
    - You rush through the test just to get it over with (probably because you want to get rid of the anxiety you're experiencing).
    - You have difficulty concentrating or focusing your attention while answering test questions.
    - Even though you studied and know the material, you go blank during the exam and forget what you studied. (However, you're able to remember the information after you turn in your test and leave the test situation.)

To minimize test anxiety, consider the following practices and strategies:

2. **Avoid cramming for exams.** Research indicates that college students who display greater amounts of procrastination experience higher levels of test anxiety (Rothblum, Solomon, & Murakami, 1986). High levels of pre-test tension associated with rushing and late-night cramming are likely to carry over to the test itself, resulting in higher levels of test-taking tension. Furthermore, loss of sleep caused by previous-night cramming results in lost dream (REM) sleep, which, in turn, elevates anxiety levels the following day—test day.

3. **Use effective test-preparation strategies prior to the exam.** Test-anxiety research indicates that college students who prepare well for exams not only achieve higher test scores, but also experience lower levels of test anxiety (Zohar, 1998). Other research findings demonstrate that using effective study strategies prior to the exam, such as those discussed in Chapter 6, reduces test anxiety during the exam (Benjamin, McKeachie, Lin, & Holinger, 1981; Jones & Petruzzi, 1995; Zeidner, 1995)

4. **During the exam, concentrate on the here and now.** Devote your attention fully to answering the test question that you're currently working on; don't spend time thinking (and worrying) about the test's outcome and what your grade will be.

5. **Stay focused on the test in front of you, not the students around you.** Don't spend valuable test time looking at what others are doing and wondering whether they're doing better than you are. If you came to the test well prepared and still find the test difficult, it's very likely that other students are finding it difficult too. If you happen to notice that other students are finishing before you do, don't assume that they breezed through the test or that they're smarter than you. Their faster finish may simply reflect the fact that they didn't know many of the answers and decided to give up and get out, rather than prolong the agony.

6. **Don't spend a lot of time focusing on the amount of time left in the exam.** Repeatedly checking the time during the test can disrupt the flow of your thought process and increase your stress level. Although it's important that you remain aware of how much time remains to complete the exam, only check the time periodically, and do your time-checking after you've completed answering a question so you don't disrupt or derail your train of thought.

7. **Control your thoughts by focusing on what you're getting right, rather than worrying about what answers you don't know and how many points you're losing.** Our thoughts influence our emotions (Ellis, 1995), and positive emotions, such as those associated with optimism and a sense of accomplishment, can improve mental performance by enhancing the brain's ability to process, store, and retrieve information (Rosenfield, 1988). Keep in mind that college exams are often designed to be more difficult than high school tests, so it's less likely that students will get 90 to 100 percent of the total points. You can still achieve a good grade on a college test without having to achieve a near-perfect test score.

8. **Remember that if you're experiencing a *moderate* amount of stress during the exam, this isn't abnormal or an indication that you're suffering from test anxiety.** If you're experiencing moderate levels of tension, it indicates that you're motivated and want to do well. In fact, research shows that experiencing *moderate* levels of tension during tests and other performance-evaluation situations serves to maximize alertness, concentration, and memory (Sapolsky, 2004).

9. **Don't forget that it's just a test: it's not a measure of your ability or character.** An exam is not a measure of your overall intelligence, your overall academic ability, or your quality as a person. In fact, a test grade may be less of an indication of your effort or ability than the level of complexity of the particular content covered by the test material or the nature of the test itself. Furthermore, one low grade on one particular test doesn't mean you're not capable of doing good work and are going to end up with a poor grade in the course, particularly if you use the results as feedback to improve your next test performance (see pp. 176–177).

One final note on the topic of test anxiety: if you continue to experience test anxiety after implementing the above strategies, don't hesitate to seek assistance from a professional in your Learning (Academic Support) Center or Personal Counseling Office.

Summary and Conclusion

Improving performance on college exams involves strategies used in advance of the test, during the test, and after test results are returned. Good test performance begins with good test preparation and adjustment of your study strategy to the type of test you'll be taking (e.g., multiple-choice or essay test).

You can learn and improve your grades not only by preparing for tests but also by reviewing your tests and using them as feedback to apply as you continue in the course. Past mistakes shouldn't be ignored or neglected; they should be detected and corrected so that they're not replayed on future tests.

Learning More through the World Wide Web

Internet-Based Resources for Further Information on Test-Taking Skills

For additional information related to ideas discussed in this chapter, we recommend the following Web sites:

Test-Taking Strategies:

www.muskingum.edu/~cal/database/general/testtaking.html

web.mit.edu/arc/learning/modules/test/testtypes.html

Overcoming Test Anxiety:

www.studygs.net/tstprp8.htm

www.swccd.edu/~asc/lrnglinks/test_anxiety.html

Chapter 9 Exercises

9.1 Midterm Self-Evaluation

Since you are near the midpoint of this textbook, you may be near the midpoint of your first term in college. At this time of the term you are likely to experience the midterm crunch—a wave of midterm exams and due dates for certain papers and projects. This may be a good time to step back and assess your academic progress thus far.

Use the form that follows to list the courses you're taking this term and the grades you are currently receiving in each of these courses. If you do not know what your grade is, take a few minutes to check your syllabus for your instructor's grading policy and add up your scores on completed tests and assignments; this should give you at least a rough idea of where you stand in your courses. If you're having difficulty determining your grade in any course, even after checking your course syllabus and returned tests or assignments, then ask your instructor how you could estimate your current grade.

Course No.	Course Title	Instructor	Grade
1.			
2.			
3.			
4.			
5.			

Self-Assessment Questions

1. Were these the grades you were hoping for? Are you pleased or disappointed by them?

2. Were these the grades you expected to get? If not, were they better or worse than expected?

3. Do you see any patterns in your performance that suggest things you are doing well or things that you need to improve?

4. If you had to pinpoint one action you could immediately take to improve your lowest course grades, what would it be?

9.2 Calculating Your Midterm Grade Point Average

Use the information in Snapshot Summary 9.2 to calculate what your grade point average (GPA) will be if these grades turn out to be your final course grades for the term.

9.2 How to Compute Your Grade Point Average (GPA)

Most colleges and universities use a grading scale that ranges from 0 to 4.0 to calculate a student's grade point average (GPA) or quality point average (QPA). Some schools use letter grades only, while other institutions use letter grades with pluses and minuses.

Grading System Using Letters Only
Grade = Point value

A	=	4
B	=	3
C	=	2
D	=	1
F	=	0

GRADE POINTS Earned Per Course = Course Grade Multiplied by the Number of Course Credits (Units)

GRADE POINT AVERAGE (GPA) = $\dfrac{\text{Total Number of Grade Points for All Courses}}{\text{Divided by Total Number of Course Units}}$

SAMPLE/EXAMPLE

Course	Units	×	Grade	=	Grade Points
Roots of Rock 'n' Roll	3	×	C (2)	=	6
Daydreaming Analysis	3	×	A (4)	=	12
Surfing Strategies	1	×	A (4)	=	4
Wilderness Survival	4	×	B (3)	=	12
Sitcom Analysis	2	×	D (1)	=	2
Love and Romance	3	×	A (4)	=	12
	16				**48**

GPA $= \dfrac{48}{16} = 3.0$

1. What is your overall GPA at this point in the term?

2. At the start of this term, what GPA were you hoping to attain?

3. Do you think your actual GPA at the end of the term will be higher or lower than it is now? Why?

Notes: It's normal for GPAs to be lower in college than they were in high school, particularly during the first year of college. Here are the results of one study that compared students' high school GPAs with the GPAs after their first year of college:

- 29 percent of beginning college students had GPAs of 3.75 or higher in high school, but only 17 percent had GPAs that high at the end of their first year of college.
- 46 percent had high school GPAs between 3.25 and 3.74, but only 32 percent had GPAs that high after the first year of college (National Resource Center for the First-Year Experience and Students in Transition, 2004).

9.3 Preparing an Oral Presentation on Student Success

1. Scan this textbook and identify a chapter topic or chapter section that you find most interesting or think is most important to you.

2. Create an introduction for a class presentation on this topic that:

    a. provides an overview or sneak preview of what you will cover in your presentation;

    b. grabs the attention of your audience (your classmates); and

    c. demonstrates the topic's relevance or importance for your audience.

3. Create a conclusion to your presentation that:

    a. relates back to your introduction;

    b. highlights your most important point or points; and

    c. leaves a memorable last impression.

Bad Feedback: Shocking Midterm Grades

Joe Frosh has enjoyed his first weeks on campus. He has met lots of interesting people and feels that he fits in socially. He's also very pleased to discover that his college schedule doesn't require him to be in class for five to six hours per day, like it did in high school. This is the good news. The bad news is that unlike high school, where his grades were all As and Bs, his first midterm grades in college are three Cs, one D, and one F. He's stunned and a bit depressed by his midterm grades because he thought he was doing well. Since he never received grades this low in high school, he's beginning to think that he's not college material and may flunk out.

Discussion Questions

1. What factors may have caused or contributed to Joe's bad start?

2. What are Joe's options at this point?

3. What do you recommend Joe do right now to get his grades up and avoid being placed on academic probation?

4. What might Joe do in the future to prevent this midterm setback from happening again?

Chapter 9 Reflection

What are some ways that you currently prepare for tests that do not seem to be working? Why do you think these methods of preparing for tests do not work?

List and explain three ways you can change your current methods of preparing for tests that you believe will help you perform better on tests.

1.

2.

3.

What are two things you can do during the test that will help you perform better?

1.

2.

What are two things you can do after you get your test back that can help you perform better on future tests?

1.

2.

Diversity and the Community College Experience

Appreciating the Value of Human Differences for Promoting Learning and Personal Development

---

THOUGHT STARTER | *Journal Entry* **10.1**

LEARNING GOAL

To appreciate the value of human differences and acquire skills for making the most of diversity in college and beyond.

Complete the following sentence:

When I hear the word *diversity*, the first thoughts that come to my mind are . . .

_____

_____

_____

_____

_____

_____

The Spectrum of Diversity

The word *diversity* derives from the Latin root *diversus*, meaning "various." Thus, human diversity refers to the variety of differences that exist among the people that comprise humanity (the human species). In this chapter, we use *diversity* to refer primarily to differences among the major groups of people who, collectively, comprise humankind or humanity. The relationship between diversity and humanity is represented visually in Figure 10.1.

The relationship between humanity and human diversity is similar to the relationship between sunlight and the spectrum of colors. Just as the sunlight passing through a prism is dispersed into all groups of colors that make up the visual spectrum, the human species that's spread across the planet is dispersed into all groups of people that make up the human spectrum (humanity).

As you can see in Figure 10.1, groups of people differ from one another in numerous ways, including physical features, religious beliefs, mental and physical abilities, national origins, social backgrounds, gender, sexual orientation, and other personal dimensions.

"We are all brothers and sisters. Each face in the rainbow of color that populates our world is precious and special. Each adds to the rich treasure of humanity."

—Morris Dees, civil rights leader and cofounder of the Southern Poverty Law Center

FIGURE 10.1

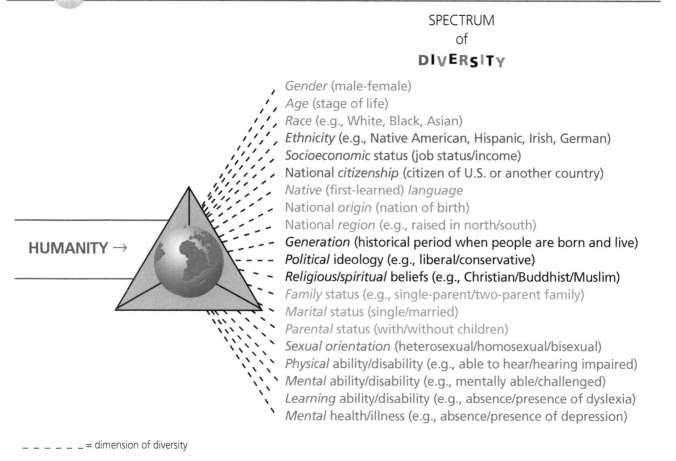

SPECTRUM
of
DIVERSITY

Gender (male-female)
Age (stage of life)
Race (e.g., White, Black, Asian)
Ethnicity (e.g., Native American, Hispanic, Irish, German)
Socioeconomic status (job status/income)
National *citizenship* (citizen of U.S. or another country)
Native (first-learned) *language*
National *origin* (nation of birth)
National *region* (e.g., raised in north/south)
Generation (historical period when people are born and live)
Political ideology (e.g., liberal/conservative)
Religious/spiritual beliefs (e.g., Christian/Buddhist/Muslim)
Family status (e.g., single-parent/two-parent family)
Marital status (single/married)
Parental status (with/without children)
Sexual orientation (heterosexual/homosexual/bisexual)
Physical ability/disability (e.g., able to hear/hearing impaired)
Mental ability/disability (e.g., mentally able/challenged)
Learning ability/disability (e.g., absence/presence of dyslexia)
Mental health/illness (e.g., absence/presence of depression)

HUMANITY →

_ _ _ _ _ _ = dimension of diversity

*This list represents some of the major dimensions of human diversity; it does not represent a complete list of all possible forms of human diversity. Also, disagreement exists about certain dimensions of diversity (e.g., whether certain groups should be considered races or ethnic groups).

© Kendall Hunt

Humanity and Diversity

Think About It ———————————————— *Journal Entry* **10.2**

Look at the diversity spectrum in Figure 10.1 and look over the list of groups that make up the spectrum. Do you notice any groups that are missing from the list that should be added, either because they have distinctive backgrounds or because they have been targets of prejudice and discrimination?

_____

_____

_____

_____

_____

Since diversity has been interpreted (and misinterpreted) in different ways by different people, we begin by defining some key terms related to diversity that should lead to a clearer understanding of its true meaning and value.

What Is Race?

A racial group (race) is a group of people who share some distinctive physical traits, such as skin color or other facial characteristics. The U.S. Census Bureau (2010) identifies four races: White, Black, Asian, and American Indian or Alaska Native. However, as Anderson and Fienberg (2000) caution, racial categories are social-political constructs (concepts) that are not scientifically based but socially determined. There continues to be disagreement among scholars about what groups of people constitute a human "race" or whether distinctive races exist (Wheelright, 2005). No specific genes differentiate one race from another. In other words, you couldn't do a blood test or any type of internal genetic test to determine a person's race. Humans have simply decided to categorize people into races on the basis of certain external differences in physical appearance, particularly the color of their outer layer of skin. The U.S. Census Bureau could just as easily have divided people into categories based on such physical characteristics as eye color (blue, brown, and green) or hair texture (straight, wavy, curly, and frizzy).

Author's Experience My mother was from Alabama and was dark in skin color, with high cheekbones and long curly black hair. My father stood approximately six feet tall and had light brown straight hair. His skin color was that of a Western European with a slight suntan. If you did not know that my father was of African American descent, you would not have thought of him as Black. All of my life I have thought of myself as African American, and all of the people who are familiar with me thought of me as African American. I have lived half of a century with that as my racial description. Several years ago, after carefully looking through records available on births and deaths in my family history, I discovered that fewer than 50 percent of my ancestors were of African lineage. Biologically, I am no longer Black. Socially and emotionally, I still am. Clearly, race is more of a social concept than a biological fact.

Aaron Thompson

The differences in skin color that now occur among humans are likely due to biological adaptations that evolved over long periods among groups of humans who lived in regions of the world with different climatic conditions. For instance, darker skin tones developed among humans who inhabited and reproduced in hotter regions nearer the equator (e.g., Africa), where darker skin enabled them to adapt and survive by providing their bodies with better protection from the potentially damaging effects of the sun (Bridgeman, 2003) and allowing their bodies to better use the vitamin D supplied by sunlight (Jablonski & Chaplin, 2002). In contrast, lighter skin tones developed over time among humans inhabiting colder climates that were farther from the equator (e.g., Scandinavia) to enable their bodies to absorb greater amounts of sunlight, which was in shorter supply in their region of the world.

While humans may display diversity in skin color or tone, the biological reality is that all members of the human species are remarkably similar. More than 98 percent of the genes that make up humans from different racial groups are the same (Bridgeman, 2003; Molnar, 1991). This large amount of genetic overlap among humans accounts for the many similarities that exist, regardless of what differences in color appear at the surface of skin. For example, all humans have similar external features that give them a "human" appearance and clearly distinguish people from other animal species, all humans have internal organs that are similar in structure and function, and no matter what the color of the outer layer of skin, when it's cut, all humans bleed in the same color.

Author's Experience I was proofreading this chapter while sitting in a coffee shop in the Chicago O'Hare airport. I looked up from my work for a second and saw what appeared to be a White girl about 18 years old. As I lowered my head to return to my work, I did a double-take to look at her again because something about her seemed different or unusual. When I looked at her more closely the second time, I noticed that although she had light skin, the features of her face and hair appeared to be those of an African American. After a couple of seconds of puzzlement, I figured it out: she was an *albino* African American. That satisfied me for the moment, but then I began to wonder: Would it still be accurate to say that she was "Black" even though her skin was light? Would her hair and facial features be sufficient for her to be considered or classified as Black? If yes, then what about someone who had a dark skin tone but did not have the typical hair and facial features characteristic of Black people? Is skin color the defining feature of being African American, or are other features equally important? I was unable to answer these questions, but I found it amusing that these thoughts were taking place while I was working on a book dealing with diversity. Later, on the plane ride home, I thought again about that albino African American girl and realized that she was a perfect example of how classifying people into races is based not on objective, scientifically determined evidence but on subjective, socially constructed categories.

— *Joe Cuseo*

Think About It — *Journal Entry* **10.3**

What race do you consider yourself to be? Would you say you identify strongly with your race, or are you rarely conscious of it? Explain.

_____

_____

_____

_____

_____

_____

What Is Culture?

Culture may be defined as a distinctive pattern of beliefs and values learned by a group of people who share the same social heritage and traditions. In short, culture is the whole way in which a group of people has learned to live (Peoples & Bailey, 1998); it includes style of speaking (language), fashion, food, art, music, values, and beliefs.

A major advantage of culture is that it helps bind its members together into a supportive, tight-knit community; however, it can also blind them to other cultural perspectives. Since culture shapes the way people think, it can cause groups of people to view the world solely through their own cultural lens or frame of reference

© steven r. hendricks, 2013. Under license from Shutterstock, Inc.

Cultural differences can exist within the same society (multicultural society), within a single nation (domestic diversity), or across different nations (international diversity).

FIGURE   10.2

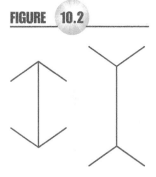

Optical Illusion

(Colombo, Cullen, & Lisle, 1995). Optical illusions are a good illustration of how cultural perspectives can blind people or lead them to inaccurate perceptions. For instance, compare the lengths of the two lines in Figure 10.2.

If you perceive the line on the right to be longer than the line on the left, welcome to the club. Virtually all Americans and people from Western cultures perceive the line on the right to be longer. Actually, both lines are equal in length. (If you don't believe it, take out a ruler and check it out.) Interestingly, this perceptual error is not made by people from non-Western cultures that live in environments populated with circular structures rather than structures with linear patterns and angled corners, like Westerners use (Segall, Campbell, & Herskovits, 1966).

The key point underlying this optical illusion is that cultural experiences shape and sometimes distort perceptions of reality. We think we are seeing things objectively or "as they really are," but we are often seeing things subjectively from our limited cultural vantage point. Being open to the viewpoints of diverse people who perceive the world from different cultural vantage points widens our range of perception and helps us overcome our "cultural blind spots." As a result, we tend to perceive the world around us with greater clarity and accuracy.

Remember

The reality of our own culture is not the reality of other cultures. Our perceptions of the outside world are shaped (and sometimes distorted) by our prior cultural experiences.

What Is an Ethnic Group?

An ethnic group (ethnicity) is a group of people who share the same culture. Thus, *culture* refers to *what* an ethnic group has in common and *ethnic group* refers to a group of people *who* share the same culture. Unlike a racial group, whose members share physical characteristics that they are born with and that have been passed on biologically, an ethnic group's shared characteristics have been passed on through socialization—that is, their common characteristics have been *learned* or acquired through shared social experiences.

Currently, European Americans are the majority ethnic group in the United States because they account for more than 50 percent of the American population. Native Americans, African Americans, Hispanic Americans, and Asian Americans are considered to be ethnic minority groups because each of these groups represents less than 50 percent of the American population.

Think About It ———————————— *Journal Entry* **10.4**

Which ethnic group or groups do you belong to or identify with? What are the most common cultural values shared by your ethnic group or groups?

_____

_____

_____

_____

_____

_____

As with the concept of race, whether a particular group of people is defined as an ethnic group can be arbitrary, subjective, and interpreted differently by different groups of people. Currently, the only races recognized by the U.S. Census Bureau are White, Black, and Asian; Hispanic is not defined as a race but is classified as an ethnic group. However, among those who checked "some other race" in the 2000 census, 97 percent were Hispanic. This fact has been viewed by Hispanic advocates as a desire for their "ethnic" group to be reclassified as a racial group (Cianciotto, 2005).

This disagreement illustrates how difficult it is to conveniently categorize groups of people into particular racial or ethnic groups. The United States will continue to struggle with this issue because the ethnic and racial diversity of its population is growing and members of different ethnic and racial groups are forming cross-ethnic and interracial families. Thus, it is becoming progressively more difficult to place people into distinct categories based on their race or ethnicity. For example, by 2050, the number of people who will identify themselves as being of two or more races is projected to more than triple, growing from 5.2 million to 16.2 million (U.S. Census Bureau, 2008).

What Is Humanity?

It is important to realize that human *variety* and human *similarity* exist side by side and complement each other. Diversity is a "value that is shown in mutual respect and appreciation of similarities and differences" (Public Service Enterprise Group, 2009.) Experiencing diversity not only enhances our appreciation of the unique features of different cultures, but also provides us with a larger perspective on the universal aspects of the human experience that are common to all humans, no matter what their particular cultural background may be. For example, despite our racial and cultural differences, all people express the same emotions with the same facial expressions (see Figure 10.3).

FIGURE 10.3

Humans all over the world display the same facial expressions when experiencing certain emotions. See if you can detect the emotions being expressed in the following faces. (To find the answers, turn your book upside down.)

All images © JupiterImages Corporation.

Answers: The emotions shown. Top, left to right: anger, fear, and sadness. Bottom, left to right: disgust, happiness, and surprise.

Think About It —— *Journal Entry* 10.5

List three human experiences that you think are universal—that is, they are experienced by all humans in all cultures:

1. _____

2. _____

3. _____

Other human characteristics that anthropologists have found to be shared across all groups of people in every corner of the world include storytelling, poetry, adornment of the body, dance, music, decoration of artifacts, families, socialization of children by elders, a sense of right and wrong, supernatural beliefs, explanations of diseases and death, and mourning of the dead (Pinker, 1994). Although different ethnic groups may express these shared experiences in different ways, these universal experiences are common to all humans.

Remember

Diversity represents variations on the common theme of humanity. Although people have different cultural backgrounds, they are still cultivated from the same soil—they are all grounded in the common experience of being human.

"We are all the same, and we are all unique."

—Georgia Dunston, African American biologist and research specialist in human genetics

Thus, different cultures associated with different ethnic groups may be viewed simply as variations on the same theme: being human. You may have heard the question "We're all human, aren't we?" The answer to this important question is "yes and no." Yes, we are all the same, but not in the same way.

A good metaphor for understanding this apparent contradiction is to visualize humanity as a quilt in which we are all joined together by the common thread of humanity—by the common bond of being human. Yet the different patches that make up the quilt represent diversity—the distinctive or unique cultures that comprise our common humanity. The quilt metaphor acknowledges the identity and beauty of all cultures. It differs from the old American melting pot metaphor, which viewed differences as something that should be melted down or eliminated, or the salad bowl metaphor, which suggested that America is a hodgepodge or mishmash of different cultures thrown together without any common connection. In contrast, the quilt metaphor suggests that the cultures of different ethnic groups should be recognized and celebrated. Nevertheless, our differences can be woven together to create a unified whole—as in the Latin expression *E pluribus unum* ("Out of many, one"), the motto of the United States, which you will find printed on all U.S. coins.

"We have become not a melting pot but a beautiful mosaic."

—Jimmy Carter, 39th president of the United States and winner of the Nobel Peace Prize

To appreciate diversity and its relationship to humanity is to capitalize on the power of our differences (diversity) while still preserving our collective strength through unity (humanity).

Remember

By learning about diversity (our differences), we simultaneously learn about our commonality (our shared humanity).

Author's Experience   When I was 12 years old and living in New York City, I returned from school one Friday afternoon and my mother asked me if anything interesting happened at school that day. I mentioned to her that the teacher went around the room, asking students what we had eaten for dinner the night before. At that moment, my mother began to become a bit agitated and nervously asked me, "What did you tell the teacher?" I said, "I told her and the rest of the class that I had pasta last night because my family always eats pasta on Thursdays and Sundays." My mother exploded and fired back at me, "Why couldn't you tell her that we had steak or roast beef?" For a moment, I was stunned and couldn't figure out what I had done wrong or why I should have lied about eating pasta. Then it suddenly dawned on me: My mother was embarrassed about being an Italian American. She wanted me to hide our family's ethnic background and make it sound like we were very "American." After this became clear to me, a few moments later, it also became clear to me why her maiden name was changed from the Italian-sounding DeVigilio to the more American-sounding Vigilis and why her first name was changed from Carmella to Mildred. Her family wanted to minimize discrimination and maximize their acculturation (absorption) into American culture.

I never forgot this incident because it was such an emotionally intense experience. For the first time in my life, I became aware that my mother was ashamed of being a member of the same group to which every other member of my family belonged, including me. After her outburst, I felt a combined rush of astonishment and embarrassment. However, these feelings eventually faded and my mother's reaction ended up having the opposite effect on me. Instead of making me feel inferior or ashamed about being Italian American, her reaction that day caused me to become more aware of, and take more pride in, my Italian heritage.

As I grew older, I also grew to understand why my mother felt the way she did. She grew up in America's "melting pot" era—a time when different American ethnic groups were expected to melt down and melt away their ethnicity. They were not to celebrate diversity: they were to eliminate it.

Joe Cuseo

What Is Individuality?

It's important to keep in mind that *individual* differences within the same racial or ethnic group are greater than the *average* differences between two different groups. For example, although you live in a world that is conscious of differences among races, differences in physical attributes (e.g., height and weight) and behavior patterns (e.g., personality characteristics) among individuals within the same racial group are greater than the average differences among various racial groups (Caplan & Caplan, 1994).

As you proceed through this book, keep in mind the following distinctions among humanity, diversity, and individuality:

- **Diversity.** We are all members of *different groups* (e.g., different gender and ethnic groups).
- **Humanity.** We are all members of the *same group* (the human species).
- **Cultural competence.** The ability to *appreciate and capitalize* on human differences by interacting effectively with people from diverse cultural backgrounds.
- **Individuality.** We are all *unique individuals* who differ from other members of any group to which we may belong.

"Every human is, at the same time, like all other humans, like some humans, and like no other human."

—Clyde Kluckholn, American anthropologist

Major Forms or Types of Diversity

International Diversity

Moving beyond our particular countries of citizenship, we are also members of an international world that includes multiple nations. Global interdependence and international collaboration are needed to solve current international problems, such as global warming and terrorism. Communication and interaction across nations are now greater than at any other time in world history, largely because of rapid advances in electronic technology (Dryden & Vos, 1999; Smith, 1994). Economic boundaries between nations are also breaking down due to increasing international travel, international trading, and development of multinational corporations. Today's world really is a "small world after all," and success in it requires an international perspective. By learning from and about different nations, you become more than a citizen of your own country; you become cosmopolitan—a citizen of the world.

Taking an international perspective allows you to appreciate the diversity of humankind. If it were possible to reduce the world's population to a village of precisely 100 people, with all existing human ratios remaining the same, the demographics of this "world village" would look something like this:

61 would be Asians, 13 Africans, 12 Europeans, 9 Latin Americans, and 5 from the USA and Canada
50 would be male, 50 would be female
75 would be non-white; 25 white
67 would be non-Christian; 33 would be Christian
80 would live in substandard housing
16 would be unable to read or write
50 would be malnourished and 1 dying of starvation
33 would be without access to a safe water supply
39 would lack access to improved sanitation
24 would not have any electricity (and of the 76 that did have electricity, most would only use it for light at night)
 8 people would have access to the Internet
 1 would have a college education
 1 would have HIV
 2 would be near birth; 1 near death
 5 would control 32 percent of the entire world's wealth; all 5 would be U.S. citizens
48 would live on less than US$ 2 a day
20 would live on less than US$ 1 a day

Source: Family Care Foundation (2005).

Ethnic and Racial Diversity

America is rapidly becoming a more racially and ethnically diverse nation. In 2008, the minority population in the United States reached an all-time high of 34 percent of the total population. The population of ethnic minorities is now growing at a much faster rate than the White majority. This trend is expected to continue, and by the middle of the 21st century, the minority population will have grown from one-third of the U.S. population to more than one-half (54 percent), with more than 60 percent of the nation's children expected to be members of minority groups (U.S. Census Bureau, 2008).

By 2050, the U.S. population is projected to be more than 30 percent Hispanic (up from 15 percent in 2008), 15 percent Black (up from 13 percent), 9.6 percent Asian (up from 5.3 percent), and 2 percent Native American (up from 1.6 percent). The native Hawaiian and Pacific Islander population is expected to more than double between 2008 and 2050. In the same time frame, the percentage of Americans who are White will drop from 66 percent (2008) to 46 percent (2050). As a result of these population trends, ethnic and racial minorities will become the "new majority" because they will constitute the majority of Americans by the middle of the 21st century. (See Figure 10.4.)

Socioeconomic Diversity

Diversity also appears in the form of socioeconomic status or social class, which is typically stratified (divided) into lower, middle, and upper classes, depending on

FIGURE 10.4

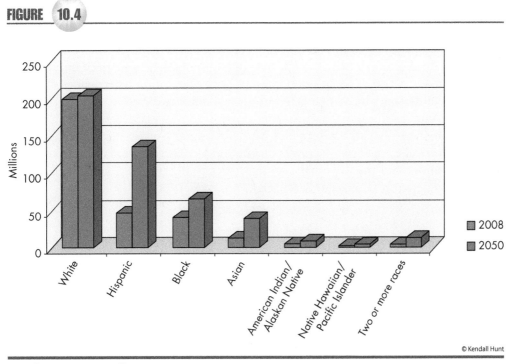

The "New Majority"

level of education and income. Groups occupying lower social strata have significantly fewer social and economic opportunities or privileges (Feagin & Feagin, 2007).

According to U.S. Census figures, the wealthiest 20 percent of the American population controls approximately 50 percent of the country's total income, and the 20 percent of Americans with the lowest income controls only 4 percent of the nation's income. Sharp discrepancies also exist in income level among different racial, ethnic, and gender groups. In 2007, Black households had the lowest median income ($33,916), compared to a median income of $54,920 for non-Hispanic White households (Annual Social and Economic Supplement, 2008).

Poverty continues to be a problem in America. In 2007, 12.5 percent of Americans (37.3 million people) lived below the poverty line, making the United States one of the most impoverished of all developed countries in the world (Shah, 2008). Although all ethnic and racial groups experience poverty, minority groups experience poverty at significantly higher rates than the White majority. In 2007, poverty rates for different ethnic and racial groups were as follows:

- Whites: 8.2 percent
- Asians: 10.2 percent
- Hispanics: 21.5 percent
- Blacks: 24.5 percent

Source: U.S. Census Bureau (2008).

It's estimated that 600,000 families and 1.25 million children are now homeless, accounting for roughly 50 percent of the homeless population. Typically, these families comprise a mother and two children under the age of five (National Alliance to End Homelessness, 2007).

Generational Diversity

Humans are also diverse with respect to the generation in which they grew up. *Generation* refers to a group of individuals born during the same historical period whose attitudes, values, and habits have been shaped by events that took place in the world during their formative years of development. Each generation experiences different historical events, so it's likely that generations will develop different attitudes and behaviors as a result.

Snapshot Summary 10.1 provides a brief summary of the major generations, the key historical events that occurred during the formative periods of the people in each generation, and the personal characteristics that have been associated with a particular generation (Lancaster & Stillman, 2002).

Snapshot Summary

10.1 Generational Diversity

- **The Traditional Generation, a.k.a. the Silent Generation** (born 1922–1945). This generation was influenced by events such as the Great Depression and World Wars I and II. Characteristics associated with this generation include loyalty, patriotism, respect for authority, and conservatism.

- **The Baby Boomer Generation** (born 1946–1964). This generation was influenced by events such as the Vietnam War, Watergate, and the human rights movement. Characteristics associated with this generation include idealism, importance of self-fulfillment, and concern for equal rights.

- **Generation X** (born 1965–1980). This generation was influenced by Sesame Street, the creation of MTV, AIDS, and soaring divorce rates that produced the first "latchkey children"—youngsters who let themselves into their homes after school with their own keys because their mothers were working outside the home. Characteristics associated with this generation include self-reliance, resourcefulness, and being comfortable with change.

- **Generation Y, a.k.a. Millennials** (born 1981–2002). This generation was influenced by the September 11, 2001, terrorist attack on the United States, the shooting of students at Columbine High School, and the collapse of the Enron Corporation. Characteristics associated with this generation include a preference for working and playing in groups, being technologically savvy, and a willingness to provide volunteer service in their community (the civic generation). They are also the most ethnically diverse generation, which may explain why they are more open to diversity and see it as a positive experience.

Diversity and the College Experience

There are more than 3,000 public and private colleges in the United States. They vary in size (small to large) and location (urban, suburban, and rural), as well as in their purpose or mission (research universities, comprehensive state universities, liberal arts colleges, and community colleges). This variety makes the American higher education system the most diverse and accessible in the world. The diversity of educational opportunities in American colleges and universities reflects the freedom of opportunity in the United States as a democratic nation (American Council on Education, 2008).

The U.S. system of higher education is also becoming more diverse with respect to the people enrolled in the system. (See Snapshot Summary 10.2 for recent statistics related to diversity in U.S. community colleges.) The ethnic and racial diversity of students in American colleges and universities is rapidly rising. In 1960, Whites made up almost 95 percent of the total college population; in 2005, that percentage

Snapshot Summary

10.2   Diversity in America's Community Colleges

58% of community college students are women

53% are 22 years of age or older

Among full-time students, 50% are employed part-time and 27% are employed full-time

Among part-time students, 50% are employed full-time and 33% are employed part-time

39% are the first in their family to attend college

36% are members of a minority ethnic or racial group

17% are single parents

Source: American Association of Community Colleges (2009).

had decreased to 69 percent. At the same time, there was an increase in the percentage of Asian, Hispanic, Black, and Native American students attending college (Chronicle of Higher Education, 2003).

The rise in ethnic and racial diversity on American campuses is particularly noteworthy when viewed in light of the historical treatment of minority groups in the United States. In the early 19th century, education was not a right but a privilege available only to those who could afford to attend private schools. Members of certain minority groups were left out of the educational process altogether or were forced to be educated in racially segregated settings. For example, Americans of color were once taught in separate, segregated schools that were typically inferior in terms of educational facilities. This continued until the groundbreaking U.S. Supreme Court ruling in *Brown v. Board of Education* in 1954, which changed the face of education for people of color by ruling that "separate educational facilities are inherently unequal." The decision made it illegal for Kansas and 20 other states to deliver education in segregated classrooms.

"Of all the civil rights for which the world has struggled and fought for 5,000 years, the right to learn is undoubtedly the most fundamental."

—W. E. B. DuBois, African American sociologist, historian, and civil rights activist

Think About It ——————————— *Journal Entry* 10.6

1. Are you the first in your family to attend college?

_____

2. Whether yes or no, how does that make you feel?

_____

_____

_____

_____

_____

Author's Experience   My mother was a direct descendent of slaves and moved with her parents from the Deep South at the age of 17. My father lived in an all-Black coal mining camp, into which my mother and her family moved in 1938. My father remained illiterate because he was not allowed to attend public schools in eastern Kentucky.

In the early 1960s my brother, my sister, and I were integrated into the White public schools. Physical violence and constant verbal harassment caused many other Blacks to forgo their education and opt for jobs in the coal mines at an early age. But my father remained constant in his advice to me: "It doesn't matter if they call you n____; but don't you ever let them beat you by walking out on your education." He would say to me, "Son, you will have opportunities that I never had. Just remember, when you do get that education, you'll never have to go in those coal mines and have them break your back. You can choose what you want to do, and then you can be a free man."

My parents, who could never provide me with monetary wealth, truly made me proud of them by giving me the gift of insight and an aspiration for achievement.

— Aaron Thompson

Think About It ——————————————— *Journal Entry* 10.7

1. What diverse groups do you see represented on your campus?

   _____

   _____

   _____

2. Are there groups on your campus that you did not expect to see or to see in such large numbers?

   _____

   _____

   _____

3. Are there groups on your campus that you expected to see but do not see or see in smaller numbers than you expected?

   _____

   _____

   _____

The Benefits of Experiencing Diversity

Diversity Promotes Self-Awareness

Learning from people with diverse backgrounds and experiences sharpens your self-knowledge and self-insight by allowing you to compare and contrast your life experiences with others whose life experiences differ sharply from your own. This comparative perspective gives you a reference point for viewing your own life, which places you in a better position to see more clearly how your unique cultural background has influenced the development of your personal beliefs, values, and lifestyle. By viewing your life in relation to the lives of others, you see more clearly what is distinctive about yourself and how you may be uniquely advantaged or disadvantaged.

When students around the country were interviewed about their diversity experiences in college, they reported that these experiences often helped them learn more about themselves and that their interactions with students from different races and ethnic groups produced "unexpected" or "jarring" self-insights (Light, 2001).

Remember

The more opportunities you create to learn from others who are different from yourself, the more opportunities you create to learn about yourself.

Diversity Stimulates Social Development

Interacting with people from various groups widens your social circle. By widening the pool of people with whom you have contact, you increase your capability and confidence in relating to people with varied life experiences, as well as your ability to converse with people on a wider range of topics. Just as seeking variety in what you eat provides greater stimulation to your taste buds, seeking variety in the people with whom you interact stimulates your social life and social skills. Research indicates that students who have more diversity experiences in college report higher levels of satisfaction with their college experience (Astin, 1993).

Diversity Enriches a College Education

Diversity magnifies the power of a college education because it helps liberate you from the tunnel vision of ethnocentric (culture-centered) and egocentric (self-centered) thinking, enabling you to get beyond yourself and your own culture to see yourself in relation to the world around you. Just as the various subjects you take in the college curriculum open your mind to multiple perspectives, so does your experience with people from varied backgrounds; it equips you with a wide-focus lens that allows you to take a multicultural perspective. A multicultural perspective helps you become aware of cultural "blind spots" and avoid the dangers of groupthink— the tendency for tight, like-minded groups of people to think so much alike that they overlook flaws in their own thinking that can lead to poor choices and faulty decisions (Janis, 1982).

Diversity Strengthens Learning and Critical Thinking

Research consistently shows that we learn more from people who are different from us than we do from people who are similar to us (Pascarella, 2001; Pascarella & Terenzini, 2005). When your brain encounters something that is unfamiliar or different than you're accustomed to, you must stretch beyond your mental comfort zone and work harder to understand it because doing so forces you to compare and contrast it to what you already know (Acredolo & O'Connor, 1991; Nagda, Gurin, & Johnson, 2005). This mental "stretch" requires the use of extra psychological effort and energy, which strengthens and deepens learning.

Diversity Promotes Creative Thinking

"When the only tool you have is a hammer, you tend to see every problem as a nail."

—Abraham Maslow, humanistic psychologist, best known for his self-actualization theory of achieving human potential

Experiences with diversity supply you with a broader base of knowledge and wider range of thinking styles that better enable you to think outside your own cultural box or boundaries. In contrast, limiting your number of cultural vantage points is akin to limiting the variety of mental tools you can use to solve new problems, thereby limiting your creativity.

Drawing on different ideas from people with diverse backgrounds and bouncing your ideas off them is a great way to generate energy, synergy, and serendipity—unanticipated discoveries and creative solutions. People who approach problems from diverse perspectives are more likely to look for and discover "multiple partial solutions" (Kelly, 1994). Diversity expands students' capacity for viewing issues or problems from multiple vantage points, equipping them with a wider variety of approaches to solving unfamiliar problems they may encounter in different contexts and situations.

Diversity Enhances Career Preparation and Success

Learning about and from diversity has a practical benefit: it better prepares you for the world of work. Whatever career you may choose to pursue, you are likely to find yourself working with employers, employees, co-workers, customers, and clients from diverse cultural backgrounds. America's workforce is now more diverse than at any other time in the nation's history, and it will grow ever more diverse. For example, the percentage of America's working-age population that represents members of minority groups is expected to grow from 34 percent in 2008 to 55 percent in 2050 (U.S. Bureau of Labor Statistics, 2008).

In addition to increasing diversity in America, today's work world is characterized by a global economy. Greater economic interdependence among nations, more international trading (imports and exports), more multinational corporations, and almost-instantaneous worldwide communication increasingly occur—thanks to advances in the World Wide Web (Dryden & Vos, 1999; Smith, 1994). Because of these trends, employers of college graduates now seek job candidates with the following skills and attributes: sensitivity to human differences, the ability to understand and relate to people from different cultural backgrounds, international knowledge, and foreign language skills (Fixman, 1990; National Association of Colleges & Employers, 2003; Office of Research, 1994; Smith, 1997). In one national survey, policymakers, business leaders, and employers all agreed that college graduates should be more than just "aware" or "tolerant" of diversity: they should have *experience* with diversity (Education Commission of the States, 1995).

"Empirical evidence shows that the actual effects on student development of emphasizing diversity and of student participation in diversity activities are overwhelmingly positive."

—Alexander Astin, *What Matters in College* (1993)

The wealth of diversity on college campuses today represents an unprecedented educational opportunity. You may never again be a member of a community that includes so many people from such a rich variety of backgrounds. Seize this opportunity! You're now in the right place at the right time to experience the people and programs that can infuse and enrich the quality of your college education with diversity.

Stumbling Blocks and Barriers to Experiencing Diversity

Stereotypes

The word *stereotype* derives from a combination of two roots: *stereo* (to look at in a fixed way) and *type* (to categorize or group together, as in the word *typical*). Thus, stereotyping is viewing individuals of the same type (group) in the same (fixed) way.

In effect, stereotyping ignores or disregards a person's individuality; all people who share a similar group characteristic (e.g., race or gender) are viewed as having the same personal characteristics, as in the expression, "You know what they are like; they're all the same." Stereotypes involve bias, which literally means "slant." A bias can be either positive or negative. Positive bias results in a favorable stereotype (e.g., "Italians are great lovers"); negative bias produces an unfavorable stereotype (e.g., "Italians are in the Mafia"). Snapshot Summary 10.3 lists some common stereotypes.

Snapshot Summary

10.3 Examples of Common Stereotypes

Muslims are terrorists.

Whites can't jump (or dance).

Blacks are lazy.

Asians are brilliant in math.

Irish are alcoholics.

Gay men are feminine; lesbian women are masculine.

Jews are cheap.

Hispanic men are abusive to women.

Men are strong.

Women are weak.

Think About It ———————————— *Journal Entry*  **10.8**

1. Have you ever been stereotyped, such as based on your appearance or group membership? If so, how did it make you feel and how did you react?

   _____

   _____

   _____

   _____

2. Have you ever unintentionally perceived or treated someone in terms of a group stereotype rather than as an individual? What assumptions did you make about that person? Was that person aware of, or affected by, your stereotyping?

   _____

   _____

   _____

   _____

Whether you are male or female, don't let gender stereotypes limit your career options.

Author's Experience When I was six years old, I was told by another six-year-old from a different racial group that all people of my race could not swim. That six-year-old happened to be of a different racial group. Since I could not swim at that time and she could, I assumed she was correct. I asked a boy, who happened to be of the same racial group as that little girl, if that statement were true; he responded: "Yes, it is true." Since I was from an area where few other African Americans were around to counteract this belief about Blacks, I bought into this stereotype for a long time until I finally took swimming lessons as an adult. I am now a lousy swimmer after many lessons because I did not even attempt to swim until I was an adult. The moral of this story is that group stereotypes can limit the confidence and potential of individuals who are members of the stereotyped group.

— *Aaron Thompson*

"Let us all hope that the dark clouds of racial prejudice will soon pass away and the deep fog of misunderstanding will be lifted from our fear-drenched communities, and in some not too distant tomorrow the radiant stars of love and brotherhood will shine over our great nation."
—Martin Luther King, Jr., civil rights activist and clergyman

Prejudice

If virtually all members of a stereotyped group are judged or evaluated in a negative way, the result is prejudice. (The word *prejudice* literally means to "pre-judge.") Technically, prejudice may be either positive or negative; however, the term is most often associated with a negative prejudgment or stigmatizing—associating inferior or unfavorable traits with people who belong to the same group. Thus, prejudice may be defined as a negative judgment, attitude, or belief about another person or group of people, which is formed before the facts are known. Stereotyping and prejudice often go hand in hand because individuals who are placed in a negatively stereotyped group are commonly prejudged in a negative way.

Someone with a prejudice toward a group typically avoids contact with individuals from that group. This enables the prejudice to continue unchallenged because there is little or no chance for the prejudiced person to have positive experiences with a member of the stigmatized group that could contradict or disprove the prejudice. Thus, a vicious cycle is established in which the prejudiced person continues to avoid contact with individuals from the stigmatized group, which, in turn, continues to maintain and reinforce the prejudice.

"'See that man over there?'
'Yes.'
'Well, I hate him.'
'But you don't know him.'
'That's why I hate him.'"
—Gordon Allport, *The Nature of Prejudice* (1954)

Discrimination

Literally translated, the term *discrimination* means "division" or "separation." Whereas prejudice involves a belief or opinion, discrimination involves an *action* taken toward others. Technically, discrimination can be either negative or positive—for example, a discriminating eater may be careful about eating only healthy foods. However, the term is most often associated with a negative action that results in a prejudiced person treating another person, or group of people, in an unfair way. Thus, it could be said that discrimination is prejudice put into action. Hate crimes are examples of extreme discrimination because they are acts motivated solely by prejudice against members of a stigmatized group. Victims of hate crimes may have their personal property damaged or they may be physically assaulted, sometimes referred to as "gay bashing" if the victim is a homosexual. Other forms of discrimination are more subtle and may take place without people being fully aware that they are discriminating. For example, evidence shows that some White, male college professors tend to treat female students and students from ethnic or racial minority groups differently than they do males and nonminority students. In particular, females and minority students in classes taught by White, male instructors tend to:

- Receive less eye contact from the instructor;
- Be called on less frequently in class;
- Be given less time to respond to questions asked by the instructor in class; and
- Have less contact with the instructor outside of class (Hall & Sandler, 1982, 1984; Sedlacek, 1987; Wright, 1987).

"A lot of us never asked questions in class before—it just wasn't done, especially by a woman or a girl, so we need to realize that and get into the habit of asking questions and challenging if we want to—regardless of the reactions of the profs and other students."
—Adult female college student (Wilkie & Thompson, 1993)

In most of these cases, the discriminatory treatment received by these female and minority students was subtle and not done consciously or deliberately by the instructors (Green, 1989). Nevertheless, these unintended actions are still discriminatory, and they may send a message to minority and female students that their ideas are not worth hearing or that they are not as capable as other students (Sadker & Sadker, 1994).

"The best way to beat prejudice is to show them. On a midterm, I got 40 points above the average. They all looked at me differently after that."
—Mexican American student (Nemko, 1988)

Think About It ————————————— *Journal Entry* **10.9**

Prejudice and discrimination can be subtle and only begin to surface when the social or emotional distance among members of different groups grows closer. Rate your level of comfort (high, moderate, or low) with the following situations.

Someone from another racial group:

1. Going to your school	high	moderate	low
2. Working in your place of employment	high	moderate	low
3. Living on your street as a neighbor	high	moderate	low

4. Living with you as a roommate	high	moderate	low
5. Socializing with you as a personal friend	high	moderate	low
6. Being your most intimate friend or romantic partner or	high	moderate	low
7. Being your partner in marriage	high	moderate	low

For any item you rated "low," what do you think was responsible for the low rating?

_____

_____

_____

_____

_____

_____

Snapshot Summary

10.4 Stereotypes and Prejudiced Belief Systems about Group Inferiority

- **Ableism.** Prejudice or discrimination toward people who are disabled or handicapped—physically, mentally, or emotionally. For example, someone shows ableism by avoiding interaction with handicapped people because of anxiety about not knowing what to say or how to act around them.
- **Ageism.** Prejudice or discrimination based on age, particularly toward the elderly. For example, an ageist might believe that all "old" people are bad drivers with bad memories.

"The Constitution of the United States knows no distinction between citizens on account of color."

—Frederick Douglass, abolitionist, author, advocate for equal rights for all people, and former slave

- **Anti-Semitism.** Prejudice or discrimination toward Jews or people who practice the religion of Judaism. For example, someone could claim to hate Jews because they're the ones who "killed Christ."
- **Classism.** Prejudice or discrimination based on social class, particularly toward people of low socioeconomic status. For example, a classist might focus only on the contributions made by politicians and wealthy industrialists to America, ignoring the contributions of poor immigrants, farmers, slaves, and pioneer women.

- **Ethnocentrism.** Considering one's own culture or ethnic group to be "central" or "normal," and viewing different cultures as "deficient" or "inferior." For example, people who are ethnocentric might claim that another culture is "weird" or "abnormal" for eating certain animals that they consider unethical to eat, even though they eat certain animals that the other culture would consider unethical to eat.

Student Perspective

"I would like to change the entire world, so that we wouldn't be segregated by continents and territories."

—College sophomore

- **Genocide.** Mass murdering of one group by another group. An example is the Holocaust during World War II, in which millions of Jews were murdered. Other examples include the murdering of Cambodians under the Khmer Rouge, the murdering of Bosnian Muslims in the former country of Yugoslavia, and the slaughter of the Tutsi minority by the Hutu majority in Rwanda.

- **Heterosexism.** Belief that heterosexuality is the only acceptable sexual orientation. For example, using the slang "fag" or "queer" as an insult or put-down or believing that gays should not have the same legal rights and opportunities as heterosexuals shows heterosexism.
- **Homophobia.** Extreme fear or hatred of homosexuals. For example, people who engage in gay bashing (acts of violence toward gays) or who create and contribute to antigay Web sites show homophobia.
- **Nationalism.** Excessive interest and belief in the strengths of one's own nation without acknowledging its mistakes or weaknesses, the needs of other nations, or the common interests of all nations. For example, "blind patriotism" blinds people to the shortcomings of their own nation, causing patriots to view any questioning or criticism of their nation as disloyalty or "unpatriotic" (as in the slogans "America: right or wrong" and "America: love it or leave it!").

- **Racism.** Prejudice or discrimination based on skin color. For example, Cecil Rhodes (Englishman and empire builder of British South Africa), once claimed, "We [the British] are the finest race in the world and the more of the world we inhabit the better it is for the human race." Currently, racism is exemplified by the Ku Klux Klan, a domestic terrorist group that believes in the supremacy of the White race and considers all other races to be inferior.
- **Regionalism.** Prejudice or discrimination based on the geographical region of a nation in which an individual has been born and raised. For example, a Northerner might think that all Southerners are racists.
- **Religious bigotry.** Denying the fundamental human right of other people to hold religious beliefs or to hold religious beliefs that differ from one's own. For example, an atheist might force nonreligious (secular) beliefs on others, or a member of a religious group may believe that people who hold different religious beliefs are immoral or sinners.
- **Sexism.** Prejudice or discrimination based on sex or gender. For example, a sexist might believe that no one should vote for a female president because she would be too "emotional."
- **Terrorism.** Intentional acts of violence against civilians that are motivated by political or religious prejudice. An example would be the September 11, 2001, attacks on the United States.
- **Xenophobia.** Extreme fear or hatred of foreigners, outsiders, or strangers. For example, someone might believe that all immigrants should be kept out of the country because they will increase the crime rate.

Think About It ——————— *Journal Entry* 10.10

1. Have you ever held a prejudice against a particular group of people?

_____

2. If you have, what was the group, and how do you think your prejudice developed?

_____

_____

_____

_____

_____

_____

The following practices and strategies may be used to accept and appreciate individuals from other groups toward whom you may hold prejudices, stereotypes, or subtle biases that bubble beneath the surface of your conscious awareness:

1. **Consciously avoid preoccupation with physical appearances.** Go deeper and get beneath the superficial surface of appearances to judge people not in terms of how they look, but in terms of who they are and how they act. Remember the old proverb "It's what's inside that counts." Judge others by the quality of their personal character, not by the familiarity of their physical characteristics.
2. **Perceive each person with whom you interact as a unique human being.** Make a conscious effort to see each person with whom you interact not merely as a member of a group, but as a unique individual. Form your impressions of each person case by case rather than by using some rule of thumb.

This may seem like an obvious and easy thing to do, but research shows that humans have a natural tendency to perceive and conceive of individuals who are members of unfamiliar groups as being more alike (or all alike) than members of their own group (Taylor, Peplau, & Sears, 2006). Thus, you may have to consciously resist this tendency to overgeneralize and "lump together" individuals into homogeneous groups and make an intentional attempt to focus on treating each person you interact with as a unique human.

> **Remember**
>
> *While it is valuable to learn about different cultures and the common characteristics shared by members of the same culture, differences exist among individuals who share the same culture. Don't assume that all individuals from the same cultural background share the same personal characteristics.*

Interacting and Collaborating with Members of Diverse Groups

Once you overcome your biases and begin to perceive members of diverse groups as unique individuals, you are positioned to take the next step of interacting, collaborating, and forming friendships with them. Interpersonal contact between diverse people takes you beyond multicultural awareness and moves you up to a higher level of diversity appreciation that involves intercultural interaction. When you take this step to cross cultural boundaries, you transform diversity appreciation from a value or belief system into an observable action and way of living.

Your initial comfort level with interacting with people from diverse groups is likely to depend on how much experience you have had with diversity before college. If you have had little or no prior experience interacting with members of diverse groups, it may be more challenging for you to initiate interactions with diverse students on campus.

However, if you have had little or no previous experience with diversity, the good news is that you have the most to gain from experiencing diversity. Research consistently shows that when humans experience social interaction that differs radically from their prior experiences, they gain the most in terms of learning and cognitive development (Piaget, 1985; Acredolo & O'Connor, 1991).

Think About It —————————————— *Journal Entry* 10.11

Rate the amount or variety of diversity you have experienced in the following settings:

1. The high school you attended   high   moderate   low
2. The college or university you now attend   high   moderate   low
3. The neighborhood in which you grew up   high   moderate   low
4. Places where you have worked or been employed   high   moderate   low

Which setting had the most and which had the least diversity?

_____

_____

_____

What do you think accounts for this difference?

_____

_____

_____

_____

_____

_____

What follows is a series of strategies for meeting and interacting with people from diverse backgrounds:

1. **Intentionally create opportunities for interaction and conversation with individuals from diverse groups.** Consciously resist the natural tendency to associate only with people who are similar to you. One way to do this is by intentionally placing yourself in situations where individuals from diverse groups are nearby and potential interaction can take place. Research indicates that meaningful interactions and friendships are more likely to form among people who are in physical proximity to one another (Latané, Liu, Nowak, Bonevento, & Zheng, 1993). Studies show that stereotyping and prejudice can be sharply reduced if contact between members of different racial or ethnic groups is frequent enough to allow time for the development of friendships (Pettigrew, 1998). You can create this condition in the college classroom by sitting near students from different ethnic or racial groups or by joining them if you are given the choice to select whom you will work with in class discussion groups and group projects.

2. **Take advantage of the Internet to "chat" with students from diverse groups on your campus or with students in different countries.** Electronic communication can be a more convenient and more comfortable way to initially interact with members of diverse groups with whom you have had little prior experience.

After you've communicated successfully *online*, you may then feel more comfortable about interacting with them *in person*. Online and in-person interaction with students from other cultures and nations can give you a better understanding of your own culture and country, as well as increase awareness of its customs and values that you may have taken for granted (Bok, 2006).

3. **Seek out the views and opinions of classmates from diverse backgrounds.** For example, during or after class discussions, ask students from different backgrounds if there was any point made or position taken in class that they would strongly question or challenge. Seeking out divergent (diverse) viewpoints has been found to be one of the best ways to develop critical thinking skills (Kurfiss, 1988).

4. **Join or form discussion groups with students from diverse backgrounds.** You can gain exposure to diverse perspectives by joining or forming groups of students who differ from you in terms of such characteristics as gender, age, race, or ethnicity. You might begin by forming discussion groups composed of students who differ in one way but are similar in another way. For instance, form a learning group of students who have the same major as you do but who differ with respect to race, ethnicity, or age. This strategy gives the diverse members of your group some common ground for discussion (your major) and can raise your group's awareness that although you may be members of different groups, you can, at the same time, be similar with respect to your educational goals and life plans.

Remember

Including diversity in your discussion groups not only provides social variety, but also promotes the quality of the group's thinking by allowing its members to gain access to the diverse perspectives and life experiences of people from different backgrounds.

5. **Form collaborative learning teams.** A learning team is more than a discussion group or a study group. It moves beyond discussion to collaborative learning—in other words, members of a learning team "colabor" (work together) as part of a joint and mutually supportive effort to reach the same goal. Studies show that when individuals from different ethnic and racial groups work collaboratively toward the attainment of a common goal, it reduces racial prejudice and promotes interracial friendships (Allport, 1954; Amir, 1976). These positive findings may be explained as follows: if individuals from diverse groups work together on the same team, no one is a member of an "out" group: instead, all are members of the same "in" group (Pratto et al., 2000; Sidanius et al., 2000).

Summary and Conclusion

Diversity refers to differences among groups of people who, together, comprise humanity. Experiencing diversity enhances our appreciation of the unique features of different cultures, and it provides us with a larger perspective on those aspects of the human experience that are common to all people, no matter what their particular cultural background happens to be.

Culture is a distinctive pattern of beliefs and values learned by a group of people who share the same social heritage and traditions. A major advantage of culture is that it helps bind groups of people into supportive, tight-knit communities. However, it can also lead its members to view the world solely through their own cultural lens, known as ethnocentrism, which can blind them from seeing the world and from taking on other cultural perspectives. Ethnocentrism can contribute to stereotyping—viewing individual members of the same group in the same way and thinking they all have similar personal characteristics.

If members of a stereotyped group are judged or evaluated in a negative way, the result is prejudice—a negative prejudgment about another person or group of people, which is formed before the facts are known. Stereotyping and prejudice often go hand in hand because if the stereotype is negative, individual members of the stereotyped group are then prejudged in a negative way. Discrimination takes prejudice one step further by converting the negative prejudgment into action that results in unfair treatment of others. Thus, discrimination is prejudice put into action.

If stereotyping and prejudice are overcome, you are then positioned to experience diversity and reap its multiple benefits, which include sharpened self-awareness, social stimulation, broadened personal perspectives, deeper learning and higher-level thinking, and career success.

College campuses today have such diversity that the educational opportunities available are unprecedented. This may be the only time in your life when you are part of an organization or community that includes so many diverse members. Seize this unique opportunity to experience the diversity of people and programs available to you and profit from the power of diversity.

Learning More through the World Wide Web

Internet-Based Resources for Further Information on Diversity

For additional information related to the ideas discussed in this chapter, we recommend the following Web sites:

www.tolerance.org

www.amnesty.org

www.amnesty.org/en/universal-declaration-human-rights-anniversary/declaration-text

10.1 Multigroup Self-Awareness

You can be members of multiple groups at the same time, and your membership in these groups can influence your personal development and self-identity. In the figure that follows, consider the shaded center circle to be yourself and the six nonshaded circles to be six groups you belong to that you think have influenced your personal development or personal identity.

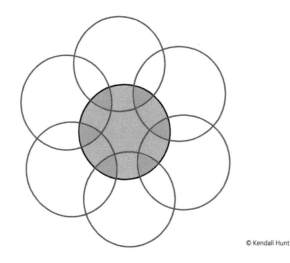

© Kendall Hunt

Fill in the nonshaded circles with the names of groups to which you belong that have had the most influence on your personal development. You can use the diversity spectrum that appears on the first page of this chapter to help you identify different groups. Do not feel you have to come up with six groups and fill all six circles. What is more important is to identify those groups that have had a significant influence on your personal development or identity.

Self-Assessment Questions

1. Which one of your groups has had the greatest influence on your personal identity, and why?

2. Have you ever felt limited or disadvantaged by being a member of any group or groups?

3. Have you ever felt that you experienced advantages or privileges because of your membership in any group or groups?

10.2 Switching Group Identity

Imagine you were to be born again as a member of a different racial or ethnic group.

1. What group would you want it to be? Why?

2. With your new group identity, what things would change in your personal life?

3. What things would remain the same in your life even though your group identity has changed?

Source: Adapted from University of New Hampshire Office of Residential Life (2001).

10.3 Intercultural Interview

Find a student, faculty member, or administrator on campus whose cultural background is different from yours, and ask if you can interview that person about his or her culture. Use the following questions in your interview:

1. How is "family" defined in your culture, and what are the traditional roles and responsibilities of different family members?

2. What are the traditional gender (male vs. female) roles associated with your culture? Are they changing?

3. What is your culture's approach to time? (Is there an emphasis on punctuality? Is doing things fast valued or frowned upon?)

4. What are your culture's staple foods or favorite foods?

5. What cultural traditions or rituals are highly valued and commonly practiced?

6. What special holidays are celebrated?

10.4 Hidden Bias Test

Go to www.tolerance.org/activity/test-yourself-hidden-bias and take one or more of the hidden bias tests on the Web site. These tests assess subtle bias with respect to gender, age, Native Americans, African Americans, Asian Americans, religious denominations, sexual orientations, disabilities, and body weight. You can assess whether you have a bias toward any of these groups.

Self-Assessment Questions

1. Did the results reveal any bias that you were unaware of?

2. Did you think the assessment results were accurate or valid?

3. What do you think best accounts for or explains your results?

4. If your parents and best friends took the test, how do you think their results would compare with yours?

Hate Crime: A Racially Motivated Murder

Jasper County, Texas, has a population of approximately 31,000 people. In this county, 80 percent of the people are White, 18 percent are Black, and 2 percent are of other races. The county's poverty rate is considerably higher than the national average, and its average household income is significantly lower. In 1998, the mayor, president of the Chamber of Commerce, and two councilmen were Black. From the outside, Jasper appeared to be a town with racial harmony, and its Black and White leaders were quick to state there was racial harmony in Jasper.

However, on June 7, 1998, James Byrd Jr., a 49-year-old African American male, was walking home along a road one evening and was offered a ride by three White males. Rather than taking Byrd home, Lawrence Brewer (31), John King (23), and Shawn Berry (23), three individuals linked to White supremacist groups, took Byrd to an isolated area and began beating him. They then dropped his pants to his ankles, painted his face black, chained Byrd to their truck, and dragged him for approximately three miles. The truck was driven in a zigzag fashion to inflict maximum pain on the victim. Byrd was decapitated after his body collided with a culvert in a ditch alongside the road. His skin, arms, genitalia, and other body parts were strewn along the road, while his torso was found dumped in front of a Black cemetery. Medical examiners testified that Byrd was alive for much of the dragging incident.

While in prison awaiting trial, Brewer wrote letters to King and other inmates. In one letter, Brewer wrote: "Well, I did it and am no longer a virgin. It was a rush and I'm still licking my lips for more." Once the trials were completed, Brewer and King were sentenced to death. Both Brewer and King, whose bodies were covered with racist tattoos, had been on parole before the incident, and they had previously been cellmates. King had spent an extensive amount of time in prison, where he began to associate with White males in an environment in which each race was pitted against the other.

As a result of the murder, Byrd's family created the James Byrd Foundation for Racial Healing in 1998. On January 20, 1999, a wrought iron fence that separated Black and White graves for more than 150 years in Jasper Cemetery was removed in a special unity service. Members of the racist Ku Klux Klan have since visited the gravesite of Byrd several times, leaving racist stickers and other marks that have angered the Jasper community and Byrd's family.

Sources: *San Antonio Express News* (September 17, 1999), *Louisiana Weekly* (February 3, 2003), *Houston Chronicle* (June 14, 1998).

Discussion Questions

1. What factors do you think were responsible for causing this incident to take place?

2. Could this incident have been prevented? If yes, how? If no, why not?

3. What do you think will be the long-term effects of this incident on the town?

4. How likely do you think it is that an incident like this could take place in your hometown or near your college campus?

5. If this event took place in your hometown, how would you and members of your family and community react?

Chapter 10 Reflection

After reading this chapter, has your definition of *diversity* changed? Explain.

List and describe five ways appreciating diversity will assist you in being successful in college and/or in life.

1.

2.

3.

4.

5.

Are there any areas of diversity you feel you need to be more comfortable with? What are the areas and HOW will you become more comfortable with them?

Financial Literacy

Managing Money and Minimizing Debt: Balancing Saving, Spending, Learning, and Earning

11

LEARNING GOAL

To become more self-aware, knowledgeable, and strategic with respect to managing your money and financing your college education.

Complete the following sentence with the first thought that comes to your mind:

For me, money is . . .

_____

_____

_____

_____

_____

_____

In addition to managing time, a personal resource you need to manage to be successful in college (and life) is money. Managing time and managing money have a lot in common. Both require self-awareness of how these resources are spent; both can be saved, or else you could run out of either one of them. Poor time management can also cost people money. For example, a report from H & R Block indicates that procrastinating on filing tax returns costs Americans an average of $400 a year due to errors resulting from last-minute rushing to meet the deadline (Kasper, 2004). How you spend your time and money often represents the true test of what really matters to you and what you truly value.

Beginning college often means the beginning of greater personal independence and greater demands for economic self-sufficiency, critical thinking about consumerism, and effective management of personal finances. The importance of money management for college students is growing for two major reasons. One is the rising cost of a college education, which is causing more students to work while in college and to work more hours per week (Levine & Cureton, 1998). The rising cost of a college education is also requiring students to make more complex decisions about what options (or combination of options) they will use to meet their college expenses. Unfortunately, research indicates that many students today are not choosing financial strategies that contribute most effectively to their educational success in college and their long-term financial success after college (King, 2005).

From *Thriving in the Community College & Beyond*, Second Edition by Joseph B. Cuseo, Aaron Thompson, Julie A. McLaughlin, and Steady H. Moono. Copyright © 2013 by Kendall Hunt Publishing Company. Reprinted by permission.

A second reason money management is growing in importance for college students is the availability and convenience of credit cards. For students today, credit cards are easy to get, easy to use, and easy to abuse. College students can do everything right, such as getting solid grades, getting involved on campus, and getting work experience before graduating, but a poor credit history due to irresponsible use of credit cards in college can reduce students' chances of obtaining credit after college and their chances of being hired after graduation. Credit reporting agencies or bureaus collect information about how well you make credit card payments and report your credit score to credit card companies and banks. Potential employers will check your credit score as an indicator or predictor of how responsible you will be as an employee because of a statistical relationship between using a credit card responsibly and being a responsible employee. Thus, being irresponsible with credit while you're in college can affect your ability to land a job after (or during) college. Your credit score report will also affect your likelihood of qualifying for car loans and home loans, as well as your ability to rent an apartment (Pratt, 2008).

Furthermore, research indicates that accumulating high levels of debt while in college is associated with higher levels of stress (Kiecolt et al., 1986), lower academic performance (Susswein, 1995), and greater risk of withdrawing from college (Ring, 1997). On the positive side of the ledger, studies show that when students learn to use effective money-management strategies, they can decrease unnecessary spending, prevent accumulation of significant debt, and reduce personal stress (Health & Soll, 1996; Walker, 1996).

"If we command our wealth, we shall be rich and free; if our wealth commands us, we are poor indeed."

—Edmund Burke, 18th-century author, political philosopher, and supporter of the American Revolution

Student Perspective

"My money-management skills are poor. If I have money, I will spend it unless somebody takes it away from me. I am the kind of person who lives from paycheck to paycheck."

—First-year student

Strategies for Managing Money Effectively

Developing Financial Self-Awareness

Developing any good habit begins with the critical first step of self-awareness. Developing the habit of effective money management begins with awareness of your cash flow—the amount of money you have flowing in and flowing out. As illustrated in Figure 11.1, cash flow can be tracked by:

- Watching how much money you have coming in (income) versus going out (expenses or expenditures); and
- Watching how much money you have accumulated but not spent (savings) versus how much money you've borrowed but not paid back (debt).

FIGURE 11.1

Income ←——→ Expenses

Savings ←——→ Debt

Two Key Avenues of Cash Flow

Income for college students typically comes from one or more of the following sources:

- Scholarships or grants, which don't have to be paid back
- Loans, which must be repaid
- Salary earned from part-time or full-time work
- Personal savings
- Gifts or other forms of monetary support from parents and other family members

Your sources of expenses or expenditures may be classified into three categories:

1. **Basic needs or essential necessities.** Expenses that tend to be fixed because you cannot do without them (e.g., expenses for food, housing, tuition, textbooks, phone, transportation to and from school, and health-related costs).

2. **Incidentals or extras.** Expenses that tend to be flexible because spending money on them is optional or discretionary (i.e., you choose to spend at your own discretion or judgment); these expenses typically include:

   a. Money spent on entertainment, enjoyment, or pleasure (e.g., music, movies, and spring-break vacations); and

   b. Money spent primarily for reasons of promoting personal status or self-image (e.g., buying expensive brand-name products, fashionable clothes, jewelry, and other personal accessories).

3. **Emergency expenses.** Unpredicted, unforeseen, or unexpected costs (e.g., money paid for doctor visits and medicine resulting from illnesses or accidents, your car breaking down).

Think About It ———————————— *Journal Entry* **11.2**

1. What do you estimate to be your two or three most expensive incidentals (optional purchases)?

   _____

   _____

   _____

2. Do you think you should reduce these expenses or eliminate them altogether? Explain.

   _____

   _____

   _____

3. How can you do this?

   _____

   _____

   _____

Developing a Money-Management Plan

Once you're aware of the amount of money you have coming in (and from what sources) and the amount of money you're spending (and for what reasons), the next step is to develop a plan for managing your cash flow. The bottom line is to ensure that the money coming in (income) is equal to or greater than the money going out (expenses). If the amount of money you're spending exceeds the amount you have coming in, you're "in the red" or have negative cash flow.

Student
Perspective

"I keep track of my money on Excel."

—First-year student

Strategic Selection and Use of Financial Tools for Tracking Cash Flow

Several financial tools or instruments can be used to track your cash flow and manage your money. These cash-flow instruments include:

- Checking accounts
- Credit cards
- Debit cards

Checking Account

Long before credit cards were created, a checking account was the method most people used to keep track of their money. Many people still use checking accounts in addition to (or instead of) credit cards.

A checking account may be obtained from a bank or credit union; its typical costs include a deposit ($20 to $25) to open the account, a monthly service fee (e.g., $10), and small fees for checks. Some banks charge customers a service fee based on the number of checks written, which is a good option if you don't plan to write many checks each month. If you maintain a high enough balance of money deposited in your account, the bank may not charge any extra fees, and if you're able to maintain an even higher balance, the bank may also pay you interest—known as an interest-bearing checking account.

Along with your checking account, banks usually provide you with an automatic teller machine (ATM) card that you can use to get cash. Look for a checking account that does not charge you fees for ATM transactions but provides this as a free service with your account. Also, look for a checking account that doesn't charge you if your balance drops below a certain minimum figure.

Strategies for Using Checking Accounts Effectively

- Whenever you write a check or make an ATM withdrawal, immediately subtract its amount from your balance—i.e., the amount of money remaining in your account—to determine your new balance.
- Keep a running balance in your checkbook to ensure that you know exactly how much money you have in your account at all times. This will reduce the risk that you'll write a check that "bounces" (i.e., a check that you don't have enough money in the bank to cover). If you do bounce a check, you'll probably have to pay a charge to the bank and possibly to the business that attempted to cash your bounced check.
- Double-check your checkbook balance with each monthly statement you receive from the bank. Be sure to include the service charges your bank makes to your account that appear on your monthly statement. This practice will make it easier to track errors—on either your part or the bank's part. (Banks can and do make mistakes occasionally.)

Advantages of a Checking Account

A checking account has several advantages:

- You can carry checks instead of cash.
- You have access to cash at almost any time through an ATM.

- It allows you to keep a visible track record of income and expenses in your checkbook.
- A properly managed checking account can serve as a good credit reference for future loans and purchases.

Credit Card (e.g., MasterCard®, Visa®, or Discover®)

A credit card is basically money loaned to you by the credit card company that issues you the card, which you pay back to the company monthly. You can pay the whole bill or a portion of the bill each month—as long as some minimum payment is made. However, for any remaining (unpaid) portion of your bill, you are charged a high interest rate, which is usually about 18 percent. This results in your paying much more for the item than it is actually worth.

Strategies for Selecting a Credit Card

If you decide to use a credit card, pay attention to its annual percentage rate (APR). This is the interest rate you pay for previously unpaid monthly balances, and it can vary depending on the credit card company. Credit card companies also vary in terms of their annual service fees. You will likely find companies that charge higher interest rates tend to charge lower annual fees, and vice versa. As a general rule, if you expect to pay the full balance every month, you're probably better off choosing a credit card that does not charge you an annual service fee. On the other hand, if you think you'll need more time to make the full monthly payments, you may be better off with a credit card company that offers a low interest rate.

Another feature that differentiates one credit card company from another is whether or not you're allowed a "grace period"—i.e., a certain period of time after you receive your monthly statement during which you can pay back the company without paying added interest fees. Some companies may allow you a grace period of a full month, while others may provide none and begin charging interest immediately after you fail to pay on the bill's due date.

Credit cards may also differ in terms of their credit limit (a.k.a. a credit line or line of credit), which refers to the maximum amount of money the credit card company will make available to you. If you are a new customer, most companies will set a credit limit beyond which you will not be granted any additional credit.

Advantages of a Credit Card

If a credit card is used responsibly, it has some key advantages as a money-management tool. Its features can provide the following advantages:

- It helps you track your spending habits because the credit card company sends you a monthly statement that includes an itemized list of all your card-related purchases. This list provides you with a paper trail of *what* you purchased that month and *when* you purchased it.
- It provides the convenience of making purchases online, which may save you some time and money that would otherwise be spent traveling to and from stores.
- It allows access to cash whenever and wherever you need it, because any bank or ATM that displays your credit card's symbol will give you cash up to a certain limit, usually for a small transaction fee. Keep in mind that some credit card companies charge a higher interest rate for cash advances than purchases.

- It enables you to establish a personal credit history. If you use a credit card responsibly, you can establish a good credit history that can be used later in life for big-ticket purchases such as a car or home. In effect, responsible use of a credit card shows others from whom you wish to seek credit (borrow money) that you're financially responsible.

> **Remember**
>
> *Do not buy into the belief that the only way you can establish a good credit history is by using a credit card. It's not your only option; you can establish a good credit history through responsible use of a checking account and by paying your bills on time.*

Strategies for Using Credit Cards Responsibly

While there may be advantages to using a credit card, you only reap those advantages if you use your card strategically. If not, the advantages of a credit card will be quickly and greatly outweighed by its disadvantages. Listed here are some key strategies for using a credit card in a way that maximizes its advantages and minimizes its disadvantages.

1. **Use a credit card only as a convenience for making purchases and tracking the purchases you make; do not use it as a tool for obtaining a long-term loan.** A credit card's main money-management advantage is that it allows you to make purchases with plastic instead of cash. The credit card allows you the convenience of not carrying around cash and enables you to receive a monthly statement of your purchases from the credit card company, which makes it easier for you to track and analyze your spending habits.

   The "credit" provided by a credit card should be seen simply as a short-term loan that must be paid back at the end of every month.

> **Remember**
>
> *Do not use credit cards for long-term credit or long-term loans because their interest rates are outrageously high. Paying such a high rate of interest for a loan represents an ineffective (and irresponsible) money-management strategy.*

2. **Limit yourself to one card.** The average college student has 2.8 credit cards (United College Marketing Service, as cited in Pratt, 2008). More than one credit card just means more accounts to keep track of and more opportunities to accumulate debt. You don't need additional credit cards from department stores, gas stations, or any other profit-making business because they duplicate what your personal credit card already does (plus they charge extremely high interest rates for late payments).

3. **Pay off your balance each month in full and on time.** If you pay the full amount of your bill each month, this means that you're using your credit card effectively to obtain an interest-free, short-term (one-month) loan. You're just paying principal—the total amount of money borrowed and nothing more. However, if your payment is late and you need to pay interest, you end up paying more for the items you purchased than their actual ticket price. For instance, if you have an unpaid balance of $500 on your monthly credit card bill for merchandise purchased the previous month and you are charged the typical 18 percent credit card interest rate for late payment, you end up paying $590: $500 (merchandise) + $90 (18 percent interest to the credit card company).

Credit card companies make their money or profit from the interest they collect from cardholders who do not pay back their credit on time. Just as procrastinating about doing your work is a poor time-management habit, procrastinating about paying your credit card bills is a poor money-management habit that can cost you dearly in the long run because of the high interest rate you pay.

Pay your total balance on time and avoid paying these huge interest rates to credit card companies, which allow them to get rich at your expense. If you cannot pay the total amount owed at the end of the month, pay off as much of it as you possibly can, rather than making the minimum monthly payment. If you keep making only the minimum payment each month and continue using your credit card, you'll begin to pile up huge amounts of debt.

Remember

If you keep charging on your credit card while you have an unpaid balance or debt, you no longer have a grace period to pay back your charges: instead, interest is charged immediately on all your purchases.

Snapshot Summary

11.1 Credit Cardholders' Bill of Rights Act of 2009

Congress passed legislation in 2009 that enacted certain protections for consumers who use credit cards. Here are the specific reforms that affect college students:

- Creditors are forbidden from offering credit to consumers under the age of 18 (unless they are emancipated under state law, or the consumer's parent or legal guardian is the primary account holder).
- College students without a cosigner will have their credit line limited to the greater amount of 20 percent of their annual gross income or $500. The collective amount of credit available on all credit cards will be limited to 30 percent of the student's annual gross income.
- Creditors are not allowed to open a credit-card account for a college student who does not have a verifiable annual gross income or already has a credit-card account with that creditor or any of its affiliates (Chan, 2009).

Think About It ———————— Journal Entry 11.3

1. Do you have a credit card? Do you have more than one?

   _____

2. If you have at least one credit card, do you pay off your entire balance each month?

   _____

3. If you don't pay off your entire balance each month, what would you say is your average unpaid balance per month?

   _____

4. What changes would you have to make in your money-management habits to be able to pay off your entire balance each month?

   _____

   _____

Debit Card

A debit card looks almost identical to a credit card (e.g., it has a MasterCard or Visa logo), but it works differently. When you use a debit card, money is immediately taken out or subtracted from your checking account. Thus, you're only using money that's already in your account (rather than borrowing money), and you don't receive a bill at the end of the month. If you attempt to purchase something with a debit card that costs more than the amount of money you have in your account, your card will not allow you to do so. Just like a bounced check, a debit card will not permit you to pay out any money that is not in your account. Like a check or ATM withdrawal, a purchase made with a debit card should immediately be subtracted from your balance.

Like a credit card, a major advantage of the debit card is that it provides you with the convenience of "plastic"; unlike a credit card, it prevents you from spending beyond your means and accumulating debt. For this reason, financial advisors often recommend using a debit card rather than a credit card (Knox, 2004; Tyson, 2003).

Snapshot Summary

11.2 Financial Literacy: Understanding the Language of Money Management

As you can tell from the number of financial terms used in this chapter, there is a fiscal vocabulary or language that we need to master in order to fully understand our financial options and transactions. In other words, we need to become *financially literate*. As you read the financial terms listed below, place a checkmark next to any term whose meaning you didn't already know.

Account. A formal business arrangement in which a bank provides financial services to a customer (e.g., checking account or savings account).

Annual percentage rate (APR). The interest rate that must be paid when monthly credit card balances are not paid in full.

Balance. The amount of money in a person's account or the amount of unpaid debt.

Bounced check. A check written for a greater amount of money than the amount contained in a personal checking account, which typically requires the person to pay a charge to the bank and possibly to the business that attempted to cash the bounced check.

Budget. A plan for coordinating income and expenses to ensure that sufficient money is available to cover personal expenses or expenditures.

Cash flow. Amount of money flowing in (income) and flowing out (expenses). "Negative cash flow" occurs when the amount of money going out exceeds the amount coming in.

Credit. Money obtained with the understanding that it will be paid back, either with or without interest.

Credit line (a.k.a. credit limit). The maximum amount of money (credit) made available to a borrower.

Debt. Amount of money owed.

Default. Failure to meet a financial obligation (e.g., a student who fails to repay a college loan "defaults" on that loan).

Emergency student loan. Immediate, interest-free loans provided by a college or university to help financially strapped students cover short-term expenses (e.g., cost of textbooks) or deal with financial emergencies (e.g., accidents and illnesses). Emergency student loans are typically granted within 24–48 hours, sometimes even the same day, and usually need to be repaid within two months.

Deferred student payment plan. A plan that allows student borrowers to temporarily defer or postpone loan payments for some acceptable reason (e.g., to pursue an internship or to do volunteer work after college).

Estimated family contribution (EFC). The amount of money the government has determined a family can contribute to the educational costs of the family member who is attending college.

Fixed interest rate. A loan with an interest rate that will remain the same for the entire term of the loan.

Grace period. The amount of time after a monthly credit card statement has been issued during which the credit card holder can pay back the company without paying added interest fees.

Grant. Money received that doesn't have to be repaid.

Gross income. Income generated before taxes and other expenses are deducted.

Insurance premium. The amount paid in regular installments to an insurance company to remain insured.

Interest. The amount of money paid to a customer for deposited money (as in a bank account) or money paid by a customer for borrowed money (e.g., interest on a loan). Interest is usually calculated as a percentage of the total amount of money deposited or borrowed.

Interest-bearing account. A bank account that earns interest if the customer keeps a sufficiently large sum of money in the bank.

Loan consolidation. Consolidating (combining) separate student loans into one larger loan to make the process of tracking, budgeting, and repayment easier. Loan consolidation typically requires the borrower to pay slightly more interest.

Loan premium. The amount of money loaned without interest.

Merit-based scholarship. Money awarded to a student on the basis of performance or achievement that doesn't have to be repaid.

Need-based scholarship. Money awarded to a student on the basis of financial need that doesn't have to be repaid.

Net income. Money earned or remaining after all expenses and taxes have been paid.

Principal. The total amount of money borrowed or deposited, not counting interest.

Variable interest rate. An interest rate on a loan that can vary or be changed by the lender.

Yield. Revenue or profit produced by an investment beyond the original amount invested. For example, the higher lifetime income and other monetary benefits acquired from a college education that exceed the amount of money invested in or spent on a college education.

Think About It — Journal Entry 11.4

1. Which of the terms in the above list were new to you?

_____

_____

2. Do any of these terms apply to your current financial situation or money-management plans? Explain.

_____

_____

_____

_____

_____

_____

Sources of Income for Financing Your College Education

Free Application for Federal Student Aid (FAFSA)

The Free Application for Federal Student Aid (FAFSA) is the application used by the U.S. Department of Education to determine aid eligibility for students. A formula is used to determine each student's estimated family contribution (EFC), which is the amount of money the government has determined a family can contribute to the educational costs of the student. No fee is charged to complete the application, and you should complete it annually to determine your eligibility to receive financial aid, whether you believe you are eligible or not. See the Financial Aid Office on your campus for the FAFSA form and for help in completing the form.

Scholarships

Scholarships are available from many sources, including the institution you choose to attend. They are awarded based on various criteria that may include a written essay, ACT or SAT scores, and high school grade point average (GPA). In addition to academic scholarships, scholarships are awarded based on organizations you may have been a part of, race or ethnicity, the region of the country you live in, athletics, artistic talents, and so on. It is important to remember that all scholarships are competitive and deadlines are observed by the awarding agencies or institutions. Be aware of the application material deadlines and submit your materials well in advance of these deadlines.

You should contact the Financial Aid Office of the institution you are attending to find available scholarships. You can also conduct an Internet search to find many sites that offer scholarship information (like www.fastweb.com), but it is important to remember that you should not enter credit card or bank account information on any site.

Grants

Grants are considered to be gift aid, which typically does not have to be repaid. About two-thirds of all college students receive grant aid, which, on average, reduces their tuition bills by more than half. The Federal Pell Grant is the largest grant program; it provides need-based aid to low-income undergraduate students. The amount of the grant depends on criteria such as: (1) the anticipated contribution of the family to the student's education (EFC), (2) the cost of the postsecondary institution that the student is attending, and (3) the enrollment status of the student (part-time or full-time). Even though grants do not need to be paid back, students must maintain certain academic standards to remain eligible to receive their grant money.

Veterans' Benefits

If you are currently a veteran, you may be eligible for the GI Bill benefits.

What Is the Montgomery GI Bill–Active Duty?

The Montgomery GI Bill–Active Duty, called MGIB for short, provides up to 36 months of education benefits to eligible veterans. Benefits may include, but are not limited to, tuition and fees, a housing allowance, and a books and supplies stipend. Veterans must maintain certain academic standards to receive the benefits. Visit the Office of Veterans Affairs on your campus to get more information (see the following Web site for more detail: http://www.vba.va.gov/VBA/benefits/factsheets/index. asp#BM4).

Loans

Student loans need to be repaid once a student graduates from college (or stops out for a certain period of time). To apply for the types of loans listed below, you must complete the FAFSA form.

- **The Federal Perkins Loan** is a 5 percent simple-interest loan awarded to exceptionally needy students. The repayment for this loan begins 9 months after a student is no longer enrolled at least half-time.
- **The Federal Subsidized Stafford Loan** is available to students enrolled at least half-time and has a fixed interest rate that's established each year on July 1. The federal government pays the interest on the loan while the student is enrolled. The repayment for this loan begins six months after a student is no longer enrolled half-time.
- **The Federal Unsubsidized Stafford Loan** is a loan that's not based on need and has the same interest rate as the Federal Subsidized Stafford Loan. Students are responsible for paying the interest on this loan while they're enrolled in college. The loan amount limits for Stafford loans are based on the classification of the student (e.g., freshman or sophomore).

Be responsible with your student loans and only take the loan out in the amount that you need! (You don't have to take the full amount.) Many students are unaware that government student loans cannot be written off in bankruptcy!

Keep in mind that federal and state regulations require that if you are receiving financial aid, you must maintain "satisfactory academic progress." In most cases this means that you must do the following:

1. **Maintain a satisfactory GPA.** Your entire academic record will be reviewed, even if you have paid for any of the classes with your own resources.
2. **Make satisfactory academic progress.** Your academic progress will be evaluated at least once per year, usually at the end of each spring semester. You will need to successfully pass a certain percentage of the courses you take.
3. **Complete a degree or certificate program within an established period of time.** Check with your institution's Financial Aid Office for details.

Snapshot Summary

11.3 Federal Loan versus Private Loan: A Critical Difference

Private loans and federal loans are totally different and unrelated types of loans. Here are the key differences:

Federal loans have fixed interest rates that are comparatively low (currently less than 7 percent).

Private loans have variable interest rates that are very high (currently more than 15 percent) and can go higher at any time.

Source: Kristof (2008).

Note: Despite the high cost of private loans, they are the fastest-growing type of loans taken out by college students, largely because of aggressive, misleading, and sometimes irresponsible or unethical advertising on loan-shopping Web sites. Students sometimes think they're getting a federal loan only to find out later they have taken on a more expensive private loan.

> **Remember**
>
> *Private lenders are like credit card companies: they charge extremely high interest rates, and they can go even higher at any time. They should not be used as a primary loan to help pay for college; they should only be used as a last resort when no other options are available for covering your college expenses.*

Student Loans and Credit Scores

Be aware that student loans are a type of loan and can have an effect on your credit score. For many community college students, credit is now a reality and will be for the rest of you when you graduate from college. College loans can hurt or enhance your credit score depending on how you treat the loan.

Your credit score is a number that tells lenders and creditors how financially responsible you are. It assists them in judging the level of risk you present to them as a borrower.

This score will dictate how easily you can obtain credit cards, loans, houses, renting an apartment, etc. The score is based on the following percentages:

- 35% based on payment history: how consistently you pay bills on time.
- 30% based on how much you currently owe.
- 15% based on credit history: have you had credit before and handled it responsibly?
- 10% based on new credit: how many new applications and acceptances of other credit you've had.
- 10% based on types of credit: credit card, student loan, auto loan, etc.

Thus, having loans (including student loans) can be good or bad and sometimes both, depending on how you use them and how you repay them. Making your student loan payments in full and on time each month will assist your credit score and helps you to establish a good credit history. However, missing payments or not paying at all can be devastating to your credit and credit score.

Salary Earnings

If you find yourself relying on your salary to pay for college tuition, check with your employer to see whether the company offers tuition reimbursement. You should also check with the Billing Office on your campus to determine whether payment plans are available for tuition costs. These plans may differ in terms of how much is due, deadlines for payments, and how any remaining debt owed to the institution is dealt with at the end of the term. You may find that the institution you are attending will not allow you to register for the following term until the previous term is completely paid for.

Research shows that when students work on campus (versus off campus) they are more likely to succeed in college (Astin, 1993; Pascarella & Terenzini, 1991, 2005). This is probably because students become more connected to the college when they work on campus (Tinto, 1993) and because on-campus employers are more flexible than off-campus employers in allowing students to meet their academic commitments while they are employed. For instance, campus employers are more willing to schedule students' work hours around their class schedules and allow students to modify their work schedules when their academic workload increases (e.g., midterm and finals). Thus, we strongly encourage you to seek on-campus employment and capitalize on its capacity to promote your academic success.

Think About It ──────────────── *Journal Entry* **11.5**

Do you need to work part-time to meet your college expenses?

_____

If yes, do you have to work more than 15 hours per week to make ends meet?

_____

If yes, is there anything you can do to change that?

_____

_____

_____

Monetary Gifts from Family or Friends

Money received as a gift from family or friends who are supporting your education should be used wisely. Although necessities such as food and transportation support your academic goals, money given to you by friends or family members should be used to pay for tuition and textbooks first. Remaining funds can be used for other expenses.

Financial Tools for Saving Money

If you're taking in more money than you're spending, you are saving money, and you can invest the money you've saved in an account that will allow you to earn interest on your savings. This account can help you build up a cash reserve that can be used for future needs or used immediately for emergencies.

> "A penny saved is a penny earned."
>
> —Benjamin Franklin, 18th-century inventor, newspaper writer, and signer of the *Declaration of Independence*

Savings Account

A savings account can be opened at virtually any bank and will earn you interest on the money placed in your account. Usually, no minimum amount of money needs to be deposited to open a savings account, and you don't need to maintain a minimum amount of money in the account.

Money-Saving Strategies and Habits

The ultimate goal of money management is to save money and avoid debt. Here are some specific strategies for accomplishing this goal:

1. **Prepare a personal budget.** A budget is simply a plan for coordinating income and expenses to ensure that your cash flow leaves you with sufficient money to cover your expenses. A budget helps you maintain awareness of your financial state or condition; it enables you to be your own accountant by keeping an accurate account of your money.

Just like managing and budgeting your time, the first step in managing and budgeting your money involves prioritizing. In the case of money management, prioritizing first involves identifying your most important expenses—necessities that are indispensable and that you must have to survive, as opposed to incidentals that are dispensable because you can live without them.

Some people can easily confuse essentials (needs) and incidentals (wants). For instance, if a piece of merchandise happens to be on sale, what this means is that it may be a great bargain for consumers who may want to purchase it; however, it doesn't mean that you need to consume (purchase) it before somebody else does.

Remember

Remaining consciously aware of the distinction between life's essentials *that must be purchased and* incidentals *that may or may not be purchased is an important first step toward preparing an effective budget that enables you to save money and escape debt.*

Author's Experience Since I was a student who had to manage my own college expenses, I became an expert in managing small budgets. The first thing I always took care of was my tuition. I was going to go to school even if I starved. The next thing I budgeted for was my housing, then food (since I worked in a grocery store, someone would feed me), and then transportation and clothing needs. If I ran out of money, I would then work additional hours if it did not interfere with my academics. I clearly understood that I was working to make a better life for myself and not to just have money to spend at that time. To be successful, I had to be a great money manager because there was so little of it to manage. This took a lot of focus and strong will, but did it ever pay off? Absolutely.

Aaron Thompson

You need to be aware of whether you're spending money on *impulse* and out of *habit* or out of need and after thoughtful reflection. The truth is that humans spend money for a host of psychological reasons (conscious or subconscious), many of which are unrelated to actual need. For example, they spend to build their self-esteem or self-image, to combat personal boredom, or to seek stimulation and an emotional "high" (Furnham & Argyle, 1998). Furthermore, people can become obsessed with spending money, shop compulsively, and become addicted to purchasing products. Just as Alcoholics Anonymous (AA) exists as a support group for alcoholics, Debtors Anonymous exists as a support group for shopaholics and includes a 12-step recovery program similar to AA.

2. **Make all your bills visible and pay them off as soon as possible.** When your bills are visible, they become memorable and you're less likely to forget to pay them or forget to pay them on time. To increase the visibility of your bill payments, keep a financial calendar on which you record key fiscal deadlines for the academic year (e.g., due dates for tuition payments, residential bills, and financial aid applications). Also, try to get in the habit of paying a bill as soon as you open it and have it in your hands, rather than setting it aside and running the risk of forgetting to pay it or losing it. Most companies will charge a late fee if you don't pay your bill on time.

3. **Live within your means.** This strategy is simple: don't purchase what you can't afford. If you are spending more money than you're taking in, it means you're living *beyond* your means. To begin living *within* your means, you have two options:

   a. Decrease your expenses (e.g., reduce your spending); or
   b. Increase your income.

Since most college students are already working while attending college (Orszag, Orszag, & Whitmore, 2001) and working so many hours that it's interfering with their academic performance or progress (King, 2005), the best option for most college students who find themselves in debt is to reduce their spending and begin living within their means.

Author's Experience   When I was young, my mom was always cutting out coupons and looking for what was on sale. If it was not on sale or she did not have a coupon, she usually did not buy it. As a child, it drove me nuts and I thought she was crazy! Now that I am older, I find I am a lot like her when it comes to money. I am always looking for coupons and I rarely buy anything if it is not on sale. Even when I do buy something, I stop and think, "Do I really need this?" or "How much use will I get out of this?" It is because of this that I am able to save up some of my money and do things I really enjoy (season tickets for football games, traveling, etc.), and I am thankful my mom taught me how to save.

Julie McLaughlin

"We choose to spend more money than we have today. Choose debt, or choose freedom, it's your choice."
—Bill Pratt, *Extra Credit: The 7 Things Every College Student Needs to Know About Credit, Debt, and Cash* (2008)

Think About It ——————— *Journal Entry* 11.6

Are you working for money while attending college?

_____

If you're not working, are you sacrificing anything that you want or need because you lack money?

_____

If you are working,

1. How many hours per week do you currently work?

_____

2. Do you think that working is interfering with your academic performance or progress? Explain.

_____

_____

_____

"It is preoccupation with possessions, more than anything else, that prevents us from living freely and nobly."
—Bertrand Russell, British philosopher and mathematician

3. Would it be possible for you to reduce the number of weekly hours you now work and still be able to make ends meet?

_____

_____

_____

4. **Economize.** By being intelligent consumers who use critical thinking skills when purchasing products, you can be frugal or thrifty without compromising the quality of your purchases. For example, you can pay less to see the same movie in the late afternoon than you would pay at night. Also, why pay more for brand-name products that are the same as products with a different name? Why pay 33 percent more for Advil® or Tylenol® when the same amount of pain-relieving ingredient (ibuprofen or acetaminophen) is contained in generic brands? Often, what you're paying for when you buy brand-name products is all the advertising these companies pay to the media and to celebrities to publicly promote their products. (That's why people instantly recognize them as familiar brand-name products.)

Remember

Advertising creates product familiarity, not product quality. The more money manufacturers pay for advertising and creating a well-known brand, the more money you pay for the product—not necessarily because you're acquiring a product of higher quality, but most often because you're covering its high cost of advertising.

5. **Downsize.** Cut down or cut out spending for products that you don't need. Don't engage in conspicuous consumption just to "keep up with the Joneses" (your neighbors or friends), and don't allow peer pressure to determine your spending habits. Let your spending habits reflect your ability to think critically rather than your tendency to conform socially.

6. **Live with others rather than living alone.** Although you lose privacy when you share living quarters with others, you save money; if you enjoy the company of those you live with, it also has social benefits.

7. **Give gifts of time rather than money.** Spending money on gifts for family, friends, and romantic partners is not the only way to show that you care. The point of gift giving is not to show others you aren't cheap or to show off your lavish spending skills. Instead, show off your social sensitivity by doing something special or making something meaningful for them. Gifts of time and kindness can often be more personal and more special than store-bought gifts.

Author's Experience When my wife (Mary) and I were first dating, she was aware that I was trying to gain weight because I was on the thin side. (All right, I was skinny.) One day when I came home from school, I found this hand-delivered package in front of my apartment door. I opened it up and there was a homemade loaf of whole wheat bread made from scratch by Mary. That gift didn't cost her much money, but she took the time to do it and remembered to do something that was important to me (gaining weight), which really touched me; it's a gift I've never forgotten. Since I eventually married Mary and we're still happily married, I guess you could say that inexpensive loaf of bread was the "gift that kept on giving."

Joe Cuseo

8. **Develop your own set of money-saving strategies and habits.** You can save money by starting to do little things that eventually turn into regular money-saving habits, which can add up to big savings over time. Consider the following list of habit-forming tips for saving money that were suggested by students in a first-year seminar class:

- Don't carry a lot of extra money in your wallet. (It's just like food: if it's easy to get to, you'll be more likely to eat it up.)
- Shop with a list—get in, get what you need, and get out.
- Put all your extra change in a jar.

- Put extra cash in a piggy bank that requires you to smash the piggy to get at it.
- Seal your savings in an envelope.
- Immediately get extra money into the bank (and out of your hands).
- Bring (don't buy) your lunch.
- Hide your credit card or put it in the freezer so that you don't use it on impulse.
- Use cash (instead of credit cards) because you can give yourself a set amount of cash and can clearly see how much of it you have at the start of a week and how much is left at any point during the week.
- If your employer has a direct deposit option, use it! This way your money goes directly into your account and you'll be less tempted to spend it.
- Identify wants vs. needs.
- Use Groupon, coupons, etc., whenever possible.

"The safest way to double your money is to fold it over and put it in your pocket."
—Kin Hubbard, American humorist, cartoonist, and journalist

Think About It — **Journal Entry 11.7**

Do you use any of the strategies on the preceding list? Which ones?

_____

_____

Have you developed any effective strategies that do not appear on the list? What are they?

_____

_____

_____

Author's Experience   When I was four years old living in the mountains of Kentucky, it was safe for a young lad to walk the railroad tracks and roads alone. My mother knew this and would send me to the general store to buy various small items we needed for our household. Since we had little money, she was aware that we had to be cautious and only spend money on the essential necessities we needed to survive. I could only purchase items from the general store that I could carry back home by myself and the ones my mother strictly ordered me to purchase. Most of these items cost less than a dollar, and in many cases you could buy multiple items for that dollar in the early 1960s. At the store I would hand my mother's handwritten list to the owners. They would pick the items for me, and we would exchange the items for my money. On the checkout counter were jars with different kinds of candy or gum. You could buy two pieces for a penny. As a hardworking boy who was doing a good deed for his parents, I didn't think there would be any harm in rewarding myself with two pieces of candy after doing a good deed. After all, I could devour the evidence of my disobedience on my slow walk home. Upon my return, my mother, being the protector of the vault and the sergeant-of-arms in our household, would count each item I brought home to make sure I had been charged correctly. She always found that I had either been overcharged by a cent or that I had spent a cent. In those days, parents believed in behavior modification. After she gave me a scolding, she would say, "Boy, you better learn how to count your money if you're ever going to be successful in life." I learned the value of saving money and the discomfort of overspending at a young age.

Aaron Thompson

9. **When making purchases, always think in terms of their long-term total cost.** It's convenient and tempting for consumers to think in the short term ("I see it; I like it; I want it; and I want it now"). However, long-term thinking is one of the essential keys to successful money management and financial planning. Those small (monthly) installment plans that businesses offer to get you to buy expensive products may make the cost of those products appear attractive and affordable in the short run. However, when you factor in the interest rates you pay on monthly installment plans, plus the length of time (number of months) you're making installment payments, you get a more accurate picture of the product's total cost over the long run. This longer-range perspective can quickly alert you to the reality that a product's sticker price represents its partial and seemingly affordable short-term cost, but its long-term total cost is much less affordable (and perhaps out of your league).

Furthermore, the long-term price for purchases sometimes involves additional "hidden costs" that don't relate directly to the product's initial price but that must be paid for the product's long-term use. For example, the sticker price you pay for clothes does not include the hidden, long-term costs that may be involved if those clothes require dry cleaning. By just taking a moment to check the inside label, you can save yourself this hidden, long-term cost by purchasing clothes that are machine washable. Or, to use an example of a big-ticket purchase, the extra money spent to purchase a new car (instead of a used car) includes not only paying a higher sticker price but also paying the higher hidden costs of licensing and insuring the new car, as well as any interest fees if the new car was purchased on an installment plan. When you count these hidden, long-term costs in a new car's total cost, buying a good used car is a more effective money-saving strategy than buying a new one.

> **Remember**
>
> *Avoid buying costly items impulsively. Instead, take time to reflect on the purchase you intend to make, do a cost analysis of its hidden or long-term costs, and then integrate these invisible costs with the product's sticker price to generate an accurate synthesis and clearer picture of the product's total cost.*

Long-Range Financial Planning: Financing Your College Education

An effective money-management plan should be time-sensitive and include the following financial planning time frames:

- Short-range financial plan (e.g., weekly income and expenses)
- Mid-range financial plan (e.g., monthly income and expenses)
- Long-range financial plan (e.g., projected or anticipated income and expenses for the entire college experience)
- Extended long-range financial plan (e.g., expected income and debt after graduation, including a plan for repayment of any college loans)

Thus far, our discussion has focused primarily on short- and mid-range financial planning strategies that will keep you out of debt monthly or yearly. We turn now to issues involving long-term financial planning for your entire college experience. While no one "correct" strategy exists for financing a college education that works best for all students, some important research findings relate to the effectiveness of different financing strategies that college students have used, which you should be aware of when doing long-range financial planning for college and beyond.

Research shows that obtaining a student loan and working no more than 15 hours per week is an effective long-range strategy for students to finance their college education and meet their personal expenses. Students who use this strategy are more likely to graduate from college, graduate in less time, and graduate with higher grades than students who work part-time for more than 15 hours per week while attending college full time, or students who work full time and attend college part time (King, 2002; Pascarella & Terenzini, 2005).

Studies also show that borrowing money in the form of a student loan and working part-time for 15 or fewer hours per week is the most effective financial strategy for students at *all income levels,* and it is *especially effective for students with low incomes.* Unfortunately, less than 6 percent of all first-year students use this strategy. Instead, almost 50 percent of first-year students choose a strategy that research shows to be least associated with college success: borrowing nothing and trying to work more than 15 hours per week. Students who use this strategy increase their risk of lowering their grades significantly and withdrawing from college altogether (King, 2005), probably because they have difficulty finding enough time to handle the amount of academic work required by college on top of working outside of college for more than 15 hours per week. Thus, a good strategy for balancing learning and earning would be to try to limit work for pay to 15 hours per week (or as close to 15 hours as possible) because working longer hours may increase your temptation to switch from full-time to part-time enrollment, which can increase your risk of delaying graduation or not graduating (Pascarella & Terenzini, 2005).

Other students decide to finance their college education by working full time and going to college part time. These students believe it will be less expensive in the long run to attend college part time because it will allow them to avoid any debt from student loans. However, studies show that when students go to college part time so that they can work full time, it significantly lengthens their time to degree completion and sharply reduces the likelihood that they will ever complete a college degree (Orszag et al., 2001).

Students who manage to eventually graduate from college, but take longer to do so because they have worked more than 15 hours per week for extra income, eventually lose money in the long run. The longer they take to graduate, the longer they must wait to "cash in" on their college degrees and enter higher-paying, full-time positions that a college diploma would allow them to enter. The pay per hour for most part-time jobs that students hold while working in college is less than half what they will earn from working in full-time positions as college graduates (King, 2005).

Furthermore, studies show that two out of three college students have at least one credit card and nearly one-half of students with credit cards carry an average balance of more than $2,000 per month (Mae, 2005). Debt this high is likely to push many students into working more than 15 hours a week to pay it off ("I owe, I owe, so off to work I go"). This often results in their taking a longer time to graduate and earn a college graduate's salary, because they enroll in fewer courses per term so that they have extra work time to earn enough money to pay off their credit card debt.

Instead of these students paying almost 20 percent interest to credit card companies for their monthly debt, they would be better off obtaining a student loan at a much lower interest rate and which they don't begin to pay back until six months after graduation—when they'll be making more money in full-time positions as college graduates. Despite the clear advantages of student loans compared to credit card loans, only about 25 percent of college students who use credit cards take out a student loan (King, 2002).

Keep in mind that not all debt is bad. Debt can be good if it represents an investment in something that will appreciate with time (i.e., something that will gain in value and eventually turn into profit for the investor). Purchasing a college education on credit is a good investment because, over time, it will appreciate—in the form of higher salaries for the remainder of the life of the investor (the college graduate). In contrast, purchasing a new car is a bad long-term investment because it immediately begins to depreciate or lose monetary value once it is purchased. The instant you drive that new car off the dealer's lot, you immediately become the proud owner of a used car that's worth much less than what you just paid for it.

> "Unlike a car that depreciates in value each year that you drive it, an investment in education yields monetary, social, and intellectual profit. A car is more tangible in the short term, but an investment in education (even if it means borrowing money) gives you more bang for the buck in the long run."
>
> —Eric Tyson, financial counselor and national bestselling author of *Personal Finance for Dummies* (2003)

Think About It — Journal Entry 11.8

In addition to college, what might be other good long-term investments for you to make now or in the near future?

_____

_____

_____

_____

_____

_____

You may have heard the expression that "time is money." One way to interpret this expression is that the more money you spend, the more time you must spend making money. If you're going to college, spending more time to earn money to cover your spending habits often means spending less time studying, learning, completing classes, and earning good grades. You can avoid this vicious cycle by viewing academic work as work that "pays" you back in terms of completed courses and higher grades. If you put in more academic time to complete more courses within less time and earn better grades, you're paid back by increasing the likelihood you will graduate sooner and start earning the full-time salary of a college graduate—which will pay you about twice as much money per hour as you'll earn doing part-time work without a college degree (not to mention fringe benefits such as medical insurance, dental insurance, and paid vacation time). Furthermore, the time you put into earning higher grades while in college should pay off immediately in your first full-time position after college, because research shows that students in the same field who graduate with higher grades are offered higher starting salaries (Pascarella & Terenzini, 2005).

> "I invested in myself—in study, in mastering my tools, in preparation. Many a man who is putting a few dollars a week into the bank would do much better to put it into himself."
>
> —Henry Ford, founder of Ford Motor Co. and one of the richest people of his generation

.Remember

Work for better grades now; work for better pay later.

You may need to delay your immediate material desires and consumer gratification by not purchasing high-priced products until later in life. Ultimately, financing a college education may require that you give serious thought to your current lifestyle choices and make firm decisions about what you can live without at the moment. For example, a new set of wheels or a more spacious apartment may have to wait until you graduate.

Finally, be sure you take full advantage of your Financial Aid Office during your time in college. This is the campus resource that has been designed specifically to help you finance your college education. If you are concerned about whether you are using the most effective strategy for financing your education, make an appointment of see a professional in your Financial Aid Office. Also, periodically check with this office to see whether you qualify for additional sources of income, such as:

- Part-time employment on campus;
- Low-interest loans;
- Grants; or
- Scholarships.

Keep a watchful eye out for notices posted near your Financial Aid Office about financial aid reminders, application deadlines and updates, money-management workshops, and on-campus employment.

WHO'S IN CHARGE?

Financial Priorities

It is the first week of the term and you still don't have your books. You are getting irritated because your instructors are telling you that you are already falling behind and if you don't get your books soon, you will fail the class! You explain that you don't have the money right now and next week you need to get your nails done and buy an iPod® because your daughter broke yours. You think your instructors are plain mean and don't want to help you. Who is really at fault here? What could have been done differently in this situation?

Summary and Conclusion

The following key strategies for effectively managing money were recommended in this chapter:

- Develop financial self-awareness. Become aware of the amount of money you have flowing in and out.
- Develop a money-management plan. Ensure that the money coming in (income) is equal to or greater than the money going out (expenses).
- Use available financial tools and instruments to track your cash flow and manage your money, such as checking accounts, credit cards, charge cards, and debit cards.
- Explore all sources of income for financing your college education, including the FAFSA, scholarships, grants, loans, monetary gifts from family or friends, salary earnings, and personal savings.

- Use available financial tools for saving money, such as savings accounts and money-market accounts.
- Prepare a personal budget. A simple plan lets you coordinate income and expenses to ensure that your cash flow leaves you with sufficient money to cover your expenses. It enables you to be your own accountant by keeping an accurate account of your money.
- Make all your bills visible and pay them off quickly. When your bills are visible, you're less likely to forget to pay them on time.
- Live within your means. Don't purchase what you can't afford.
- Economize by using critical thinking skills when purchasing products. You can be frugal or thrifty without compromising quality.
- Downsize. Cut down or cut out spending for unneeded products. Let your spending habits reflect your ability to think critically rather than a tendency to be influenced by peer pressure.
- Live with others rather than living alone. Sharing translates to saving, and if you enjoy the company of those you live with, shared living quarters have social benefits.
- Give gifts of time rather than money. Gifts of time and kindness can often be more personal and more special than store-bought gifts.
- Work for better grades now; work for better pay later. Taking out a student loan and working part-time for 15 or fewer hours per week is the most effective financial strategy for students at all income levels.
- Take full advantage of your Financial Aid Office during your time in college. Check periodically with this office to see whether you qualify for additional sources of income, such as part-time employment on campus, low-interest loans, grants, or scholarships.

Managing money is a key personal resource that can promote or sabotage your success in college and in life beyond college. As with time management, if you effectively manage your money and gain control of how you spend it, you can gain greater control over the quality of your life. On the other hand, if you ignore it or abuse it, you raise your level of debt and stress and lower your level of performance. Research shows that accumulating high levels of debt while in college is associated with higher levels of stress, lower academic performance, and greater risk of withdrawing from college. However, the good news is that students who learn to use effective money-management strategies are able to reduce unnecessary spending, accumulation of debt, and stress while improving the quality of their academic performance.

Learning More through the World Wide Web

Internet-Based Resources for Further Information on Money Management

For additional information related to the ideas discussed in this chapter, we recommend the following Web sites:

www.360financialliteracy.org/Life-Stages/College-Students

finance.youngmoney.com/Money-Management/

studentaid.ed.gov/home

11.1 Self-Assessment of Financial Attitudes and Habits

Answer the following questions as accurately and honestly as possible.

		Agree	Disagree
1.	I pay my rent or mortgage on time each month.	_____	_____
2.	I avoid maxing out or going over the limit on my credit cards.	_____	_____
3.	I balance my checkbook each month.	_____	_____
4.	I set aside money each month for savings.	_____	_____
5.	I pay my phone and utility bills on time each month.	_____	_____
6.	I pay my credit card bills in full each month to avoid interest charges.	_____	_____
7.	I believe it's important to buy the things I want when I want them.	_____	_____
8.	Borrowing money to pay for college is a smart thing to do.	_____	_____
9.	I have a monthly or weekly budget that I follow.	_____	_____
10.	The thing I enjoy most about making money is spending money.	_____	_____
11.	I limit myself to one credit card.	_____	_____
12.	Getting a degree will get me a good job and a good income.	_____	_____

Give yourself one point for each item that you checked "agree"—except items 7 and 10. For these items, give yourself a point if you checked "disagree."

A perfect score on this short survey would be 12.

Sources: Cude et al. (2006), Niederjohn (2008).

Self-Assessment Questions

1. What was your total score?

2. Which items lowered your score?

3. Do you see any pattern across the items that lowered your score?

4. Do you see any realistic way or ways you could improve your score on this test?

11.2 Financial Self-Awareness: Monitoring Money and Tracking Cash Flow

1. Use the worksheet on this page to estimate what your income and expenses are per month, and enter them in column 2.

2. Track your actual income and expenses for a month and enter them in column 3. (To help you do this accurately, keep a file of your cash receipts, bills paid, and checking or credit records for the month.)

3. After a month of tracking your cash flow, answer the self-assessment questions.

Financial Self-Awareness Worksheet

Income Sources	Estimate	Actual
Parents/Family		
Work/Job		
Grants/Scholarships		
Loans		
Savings		
Other:		
TOTAL INCOME		
Essentials (Fixed Expenses)		
Living Expenses: Food/Groceries		
Rent/Room & Board		
Utilities (gas/electric)		
Clothing		
Laundry/Dry Cleaning		
Phone		
Computer		
Household Items (dishes, etc.)		
Medical Insurance Expenses		
Debt Payments (loans/credit cards)		
Other:		
School Expenses: Tuition		
Books		
Supplies (print cartridges, etc.)		
Special Fees (lab fees, etc.)		
Other:		
Transportation: Public Transportation (bus fees, etc.)		
Car Insurance		
Car Maintenance		
Fuel (gas)		
Car Payments		
Other:		

Incidentals (Variable Expenses)	Estimate	Actual
Entertainment:		
Movies/Concerts		
DVDs/CDs		
Restaurants (eating out)		
Other:		
Personal Appearance/Accessories:		
Haircuts/Hairstyling		
Cosmetics/Manicures		
Fashionable Clothes		
Jewelry		
Other:		
Hobbies:		
Travel (trips home, vacations)		
Gifts		
Other:		
TOTAL EXPENSES		

Self-Assessment Questions

1. Did you enter any sources of income or expenses that were not listed on the worksheet? (If yes, what were they?)

2. Were your estimates generally accurate?

3. What specific items or areas had the largest discrepancies between what you estimated they would be and what they actually were?

4. Comparing your bottom-line totals for income and expenses, are you satisfied with how your monthly cash flow seems to be going?

5. What changes could you make to create more positive cash flow (i.e., to increase your income or savings and reduce your expenses or debt)?

6. How likely is it that you would actually make such changes?

Problems Paying for College

A college student posted the following message on the Internet:

"I went to college for one semester, failed some of my classes, and ended with 900 dollars in student loans. Now I can't even get financial aid or a loan because of some stupid thing that says if you fail a certain amount of classes you can't get aid or a loan. And now since I couldn't go to college this semester they want me to pay for my loans already, and I don't even have a job."

Any suggestions?

Discussion Questions

1. What suggestions would you offer this student? Which should the student do right now? Which should the student do eventually?

2. What should the student have done to prevent this from happening?

3. Do you think that this student's situation is common or unusual? Why?

Chapter 11 Reflection

How are you financing your college education? Do you feel this is the best way for you to pay for college? Why or why not?

Do you feel you have good or poor money management skills? Explain.

List and describe at least five principles discussed in this chapter that you can use to better manage your money.

1.

2.

3.

4.

5.

Now explain HOW you can put these principles into practice.

Health and Wellness

Body, Mind, and Spirit

12

THOUGHT STARTER | *Journal Entry* **12.1**

LEARNING GOAL

To acquire strategies for physical and mental wellness that can be applied to promote your success during the first year of college and preserve wellness during your later years in college and beyond.

What would you say are the three most important things that humans can do to preserve their health and promote their physical well-being?

1. _____

2. _____

3. _____

What Is Wellness?

Wellness may be described as a state of good health and positive well-being that promotes peak mental and physical performance by enabling different dimensions of the self to work well together.

While experts disagree on the exact number and nature of the different dimensions of wellness (President's Council on Physical Fitness and Sports, 2001), we feel that wellness is best understood and developed in terms of the following dimensions of the self:

1. **Intellectual.** Knowledge, thoughts, and self-concept
2. **Emotional.** Feelings, emotional adjustment, and mental health
3. **Social.** Interpersonal interactions and relationships
4. **Ethical.** Values and moral convictions
5. **Physical.** Bodily health and wellness
6. **Spiritual.** Beliefs about the meaning or purpose of life and the hereafter
7. **Vocational (occupational).** Career development and satisfaction
8. **Personal.** Self-concept, personal identity, and personal habits (e.g., how time and money are spent)

Your "self" is composed of multiple elements or dimensions, and each of them can affect your health, success, and happiness. As can be seen in Figure 12.1, numerous elements of the self join together to form the wellness wheel. The development of all these elements is a primary goal of wellness and that of a well-rounded college education.

"Wellness is an integrated method of functioning, which is oriented toward maximizing the potential of the individual."

—H. Joseph Dunn, originator of the term "wellness"

FIGURE 12.1

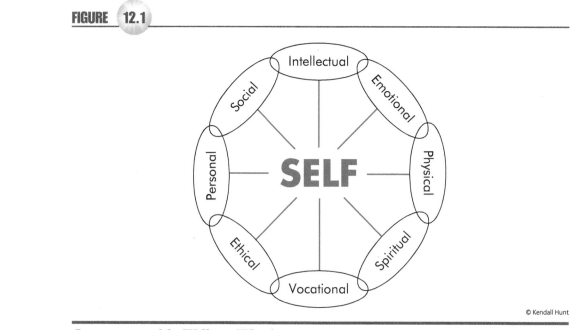

© Kendall Hunt

Components of the Wellness Wheel

Student Perspective

People are not just thinking (intellectual) or working (vocational) beings: they are also social, emotional, physical, ethical, and spiritual beings. In Figure 12.1, these dimensions of the self are joined or linked to show they are interrelated and do not work independently; rather, they work interdependently to affect an individual's development and well-being (Love & Love, 1995). For instance, your emotional state can be influenced by your social relationships (e.g., whether you feel lonely or loved), your intellectual performance can be influenced by your emotional state (e.g., whether you are relaxed or anxious), and your social relationships can be influenced by your physical condition (e.g., whether you have a positive or negative physical self-image). If one link in the chain is strengthened or weakened, other dimensions of the self are likely to be simultaneously strengthened or weakened.

Research strongly suggests that quality of life depends on attending to and integrating all important elements of the self. It has been found that people who are healthy (physically and mentally) and successful are typically individuals who have effectively attended to and blended all key dimensions of the self, enabling them to lead well-balanced and well-rounded lives (Covey, 1990; Goleman, 1995; Heath, 1977).

Since wholeness is essential for wellness, success, and happiness, read carefully the following descriptions and skills associated with each of the eight elements of holistic development. **As you read the skills listed beneath each element, place a checkmark in the space next to any skill that is particularly important to you.** You may check more than one skill within each area.

Skills and Abilities Associated with Each Element of Wellness

1. **Intellectual development.** Acquiring knowledge and learning how to learn deeply and how to think at a higher level.

Skills and Abilities

- Becoming aware of your intellectual abilities, interests, or learning styles
- Attaining and maintaining attention and concentration
- Using effective strategies for improving long-term learning and memory
- Moving beyond memorization to think at a higher level
- Using effective research skills to obtain information from various sources and systems
- Viewing issues from multiple angles or viewpoints (psychological, social, political, economic, etc.) to attain a balanced, comprehensive perspective
- Evaluating ideas critically in terms of their truth and value
- Thinking creatively or imaginatively
- Responding rationally and constructively to differing viewpoints or opposing arguments
- Resisting persuasion tactics that appeal to emotions and responding to them logically or rationally

> "You know you've got to exercise your brain just like your muscles."
>
> —Will Rogers, Native American humorist and actor

2. **Emotional development.** Strengthening skills for understanding, controlling, and expressing emotions

Skills and Abilities

- Dealing with emotions in an honest, nondefensive manner
- Maintaining a healthy balance between emotional control and emotional expression
- Responding with empathy and sensitivity to emotions experienced by others
- Dealing effectively with depression
- Dealing effectively with anger
- Using effective stress-management strategies to control anxiety or tension
- Responding positively to life changes and challenges
- Dealing effectively with fear of failure, criticism, or poor performance
- Accepting feedback in a constructive, nondefensive manner
- Maintaining optimism and enthusiasm

> "It's not stress that kills us; it is our reaction to it."
>
> —Hans Selye, Canadian endocrinologist and author of *Stress Without Distress* (XXXX)

3. **Social development.** Enhancing the quality and depth of interpersonal relationships

Skills and Abilities

- Using effective interpersonal communication skills
- Relating effectively to others in one-to-one, small-group, and large-group situations
- Overcoming shyness or loneliness and initiating new relationships
- Forming meaningful friendships
- Handling interpersonal conflict effectively in an assertive manner rather than in a passive or aggressive manner
- Providing advice and feedback to others in a constructive and considerate manner
- Using effective collaboration and teamwork skills to work productively with others
- Relating effectively to others from different cultural backgrounds and with different personal lifestyles
- Developing leadership skills

4. **Ethical development.** Acquiring a clear value system for guiding life choices and decisions and developing moral character, or the ability to make judgments and demonstrate consistency between moral convictions (beliefs) and moral commitments (actions)

Skills and Abilities

- Being self-aware of personal values and ethical assumptions
- Making important personal choices and life decisions based on a meaningful value system (e.g., decisions about majors, careers, and relationships)
- Having the courage to think and act with personal integrity or honesty, including honesty with respect to schoolwork, both inside and outside the classroom (academic integrity)
- Using electronic technology in an ethical and responsible manner
- Fulfilling personal commitments and responsibilities to others
- Knowing how to exercise individual freedom without infringing on the rights of others
- Developing concern and commitment for human rights and social justice
- Becoming a responsible citizen

5. **Physical development.** Applying knowledge about how the human body functions to prevent disease, maintain wellness, and promote peak performance

Skills and Abilities

- Being aware of your physical condition and state of health
- Applying knowledge about exercise and fitness training to promote physical and mental health
- Understanding the role of rest and sleep patterns for promoting health and increasing energy
- Applying knowledge on nutrition and diet to enhance your health and physical performance

- Maintaining a healthy balance among work, relaxation, and recreation
- Having a healthy and positive body image
- Being aware of nutritional imbalances and eating disorders
- Being aware of the effects of drugs and alcohol on the body and on physical and mental performance
- Being knowledgeable about the biology and psychology of human sexuality and sexually transmitted diseases
- Being knowledgeable about the physical and physiological differences between the sexes and their implications for male-female relationships, orientation, and gender

6. **Spiritual development.** Searching for an answer to the "big questions," such as the meaning or purpose of life and death and nonmaterial issues that transcend human life and the physical world

Skills and Abilities

- Developing a personal philosophy or worldview about the meaning and purpose of human existence
- Appreciating what cannot be completely understood
- Appreciating the mysteries associated with the origin of the universe
- Exploring the connection between yourself and humanity

- Exploring the connection between yourself and the physical world that surrounds you
- Being open to examining questions relating to death and life after death
- Being open to examining questions about the possible existence of a supreme being or higher power
- Being aware of different approaches to spirituality and their underlying beliefs or assumptions
- Understanding the difference and relationship between faith and reason
- Being knowledgeable and tolerant of religious beliefs and practices

7. **Vocational development.** Exploring career options, making career choices wisely, and developing skills needed for lifelong career success

Skills and Abilities

- Being knowledgeable about the relationship between college majors and careers
- Using effective strategies for exploring and identifying potential careers
- Selecting career options that are consistent with your personal values, interests, and talents
- Acquiring work experience in fields that relate to your career interests
- Developing an effective resume and portfolio
- Adopting effective strategies for selecting individuals to serve as personal references and improving the quality of your letters of recommendation
- Developing effective job-search strategies
- Acquiring effective strategies for writing letters of inquiry and letters of application to potential employers
- Developing effective networking skills for making personal contacts with potential employers
- Learning strategies for effective job-interview preparation and performance

8. **Personal development.** Developing positive self-beliefs, personal attitudes, and personal habits

Skills and Abilities

- Developing a sense of personal identity and a coherent self-concept (e.g., "Who am I?")
- Finding a sense of future direction and purpose (e.g., "Who am I becoming?")
- Developing self-respect and positive self-esteem
- Acquiring self-confidence
- Developing self-efficacy, or a strong belief that events and outcomes in life can be affected or influenced by personal initiative or effort
- Setting realistic goals
- Establishing personal priorities
- Becoming self-motivated and self-disciplined
- Developing the patience and perseverance to persist on tasks despite personal setbacks or frustration
- Learning practical skills for managing personal affairs effectively and efficiently
- Becoming independent and self-reliant

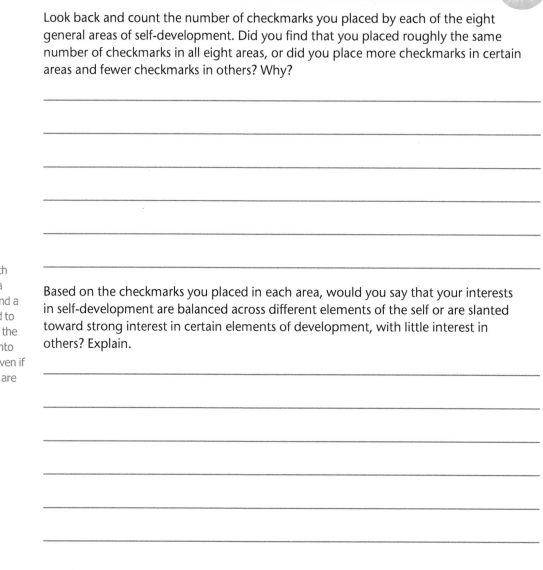

Think About It ————————————— *Journal Entry* **12.2**

Look back and count the number of checkmarks you placed by each of the eight general areas of self-development. Did you find that you placed roughly the same number of checkmarks in all eight areas, or did you place more checkmarks in certain areas and fewer checkmarks in others? Why?

_____

_____

_____

_____

_____

Based on the checkmarks you placed in each area, would you say that your interests in self-development are balanced across different elements of the self or are slanted toward strong interest in certain elements of development, with little interest in others? Explain.

_____

_____

_____

_____

_____

"Everyone is a house with four rooms: a physical, a mental, an emotional, and a spiritual. Most of us tend to live in one room most of the time, but unless we go into every room every day, even if only to keep it aired, we are not complete."
—Native American proverb

"Health is a state of complete . . . well-being, and not merely the absence of disease or infirmity."
—World Health Organization

The physical element of wellness is the focus of this chapter. It could be said that physical health is the precondition or prerequisite that enables all other elements of wellness to take place. For instance, it's hard to develop intellectually or socially if you're not well physically, and it's hard to become wealthy and wise unless you're first healthy.

However, physical wellness isn't just the absence of illness or something that's done in reaction to illness (e.g., getting well after being sick): it's something that's done proactively to prevent illness from occurring (Corbin, Pangrazi, & Franks, 2000). Wellness puts into practice two classic proverbs: "Prevention is the best medicine" and "An ounce of prevention is worth a pound of cure."

As depicted in Figure 12.2, three potential interception points for preventing illness, maintaining health, and promoting peak performance range from the reactive (after illness) to the proactive (before illness).

FIGURE 12.2

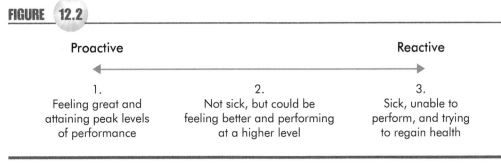

Potential Points for Preventing Illness, Preserving Health, and Promoting Peak Performance

Wellness goes beyond merely maintaining physical health to attaining quality of life, to include personal satisfaction, happiness, vitality (energy and vigor), and longevity (a longer life span).

The Relevance of Wellness for Today's College Students

When students move directly from high school to college, and move from life at home to life on campus, they're making a major move toward taking sole responsibility for their own wellness. Mom and Dad are no longer around to monitor their health habits and to remind them about what and when to eat, what hours to keep, or when to go to sleep.

In addition to receiving less guidance and supervision, new college students are making a major life transition; during times of change or transition, stress tends to increase. Bad health habits, such as poor eating habits, can further increase stress and moodiness (Khoshaba & Maddi, 2004). In contrast, maintaining good health habits is one way to both cope effectively with college stress and promote peak performance.

In the introduction to this book, we noted research that pointed to the advantages of the college experience and college degree. Among the advantages experienced by college graduates are better physical health, longer lives, and higher levels of both psychological well-being (mental health) and personal happiness (life satisfaction). This suggests that students are learning something about wellness and how to promote it by the time they graduate from college. We want you to begin learning about wellness now so that you can experience its benefits immediately and continue to experience them throughout your college years.

Think About It ———————————— *Journal Entry* **12.3**

If you could single out one thing about your physical health as something you'd like to improve or learn more about, what would it be? Explain.

_____

_____

_____

_____

Components of Physical Wellness

A healthy physical lifestyle includes four elements:

1. Supplying your body with effective fuel (nutrition).
2. Converting the fuel you consume into bodily energy (exercise).
3. Giving your body adequate rest (sleep) so that it can recover the energy it has expended.
4. Avoiding risky substances (alcohol and drugs) and risky behaviors that can threaten your health and safety.

Nutrition

Your body needs nutrients to replenish its natural biochemicals and repair its tissues. The food you put into your body supplies it with energy much like fuel does for a car. Just as high-quality gasoline can improve how well and how long your car runs, so can the consumption of high-quality (nutritious) food improve your body and mind, allowing them to function at peak capacity. Unfortunately, however, people often pay more attention to the quality of fuel they put in their cars than to the quality of food they put into their bodies. Humans often eat without any intentional planning about what they eat. They eat at places where they can get food fast, and where they can pick up food on the go, without having to move an inch to get out of their cars (and off their butts) to consume it. America has become a "fast-food nation," accustomed to consuming food that can be accessed quickly, conveniently, cheaply, and in large (super-sized) portions (Schlosser, 2001).

Even when people slow down and take time to eat, they often consume food while their attention is divided and consumed by something else (e.g., conversation, reading, or watching TV).

You should eat in a thoughtful, nutritionally conscious way; not just out of convenience, habit, or pursuit of what's most pleasant to your taste buds. You should also "eat to win" (i.e., eat the types of food that will best equip you to defeat disease and allow you to reach peak levels of physical and mental performance).

Studies show that the least nutritious and healthy foods are the very ones that receive the most media advertising (Caroli, Argentieri, Cardone, & Masi, 2004; Hill, 2002). The most frequently advertised food items that people are consuming in the largest quantities tend to be junk food (i.e., food with the least nutrients, the most calories, and the highest health risks). The advertising, availability, and convenience of high-calorie, low-cost food is contributing to Americans being heavier now than at any other time in the nation's history. In 2003, approximately 65 percent of Americans 20 years and older were either overweight—20 percent more than the ideal body weight for their height and age—or obese—30 percent more than their ideal weight (World Health Organization, 2012). This percentage has risen from 26 percent in 1976 (Hill, Wyat, Reed, & Peters, 2003). The most telling piece of evidence is the finding that when people from other countries move to America and begin to adopt American eating habits, they typically put on a significant amount of weight (Sundquist & Winkleby, 2000).

National surveys of first-year college students indicate that less than 40 percent report maintaining a healthy diet (Sax, Lindholm, Astin, Korn, & Mahoney, 2004). The phrase "freshman 15" is commonly used to describe the 15-pound weight gain

"May the sun bring you new energy by day; may the moon restore you by night. May the rain wash away your worries; may the breeze blow strength into your being. May you walk gently through the world and know its beauty all the days of your life."

—Apache Indian blessing

"If we are what we eat, then I'm cheap, fast, and easy."

—Stephen Wright, Boston-based comedian

that some students experience during their first year of college (Brody, 2003; Levitsky, Nussbaum, Halbmaier, & Mrdjenovic, 2003). For some first-year students, this weight gain may be temporary and associated with the initial transition to the college eating lifestyle (e.g., all-you-can-eat dining halls, late-night pizzas, and junk-food snacks). However, for other students, it may signal the start of a longer-lasting pattern of gaining and carrying excess weight. The disadvantage of being overweight isn't merely a matter of appearance: it's also a matter of health and survival because excess weight increases susceptibility to the leading life-threatening diseases, such as diabetes, heart disease, and certain forms of cancer.

Author's Experience   When I first went away to college, I loved that I had the freedom to eat whatever I wanted, whenever I wanted. Food (and alcohol) were always readily available. During the first 18 years of my life, I never had any issues with my weight, so I didn't really think about what I was eating while in college. The late-night pizza and ice cream runs caught up with me, and by the time I went home for the holiday break in December, I only had a few pairs of sweatpants that fit me. The fact that I was eating unhealthy foods and not exercising much had really caught up with me, and I gained over 20 pounds in four months. I have since learned how to eat healthier and exercise, but I have struggled with my weight ever since that first year of college.

— Julie McLaughlin

Think About It ——————————— Journal Entry 12.4

Have your eating habits changed since you've begun college?

_____

_____

If yes, in what way or ways have they changed?

_____

_____

_____

_____

_____

_____

Snapshot Summary

12.1   Eating Disorders

While some students experience the "freshman 15," others experience eating disorders related to weight loss and loss of control of their eating habits. The disorders described in this box are more common among females (National Institute of Mental Health, 2011). Studies show that approximately one of every three college females indicates that she worries about her weight, body image, or eating habits. Western cultures place more emphasis and pressure on females than males to maintain lighter body weight and body size.

What follows is a short summary of the major eating disorders experienced by college students. These disorders are often accompanied by emotional issues (e.g., depression and anxiety) that are serious enough to require professional treatment. The earlier these disorders are identified and treated, the better the prognosis or probability of complete and permanent recovery. The Counseling Center and Student Health Center are the key campus resources where students can seek help and treatment for any of the following eating disorders.

Anorexia Nervosa

The self-esteem of people who experience anorexia nervosa disorder is often tied closely to their body weight or shape. They see themselves as overweight and have an intense fear of gaining weight, even though they're dangerously thin. Anorexics typically deny that they're severely underweight, and even if their weight drops to the point where they may look like walking skeletons, they may continue to be obsessed with losing weight, eating infrequently, and eating in extremely small portions. Anorexics may also use other methods to lose weight, such as compulsive exercise, diet pills, laxatives, diuretics, or enemas.

Bulimia Nervosa

The eating disorder known as bulimia nervosa is characterized by repeated episodes of binge eating—consuming excessive amounts of food within a limited period of time. Bulimics tend to lose all sense of self-control during their binges, then try to compensate for overeating by engaging in behavior to purge their guilt and prevent weight gain. For example, they may purge by self-induced vomiting, consuming excessive amounts of laxatives or diuretics, using enemas, and fasting. The binge-purge pattern typically takes place at least twice a week and continues for three or more months.

Unlike anorexia, bulimia is harder to detect because bulimics' binges and purges take place secretly and their body weight looks about normal for their age and height. However, similar to anorexics, bulimics fear gaining weight, aren't happy with their bodies, and have an intense desire to lose weight.

Binge-Eating Disorder

Like bulimia, binge-eating disorder involves repeated, out-of-control binging on large quantities of food. However, unlike bulimics, binge eaters don't purge after binging episodes. For someone to be diagnosed as suffering from binge-eating disorder, that person must demonstrate at least three of the following symptoms, two or more times per week, for several months:

1. Eating more rapidly than normal
2. Eating until becoming uncomfortably full
3. Eating large amounts of food when not physically hungry
4. Eating alone because of embarrassment about others seeing how much they eat
5. Feeling guilty, disgusted, or depressed after overeating.

Since individuals suffering from these eating disorders usually don't recognize or admit their illness, friends and family members play a key role in helping them receive help before the disorder progresses to a life-threatening level. If someone you know is experiencing an eating disorder, consult with a professional at the Student Health Center or Counseling Center about strategies for approaching and encouraging this person to seek help.

Nutrition Management Strategies

The following nutrition management strategies may be used to enhance your body's ability to stay well and perform well.

1. **Develop a nutrition management plan to ensure your diet has variety and balance.** Planning what you eat is essential to ensure you eat what's best for pre-

serving health and promoting wellness. If you don't plan ahead to acquire the food you should eat, you're more likely to eat food that can be accessed conveniently and doesn't require advanced preparation. Unfortunately, the types of foods that are readily available, easily accessible, and immediately consumable are usually fast food and packaged food, which are the least healthy foods. If you're serious about eating in a way that's best for your health and performance, you need to do some nutritional planning in advance.

Figure 12.3 depicts the MyPlate chart, which is the new version of the former Food Guide Pyramid and created by the United States Department of Agriculture (USDA). Since foods vary in terms of the nature of nutrients they provide (carbohydrates, protein, and fat), no single food group can supply all the nutrients your body needs. Therefore, your diet should be balanced and include all of these food groups, but you should include them in different proportions or percentages. To find the daily amount of food you should be consuming from each of these major food groups (e.g., your age and gender), go to www.choose myplate.gov or www.cnpp.usda.gov/dietaryguidelines.htm. You can use these guidelines to create a dietary plan that ensures you consume each of these food groups every day, resulting in a balanced diet that minimizes your risk of experiencing any nutritional deficits or deficiencies. If this guide to nutrition is followed, there should be no need for you to take vitamins or dietary supplements.

FIGURE 12.3

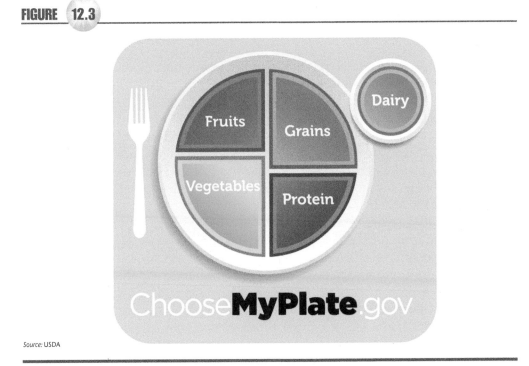

Source: USDA

MyPlate

2. **Minimize your consumption of foods whose nutritional value is low (or zero) and that increase your risk of heart disease and cancer.**

   - Reduce intake of fried and fatty foods such as pizza, hamburgers, French fries, donuts, butter, and margarine. These foods not only contain lots of calories but also can increase the risk of heart disease because they contain saturated fats and trans fats—"bad" fats that tend to stick to blood vessel walls and increase the risk of blocking normal blood flow. Saturated fats also increase the risk of certain forms of cancer, such as breast and bowel cancer. Saturated fats should comprise less than one-tenth of the total number of calories you consume (National Research Council, 1989). Even if you exercise regularly and are physically active, you still have to be conscious of the food you put into your body. Well-conditioned athletes still can be at risk for heart disease and cancer if they consume foods containing high amounts of saturated fat.

- Reduce consumption of processed foods. Processed foods were originally natural foods, but synthetic ingredients have been added to them so that they can be preserved, packaged, jarred, canned, or bottled and sold later to the public in large or bulk quantities. Processed foods contain additives that supplement natural food to preserve its shelf life, make it more pleasing to the eye, or make it more pleasing to the taste buds. These additives typically have no nutritional value and may have unknown or possibly unhealthy effects on the body. For example, processed foods often contain added sugar and salt, which tend to promote weight gain and elevate blood pressure, respectively.

  Salt and sugar are often added to processed foods just to increase their taste appeal (and sales appeal). Why do humans often find sweeter and saltier processed foods tastier than natural foods? One theory is that processed foods haven't been around as long as unprocessed "natural" foods, which have been around for millions of years and were the only foods available to and consumed by our ancient ancestors. Therefore, our taste buds may find "newer" processed foods to be more stimulating because they're different from the "old" natural foods that have been eaten for millions of years (Eaton & Konner, 1985; Simopoulos & Pavlou, 1997). Ironically, humans may have developed or evolved a taste preference for the very foods that are the least nutritious, least healthy, and highest in calories. The unfortunate consequence of all this is that the foods most likely to stimulate taste buds (and sense of smell) are the ones also most likely to inflate fat cells.

- Reduce consumption of high-fat dairy products (e.g., cheese, butter, margarine, cream, and whole milk). High-fat dairy products are high in saturated fat and sodium, both of which increase the risk of heart disease. The calcium contained in dairy products is good for you, but you're better off getting that calcium from low-fat dairy products, such as low-fat milk, yogurt, and cottage cheese.

- Minimize consumption of animal meat, particularly red meat such as hamburger and steak. Meat often contains a large amount of saturated fat, which poses a major risk for heart disease. Many people believe they must consume a substantial amount of red meat because the body needs protein. It's true that meat provides large amounts of protein, but protein should make up only 15 percent of your daily calories. Americans tend to consume about twice as much protein as their bodies need (National Research Council, 1989). Consequently, it's probably best to decrease the amount of protein you get from meat and increase the amount you get from sources that are low in saturated fat, such as plants (e.g., beans and peas), nuts (e.g., walnuts and almonds), and low-fat dairy products (e.g., low-fat milk and yogurt).

  If or when you consume meat, you can reduce its health risk by eating lean meat that has less fat and by removing any fatty skin from the meat (e.g., removing the skin from chicken or turkey). You can also reduce meat's unhealthy effects by not frying it, because the oils used in the frying process in-

"Life expectancy would grow by leaps and bounds if green vegetables smelled as good as bacon."

—Doug Larson, American cartoonist

crease the concentration of saturated fat in the meat. Instead of frying, roast, grill, bake, or broil the meat you eat.

3. **Reduce calorie intake and control weight.**

- Decrease or eliminate junk-food snacks. Replace sugary and salty snacks with healthier munchies, such as fruits, nuts, seeds, and raw vegetables. Many of these healthier snacks are as sweet, crispy, or crunchy as junk food snacks. Natural fruits can provide sweetness with more nutrients and fewer calories than processed sweets (e.g., candy bars and blended coffee drinks). Unfortunately, advertisers spend millions of dollars convincing consumers that processed sweets are "indescribably delicious." From a strictly economic standpoint, nutritious snacks represent a better financial investment because you get a bigger bang for your buck—that is, more nutrients (and less empty calories) for your snacking dollar.

Think About It — Journal Entry 12.5

What type of junk food (if any) do you currently eat? Why?

If you do eat junk food, what's the likelihood that you'll continue to do so? Why?

What could you eat instead?

- Decrease the tendency to pack most of your calories into one or two large meals per day. Most nutritionists recommend that people eat large meals less often and small meals more often. No research evidence or dietary rule supports the American habit of eating three times a day as the best nutritional practice. Six smaller meals or healthy snacks per day may be a more effective way to fuel the body than three full-sized meals (Khoshaba & Maddi, 2004). When our ancient ancestors foraged for food, it's unlikely that they ate full meals three times a day; they probably ate more frequently and in smaller portions, which provided them with a steady stream of energy throughout the day.

- Decrease the amount of juices you consume daily. They contain a large amount of calories. Eliminate sodas as they contain a large amount of sugar and empty calories.

- Reduce the total number of calories consumed during your evening meal. The meal you eat closest to bedtime should be your lightest meal with the fewest calories because you're soon going to be lying down and not expending much physical energy for seven to eight hours. Remember that calories are measures of the amount of energy contained in food. One calorie may be described as one unit or degree of energy. If you consume a unit of energy and don't use it, you don't lose it; instead, you save it or store it—as fat. In other words, much like money, if you don't spend your income (caloric intake), you tend to save it in your body's bank of fat cells. Eating lots of calories in the evening and then lying down and sleeping soon thereafter means those evening calories don't get burned as physical energy, but are stored as body fat.

- Avoid rushing out at the beginning of the day and skipping or skimping on breakfast. As the term implies, a good breakfast provides energy that enables you to break your nighttime fast at the start of the day and sustain your energy throughout the day. (It also reduces your desire for unhealthy snacks later in the day.) Your first meal of the day should be the meal at which you consume most of your daily calories because you need energy for the next 16 or so hours that you'll be awake and moving. Unfortunately, Americans tend to do it backward by skipping or skimping at breakfast and piling on calories at dinner—a time of day when they don't need many calories because they'll soon be lying down and falling asleep.

4. **Make a conscious attempt to increase consumption of natural foods that have been available to humans throughout natural history.** The following foods aren't processed foods but natural foods that have been available to, and consumed by, humans for thousands of years. As a rule, the food that was good for our ancient ancestors and the survival of our species is good for us now. These are the foods that provide humans with the best protection against their two leading killers: heart disease and cancer.

- Feast on fresh fruit. Fruit has multiple nutritional benefits, including high amounts of vitamins (especially A and C) and minerals. Many fruits also contain high amounts of fiber, which helps purify the bloodstream, lowers the bad type of cholesterol that causes heart disease, and rids the body of toxins found in the intestine. Other fruits, such as berries, are rich in antioxidants—substances known to lower the risk of cancer by attacking oxidants (toxins) in the body that can damage genetic DNA and weaken the immune system. (Blueberries are thought to contain the most antioxidants, followed by blackberries, raspberries, and strawberries.) Keep in mind that fresh fruit is superior to canned fruit, which has been processed and artificially preserved. Also, if weight control is an issue for you, fresh fruit is superior to dried fruit, which contains more calories.

- Go for fresh (or frozen) vegetables. Fresh or frozen vegetables are superior to canned and processed vegetables. The natural oils in certain vegetables (e.g., olive, corn, avocado, and soy) are rich sources of unsaturated fat. Unsaturated fats, also known as essential fatty acids, are considered to be "good" fats because they don't congregate or coagulate in your bloodstream but remain in liquid form within your system; therefore, they don't degenerate into fat on the walls of blood vessels (Erasmus, 1993). Unsaturated fats also help wash away and flush out bad fats from your bloodstream. In addition to containing unsaturated fats, many vegetables—such as raw carrots and green beans—contain fiber that reduces the risk of heart disease and certain forms of cancer.

Think About It ———————————— Journal Entry 12.6

Do you eat fresh fruit and vegetables daily?

_____

Why or why not?

_____

_____

_____

_____

_____

- Go wild on grains. Whole-wheat bread and pasta, whole-grain cereals, oatmeal, and bran are examples of healthy grains. Note that the word "whole" should appear in the product's name (e.g., "whole-wheat bread" and "whole-grain cereal"). This is the key to determining that the grain is natural and not processed; for example, whole-wheat bread is made from a natural grain, but wheat or white bread has been processed. Thus, if you're looking for unbleached, unprocessed grain bread, make sure it says "whole wheat."

   Natural grains contain complex carbohydrates, which the body uses to produce steady, ongoing energy. Complex carbohydrates are called "complex" because their molecular structure is harder for the body to digest and break down into blood sugar. Their more complex molecular structure slows the digestion process; as a result, they're absorbed into the bloodstream more slowly, which allows them to deliver energy to the body more gradually and evenly over an extended period (similar to a coated pill or time-released capsule). Thus, grains are an excellent source of food for producing the steady, long-term energy necessary for athletic activities that require endurance and stamina. Grains are also high in fiber, which helps fight heart disease and certain forms of cancer. Lastly, many complex carbohydrates contain an amino acid that helps manufacture serotonin, a brain chemical associated with relaxation and feelings of emotional serenity (DesMaisons, 1998).

- Feed freely on fish. Fish are high in protein and low in saturated fat, and the natural oil in fish is high in unsaturated fat, which flushes out and washes away cholesterol-forming fats from the bloodstream (Khoshaba & Maddi, 2004). Thus, a diet high in unsaturated fats (and low in saturated fats) reduces risk for cardiovascular disease such as high blood pressure, heart attacks, and strokes. This explains why fish-eating Eskimos have a significantly lower rate of cardiovascular disease than non-Eskimos (Feskens & Kromhout, 1993). However, be cautious about eating too much fish that could contain high levels of mercury, such as shark, swordfish, red snapper, and orange roughy. Eating a variety of fish will help minimize this risk (American Heart Association, 2006).

- Consume lots of legumes. The word *legumes* derives from the Latin root *legumend,* meaning "to gather." This group includes plants and seeds, such as beans (black, red, and navy), lentils, Brussels sprouts, peas, and peanuts. Such foods are great sources of fiber, protein, iron, and B vitamins; plus, they are naturally cholesterol-free and low in saturated fat. The natural oil contained in these foods contains unsaturated fats—"good" fats that can reduce buildup of bad cholesterol in the bloodstream. It's interesting to note that in developing countries, where there is less affluence than in the United States, people rely mainly on legumes, grains, fruits, and vegetables. Despite their poorer economies and poorer medical care, people living in underdeveloped countries have significantly lower rates of heart disease and diet-related cancers than do people living (and eating) in the United States (U.S. Department of Health & Human Services, 2000).

- Drink more water. Most people don't get the recommended amount of water (seven 8-ounce glasses per day). You need to hydrate your body. The body uses water much like a car uses motor oil and transmission fluid, to drive nutrients (fuel) to their proper destinations and to drive waste products out of the system. Water also improves your nervous system's ability to conduct electrochemical signals, which may benefit the brain's ability to process information more easily and more rapidly. In addition to its internal benefits, water has the cosmetic benefit of improving the appearance of your skin. The multiple health benefits of water suggest that you shouldn't drink water only when you're feeling thirsty, but should get into a routine of drinking water regularly throughout the day.

- If you're a woman, make a conscious effort to consume more calcium. Females should take in at least 1,200 mg of calcium per day (Gershoff & Whitney, 1996) to reduce the risk of osteoporosis (thinning of bones and loss of bone mass or density), which increases risk for fractures and curvature of the upper spine. Although osteoporosis can happen in men as well as women, it occurs more often among females. It's estimated that one of three women over the age of 40 will develop osteoporosis (Bohme & Budden, 2001). Because societal pressures make women more weight-conscious than men, females may try to avoid high-calcium dairy products because they're high in calories. However, low-fat, low-calorie dairy products, such as cottage cheese and low-fat yogurt, can contain lots of calcium without lots of calories. Sizable amounts of calcium are also found in other low-calorie foods, such as certain fish (e.g., salmon), vegetables (e.g., broccoli), and fruit (e.g., oranges; Gershoff & Whitney, 1996). Women can also ensure that they get their optimum level of calcium each day by taking calcium dietary supplements.

Student
Perspective

"I always drink lots of water and I try to eat as much fruit and veggies as I can with each meal."

—First-year student

5. **Maintain self-awareness of your eating habits.** The first step toward effective nutrition management is to become fully aware of your current eating habits. People often make decisions about what to eat without giving it much thought or even without conscious awareness. You can increase awareness of your eating habits by simply taking a little time to read the labels on the food products before you put them into your shopping cart and into your body. Keeping a nutritional log or journal of what you eat in a typical week to track its nutrients and caloric content is also an effective way to become self-aware of your eating habits.

Another thing to be aware of is your family history. Have members of your immediate and extended family shown tendencies toward heart disease? Diabetes? Cancer? If so, intentionally adopt a diet that will reduce your risk for developing the types of illnesses that you may have the genetic potential to develop.

| Think About It ——————————— *Journal Entry* **12.7** |

Are you aware of any disease or illness that tends to run in your family?

_____

If yes, is there anything you can do with respect to your diet that may decrease your risk of experiencing this disease or illness?

_____

_____

_____

_____

_____

_____

Exercise and Fitness

Wellness depends not only on fueling the body but also on moving it. The benefits of physical exercise for improving the longevity and quality of human life are simply extraordinary. The health-promoting power of exercise is not surprising, because physical activity was something that our early ancestors did daily to stay alive. They had no motorized vehicles to move them from point A to point B, and no one sold or served them food. Exercise was part of their daily survival routine of roaming and rummaging for fruit, nuts, and vegetables to eat or running after and tracking down animals for meat to eat. Just as eating natural (unprocessed) food is better for your health because it's long been part of human history and has contributed to the survival of the human species, so too is exercise a "natural" health-promoting activity that has made the same contribution (Booth & Vyas, 2001). If done regularly, exercise may well be the most effective "medicine" available to humans for preventing disease and preserving lifelong health.

"If exercise could be packaged into a pill, it would be the single most widely prescribed and beneficial medicine in the nation."

—Robert N. Butler, former director of the National Institute of Aging

Author's Experience I kept in shape when I was young by playing sports such as basketball and baseball. Every chance that made itself available to my schedule, I would play these sports for hours at a time. I enjoyed it so much that I did not realize I was exercising. My body fat was practically nonexistent, energy was ever flowing, and my skills in basketball were always growing. As a middle-aged person, I realize I can no longer do the activities I did for fun as a young person because age has caught up with me. At this point in my life, I attempt to remain active to keep my body fat in a reasonable double-digit category. This takes good scheduling, forethought, and strong will.

— Aaron Thompson

Benefits of Exercise for the Body

1. **Exercise promotes cardiovascular health.** Exercise makes for a healthy heart. The heart is a muscle, and like any other muscle in the body, its size and strength are increased by exercise. A bigger and stronger heart can pump more blood per beat, which reduces the risk for heart disease and stroke (loss of oxygen to the brain) by increasing circulation of oxygen-carrying blood throughout the body and by increasing the body's ability to dissolve blood clots (Khoshaba & Maddi, 2004).

   Exercise further reduces the risk of cardiovascular disease by decreasing the level of triglycerides (clot-forming fats) in the blood, increasing the levels of "good" cholesterol (high-density lipoproteins), and preventing "bad" cholesterol (low-density lipoproteins) from sticking to and clogging up blood vessels.

2. **Exercise stimulates the immune system.** Exercise improves the functioning of the immune system and enables you to better fight off infectious diseases (e.g., colds and the flu) for the following reasons:

   - Exercise reduces stress, which normally weakens the immune system.
   - Exercise increases breathing rate and blood flow throughout the body; which helps flush out germs from your system by increasing the circulation of antibodies carried through the bloodstream.
   - Exercise increases body temperature, which helps kill germs—similar to how a low-grade fever kills germs when you're sick (May, 2004).

3. **Exercise strengthens muscles and bones.** Exercise reduces muscle tension, which helps prevent muscle strain and pain. For example, strengthening abdominal muscles reduces the risk of developing lower back pain. Exercise also maintains bone density and reduces the risk of osteoporosis (brittle bones that bend and break easily). It's noteworthy that bone density before age 20 affects a person's bone density for the remainder of life. Thus, engaging in regular exercise early in life pays long-term dividends by preventing bone deterioration throughout life.

Think About It ———————————— *Journal Entry* **12.8**

Have your exercise habits changed (for better or worse) since you've begun college?

_____

_____

_____

Why or why not?

_____

_____

_____

_____

_____

_____

4. **Exercising promotes weight loss and weight management.** The increasing national trend toward weight gain is due not only to Americans consuming more calories but also to reduced levels of physical activity (American Obesity Association, 2002). Much of this reduction in physical activity results from the emergence of modern technological conveniences that have made it easier for humans to go about their daily business without exerting themselves in the slightest. For example, almost all TVs now come with remote controls so that you don't have to move to change channels, change volume, or turn it on and off. Children now have video games galore that are played virtually so that they can have fun playing without getting up, running around, or jumping up and down. Consequently, people are playing double jeopardy with their health by eating more and moving less.

Exercise is superior to dieting in one major respect: it raises the body's rate of metabolism (i.e., the rate at which consumed calories are burned as energy rather than stored as fat). In contrast, low-calorie dieting lowers the body's rate of metabolism (Leibel, Rosenbaum, & Hirsch, 1995) and slows the rate at which calories are burned. After two to three weeks of low-calorie dieting without exercising, the body saves more of the calories it does get by storing them as fat. This happens because long-term low-calorie dieting makes the body "think" it's starving; it therefore tries to compensate and increase its chances of survival by saving more calories as fat so that they can be used for future energy (Bennet & Gurin, 1983). In contrast, exercise speeds up basal metabolism—the body's rate of metabolism when it is resting. Thus, in addition to burning fat directly while exercising, exercise burns fat by continuing to keep the body's metabolic rate higher after you stop exercising and move on to do more sedentary things.

Benefits of Exercise for the Mind

In addition to the multiple benefits of exercise for the body, there are numerous benefits for the mind. What follows is a summary of the powerful benefits of physical exercise for mental health and mental performance. For people who believe that exercise isn't all that good for them and still cling to this belief after reading the following sections, it may be safe to conclude that they are in denial.

1. **Exercise increases mental energy and improves mental performance.** Have you ever noticed how red your face gets when you engage in strenuous physical activity? This rosy complexion occurs because physical activity pumps enormous amounts of blood into your head region, resulting in more oxygen reaching your brain. Exercise increases the heart's ability to pump blood throughout the body and into the brain, and since the brain consumes more oxygen than any other part of the body, it's easy to see why it's the bodily organ that benefits the most from exercise. Moreover, exercise increases production of a brain chemical called norepinephrine, which helps form physical connections between brain cells (Howard, 2000). As mentioned in Chapter 6, these are the connections that provide the biological basis of learning and memory.

2. **Exercise elevates mood.** Exercise increases the release of endorphins (morphine-like chemicals found in the brain that produce a natural high) and serotonin (a mellowing brain chemical that reduces feelings of tension, anxiety, and depression). For these reasons, psychotherapists prescribe exercise for patients experiencing mild forms of anxiety or depression (Johnsgard, 2004). Studies show that people who exercise regularly tend to report feeling "happier" (Myers, 1993).

3. **Exercise strengthens self-esteem.** Exercise improves self-esteem by giving you a sense of personal achievement or accomplishment by improving your physical self-image (e.g., improved weight control, body tone, and skin tone).

4. **Exercise deepens and enriches the quality of sleep.** Research on the effects of exercise on sleep indicates that if exercise is engaged in at least three hours before bedtime, it helps people fall asleep, stay asleep, and sleep more deeply (Singh, Clements, & Fiatarone, 1997). Therefore, exercise is a common component of treatment programs for people experiencing insomnia (Dement & Vaughan, 2000).

> "It is exercise alone that supports the spirits, and keeps the mind in vigor."
>
> —Marcus Cicero, ancient Roman orator and philosopher

Guidelines and Strategies for Effective Exercise

Specific exercises vary in terms of what they do to and for the body. Nevertheless, some general guidelines and strategies, such as those discussed here, can be applied to any exercise routine or personal fitness program.

1. **Warm up before exercising and cool down after exercising.** Start with a 10-minute warm-up of low-intensity movements that are similar to the ones you'll be using in the actual exercise. This increases circulation of blood to the muscles that you'll be exercising and reduces muscle soreness and your risk of muscle pulls.

    End your exercise routine with a 10-minute cool-down, during which you stretch the muscles that you used while exercising. Stretch the muscle until it burns a little bit, and then release it. Cooling down after exercise improves circulation to the exercised muscles and enables them to return more gradually to a tension-free state, which will minimize the risk of muscle tightness, cramps, pulls, or tears.

2. **Engage in cross-training to attain total body fitness.** A balanced, comprehensive fitness program is one that involves cross-training—combining different exercises to achieve overall bodily fitness. For instance, combine exercises that promote:

    -   Endurance and weight control (e.g., running, cycling, or swimming);
    -   Muscle strength and tone (e.g., weight training, push-ups, or sit-ups); and
    -   Flexibility (e.g., yoga, Pilates, or tai chi).

A total fitness plan also includes exercising various muscle groups rotationally (e.g., upper-body muscles one day, lower-body muscles the next), which allows your muscle tissue extra time to rest and fully repair itself before it's exercised again.

3. **Exercising with regularity and consistency is as important as exercising with intensity.** Doing exercise regularly, and allowing strength and stamina to increase gradually, is the key to attaining fitness and avoiding injury. One strategy you can use to be sure that you're training your body, rather than straining and overextending it, is to see whether you can talk while you're exercising. If you can't continue speaking without having to catch your breath, you may be overdoing it. Drop the intensity level and allow your body to adapt or adjust to a less strenuous level. After continuing at this lower level awhile, try again at the higher level while trying to talk simultaneously. If you can do both, then you're ready to continue at that level for some time. Thus, you can gradually increase the intensity, frequency, or duration of your exercise routine to a level that produces maximum benefits with minimal post-exercise strain or pain.

Author's Experience   I had a habit of exercising too intensely—to the point where I overfatigued my muscles and left my body feeling sore for days after I worked out. Like many people, I exercise while listening to music to make the exercise routine more stimulating. I've since discovered that listening to music through headphones while exercising may help me determine whether I'm overdoing it. If I can't sing along with the music without having to stop and catch my breath, then I know I'm overdoing it. This strategy has helped me manage my exercise intensity level and reduce my day-after-exercise soreness. (Plus, I've gained more confidence as a singer. My singing sounds better to me when my ears are covered with headphones.)

— Joe Cuseo

4. **Take advantage of exercise and fitness resources on your campus.** You paid for use of the campus gym or recreation center with your college tuition, so take advantage of this and other exercise resources on campus. Also, consider taking physical education courses offered by your college. They may count toward your college degree, and typically they carry one unit of credit so that they can be easily added to your course schedule. If exercise-related groups or clubs meet on campus, consider joining them; they can provide you with a motivating support group that can convert your exercise routine from an experience that's done alone to a social experience with others.

5. **Take advantage of natural opportunities for physical activity that present themselves during the day.** Exercise can take place outside a gym or fitness center and outside scheduled workout times. Opportunities for exercise often occur naturally as you go about your daily activities. For example, if you can walk or ride your bike to class, do that instead of driving a car or riding a bus. If you can climb some stairs instead of taking an elevator, take the route that's more physically challenging and requires more bodily activity.

6. **Use exercise as a strategy for improving your academic performance.** Two simple strategies can be used to combine physical activity with mental activity in a way that may improve your academic performance:

   • Take study breaks that involve physical activity (e.g., a short jog or brisk walk). Study breaks that include physical activity not only refresh the mind by giving it a break from studying but also stimulate the mind by increasing blood flow to your brain, which will help you retain what you've already studied and regain concentration for what you're about to study.

- Before exams, take a brisk walk. This will increase mental alertness by increasing oxygen flow to the brain; it will also decrease tension by increasing the brain's production of emotionally "mellowing" brain chemicals (e.g., serotonin and endorphins).

Think About It ———————— Journal Entry 12.9

Do you have a regular exercise routine?

_____

If no, why not?

_____

_____

_____

_____

_____

If yes, what do you do and how often do you do it?

_____

_____

_____

_____

_____

What more could you do to improve your:

1. Endurance

_____

_____

_____

2. Strength

_____

_____

_____

3. Flexibility

_____

_____

_____

Rest and Sleep

Sleep experts agree that humans in today's information-loaded, multitasking world aren't getting the quantity and quality of sleep needed to perform at peak levels (Mitler, Dinges, & Dement, 1994).

We often underestimate the power of sleep and think we can cheat on sleep without compromising the quality of our lives. As discussed below, sleep has multiple benefits for the body and mind, which strongly suggests that good sleep habits are necessary for ensuring our physical and mental well-being.

The Value and Purpose of Sleep

Resting and reenergizing the body are the most obvious purposes of sleep (Dement & Vaughan, 1999). However, other benefits of sleep are less well known but equally important for physical and mental health (Dement & Vaughan, 2000; Horne, 1988). Some of these key, less apparent benefits of sleep are described here.

1. **Sleep restores and preserves the power of the immune system.** Studies show that when humans and other animals lose sleep, their production of disease-fighting antibodies is reduced and they become more susceptible to illness, such as common colds and the flu (Blakeslee, 1993).

2. **Sleep helps you cope with daily stress.** Sleep research shows that the amount of time we spend in dream sleep increases when we are experiencing stress (Greenberg, Pillard, & Pearlman, 1972). When you lose dream sleep, emotional problems such as anxiety and depression worsen (Voelker, 2004). It's thought that the biochemical changes that take place in your brain during dream sleep repair imbalances in brain chemistry that would otherwise trigger feelings of anxiety or depression. Getting quality sleep, especially dream sleep, is essential for maintaining a good mood and a positive frame of mind. Indeed, research reveals that people who sleep well are more likely to report that they are happy (Myers, 1993).

"Sleep deprivation is a major epidemic in our society. Americans spend so much time and energy chasing the American dream that they don't have much time left for actual dreaming."

—William Dement, pioneering sleep researcher and founder of the American Sleep Disorders Association

3. **Sleep helps the brain form and store memories.** Studies show that loss of dream sleep at night results in poorer memory for information learned earlier in the day (Peigneux, Laureys, Delbeuck, & Maquet, 2001). For instance, adolescents who get minimal sleep have a more difficult time retaining new information learned in school (Horne, 1988).

Importance of Sleep for College Students

College students, in particular, tend to have poor sleep habits. Heavier academic workloads, more opportunities to socialize, and course schedules that provide more opportunity to procrastinate can result in last-minute, late-night, or all-night study binges that lead to irregular sleep schedules and regular sleep loss.

How much sleep do you need or should you get? The answer to this question lies in your genes and varies from person to person. On average, adults need seven to eight hours of sleep each day and teenagers need slightly more—about nine hours (Roffwarg, Muzio, & Dement, 1966). Research shows that college students get an average of less than seven hours of sleep each night (Hicks, as cited in Zimbardo, Johnson, & Weber, 2006), which means that they're not getting the amount of sleep needed for optimal academic performance.

Attempting to train your body to sleep less is likely to be an exercise in futility, because what you're actually trying to do is force your body to do something that it's not naturally (genetically) inclined to do. Eventually, you pay the price for the sleep you've lost with lower energy and poorer performance. When your body is deprived of its needed amount of sleep, it accumulates "sleep debt," which, like financial debt, must be eventually paid back at a later time (Dement & Vaughan, 1999). If your sleep debt isn't repaid, it will catch up with you and you will pay the consequences in terms of impaired health, mood, and performance (Van Dongen, Maislin, Mullington, & Dinges, 2003). For example, studies show that the effects of sleep loss on driving an automobile are similar to the effects of alcohol (Arnedt, Wilde, Munt, & MacLean, 2001; Fletcher, Lamond, Van den Heuvel, & Dawson, 2003), and sleep-deprived students have been found to earn lower grades than students who get sufficient sleep (Spinweber, as cited in Zimbardo et al., 2006).

Student Perspective

"I 'binge' sleep. I don't sleep often and then I hibernate for like a day or two."

—First-year student

Student Perspective

"I'm not getting enough sleep. I've been getting roughly 6–7 hours of sleep on weekdays. In high school, I would get 8–9 hours of sleep."

—First-year student

Student Perspective

"First of all, you should probably know that your body will not function without sleep. I learned that the hard way."

—Words written by a first-year student in a letter of advice to new college students

Think About It — Journal Entry 12.10

What amount of sleep per night do you think you need to perform at your highest level?

_____

_____

How many nights per week do you typically get this amount of sleep?

_____

_____

If you're not getting this optimal amount of sleep each night, what is preventing you from doing so?

_____

_____

_____

_____

_____

_____

Strategies for Improving Sleep Quality

Since sleep has powerful benefits for both the body and the mind, if you can improve the quality of your sleep, you can improve your physical and mental well-being. Listed here is a series of strategies for improving sleep quality that should also improve your health and performance.

1. **Increase awareness of your sleep habits by keeping a sleep log or sleep journal.** In your sleep journal, note nights when you slept well or poorly and what you did before going to bed on those nights. Tracking your sleep experiences in a journal may enable you to find patterns that reveal relationships among things you do (or don't do) during the day when you sleep well. If you detect such a pattern, you may have detected a routine you could follow regularly to ensure that you consistently get high-quality sleep.

2. **Attempt to get into a regular sleep schedule by going to sleep and getting up about the same times each day.** Irregular sleep schedules can disrupt the quality of sleep. This is what happens to people who experience jet lag. Traveling to a new time zone often requires travelers to change their sleep schedules to accommodate the time shift, which can disrupt the quality of their sleep (Rader & Hicks, 1987). Your body likes to work on a biological rhythm of set cycles; if you can get your body on a regular sleep schedule, you're more likely to establish a biological rhythm that makes it easier for you to fall asleep, stay asleep, and wake up naturally from sleep according to your internal alarm clock.

   Establishing a stable sleep schedule is particularly important around midterms and finals. Unfortunately, these are the times during the term when students often disrupt their normal sleep patterns by cramming in last-minute studying, staying up later, getting up earlier, or not going to sleep. Sleep research shows that if you want to be at your physical and mental best for upcoming exams, you should get yourself on a regular sleep schedule of going to bed about the same time and getting up about the same time for at least one week before your exams (Dement, 1999).

3. **Sleep in the same place each night.** People are creatures of habit, and if your brain gets in the habit of associating the same environmental cues (e.g., sights, smells, and sounds) with falling asleep, you're more likely to fall asleep when you find yourself in that same environment. When you repeatedly sleep in the same environment (e.g., the same room, the same side of the bed, and the same sound

of a humming fan), these sensations become repeatedly paired or associated with sleep and your body is more likely to respond to those associations by falling asleep (Hauri & Linde, 1996).

4. **Attempt to get into a relaxing bedtime ritual each night.** Taking a hot bath or shower, consuming hot milk, or listening to relaxing music are bedtime rituals that can get you into a worry-free state and help you fall asleep sooner. Also, making a list of things you intend to do the next day before going to bed may help you relax and fall asleep because you can go to bed with the peace of mind that comes from being organized and ready to handle the following day's tasks.

    Light studying or reviewing previously studied material may also be good to do at bedtime because sleep can help you better retain what you've experienced just before going to sleep. Many years of studies show that the best thing you can do after attempting to learn something is to "sleep on it," probably because your brain can then focus on processing it without interference from outside distractions (Jenkins & Dallenbach, 1924).

5. **Make sure the temperature of your sleep room is not too warm (no higher than 70 degrees).** Warm temperatures often make people feel sleepy, but they usually don't help them stay asleep or sleep well. This is why people have trouble sleeping on hot summer evenings. High-quality, uninterrupted sleep is more likely to take place at cooler, more comfortable room temperatures (Coates, 1977).

6. **Avoid intense mental activity just before going to sleep.** Light mental work may serve as a relaxing presleep ritual, but cramming intensely for a difficult exam or doing intensive writing before bedtime is likely to generate a state of mental arousal, which will interfere with your ability to "wind down" and fall asleep.

7. **Avoid intense physical exercise before going to sleep.** Physical exercise generates an increase in muscle tension and mental energy (oxygen flow to the brain), which energizes you and keeps you from falling asleep. If you're going to exercise in the evening, it should be done at least three hours before bedtime (Hauri & Linde, 1996).

8. **Avoid consuming sleep-interfering foods, beverages, or drugs in late afternoon or evening.** In particular, avoid the following substances near bedtime:

    *   **Caffeine.** Because it works as a stimulant drug for most people, caffeine is likely to stimulate your nervous system and keep you awake.
    *   **Nicotine.** This stimulant drug is also likely to reduce the depth and quality of your sleep.
    *   **Alcohol.** This drug will make you feel sleepy in larger doses, but smaller doses can have a stimulating effect; furthermore, alcohol in all doses disrupts the quality of sleep by reducing the amount of time you spend in dream-stage sleep (marijuana does the same).

Remember

Things that make you feel sleepy (e.g., warm room temperature or alcohol consumption) often won't improve the depth and quality of your sleep.

Alcohol, Drugs, and Risky Behavior

In addition to putting healthy nutrients into your body, exercising it, and resting it, two other elements can help you maintain physical wellness: (1) keeping risky substances out of your body, and (2) keeping away from risky behaviors that jeopardize your body. New college students are often confronted with new choices to make about what risks to take, or not to take, during their first year of college.

Alcohol Use among College Students

In the United States, alcohol is a legal beverage (drug) for people 21 years of age and older. However, whether you're of legal age or not, it's likely that alcohol has already been available to you and will continue to be available to you when you're in college. Since it's a substance commonly accessible at college parties and social gatherings, you'll be confronted with two sets of decisions about alcohol:

1. To drink or not to drink
2. To drink responsibly or irresponsibly (i.e., drinking to get drunk or escape problems)

If you decide to drink, here are some quick tips for drinking responsibly:

- Don't drink with the intention of getting intoxicated; set a limit for how much you will drink. (Use alcohol as a beverage, not as a mind-altering drug.)
- Drink slowly. (Sip, don't gulp, and avoid "shotgunning" or "chug-a-lugging" drinks.)
- Space out your drinks over time. (This gives your body time to metabolize the alcohol and keeps your blood alcohol level manageable.)
- Alternate water and alcoholic drinks.
- Eat well before you drink and snack while you're drinking. (This will lower your peak blood alcohol level.)

Naturally, the best way to avoid irresponsible drinking is to not to drink at all. This is the safest option, particularly if your family has a history of alcohol abuse. If you choose to drink, make sure that it's *your* choice, not a choice imposed on you through social pressure or the need to conform. Research indicates that first-year college students drink more than they did in high school and that alcohol abuse is higher among first-year college students than students at more advanced stages of their college experience.

The most common reason why first-year students drink is to "fit in" or to feel socially accepted. However, college students overestimate the number of their peers who drink and the total amount they drink; this overestimation can lead them to believe that if they don't conform to this "norm," they're not "normal" (DeJong & Linkenback, 1999). Student beliefs that college partying and college drinking go hand in hand may also be exaggerated by media portrayals of college students as wild party animals. Popular magazines rank the "top party schools," DVDs depict female college students who've "gone wild," and popular movies have been made whose entire plots revolve around the drunken escapades of college students (*Animal House, Spring Break I, II*, etc.).

College students' expectation that they should drink (and drink to excess) accounts, at least in part, for the fact that the number one drug problem on college campuses is *binge drinking*—periodic drinking episodes during which a large amount of alcohol (four or five drinks) is consumed in a short period of time, resulting in an acute state of intoxication—i.e., a drunken state. Although alcohol is a legal substance (if you're 21 or older) and it's a substance that's consumed as a beverage rather than injected, smoked, or snorted, alcohol is still a mind-altering substance when consumed in large quantities (doses). Just as THC is the mind-altering ingredient in marijuana, ethyl alcohol is the mind-altering ingredient in beer, wine, and hard liquor (see Figure 12.4).

FIGURE 12.4

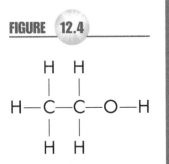

Ethyl Alcohol: The Mind-Altering Ingredient Contained in Alcohol

WHO'S IN CHARGE?

Drugs and Alcohol

It's "Thirsty Thursday" and your friend convinces you to go to a party with him. You tell him that you have class at 9:00 and you cannot miss it. He assures you that you will be home before midnight. You go to the party and you are having a great time. Everyone is drinking so you decide you should join in (even though you are underage). You drink more than your fair share and stumble in at 3 a.m. Your friend makes sure you get to bed OK and even sets your alarm for 8:30 so that you can make it to your 9:00 class. You are sick all night because you drank too much and you pass out on the bathroom floor. You finally get up around 11:00 and realize you missed class. You hear from a classmate that the teacher gave a pop quiz. You are irate with your friend because it is all his fault that you missed class and the quiz! Could you have handled this situation differently? If so, how? Who really is to blame for you missing class and the quiz?

Alcohol abuse is like any other form of drug abuse. Approximately 7 to 8 percent of people who drink develop alcohol addiction or dependency, i.e., alcoholism. Although binge drinking may not be alcoholism, it's still a form of alcohol abuse because it has direct, negative effects on the drinker's:

- Behavior—e.g., drunk-driving accidents and deaths,
- Body—e.g., acute alcohol withdrawal syndrome, better known as a hangover, and
- Mind—e.g., memory loss ("blackouts").

Research indicates that repeatedly getting drunk can reduce the size and effectiveness of the part of the brain involved with memory formation, which has led some researchers to the conclusion that the more often a person gets drunk, the dumber that person gets.

Furthermore, binge drinking can have indirect negative effects on health and safety by reducing the drinker's inhibitions about engaging in risk-taking behavior, which, in turn, increases the risk of personal accidents, injuries, and illnesses. Arguably, no other drug reduces a person's inhibitions as dramatically as alcohol. After consuming a significant amount of alcohol, people can become much less cautious about doing things they normally wouldn't do. This chemically induced sense of courage (sometimes referred to as "liquid courage") can override the process of logical thinking and decision making, increasing the drinker's willingness to engage in irrational risk-taking behavior. Typically, binge drinkers become less inhibited about engaging in reckless driving, increasing the risk of accidental injury or death, and less cautious about engaging in reckless (unprotected) sex, increasing the risk of accidental pregnancy or contracting sexually transmitted infections (STIs). It could be said that binge drinkers think they've become invincible, immortal, and infertile.

It's noteworthy that the legal age for consuming alcohol was once lowered to 18 years; it was raised back to 21 because the number of drunk-driving accidents and deaths among teenage drinkers increased dramatically when the legal age was lowered. Traffic accidents still account for more deaths of Americans between the ages of 15 and 24 than any other single cause.

When teenagers gain independence and acquire their first taste of new freedoms, they often take the newfound freedom beyond moderation and push it to the outer limits—for example, driving as fast as they can and drinking as much as they can—perhaps to prove to themselves and others how much freedom they now have. It's as if the more risks they take with their new freedom, the more of it they think they have. In the case of freedom to drink and freedom to drive, the two can be a dangerous (or deadly) combination.

Since alcohol is a depressant drug, it depresses (slows) the nervous system. This can increase the probability of aggressive and sexual behavior by slowing signals normally sent from the upper, front part of the brain (the "human brain"), which is responsible for rational thinking and inhibits or controls the lower, middle part of the brain (the "animal brain") that is responsible for basic animal drives, such as sex and aggression (see Figure 12.5). When the upper (rational) brain's messages are slowed by alcohol, the animal brain is freed from the signals that normally restrain or inhibit it, allowing its basic drives to be released or expressed. Thus, the less inhibited drinker is more likely to engage in aggressive or sexual behavior.

FIGURE 12.5

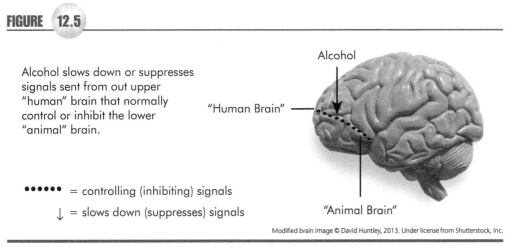

Alcohol slows down or suppresses signals sent from out upper "human" brain that normally control or inhibit the lower "animal" brain.

"Human Brain"

Alcohol

"Animal Brain"

●●●●● = controlling (inhibiting) signals

↓ = slows down (suppresses) signals

Modified brain image © David Huntley, 2013. Under license from Shutterstock, Inc.

How Alcohol Works in the Brain to Reduce Personal Inhibitions

Sexual Assault, a.k.a. Sexual Violence

Sexual assault refers to nonconsensual (unwanted or unwilling) sexual contact, which includes rape, attempted rape, and any other type of sexual contact that a person forces on another person without their consent.

Rape is an extreme form of sexual assault or sexual violence that involves forced sexual penetration (intercourse), which takes place through physical force, by threat of bodily harm, or when the victim is incapable of giving consent due to alcohol or drug intoxication. Rape takes place in two major forms:

1. **Stranger rape.** When a total stranger forces sexual intercourse on the victim.
2. **Acquaintance rape or date rape.** The victim knows, or is dating, the person who forces unwanted sexual intercourse. It's estimated that about 85 percent of reported rapes are committed by an acquaintance. Alcohol is frequently associated with acquaintance rapes because it lowers the rapist's inhibitions and reduces the victim's ability to judge whether she is in a potentially dangerous situation. Since the victim is familiar with the offender, she may feel at fault or conclude that

what happened is not sexual assault. The bottom line: Even though the partners know each other, acquaintance rape is still rape and still a crime because it's non-consensual sex.

Recommendations for women to reduce the risk of experiencing sexual assault:

- Don't drink to excess or associate with others who drink to excess.
- Go to parties with at least one friend so you can keep an eye out for each other.
- Clearly and assertively communicate what your sexual limits are. Use "I messages" to firmly resist unwanted sexual advances by rejecting the behavior rather than the person (e.g., "I'm not comfortable with you touching me like that.").
- Remain mindful of the difference between lust and love. If you just met someone who makes sexual advances toward you, that person lusts for you but doesn't love you.
- Take a self-defense class.
- Carry mace or pepper spray.
- Leave with a friend. Use the buddy system.

Recommendations for men for reducing the risk of committing sexual assault:

- Don't assume a woman wants to have sex just because she's:
  a. very friendly or flirtatious,
  b. dressed in a provocative way, or
  c. drinking alcohol.
- If a woman says "no," don't interpret that to mean she's really saying "yes."
- Don't think that just because you're "the man," you have to be the sexual initiator or aggressor
- Don't interpret sexual rejection as personal rejection or a blow to masculinity.

Note: Title IX of the Education Amendment of 1972 is a federal civil rights law that prohibits discrimination on the basis of sex, which includes sexual harassment, rape, and sexual assault. A college or university may be held legally responsible when it knows about and ignores sexual harassment or assault in its programs or activities, whether the harassment is committed by a faculty member, staff, or a student. If you have been sexually harassed and believe that your campus has not responded effectively to your concern, you can contact or file a complaint with the Department of Education's Office of Civil Rights (www2.ed.gov/about/offices/list/ocr/docs/howto.html).

Illegal Drugs

In addition to alcohol, other substances are likely to be encountered on college campuses that are illegal for anyone to use at any age. Among the most commonly used illegal drugs are the following:

- **Marijuana (weed, pot).** Primarily a depressant or sedative drug that slows the nervous system and produces a mellow feeling of relaxation.
- **Ecstasy (X).** A stimulant typically taken in pill form that speeds up the nervous system and reduces social inhibitions.
- **Cocaine (coke, crack).** A stimulant that's typically snorted or smoked and produces a strong rush of euphoria.

- **Amphetamines (speed, meth).** A strong stimulant that increases energy and general arousal; it is usually taken in pill form but may also be smoked or injected.
- **Hallucinogens (psychedelics).** Drugs that alter or distort perception and are typically swallowed—e.g., LSD or acid and hallucinogenic mushrooms ("shrooms").
- **Narcotics (e.g., heroin and prescription pain pills).** Depressant or sedative drugs that slow the nervous system and produce feelings of relaxation. (Heroin is a particularly powerful narcotic that can either be injected or smoked, and produces an intense rush of euphoria.)
- **Date rape drugs.** Depressant (sedative) drugs that induce sleepiness, memory loss, and possible loss of consciousness; they are typically colorless, tasteless, and odorless, so they can be easily mixed into a drink without the drinker noticing it and render the drinker vulnerable to rape or other forms of sexual assault. The most common date-rape drugs are Rohypnol ("roofies") and GHB ("liquid E").

All of these drugs are potentially habit-forming, especially if they're injected intravenously (directly into a vein) or smoked (inhaled through the lungs). These routes of drug delivery are particularly dangerous because they allow the drug to reach the brain faster and with more intense impact, resulting in the drug's effect being experienced more rapidly and at a higher peak effect. However, this is followed by a rapid and sharp drop (crash) after the drug's peak effect has been experienced (see Figure 12.6). This peak-to-valley, roller-coaster effect creates a greater risk for craving and desire to use the drug again, thereby increasing the user's risk of dependency (addiction).

FIGURE 12.6

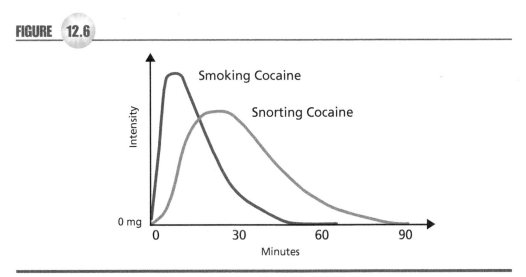

Drugs Smoked Produce a Higher and More Rapid Peak Effect

Listed here are common signs that use of any drug (including alcohol) is moving in the direction of *dependency* (*addiction*):

- Steadily using more of the drug and/or using it more often
- Difficulty cutting back (e.g., unable to use the drug less frequently or in smaller amounts)
- Difficulty controlling or limiting the amount taken after starting
- Keeping a steady supply of the drug on hand

- Spending more on the drug than you can afford
- Using the drug alone
- Hiding or hoarding the drug
- Lying about your drug use to family and friends
- Reacting angrily or defensively when questioned about drug use
- Being in denial about abusing the drug (e.g., "I don't have a problem")
- Rationalizing drug abuse (e.g., "It's no big deal; it's just part of the college experience")
- Continuing to use the drug matters more to the user than the personal and interpersonal problems caused by its use

Addiction is one major motive for repeated use of any drug. However, there are other motives underlying the desire to do drugs. A summary of the major motives for drug use is provided in Snapshot Summary 12.2.

Snapshot Summary

12.2 Drug Use among College Students: Common Causes and Major Motives

1. **Social pressure.** To fit in or be socially accepted (e.g., smoking marijuana because lots of college students seem to be doing it)
2. **Recreational (party) use.** For fun, stimulation, or pleasure (e.g., drinking alcohol at parties to loosen inhibitions and to have a good time)
3. **Experimental use.** Doing drugs out of curiosity—to test out their effects (e.g., experimenting with LSD to see what it's like to have a psychedelic or hallucinogenic experience)
4. **Therapeutic use.** Using prescription or over-the-counter drugs for medical purposes (e.g., taking Prozac for depression or Ritalin to treat attention deficit disorder)
5. **Performance enhancement.** To improve physical or mental performance (e.g., taking steroids to improve athletic performance or stimulants to stay awake all night and cram for an exam)

6. **Escapism.** To temporarily escape a personal problem or an unpleasant emotional state (e.g., taking ecstasy to escape depression or boredom)
7. **Addiction.** Physical or psychological dependence resulting from habitual use of a drug (e.g., continuing to use nicotine or cocaine because stopping will result in withdrawal symptoms such as anxiety or depression)

Student
Perspectives

"For fun." "To party." "To fit in." "To become more talkative, outgoing, and flirtatious."

"To try anything once." "To become numb." "To forget problems." "Being bored."

—Responses of freshmen and sophomores to the question "Why do college students take drugs?"

Think About It ———————————— *Journal Entry* 12.11

What drugs (if any) have you seen being used on your campus?

_____

_____

_____

_____

How would the type and frequency of drug use on your campus compare to what you saw in high school?

_____

_____

_____

_____

What motives for drug use listed in Snapshot Summary 12.2 would you say are the most common reasons for drug use on your campus?

_____

_____

_____

_____

Strategies for Minimizing or Eliminating the Negative Effects of Alcohol and Other Drugs

1. **Don't let yourself be pressured into drinking.** Keep in mind that college students tend to overestimate how much their peers drink, so don't feel you're uncool, unusual, or abnormal if you prefer not to drink.

2. **If you drink, maintain awareness of how much you're drinking while you're drinking by monitoring your physical and mental state.** Don't continue to drink after you've reached a state of moderate relaxation or a mild loss of inhibition. Drinking to the point where you're drunk or bordering on intoxication doesn't improve your physical health or your social life. You're not exactly the life of the party if you're slurring your speech, vomiting in the restroom, nodding out, or on the verge of falling sound asleep.

   The key to drinking responsibly and in moderation is to have a plan for managing your drinking. Your plan should include strategies such as:

   - Drinking slowly
   - Eating while drinking
   - Alternating between drinking alcoholic and nonalcoholic beverages
   - Tapering off your drinking after the first hour of a party or social gathering.

   Lastly, don't forget that alcohol is costly, both in money and in calories. Thus, reducing or eliminating your drinking is not only a good way to manage your health; it's also a good money-management and weight-management strategy.

3. **If you're a woman who drinks, or who frequents places where others drink, remain aware of the possibility of date-rape drugs being dropped into your drink.** Drugs such as gamma-hydroxybutyric acid (a.k.a. GHB or G) and Rohypnol (a.k.a. roofies or roaches) induce sleep and memory loss, and they are particularly powerful when taken with alcohol. To guard against this risk, don't let others give you drinks, and hold onto your drink at all times (e.g., don't leave it, go to the restroom, and come back to drink it again).

There are safer and more productive ways to blow your mind than using mind-altering substances.

Don't Blow It on Drugs

4. **If you find yourself in a situation where an illegal drug is available to you, our bottom-line recommendation is this: If you're in doubt, keep it out—don't put anything into your body that you're unsure about.** We acknowledge that the college years are a time for exploring and experimenting with different ideas, experiences, feelings, and states of consciousness. However, doing illegal drugs just isn't worth the risk. Even if you're aware of how an illegal drug affects people in general, you don't know how it will affect you in particular, because each individual has a unique genetic makeup. Furthermore, unlike legal drugs that have to pass through rigorous testing by the Food and Drug Administration before they're approved for public consumption, you can't be sure how an illegal drug has been produced and packaged from one time to the next, and you don't know if it may have been "cut" (mixed) with other substances during the production process. Thus, you're not just taking a criminal risk by using a drug that's illegal: you're also taking a health risk by consuming an unregulated substance whose effects on your body and mind are likely to be more unpredictable and potentially detrimental.

Minimize Your Risk of Contracting Sexually Transmitted Infections (STIs)

STIs represent a group of contagious infections that are spread through sexual contact. The more sexual partners you have, the greater the risk of contracting an STI. Latex condoms provide the best protection.

More than 25 different types of STIs have been identified, but the following bacteria and viruses account for the majority of infections. These infections are typically very treatable, but if they are ignored, they can lead to internal infections and possible infertility.

STIs Caused by Bacteria

Gonorrhea. This is a common STI with few symptoms but serious consequences if it is left untreated. In 2007, there were 355,991 cases reported, however the Center for Disease Control (CDC) estimates there are nearly twice as many infections annually than the number reported (Weinstock, Berman, & Cates, Jr., 2004). Men typically experience creamy, yellow-colored, pus-like discharge from the penis, and burning when urinating. Women experience few early symptoms, but the disease can lead to later pelvic infections and possible infertility. The best way to detect gonorrhea, or any other STI that produces early symptoms that are not visible, is to have a laboratory test done by a doctor or healthcare provider. Gonorrhea can be treated and completely cured with antibiotics.

Chlamydia. This is the number-one bacterial STI; it's estimated to infect more than 10 percent of college students. In 2007, there were 1,108,374 chlamydia diagnoses reported, the largest number of cases ever reported to the CDC for any condition. However, the CDC estimates that there are approximately 2.8 million new cases of chlamydia annually, meaning more than half of new cases go undiagnosed and unreported (Weinstock et al., 2004). Symptoms include a clear, mucous-like discharge and a burning sensation when urinating. Men may experience pain in the testes, and women may experience pain in the abdomen. However, women typically experience few or no early symptoms.

Genital Herpes. Typically produces painful blisters on the genitals or in the anus, which may itch and burn, especially during and following urination. Symptoms may disappear and come back, but are never cured. Later attacks tend to be less severe than the first attack. The frequency and intensity of outbreaks can be reduced with prescription medication (e.g., acyclovir capsules).

Syphilis. Men first experience ulcers (open sores) on the penis. Women may first develop ulcers in the vagina, but they can be overlooked, allowing the disease to progress. Syphilis is totally curable with antibiotics.

STIs Caused by Viruses

Human Papilloma Virus (HPV). Overall, this is the most common STI among young, sexually active people. HPV is a virus that may cause warts in the genital area, but it typically does not produce noticeable symptoms in its early stages. Sometimes, the disease may also cause lesions (abnormal tissue changes) that are not visible, but when they appear, they look like small hard, cauliflower-like spots. Men can experience warts on the penis. HPV is treatable with laser or chemical treatment, which basically burn off the lesions. If untreated, HPV can lead to cancer of the cervix in women.

Human Immunodeficiency Virus (HIV). Early symptoms include fever, night sweats, swollen lymph nodes, diarrhea, chronic fatigue, and weight loss. About one-half of people with HIV experience these flu-like symptoms, but one-half show no symptoms at all. Thus, the disease may go undetected until the person is given a blood test for some other reason. Most cases of HIV are transmitted through sexual contact; however, the disease may also be contracted through the sharing of intravenous needles. The most serious form of HIV is *Acquired Immune Deficiency Syndrome (AIDS),* which is a life-threatening condition, because the person's immune system becomes severely impaired and leaves the infected person vulnerable to cancer and diseases of the nervous system.

Hepatitis B or *Hepatitis C.* About one-half of the people with hepatitis experience flu-like symptoms, and one-half show no symptoms at all. Thus, the disease may go undetected until the person is given a blood test for some other reason.

Pubic Lice (a.k.a. "Crabs"). Caused by tiny lice that are called "crabs" (because they look like sea crabs), which breed in pubic hair around the genitals. These creatures are not dangerous but can cause intense itching.

STIs

You have been seeing a new guy for almost a month and decide you are ready to have sex. He tells you not to worry because he has been tested for STIs and the test came back clean. Since you are both really into each other and have decided to be exclusive and you are on the Pill, you decide there is no need to use a condom. Sex is so much better without them! A few weeks later you notice an odd-smelling discharge and go to the doctor only to find out you have an STI. What could you have done to prevent getting the STI? Many people blame the partner, but in this case, could the situation have been prevented? How?

Unplanned Pregnancy and Community College Students

Understanding risky behaviors regarding sexual activity is important not only because of the risk of STIs but also because of the risk of unplanned pregnancy. Having a baby can be a wonderful experience, especially when he/she is planned. However, having an unplanned baby while in college could significantly decrease your chance of successfully completing college.

Although many might think this topic is not necessary to talk about for students in community colleges, it is! The rate of unplanned pregnancies is actually increasing (and not decreasing) among 20 to 24 year olds (Guttmacher Institute, 2009). Possibly the most important thing to know regarding community college students and unplanned pregnancy is that 61 percent of women who have children after enrolling in a community college do not finish their education. This number is 65 percent higher than for women who do not have children while in college (Bradburn, 2002).

Many students believe that preventing pregnancy while in school is important. Three-quarters of students report that preventing unplanned pregnancy is important to them, and eight in 10 say that having a child while in school would make it harder to accomplish their goals. Research supports this belief. Students who are parents, particularly those who are single parents, often do not do as well in college as their peers without children (Prentice, Storin, and Robinson, 2012). Thus, having unprotected sex can lead to multiple unplanned outcomes.

Summary and Conclusion

Research findings and advice from professionals indicate that physical wellness is most effectively promoted if we adopt the following strategies with respect to our bodies:

- **Pay more attention to nutrition.** In particular, we should increase consumption of natural fruits, vegetables, legumes, whole grains, fish, and water and decrease consumption of processed, fatty, and fried foods. Although the expression "you are what you eat" may be a bit of an exaggeration, it contains a kernel of truth because the food we consume does influence our health, our emotions, and our performance.
- **Become more physically active.** To counteract the sedentary lifestyle created by life in modern society and to attain total fitness, we should engage in a balanced blend of exercises that build stamina, strength, and flexibility.
- **Don't cheat on sleep.** Humans typically do not get enough sleep to perform at their highest levels. College students, in particular, need to get more sleep and develop more regular (consistent) sleeping habits.

- **Drink alcohol responsibly or not at all.** We should avoid excessive consumption of alcohol or other mind-altering substances that can threaten our physical health, impair our mental judgment, and increase our tendency to engage in dangerous, risk-taking behavior.
- **Minimize the risk of contracting sexually transmitted infections and an unplanned pregnancy.** College students have basically three options to reduce their risk for sexually transmitted infections: (1) using latex condoms during sex; (2) limiting the number of sexual partners they have; or (3) choosing not to be sexually active. There are many birth control options to help students who are sexually active avoid an unplanned pregnancy.

In the introduction to this book, research was cited about the advantages of the college experience and college degree. Among the many benefits experienced by college graduates are health and wellness benefits: they live healthier, longer lives. This suggests that students manage to learn something about physical wellness and how to promote it by the time they graduate from college. The strategies discussed in this chapter can be implemented immediately to promote optimal health and peak performance throughout your college experience and beyond.

Learning More through the World Wide Web
Internet-Based Resources for Further Information on Health and Wellness

For additional information related to the ideas discussed in this chapter, we recommend the following Web sites:

Nutrition:

www.eatright.org

Fitness:

www.fitness.gov/home_resources.htm

Sleep:

www.sleepfoundation.org

Alcohol and Drugs:

www.drugabuse.gov

Sexual Harassment, Assault, and Abuse

www.princeton.edu/uhs/healthy-living/hot-topics/sexual-harassment-assault/

Sexual Health

www.bedsider.org

www.thenationalcampaign.org

www.studentsexlife.org

Chapter 12 Exercises

12.1 Nutritional Self-Assessment and Self-Improvement

1. Go online to www.ChooseMyPlate.gov.

2. In the boxes on the right side of the screen, fill in your age, gender, and daily level of physical activity.

3. Click "select" to get a nutritional guide that is customized to your age, gender, and exercise habits.

4. For each of the five food groups listed here, record the amount recommended for you to consume daily, and next to it, estimate the amount you now consume.

Basic Food Type	Amount Recommended	Amount Consumed
Grains		
Vegetables		
Fruits		
Milk Products		
Meat and Beans		

5. For any food group where you're consuming less than the recommended amount, use the above Web site to find foods you could consume to meet the recommended daily amount. In the space that follows, record any items that you'd be willing to consume in greater amounts to meet the daily recommendation.

_____

_____

_____

_____

_____

6. How likely is it that you'll add these food items to your regular diet? Explain.

   very likely   possibly   very unlikely

7. If you didn't answer "very likely," what would interfere or prevent you from adding these food items to your regular diet?

12.2 Wellness Self-Assessment and Self-Improvement

For each aspect of wellness listed here, rate yourself in terms of how close you are to doing what you should be doing (1 = furthest from the ideal, 5 = closest to the ideal).

	Nowhere Close to What I Should Be Doing	Not Bad but Should Be Better	Right Where I Should Be
Nutrition			
Exercise			
Sleep			
Alcohol and Drugs			
Sexual Health			

For each area in which there's a gap between where you are now and where you should be, identify the best action you could take to reduce or eliminate this gap.

Concerns about Eating: Too Much or Too Little?

The following e-mail message was sent by an underweight, 25-year-old female (Nancy) who was seeking advice:

I have a big worry: I eat normally during the day but I eat two scoops of ice cream at the end of the day followed by a large package of cookies. I am not exaggerating the situation. Last week, I could only stuff myself with two scoops of Häagen-Dazs after dinner, but these days it's getting worse—now that I can add bread and buttery cookies (a whole packet—not those mini ones, mind you). What should I do? I know that I should gain weight but I should be getting the extra pounds by more normal means like meat or milk—and I am really worried that once this binge and indulgence becomes a habit, it's difficult to get rid of.

Discussion Questions

Nancy goes on to ask the following questions about her condition. As you read each question, respond to it with the advice you think would be best.

1. Is it okay that I eat that much at the end of each day rather than distributing it equally throughout the day? (Though the former way seems better, I can tell myself, "Hey, girl, after all, you are eating less than your sister!")

2. I am eating junk food—ice cream, loads of biscuits, bread, those Garden chocolate roll cakes, chocolate fingers, chocolate McVita's, buttery cookies. . . . It seems that this is not as healthy as gaining weight by eating meat, milk, or carbohydrates. Is this true?

3. Is it unhealthy to eat just before bed?

4. Could it become difficult to stop?

5. Am I controlled by food?

6. Now that I am eating more than my sister, I am really scared, very scared indeed, not only because I am eating far more than my sister but also because I am having fat deposited in undesirable parts of my body and getting a totally worse figure than she has—that fat which I had tried so hard for three years to get rid of. Any advice?

Source: Chan and Ma (2002).

Chapter 12 Reflection

What is the one area of your health that could most affect your success in college? Explain.

What are three action steps you can take to improve in this area of health?

1.

2.

3.

Write three health goals you have set for yourself. (Remember to use the goal-setting strategies you learned about in Chapter 3.)

1.

2.

3.

Educational and Career Planning and Decision Making

Making Wise Choices about Your Courses, Major, Degree, and Career Plans

13

THOUGHT STARTER | *Journal Entry* **13.1**

LEARNING GOAL

To develop strategies for exploring different academic fields and for choosing an educational path that will enable you to achieve your personal and career goals.

1. Are you decided or undecided about a college major?

   _____

2. If you are undecided, list any subjects that might be possibilities:

   _____

   _____

3. If you are decided, what is your choice and why did you choose this major?

   _____

   _____

4. Indicate how sure you are about that choice by circling one of the following options:

   absolutely sure   fairly sure   not too sure   likely to change

   Why?

   _____

   _____

   _____

   _____

The Importance of Long-Range Educational Planning

College will allow you many choices about what courses to enroll in and what field to specialize in. By looking ahead and developing a tentative plan for your courses beyond the first term of college, you will position yourself to view your college experience as a full-length movie and get a sneak preview of the total picture. In contrast, scheduling your classes one term at a time just before each registration period (when everyone else is making a mad rush to get their advisor's signature for the following term's classes) forces you to view your academic experience as a series of short, separate snapshots that lack connection or direction.

Long-range educational planning also enables you to take a proactive approach to your future. Being proactive means you are taking early, preventative action that an-

"When you have to make a choice and don't make it, that is in itself a choice."

—William James, philosopher and one of the founders of American psychology

"Education is our passport to the future; for tomorrow belongs to the people who prepare for it today."

—Malcolm X, African American civil rights leader

Don't take the denial and avoidance approach to planning your educational future.

ticipates events before they sneak up on you and force you to react without time to plan your best strategy. As the old saying goes, "If you fail to plan, you plan to fail." Through advanced planning, you can actively take charge of your academic future and make it happen *for* you, rather than waiting and passively letting it happen *to* you.

Remember

Any long-range plan you develop is not set in stone: it can change depending on changes in your academic interests and future plans. The purpose of long-range planning is not to lock you into a particular plan but to free you from shortsightedness, procrastination, or denial about choosing to take charge of your life.

Think About It ———————————————— *Journal Entry* **13.2**

Choosing a major is a life-changing decision because it will determine what you do for the rest of your life. Would you agree or disagree with this statement? Why?

_____

_____

_____

_____

_____

_____

One important element of long-range educational planning is deciding whether you're going to continue your education beyond your community college experience by transferring to a four-year college or university and when you plan to make that transition. Some community college students plan to transfer to a four-year college before completing their associate degree at their community college. However, we strongly recommend that you complete your general education program before attempting to transfer, because multiple advantages are associated with completing 60 or more units at a two-year college and attaining an associate degree. These advantages are listed in the next section.

Advantages of Completing an Associate Degree before Transferring to a Four-Year College or University

1. **You will acquire a college degree before completing a bachelor's degree.** Regardless of whether you receive academic or cocurricular distinctions and awards, completion of an associate degree is an achievement in itself for two reasons:

    *   It indicates that you have survived the two most critical years of the college experience. Research shows that almost 75 percent of those students who withdraw from college do so during the freshman and sophomore years (American College Testing, 2009). The associate degree is evidence to four-year colleges and future employers that you have persisted through, and completed, these two critical years.
    *   The associate degree signifies that you have successfully completed the general education component of the college experience. In some ways, this is the most important component of the college experience because it represents the acquisition of breadth of knowledge and the development of essential learning skills (e.g., written and oral communication). Surveys indicate that employers look for and value these skills the most in their employees (National Association of Colleges & Employers, 2003).

    Having your associate degree after your sophomore year will also improve your job prospects during your junior and senior years of college (e.g., your chances of obtaining an internship, part-time employment during the academic year, or full-time employment during the summers between your sophomore and your junior years and between your junior and your senior years). In addition, those with an associate degree, on average, earn more than $13,000 more per year than individuals with a high school diploma (College Board, 2008). Thus, the two-year degree should not only increase your chances of being hired, but also increase the amount of pay you receive. Furthermore, this vocational advantage of earning an associate degree will be particularly important if, for some reason, you're unable to complete the bachelor's (or baccalaureate) degree or if you have to postpone its completion.

2. **You will complete general education requirements, basic skills courses, and premajor requirements before transferring.** Completing an associate degree will enable you to finish up general education requirements and skill-building courses (e.g., writing and math) in smaller classes where you are likely to receive more individual attention and more personalized feedback and academic support from instructors. Thus, you will have a broader base of knowledge and a more highly developed set of academic skills before transferring. Studies show that students who transfer to four-year institutions after completing just one year at a two-year college have a greater "dip" or drop in grade point average (GPA) than students who transfer after two years (Cuseo, 2003a; Diaz, 1992). The bigger drop in GPA for early transfers may also be due to greater culture shock ex-

perienced by students who transfer after one year because they enter four-year institutions neither as freshmen nor as juniors—the two years when most other students enter four-year colleges. Sophomore-year transfers begin their four-year college experience as interlopers or "betweeners." This can make it difficult for sophomore transfers to fit into the student culture because they have fewer peers entering with them and because orientation activities are more likely to be geared toward entering freshmen and junior transfers.

3. **You will have extra time and advisement for deciding on an academic major and a four-year college.** For students who are not sure about what their particular major will be or what particular four-year institution they should transfer to, returning to their community college for the sophomore year will provide an additional year of time and advisor contact that can be used to reach both of these important decisions. Making these two decisions is a complex and interrelated process. What major you eventually decide on may influence what college you should attend. Some academic majors may not be offered at all colleges, and the nature and quality of the same major may vary from one college to another. For example, the psychology major at College X may require different courses and have a different career-preparation emphasis than the psychology major at college Y. Also, transfer students may report different levels of satisfaction with the psychology program and the professors in the psychology department at College X than they do at College Y.

Since so many of the courses you will be taking during your last two years of college will be courses in your major, when you choose a four-year college for transfer, you're also choosing the particular department within the college that houses your particular major. Your second year at a community college can supply you with the time needed to finalize your decision about what major to declare and to consult with a network of advisors concerning what four-year colleges would be best for your particular major and your future career goals.

4. **You may have a higher college GPA at the end of your sophomore year.** It's likely that your GPA will be higher after your sophomore year at your community college than it is after your freshman year because you've made the critical first-year adjustment and have gained greater experience with the system. A higher GPA when you transfer will increase the likelihood that you will be accepted, particularly if you're applying for admission into "impacted" majors (i.e., majors that are competitive and hard to get into because they are overcrowded). It also increases your likelihood of getting a transfer scholarship when you transfer to your four-year institution.

5. **There will be less emphasis on high school grades and SAT or ACT scores by four-year colleges.** Four-year colleges and universities are less likely to place less emphasis on high school grades and SAT or ACT scores when reviewing the applications of students who've completed two full years of college than they are for students who are attempt to transfer earlier. Some four-year campuses require SAT or ACT scores for high school seniors and for students attempting to transfer after one year of college, but will not require SAT or ACT scores from transfer students who have completed two full years of college and hold an associate degree.

6. **You will have more opportunity to receive academic recognition and awards before transferring.** If you're doing well academically during your first year at your community college, returning for the sophomore year will enable you to enter the community college's honors program, take honors courses, and become

a member of the National Collegiate Honors Council and Phi Theta Kappa—an international honor society for two-year college students. If you then complete your associate degree at a community college, you become eligible for academic honors at graduation, such as graduating magna cum laude (with high distinction) or summa cum laude (with highest distinction). These awards can increase your prospects for acceptance at four-year colleges, as well as your chances for scholarships and other types of merit-based financial aid that are earmarked for junior-transfer students. These academic achievements will be listed on your transcript and will provide you with a distinctive advantage for acceptance at four-year schools, as well as increase your eligibility for entry into their honors programs. Furthermore, these accomplishments will remain on your permanent college record after you graduate with a four-year (bachelor's) degree, which should increase your job prospects after graduation and your chances for acceptance at graduate schools (e.g., to pursue a master's or doctoral degree) and professional schools (e.g., to pursue a law or medical degree).

7. **You will have opportunities and recognition for leadership activities before transferring.** If you are a first-year college student with leadership potential, or if you are committed to developing your leadership skills, you may become eligible for various resume- and character-building leadership opportunities during your sophomore year at a community college (e.g., peer tutoring or peer mentoring). At four-year colleges, sophomores are often unable to assume these leadership positions because they may be reserved for more experienced upper-division students (juniors and seniors). At your community college, you can get these experiences as a sophomore and use them to: (1) increase your chances of acceptance at four-year colleges, (2) qualify for similar leadership positions at the four-year college to which you transfer, and (3) enhance your job prospects during your last two years of college and after you complete your bachelor's degree.

8. **You will have a chance to participate in a graduation ceremony after completing the associate degree program.** Completion of an associate degree will also enable you to participate in your community college's graduation ceremony. The significance of this celebratory event should not be underestimated. This is an opportunity for you to be recognized publicly, in front of family, friends, faculty, and fellow students, for your completion of general education and for any academic and cocurricular awards you achieved along the way.

Research indicates that student involvement in college rituals or ceremonial events (such as graduation) reinforces students' motivation and commitment to continue their education and promotes their ability to persist or persevere until achieving their final degree objective (Kuh et al., 1991, 2005). Thus, participation in your community college's graduation ceremony may not only celebrate your attainment of the associate degree, but also strengthen or stimulate your drive to achieve a bachelor's degree.

Proof of the power of the graduation experience is illustrated in the following excerpt of a letter written by a student who graduated from a two-year college and transferred to a four-year campus to complete her bachelor's degree.

I graduated with my associate degree [several years ago] and I just wanted to get in touch and let you know how I am doing. I successfully graduated from USF [University of San Francisco] in 4 years (including the 2 before I transferred). During the graduation ceremony after my sophomore year, I saw some fellow students wearing the yellow shawl that represented walking with honors. I thought to myself, "I am going to walk with honors when I get my B.A." And that I did!

Who would have ever thought? [Now] I have decided that I want to go to graduate school.

—*Letter from a two-year college graduate received by Joe Cuseo*

Snapshot Summary

13.1 Tips for Students Transferring to Four-Year Colleges and Universities

The following criteria are those that most likely will be used by four-year colleges to evaluate your application and decide on your acceptance:

- **Academic record.** Colleges will look at your overall GPA and grades for courses in your chosen major.
- **Out-of-class experiences.** For example, your involvement in leadership activities and volunteer experience in the community or on campus can play a role in your acceptance to a four-year college.
- **Letters of recommendation.** Letters can come, for example, from course instructors and academic advisors. Provide the following courtesies for those you ask to write letters of recommendation for you:
  - A *fact sheet* about yourself that will enable them to cite concrete examples or evidence of your achievements and contributions (which will make the letter more powerful)
  - Give the person at least two weeks' notice.
  - A *stamped, addressed* envelope (a personal courtesy that makes the job a little easier for your reference)
  - A *thank-you note* close to the date that the letter is due (not only a nice thing to do but also a reminder in case the person has forgotten about your letter or has not yet set aside time to write it)
- **Personal statement.** In your letter of application for admission, which you write

when applying to a school, try to demonstrate your knowledge of:

- *yourself* (e.g., your personal interests, abilities, and values);
- your intended *major* (e.g., why you're interested in it and what you might do with it after graduation); and
- the *college* to which you're applying by showing that you know something specific about the school (e.g., its mission, philosophy, and programs—especially the particular program to which you're applying).

To maximize your success at four-year colleges and universities, take the initiative to connect with people who can contribute to your success, including the following:

- **Faculty.** Make sure they know who you are (e.g., sit in front of class, come up to speak with them after class, visit them in their offices, or volunteer to help them with research they're doing that you find interesting or relevant to your career interests).
- **Students in your major.** Connect with them in study groups and major clubs (psychology club, history club, etc.).
- **Career development specialists.** Connect with these professionals on strategies for enhancing your marketability after graduation. Ask them about what graduates (alumni) with your major have gone on to do and whether they can connect you with an alum in a career that you intend to pursue.

To Be or Not to Be Decided about a College Major: What the Research Shows

Studies of student decisions about a college major show that:

- Less than 10 percent of new college students feel they know a great deal about the fields that they intend to major in.
- As students proceed through the first year of college, they grow more uncertain about the majors they chose when they began college.
- More than two-thirds of new students change their minds about their majors during the first year of college.

Snapshot Summary

13.2 A Checklist of Course-Registration Reminders for Community College Students

Achieving your educational goals requires both long- and short-range planning. Your long-range plan involves completing your degree, and your short-range plan involves continuing your enrollment in college from term to term. When planning to register for the next academic term, keep the following list of reminders handy to ensure that your term-to-term transition proceeds smoothly.

- Check the registration dates and be prepared to register at the earliest date that's available to you.
- Check with an academic advisor to be sure that you're planning to take the right classes for your program, major, and any four-year school you plan to transfer to.
- Let your advisor know what your educational goals are and if you've changed your goals since the last time you registered.
- Let your advisor know the total number of hours per week you plan to work so that you create a schedule that will allow you to successfully balance schoolwork and for-pay work.

- If you're receiving financial aid, meet with a financial aid counselor or advisor to be sure that you have adequate funds to cover next term's tuition, book costs, and parking fees.
- Once you've registered, periodically check the status of your courses because last-minute changes can occur in the time and day when courses meet and it's possible that one of your courses might be canceled (e.g., due to insufficient enrollment).

Remember

Unlike in high school, summer school in college isn't something you do to make up for courses that were failed or should have been taken during the "regular" school year (fall and spring terms). Instead, it's an additional term that you can use to make further progress toward your college degree and reduce the total time it takes to complete your degree.

- Only one in three college seniors eventually major in the same fields that they chose during their first year of college (Cuseo, 2005).

These findings demonstrate that the vast majority of students entering college are not certain about their college majors. Many students don't reach their final decision about a major *before* starting their college experience; instead, they make that decision *during* their college experience. Being uncertain about a major is nothing to be embarrassed about. Being "undecided" or "undeclared" doesn't mean that you're irresponsible, clueless, or lost. Beginning college students may be undecided for very good reasons. For instance, you may be undecided simply because you have interests in various subjects; this is a healthy form of indecision because it shows that you have a range of interests and a high level of motivation to learn about different subjects. You may also be undecided simply because you're a careful, reflective thinker whose decision-making style is to gather more information before making a firm and final commitment.

In one study of students who were undecided about a major at the start of college, 43 percent had several ideas in mind but were not yet ready to commit to one of them (Gordon & Steele, 2003). These students were not clueless or lacking direction; they had some ideas but still wanted to explore them and keep their options open, which is an effective way to go about making decisions.

As a first-year student, it's only natural to be at least somewhat uncertain about your educational goals because you haven't yet experienced the variety of subjects and academic programs that make up the college curriculum, some of which you didn't know existed. In fact, one purpose of general education courses is to help new

"Not all who wander are lost."
—J. R. R. Tolkien, *The Lord of the Rings*

students develop the critical thinking skills needed to make wise choices and well-informed decisions, such as their choice of a college major.

Similarly, changing your original educational plans is not necessarily a bad thing. It may mean that you have discovered another field that's more interesting to you or that's more compatible with your personal interests and talents. It's OK to start off not knowing what your major will be or whether you want to pursue a four-year degree or a shorter-range educational goal, such as an associate degree or vocational-technical certificate. You still have time to make up your mind and to change your mind. Don't think that you must lock yourself into a particular plan and must either stick with it or drop out of college if your plans change. You can take courses that will count toward graduation, regardless of what major or educational track you end up taking.

Changing your educational plan has one downside: if you make that change late in your college experience, it can result in more time to graduation (and more tuition) because you may need to complete additional courses required for your newly chosen field.

"When you get to a fork in the road, take it."

—Yogi Berra, Hall of Fame baseball player

I've decided to change my major.

HAHAH HAHHA

Remember

As a rule, you should reach a fairly firm decision about your major during your second (sophomore) year in college. However, to reach a good decision within this time frame, the process of exploring and planning should begin now—during your first term in college.

Think About It ———————————— Journal Entry 13.3

If you've already chosen a major or specialized program, what led you to this choice?

_____

_____

_____

_____

_____

Myths about the Relationship between Majors and Careers

Good decisions are based not on misconceptions or myths, but on accurate information. Effective planning for a college major requires accurate information about the relationship between majors and careers. Unfortunately, several popular myths about the relationship between majors and careers can lead to uninformed or unrealistic choices of a college major.

Myth 1. When you choose your major, you're choosing your career. While some majors lead directly to a particular career, most do not. Majors leading directly to specific careers are called preprofessional or prevocational majors, and they include such fields as accounting, engineering, and nursing. However, most college majors don't channel you directly down one particular career path: they leave you with various career options. All physics majors don't become physicists, all philosophy majors don't become philosophers, all history majors do not become historians, and all English majors do not become Englishmen (or Englishwomen). The career paths of most college graduates are not straight lines that run directly from their majors to their careers. The trip from college to career or careers is more like climbing a tree. As illustrated in Figure 13.1, you begin with the tree's trunk—the foundation of general education (courses required of all college students, whatever their major may be)—which grows into separate limbs (different college majors) that, in turn, lead to different branches (different career paths or options).

FIGURE 13.1

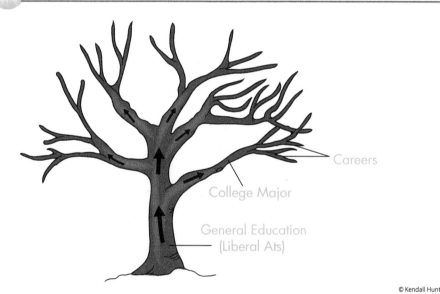

© Kendall Hunt

The Relationship between General Education (Liberal Arts), College Majors, and Careers

Note that the career branches grow from the same limb. Likewise, the same major leads to a "family" of related careers. For example, an English major often leads to careers that involve use of the written language (e.g., editing, journalism, and publishing), while a major in art leads to careers that involve use of visual media (e.g., illustration, graphic design, and art therapy). (Note that the Web site www.mymajors.com provides useful and free information on groups or families of jobs that tend to be related to different majors.)

Also, different majors can lead to the same career. For instance, many majors can lead a student to law school and to an eventual career as a lawyer; there is no undergraduate major in law or prelaw. Similarly, premed isn't a major. Although most students interested in going to medical school after college major in some field in the natural sciences (e.g., biology or chemistry), it's possible for students to go to medical school with majors in other fields, particularly if they take and do well in certain science courses that are emphasized in medical school (e.g., general biology, general chemistry, and organic and inorganic chemistry).

Thus, don't presume that your major is your career or that your major automatically turns into your career. This is one reason some students procrastinate about choosing a major; they think they are making a lifelong decision and fear that if they make the "wrong" choice they'll be stuck doing something they hate for the rest of their lives. The belief that your major becomes your career may also account for 58 percent of college graduates choosing to major in a preprofessional or prevocational field such as nursing, accounting, or engineering (Association of American Colleges & Universities, 2007). These majors have careers obviously connected to them, which reassures students (and their family members) that they will have jobs after graduation. However, although students in prevocational majors may be more likely to be hired immediately after graduation, tracking college graduates with other college majors has shown that six months after graduation they too have jobs; thus, they are not more likely to be unemployed (Pascarella & Terenzini, 2005).

Remember

Don't assume that choosing your college major means you're choosing what you'll be doing for as long as you'll be living.

Research on college graduates indicates that they change careers numerous times, and the further they continue along their career paths, the more likely they are to work in fields unrelated to their college majors (Millard, 2004). Remember that the general education curriculum is a significant part of a college education. It allows students to acquire knowledge in diverse subjects and to develop durable, transferable skills (e.g., writing, speaking, and organizing) that qualify college graduates for a diversity of careers, regardless of what their particular majors happened to be.

The order in which decisions about majors and careers are covered in this book reflects the order in which they are likely to be made in your life. For most college majors, students first decide on their majors; later, they decide on their careers. Although it is important to think about the relationship between your choice of major and your choice of career or careers, these are different choices that are usually made at different times. Both choices relate to your future goals, but they involve different time frames: choosing your major is a short-range goal, whereas choosing your career is a long-range goal.

Remember

Choosing a major and choosing a career are not always the same decision: they are often separate decisions that don't have to be made at the same time.

Myth 2. After a bachelor's degree, any further education must be in the same field as your college major. After college graduation, you have two main options or alternative paths available to you:

1. You can enter a career immediately.
2. You can continue your education in graduate school or professional school. (See Figure 13.2 for a visual map of the signposts or stages in the college experience and the basic paths available to you after college graduation.)

FIGURE 13.2

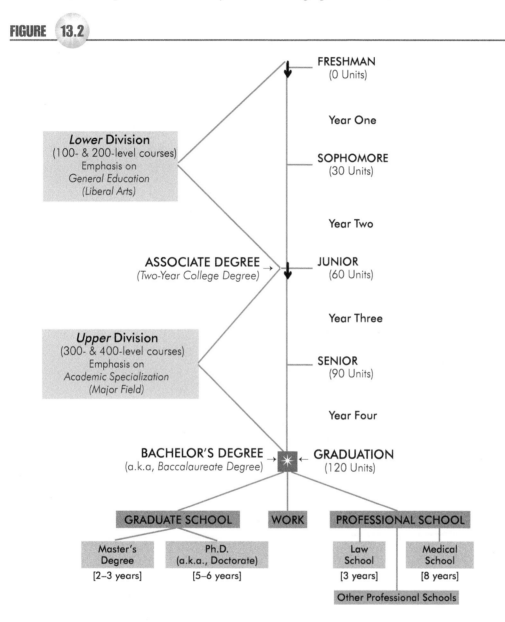

Notes

1. The total number of *general education* units and the total number of units needed to **graduate** with a bachelor's degree may vary somewhat from school to school. Also, the total number of units required for a *major* will vary somewhat from major to major and from school to school.

2. It often takes college students longer than four years to graduate due to a variety of reasons, such as working part-time and taking fewer courses per term, needing to repeat courses that were failed or dropped, or making a late change to a different major and needing to fulfill additional requirements for the new major.

3. *Graduate* and *professional* schools are options for continuing to higher levels of education after completion of an undergraduate (college) education.

4. Compared to graduate school, *professional* school involves advanced education in more "applied" professions (e.g., pharmacy or public administration).

© Kendall Hunt

Timeline to the Future: A Snapshot of the College Experience and Beyond

Once you complete a bachelor's degree, it's possible to continue your education in a field that's not directly related to your college major. This is particularly true for students who are majoring in preprofessional careers that funnel them directly into a particular career after graduation (Pascarella & Terenzini, 2005). For example, if you major in English, you can still go to graduate school in a subject other than English; you could go to law school or get a master's degree in business administration. It's common to find graduate students in masters of business administration programs who were not business majors in college (Dupuy & Vance, 1996).

Think About It ——————————— *Journal Entry* 13.4

Reflect back on the preceding timeline and Figure 13.2, which suggests that it will take you two years to complete an associate degree and four years to complete a bachelor's degree.

1. Do you see yourself completing an associate degree in two years? A bachelor's degree in four years? Why or why not?

   _____

   _____

2. Do you plan to transfer after completing an associate degree?

   _____

   If yes, to what college or university?

   _____

   If no, do you ever see yourself eventually returning to college to complete your bachelor's degree?

   _____

3. Do you see any possible interfering factors or potential obstacles that might prolong the time you need to reach your educational goals?

   _____

   _____

   _____

"We should not underestimate the ability of people to eventually obtain their college degrees. Nor should we minimize the diversity of behaviors which lead individuals to leave and eventually to return to complete their college degree programs."

—Vincent Tinto, nationally known researcher and scholar on college student success

Myth 3. You should major in business because most college graduates work in business settings. Studies show that college graduates with various majors end up working in business settings. For instance, engineering majors are likely to work in accounting, production, and finance. Liberal arts majors are likely to move on to positions in business settings that involve marketing, human resources, or public affairs (Bok, 2006; Useem, 1989). Research also reveals that the career mobility and career advancement of nonbusiness majors in the business world are equal to those attained by business majors (Pascarella & Terenzini, 1991, 2005).

Author's Experience My undergraduate degree was in political science and sociology. When I graduated from college, I spent the first eight years of my professional life becoming a corporate manager. I did not major in business, but found that my liberal arts background gave me the problem-solving and communication skills that were crucial in working with a variety of people in my profession. You do not need to major in business to be a successful business person. Indeed, employers are telling us that they are looking for those who can problem solve, critically think, write and speak well, and work with a diversity of people and thought.

Aaron Thompson

"Employers are far more interested in the prospect's ability to think and to think clearly, to write and speak well, and how (s)he works with others than in his major or the name of the school (s)he went to. Several college investigating teams found that these were the qualities on which all kinds of employers, government and private, base their decisions."

—Lauren Pope, *Looking beyond the Ivy League* (1990)

Don't restrict your choices of a major to business by believing in the myth that you must major in business to work for a business after graduation.

Myth 4. If you major in a liberal arts field, the only career available is teaching. Liberal arts majors are not restricted to teaching careers. Many college graduates with majors in liberal arts fields have proceeded to, and succeeded in, careers other than teaching. Among these graduates are such notable people as:

- Jill Barad (English major), CEO, Mattel Toys;
- Steve Case (political science major), CEO, America Online;
- Brian Lamb (speech major), CEO, C-Span; and
- Willie Brown (liberal studies major), mayor, San Francisco.

Source: Indiana University (2004).

Studies show that college graduates in liberal arts majors are just as likely to advance to the highest levels of corporate leadership as graduates majoring in preprofessional fields, such as business and engineering (Pascarella & Terenzini, 2005). If you are considering a major in a liberal arts field, you should not be dismayed or discouraged by those who may question your choice by asking, "What are you going to do with a degree in *that* major?"

Note: A good career-information Web site for liberal arts majors can be found at www.eace.org/networks/liberalarts.html.

Myth 5. Specialized skills are more important for career success than general skills. You may find that general education (liberal arts) courses are sometimes viewed by students as unnecessary requirements that they have to "get out of the way" before they can "get into what's really important"—their major or academic specialization. However, general education courses develop practical, durable, and transferable skills that supply a strong foundation for success in any career.

Also, don't forget that the general skills and qualities developed by the liberal arts increase career advancement (your ability to move up the career ladder) and career mobility (your ability to move into different career paths). Specific technical skills may be important for getting into a career, but general educational skills are more important for moving up the career ladder. The courses you take as part of your general education will prepare you for your advanced career positions, not just your first one (Boyer, 1987; Miller, 2003). Furthermore, general professional skills are growing even more important for college graduates entering the workforce in the 21st century because the demand for upper-level positions in management and leadership will exceed the supply of workers available to fill these positions (Herman, 2000).

Student Perspective

"They asked me during my interview why I was right for the job and I told them because I can read well, write well and I can think. They really liked that because those were the skills they were looking for."

—English major hired by a public relations firm (*Los Angeles Times,* April 4, 2004)

Think About It ———————————————— *Journal Entry* **13.5**

In what ways do you think your general education courses will improve your work performance in the career field you may pursue?

_____

_____

_____

_____

_____

Factors to Consider When Choosing Your Major or Field of Study

Gaining self-awareness is the critical first step in making decisions about a college major, or any other important decision. You must know yourself before you can know what choice is best for you. While this may seem obvious, self-awareness and self-discovery are often overlooked aspects of the decision-making process. In particular, you need awareness of:

- Your *interests*, what you like doing;
- Your *abilities*, what you're good at doing; and
- Your *values*, what you feel good about doing.

Research indicates that students are more likely to continue in college and graduate when they choose majors that reflect their personal interests and talents (Leuwerke et al., 2004).

"I try to do more to please myself, and making good grades and doing well in school helps my ego. It gives me confidence, and I like that feeling."

—First-year student (Franklin, 2002)

Think About It ———————————————— *Journal Entry* **13.6**

In Chapter 3 (pp. 54–55), you answered self-awareness questions related to three elements of "self": interests, abilities (talents), and values. Review your answers to these questions. Do you notice any patterns across your answers suggesting that a certain major would provide a nice "fit" or "match" with your personal interests, abilities, and values?

_____

_____

_____

_____

_____

Multiple Intelligences: Identifying Personal Abilities and Talents

One element of the self that you should be aware of when choosing a major is your mental strengths, abilities, or talents. Intelligence was once considered to be one general trait that could be detected and measured by a single intelligence test score. The singular word *intelligence* has now been replaced by the plural word *intelligences* to reflect the fact that humans can display intelligence (mental ability) in many forms other than performance on an IQ test.

Listed in Snapshot Summary 13.3 are forms of intelligence identified by Howard Gardner (1999, 2006) based on studies of gifted and talented individuals, experts in different lines of work, and various other sources. As you read through the types of intelligence, place a checkmark next to the type that you think represents your strongest ability or talent. (You can possess more than one type.) Keep your type(s) of intelligence in mind when you're choosing a college major because different majors emphasize different thinking skills. Ideally, you want to select an academic field that allows you to utilize your strongest skills and talents. Choosing a major that's compatible with your abilities should enable you to master the concepts and skills required by your major more easily and more deeply. If you follow your academic talents, you're also more likely to succeed or excel in what you do, which will bolster your academic self-confidence and motivation.

Snapshot Summary

13.3 Multiple Forms of Intelligence

- **Linguistic intelligence.** Ability to communicate through language—e.g., verbal skills in the areas of speaking, writing, listening, and reading.
- **Logical-mathematical intelligence.** Ability to reason logically and succeed in tasks that involve mathematical problem solving—e.g., making logical arguments and following logical reasoning, or ability to work well with numbers and make quantitative calculations.
- **Spatial intelligence.** Ability to visualize relationships among objects arranged in different spatial positions and the ability to perceive or create visual images—e.g., forming mental images of three-dimensional objects; detecting detail in objects or drawings; artistic talent for drawing, painting, sculpting, and graphic design; and skills related to sense of direction and navigation.
- **Musical intelligence.** Ability to appreciate or create rhythmical and melodic sounds—e.g., playing, writing, and arranging music.
- **Interpersonal (social) intelligence.** Ability to relate to others, to accurately identify others' needs, feelings, or emotional states of mind, and to effectively express emotions and feelings to others—e.g., interpersonal communication skills, ability to accurately "read" the feelings of others, and ability to meet their emotional needs.
- **Intrapersonal (self) intelligence.** Ability to introspect and understand one's own thoughts, feelings, and behavior—e.g., capacity for personal reflection, emotional self-awareness, and self-insight.

- **Bodily-kinesthetic (psychomotor) intelligence.** Ability to use one's own body skillfully and learn through bodily sensations or movements—e.g., skilled at tasks involving physical coordination, ability to work well with hands, mechanical skills, talent for building models, assembling things, and using technology.

Student Perspective

"I used to operate a printing press. In about two weeks I knew how to run it and soon after I could take the machine apart in my head and analyze what each part does, how it functioned, and why it was shaped that way."

—Response of college sophomore to the questions "What are you really good at? What comes easily or naturally to you?"

- **Naturalist intelligence.** Ability to carefully observe and appreciate features of the natural environment—e.g., keen awareness of nature or natural surroundings, and ability to understand causes and consequences of events occurring in the natural world.
- **Existential.** Ability to conceptualize phenomena and experiences that require one to go beyond sensory or physical evidence, such as questions and issues involving the origin of the universe and human life, and the purpose of human existence.

Source: Gardner (1993, 1999, 2006).

Think About It —————————— *Journal Entry* **13.7**

Which types of intelligence listed in Snapshot Summary 13.3 are your strongest areas? Which majors or fields of study do you think may be the best match for your natural talents?

_____

_____

_____

_____

_____

_____

_____

 Author's Experience   I first noticed that students in different academic fields may have different learning styles when I was teaching a psychology course that was required for students majoring in nursing and social work. I noticed that some students in class seemed to lose interest (and patience) when we got involved in lengthy class discussions about controversial issues or theories, while others seemed to love it. On the other hand, whenever I lectured or delivered information for an extended period, some students seemed to lose interest (and attention), while others seemed to get into it and took great notes. After one class period that involved quite a bit of class discussion, I began thinking about which students seemed most involved in the discussion and which seemed to drift off or lose interest. I suddenly realized that the students who did most of the talking and seemed most enthused during the class discussion were the students majoring in social work. On the other hand, most of the students who appeared disinterested or a bit frustrated were the nursing majors.

When I began to think about why this happened, it dawned on me that the nursing students were accustomed to gathering factual information and learning practical skills in their major courses and were expecting to use that learning style in my psychology course. The nursing majors felt more comfortable with structured class sessions in which they received lots of factual, practical information from the professor. On the other hand, the social work majors were more comfortable with unstructured class discussions because courses in their major often emphasized debating social issues and hearing viewpoints or perspectives.

As I left class that day, I asked myself: Did the nursing students and social work students select or gravitate toward their major because the type of learning emphasized in the field tended to match their preferred style of learning?

— Joe Cuseo

To sum up, the most important factor to consider when reaching decisions about a major is whether it is compatible with four characteristics of your self: (1) your learning style, (2) your abilities, (3) your personal interests, and (4) your values (see Figure 13.3). These four pillars provide the foundation for effective decisions about a college major.

Strategies for Discovering a Major Compatible with Your Interests, Talents, and Values

If you're undecided about a major, there's no need to feel anxious or guilty. You're at an early stage in your college experience. Although you've decided to postpone your decision about a major, this doesn't mean you're a clueless procrastinator as long as you have a plan for exploring and narrowing down your options. Just be sure that you don't put all thoughts about your major on the back burner and simply drift along until you have no choice but to make a choice. Start exploring and developing a game plan now that will lead you to a wise decision about your major.

Similarly, if you've already chosen a major, this doesn't mean that you'll never have to give any more thought to that decision or that you can just shift into cruise control and motor along a mindless ride in the major you've selected. Instead, you should continue the exploration process by carefully testing your first choice, making sure it's a choice that is compatible with your abilities, interests, and values. In other words, take the approach that it's your *current* choice; whether it becomes your firm and *final* choice will depend on how well you perform, and how interested you are, in the first courses you take in the field.

To explore and identify majors that are compatible with your personal strengths and interests, use the following strategies:

1. **Use past experience to help you choose a major.** Think about the subjects that you experienced during high school and your early time in college. As the old saying goes, "Nothing succeeds like success itself." If you have done well and continue to do well in a certain field of study, this may indicate that your natural abilities and learning style correspond well with the academic skills required by that particular field. This could translate into future success and satisfaction in the field if you decide to pursue it as a college major.

   You can enter information about your academic performance in high school courses at the Web site mymajors.com, which will analyze it and provide you with college majors that may be a good match for you (based on your academic experiences in high school).

2. **Use your elective courses to test your interests and abilities in subjects that you might consider as majors.** As the name implies, "elective" courses are those that you elect or choose to take. Your college electives come in two forms: free electives and restricted electives. *Free electives* are courses that you may elect (choose) to enroll in; they count toward your college degree but are not required for general education or your major. *Restricted electives* are courses that you must take, but you choose them from a restricted list of possible courses that have been specified by your college as fulfilling a requirement in general education or your major. For example, your campus may have a general education requirement in social or behavioral sciences that requires you to take two courses in this field, but you're allowed to choose what those two courses are from a menu of options in the field, such as anthropology, economics, political science, psychology, or sociology. If you're considering one of these subjects as a possible major, you can take an introductory course in that subject to test your interest in it while simultaneously fulfilling a general education requirement needed for graduation. This strategy will allow you to use general education as the main highway for travel toward your final destination (a college degree) while using your electives to explore side roads (potential majors) along the way. If you find one that's compatible with your talents and interests, you may have found yourself a major.

3. **Be sure you know the courses that are required for the major you're considering.** In college, it's expected that students may know the requirements for the major they've chosen. These requirements vary considerably from one major to another. Be sure to review your college catalog carefully to determine what courses are required for the major you're considering. If you have trouble tracking down the requirements in your college catalog, don't become frustrated. These catalogs are often written in a technical manner that can sometimes be hard to interpret. If you need help identifying and understanding the requirements for a major that you are considering, don't be embarrassed about seeking assistance from a professional in your school's Academic Advisement Center.

Author's Experience   As an academic advisor, I often see students who are confused about what they want to major in, especially traditionally aged (18 to 24 years old) students. I can relate to these students because I changed my major multiple times before I reached a final decision. The first piece of advice I give students about choosing majors is to use their resources (e.g., academic advisement) and to do some research on the courses required for the majors they're considering. Over the last few years, I've seen many students who want to major in forensic science—largely due to the popularity of the *CSI* shows. I then ask them how they feel about science and math, and many of these students tell me they hate those subjects. When I inform them that becoming a forensic scientist often involves a minimum of a master's in chemistry, they decide to look at other majors. Fewer surprises like this would occur if students did at least some research on what courses are required for the majors and careers they're considering.

Julie McLaughlin

Keep in mind that college majors often require courses in fields outside of the major. Such courses are designed to support the major. For instance, psychology majors are often required to take at least one course in biology, and business majors are often required to take calculus. If you are interested in majoring in a particular subject area, be sure you are fully aware of such outside requirements and are comfortable with them.

Once you've accurately identified all courses required for the major you're considering, ask yourself the following two questions:

- Do the course titles and descriptions appeal to my interests and values?
- Do I have the abilities or skills needed to do well in these courses?

You don't want to be surprised by unexpected requirements after you have already committed to a major, particularly if these unanticipated requirements do not match your personal abilities, interests, or learning styles.

4. **Talk with students majoring in the field you are considering and ask them about their experiences.** Try to speak with several students in the field so that you get a balanced perspective that goes beyond the opinion of one individual. A good way to find students in the major you're considering is to visit student clubs on campus related to the major (e.g., psychology club or history club). The following questions may be good ones to ask students in a major that you're considering:

- What first attracted you to this major?
- What would you say are the advantages and disadvantages of majoring in this field?
- Knowing what you know now, would you choose the same major again?

Also, ask students about the quality of teaching and advising in the department. Studies show that different departments within the same college or university can vary greatly in terms of the quality of teaching, as well as their educational philosophy and attitude toward students (Pascarella & Terenzini, 1991).

5. **Sit in on some classes in the field you are considering as a major.** If the class you want to visit is large, you probably could just slip into the back row and listen. However, if the class is small, you should ask the instructor's permission. When visiting a class, focus on the content or ideas being covered in class rather than the instructor's personality or teaching style. (Keep in mind that you're trying to decide whether you will major in the subject, not in the teacher.)

6. **Discuss the major you're considering with an academic advisor.** It's probably best to speak with an academic advisor who advises students in various majors rather than to someone who advises only students in their particular academic department or field. You want to be sure to discuss the major with an advisor who is neutral and will give you unbiased feedback about the pros and cons of majoring in that field.

7. **Speak with some faculty members in the department that you're considering as a major.** Consider asking them the following questions:

    - What academic skills or qualities are needed for a student to be successful in your field?
    - What are the greatest challenges faced by students majoring in your field?
    - What do students seem to like most and least about majoring in your field?
    - What can students do with a major in your field after college graduation?
    - What types of graduate programs or professional schools would a student in your major be well prepared to enter?

8. **Visit your Career Development Center.** See whether information is available on college graduates who've majored in the field you're considering and what they've gone on to do with that major after graduation. This will give you an idea about the types of careers the major can lead to or what graduate and professional school programs students often enter after completing a major in the field that you're considering.

9. **Surf the Web site of the professional organization associated with the field that you're considering as a major.** For example, if you're thinking about becoming an anthropology major, check out the Web site of the American Anthropological Association. If you're considering history as a major, look at the Web site of the American Historical Association. The Web site of a professional organization often contains useful information for students who are considering that field as a major. For example, the Web site of the American Philosophical Association contains information about nonacademic careers for philosophy majors, and the American Sociological Association's Web site identifies various careers that sociology majors are qualified to pursue after college graduation. To locate the professional Web site of the field that you might want to explore as a possible major, ask a faculty member in that field or complete a search on the Web by simply entering the name of the field followed by the word *association*.

10. **Be sure you know what academic standards must be met for you to be accepted for entry into a major.** Because of their popularity, certain college majors may be impacted or oversubscribed, which means that more students are interested in majoring in these fields than there are openings for them. Preprofessional majors that lead directly to a particular career are often the ones that become oversubscribed (e.g., accounting, education, engineering, premed, nursing, or physical therapy). On some campuses, these majors are called restricted majors, meaning that departments control their enrollment by limiting the number of students they let into the major. For example, departments may restrict entry to their major by admitting only students who have achieved an overall GPA of 3.0 or higher in certain introductory courses required by the majors, or they may

take all students who apply for the major, rank them by their GPA, and then count down until they have filled their maximum number of available spaces (Strommer, 1993).

Be sure you know whether the major you're considering is impacted or oversubscribed and whether it requires you to meet certain academic standards before you can be admitted. As you complete courses and receive grades, check to see whether you are meeting these standards. If you find yourself failing to meet these standards, you may need to increase the amount of time and effort you devote to your studies and seek assistance from your campus Learning Center. If you're working at your maximum level of effort and are regularly using the learning assistance services available on your campus but are still not meeting the academic standards of your intended major, consult with an academic advisor to help you identify an alternative field that may be closely related to the restricted major you were hoping to enter.

Think About It ————————————— *Journal Entry* **13.8**

Do you think that the major you're considering is likely to be oversubscribed (i.e., there are more students wanting to major in the field than there are openings in the courses)? Explain.

_____

_____

_____

_____

_____

_____

11. **Consider the possibility of a college minor in a field that complements your major.** A college minor usually requires about one-half the number of credits (units) required for a major. Most campuses allow you the option of completing a minor with your major. Check with your academic advisor or the course catalog of the school you're considering transferring to; if the school offers a minor that interests you, find out what courses are required to complete it.

If you have strong interests in two different fields, a minor will allow you to major in one of these fields while minoring in the other. Thus, you can pursue two fields that interest you without having to sacrifice one for the other. Furthermore, a minor can be completed at the same time as most college majors without delaying your time to graduation. (In contrast, a double major will typically lengthen your time to graduation because you must complete the separate requirements of two different majors.) You can also pursue a second field of study alongside your major without increasing your time to graduation by completing a cognate area—a specialization that requires fewer courses to complete than a minor (e.g., four to five courses instead of seven to eight courses). A concentration area may have even fewer requirements (only two to three courses).

Taking a cluster of courses in a field outside your major can be an effective way to strengthen your resume and increase your employment prospects because it demonstrates your versatility and allows you to gain experience in areas that may be missing or underemphasized in your major. For example, students majoring in the fine arts (e.g., music or theater) or humanities (e.g., English or history) may take courses in the fields of mathematics (e.g., statistics), technology (e.g., computer science), and business (e.g., economics)—none of which are emphasized by their majors.

12. **Join a professional organization as a student.** Many professional organizations offer discounted rates for students. These organizations offer opportunities for networking with those already in the profession as well as educational experiences through local, regional, and national conferences.

Think About It ———————————— *Journal Entry* **13.9**

Before you start to dig into this chapter, take a moment to answer the following questions:

1. Have you decided on a career, or are you leaning strongly toward one?

   _____

2. If yes, why have you chosen this career? (Was your decision influenced by anybody or anything?)

   _____

   _____

   _____

3. If no, are there any careers you're considering as possibilities? What are they?

   _____

   _____

   _____

   _____

The Importance of Career Planning

College graduates in the 21st century are likely to continue working until age 75 (Herman, 2000). Once you enter the workforce full time, you'll spend most of the remaining waking hours of your life working. The only other single activity that you'll spend more time doing in your lifetime is sleeping. When you consider that such a sizable portion of your life is spent working and that your career can strongly influence your sense of personal identity and self-esteem, it becomes apparent that career choice is a critical process that should begin early in your college experience.

> **Remember**
>
> *When you're doing career planning, you're also doing life planning because you are planning how you will spend most of the waking hours of your future.*

Even if you've decided on a career that you were dreaming about since you were a preschooler, the process of career exploration and planning is not complete because you still need to decide on what specialization within that career you'll pursue. For example, if you're interested in pursuing a career in law, you'll need to eventually decide what branch of law you wish to practice (e.g., criminal law, corporate law, or family law). You'll also need to decide what employment sector or type of industry you would like to work in, such as nonprofit, for-profit, education, or government. Thus, no matter how certain or uncertain you are about your career path, you'll need to begin exploring career options and start taking your first steps toward formulating a career development plan.

Strategies for Career Exploration and Development

Reaching an effective decision about a career involves the same four steps you used in the goal-setting process (see Chapter 3):

1. **Awareness of yourself.** Your personal abilities, interests, needs, and values.

2. **Awareness of your options.** The variety of career fields available to you.

3. **Awareness of what best "fits" you.** The careers that best match your personal abilities, interests, needs, and values.

4. **Awareness of the process.** How to prepare for and gain entry into the career of your choice.

Step 1. Self-Awareness

The more you know about yourself, the better your choices and decisions will be. Self-awareness is a particularly important step to take when making career decisions because the career you choose says a lot about who you are and what you want from life. Your personal identity and life goals should not be based on or built around your career choice: it should be the other way around.

> **Remember**
>
> *Your personal attributes and goals should be considered first because they provide the foundation on which you build your career choice and future life.*

One way to gain greater self-awareness of your career interests is by taking psychological tests or assessments. These assessments allow you to see how your interests in certain career fields compare with those of other students and professionals who've experienced career satisfaction and success. These comparative perspectives can give you important reference points for assessing whether your level of interest in a career is high, average, or low relative to other students and working professionals. Your Career Development Center or Counseling Center is the place on campus where you can find these career-interest tests, as well as other instruments that allow you to assess your career-related abilities and values.

When making choices about a career, you may have to consider one other important aspect of yourself: your personal needs. A "need" may be described as something stronger than an interest. When you satisfy a personal need, you are doing something that makes your life more satisfying or fulfilling. Psychologists have identified several important human needs that vary in strength or intensity from person to person. Listed in Do It Now! 13.1 are personal needs that are especially important to consider when making a career choice.

13.1   DO IT NOW!

Personal Needs to Consider When Making Career Choices

As you read the needs listed here, make a note after each one indicating how strong the need is for you (high, moderate, or low).

1. **Autonomy.** The need to work independently without close supervision or control. Individuals high in this need may experience greater satisfaction working in careers that allow them to be their own bosses, make their own decisions, and control their own work schedules. Individuals low in this need may experience greater satisfaction working in careers that are more structured and involve working with a supervisor who provides direction, assistance, and frequent feedback.

2. **Affiliation.** The need for social interaction, a sense of belonging, and the opportunity to collaborate with others. Individuals high in this need may experience greater satisfaction working in careers that involve frequent interpersonal interaction and teamwork with colleagues or co-workers. Individuals low in this need may be more satisfied working alone or in competition with others.

Student Perspective

"To me, an important characteristic of a career is being able to meet new, smart, interesting people."

—First-year student

3. **Achievement.** The need to experience challenge and a sense of personal accomplishment. Individuals high in this need may be more satisfied working in careers that push them to solve problems, generate creative ideas, and continually learn new information or master new skills. Individuals low in this need may be more satisfied with careers that don't continually test their abilities and don't repeatedly challenge them to stretch their skills with new tasks and different responsibilities.

Student Perspective

"I want to be able to enjoy my job and be challenged by it at the same time. I hope that my job will not be monotonous and that I will have the opportunity to learn new things often."

—First-year student

4. **Recognition.** The need for high rank, status, and respect from others. Individuals high in this need may crave careers that are prestigious in the eyes of friends, family, or society. Individuals with a low need for recognition would feel comfortable working in a career that they find personally fulfilling, without being concerned about how impressive or enviable their career appears to others.

5. **Sensory stimulation.** The need to experience variety, change, and risk. Individuals high in this need may be more satisfied working in careers that involve frequent changes of pace and place (e.g., travel), unpredictable events (e.g., work tasks that vary considerably), and moderate stress (e.g., working under pressure of competition or deadlines). Individuals with a low need for sensory stimulation may feel more comfortable working in careers that involve regular routines, predictable situations, and minimal amounts of risk or stress.

Student Perspective

"For me, a good career is very unpredictable and interest-fulfilling. I would love to do something that allows me to be spontaneous."

—First-year student

"Don't expect a recluse to be motivated to sell, a creative thinker to be motivated to be a good proofreader day in and day out, or a sow's ear to be happy in the role of a silk purse."

—Pierce Howard, *The Owner's Manual for the Brain* (2000)

Think About It ——————————————— *Journal Entry* **13.10**

1. Which of the five needs in Do It Now! 13.1 did you indicate as being strong personal needs? Why?

   I chose Atonomy, because I enjoy working alone, and I don't really need that many compliments

2. What career or careers do you think would best match your strongest needs?

   Music, music production

Author's Experience

While enrolled in my third year of college with half of my degree completed, I had an eye-opening experience. I wish this experience had happened in my first year, but better late than never. Although I had chosen a career during my first year of college, my decision-making process was not systematic and didn't involve critical thinking. I chose a major based on what sounded prestigious and would pay me the most money. Although these are not necessarily bad factors, my failure to use a systematic and reflective process to evaluate these factors was bad. In my junior year of college I asked one of my professors why he decided to get his Ph.D. and become a professor. He simply answered, "I wanted autonomy." This was an epiphany for me. He explained that when he looked at his life he determined that he needed a career that offered independence, so he began looking at career options that would offer that. After that explanation, *autonomy* became my favorite word, and this story became a guiding force in my life. After going through a critical self-awareness process, I determined that autonomy was exactly what I desired and a professor is what I became.

Aaron Thompson

Student Perspective

"I think that a good career has to be meaningful for a person. It should be enjoyable for the most part [and] it has to give a person a sense of fulfillment."

—First-year student

Taken altogether, four aspects of yourself should be considered when exploring careers: your personal abilities, interests, values, and needs. As illustrated in Figure 13.3, these four pillars provide a solid foundation for effective career choices and decisions. You want to choose a career that you're good at, interested in, and passionate about and that fulfills your personal needs.

Lastly, since a career choice is a long-range decision that involves life beyond college, self-awareness should involve not only reflection on who you are now but also self-projection—reflecting on how you see yourself in the future. When you engage in the process of self-projection, you begin to see a connection between where you are now and where you want or hope to be.

FIGURE 13.3

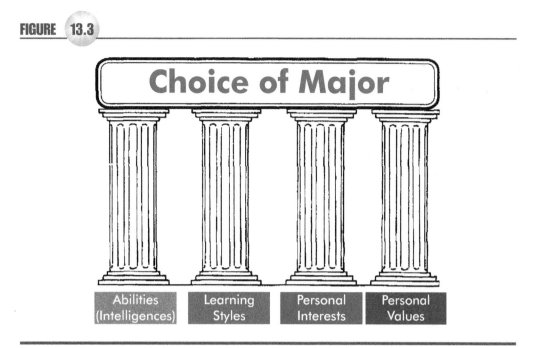

Personal Characteristics Providing the Foundation for Effective Career Choice

Think About It ————————— *Journal Entry* **13.11**

Project yourself 10 years into the future and visualize your ideal career and life.

1. What are you spending most of your time doing during your typical workday?

   _____

   _____

2. Where and with whom are you working?

   _____

3. How many hours are you working per week?

   _____

4. Where are you living?

   _____

5. Are you married? Do you have children?

   _____

6. How does your work influence your home life?

   _____

   _____

Ideally, your choice of a career should be one that leads to the best-case future scenario in which your typical day goes something like this: You wake up in the morning and hop out of bed enthusiastically, eagerly looking forward to what you'll be doing at work that day. When you're at work, time flies by, and before you know it, the day's over. When you return to bed that night and look back on your day, you feel good about what you did and how well you did it.

For this ideal scenario to have any chance of becoming a reality, or even coming close to reality, you have to select a career path that is true to yourself—a path that leads you to a career that closely matches your abilities (what you do well), your interests (what you like to do), your values (what you feel good about doing), and your needs (what brings you satisfaction and fulfillment in life).

Step 2. Awareness of Your Options

To make effective decisions about your career path, you need to have accurate knowledge about the nature of different careers and the realities of the work world. The Career Development Center is the first place to go for this information and help with career exploration and planning. In addition to helping you explore your personal career interests and abilities, the Career Development Center is your key campus resource for learning about the nature of different careers and for strategies on locating career-related work experiences.

If you were to ask people to name as many careers as they can, they wouldn't come close to naming the 900 career titles listed by the federal government in its Occupational Information Network. Many of these careers you may have never heard of, but some of them may represent good career options for you. You can learn about careers through nine major routes or avenues:

- Reading about them in books or online
- Becoming involved in cocurricular programs on campus related to career development
- Taking career development courses
- Interviewing people in different career fields
- Observing (shadowing) people at work in different careers
- Interning
- Participating in a co-op program
- Volunteering
- Working part-time

Author's Experience   When my sister was in the last year of her nursing degree, she decided she wanted to be a pediatric nurse and work at one of the top 10 pediatric hospitals in the country. At the time, I lived in a city with an excellent pediatric hospital. My sister decided to come visit me for an extended weekend and made appointments to shadow different units in that hospital on her visit. She fell in love with the place and decided she definitely wanted to work there! A few months later, when she was in her last semester of school, that hospital called her and asked if she wanted to come and interview for jobs on all four units. They'd been just as impressed with her when she shadowed as she was with them, and they made a note on her resume to call her when she was close to graduating. She interviewed and was offered all four jobs! It turned out her shadowing experience actually ended up being a "pre-interview," and she had a job before she even graduated!

— *Julie McLaughlin*

Resources on Careers

Your Career Development Center and your College Library are campus resources where you can find a wealth of reading material on careers, either in print or online. Listed here are some of the most useful sources of written information on careers:

- *Dictionary of Occupational Titles* (www.occupationalinfo.org). This is the largest printed resource on careers; it contains concise definitions of over 17,000 jobs. It also includes information on:
  - work tasks that people in the career typically perform regularly;
  - types of knowledge, skills, and abilities that are required for different careers;
  - interests, values, and needs of individuals who find working in particular careers to be personally rewarding; and
  - background experiences of people working in different careers that qualified them for their positions.
- *Occupational Outlook Handbook* (www.bls.gov/oco). This is one of the most widely available and used resources on careers. It contains descriptions of approximately 250 positions, including information on the nature of work, work conditions, places of employment, training or education required for career entry and advancement, salaries, careers in related fields, and additional sources of information about particular careers (e.g., professional organizations and governmental agencies). A distinctive feature of this resource is that it contains information about the future employment outlook for different careers.
- *Encyclopedia of Careers and Vocational Guidance* (Chicago: Ferguson Press). As the name suggests, this is an encyclopedia of information on qualifications, salaries, and advancement opportunities for various careers.
- Occupational Information Network (O*NET) Online (online.onetcenter. org). This is America's most comprehensive source of online information about careers. It contains an up-to-date set of descriptions for almost 1,000 careers, plus lots of other information similar to what you would find in the *Dictionary of Occupational Titles*.

In addition to these general sources of information, your Career Development Center and College Library should have books and other published materials related to specific careers or occupations (e.g., careers for English majors).

You can also learn a lot about careers by simply reading advertisements for position openings in your local newspaper or online, such as at www.careerbuilder.com and www.monstertrak.com. When reading position descriptions, make special note of the tasks, duties, or responsibilities they involve and ask yourself whether these positions are compatible with your personal profile of abilities, interests, needs, and values.

Career Planning and Development Programs

Periodically during the academic year, cocurricular programs devoted to career exploration and career preparation are likely to be offered on your campus. For example, the Career Development Center may sponsor career exploration or career planning workshops that you can attend for free. Also, the Career Development Center may organize a career fair on campus, at which professionals working in different career fields are given booths on campus where you can visit with them and ask questions about their careers. Research indicates that career development workshops offered on campus are effective in helping students plan for and decide on a career (Brown & Krane, 2000; Hildenbrand & Gore, 2005).

Career Development Courses

Many colleges offer career development courses for elective credit. These courses typically include self-assessment of your career interests, information about different careers, and strategies for career preparation. You should be doing career planning, so why not do it by taking a career development course that rewards you with college credit for doing it? Studies show that students who participate in career development courses experience significant benefits in terms of their career choice and career development (Pascarella & Terenzini, 2005).

Informational Interviews

One of the best and most overlooked ways to get accurate information about careers is to interview professionals who are working in career fields. Career development specialists refer to this strategy as informational interviewing. Don't assume that working professionals would not be interested in taking time out of their day to speak with a student. Most are willing to be interviewed about their careers; they often enjoy it (Crosby, 2002).

Informational interviews provide you inside information about what careers are like because you're getting that information directly from the horse's mouth. It also helps you gain experience and confidence in interview situations, which may help you prepare for future job interviews. Furthermore, if you make a good impression during informational interviews, the people you interview may suggest that you contact them again after graduation in case there are position openings. If there are openings, you might find yourself being the interviewee instead of the interviewer (and you might find yourself a job).

Because interviews are a valuable source of information about careers and provide possible contacts for future employment, we strongly recommend that you complete the information interview assignment included at the end of this chapter.

Think About It ———————————————— *Journal Entry* **13.12**

If you were to observe or interview a working professional in a career that interests you, what position would that person hold?

_____

_____

_____

_____

_____

_____

Career Observation (Shadowing)

In addition to learning about careers from reading and interviews, you can experience careers more directly by placing yourself in workplace situations or work environments that allow you to observe workers performing their daily duties. Two college-sponsored programs may be available on your campus that would allow you to observe working professionals:

- **Job Shadowing Programs.** These programs allow you to follow ("shadow") and observe a professional during a typical workday.
- **Career Development Center.** Learn about what job shadowing programs may be available on your college campus. If none are available in a career field that interests you, consider finding one on your own by using strategies similar to those we recommend for informational interviews at the end of this chapter. The only difference is that instead of asking the person for an interview, you'd be asking whether you could observe that person at work. The same person who gave you an informational interview might be willing to allow such observation. Keep in mind that one or two days of observation will give you some firsthand information about a career, but will not give you firsthand experience in that career.

Internships and Co-Ops

In contrast to job shadowing, where you observe someone at work, an internship program immerses you in the work itself and gives you the opportunity to perform career-related work duties. A distinguishing feature of internships is that you can receive academic credit and sometimes financial compensation for the work you do. An internship usually totals 120 to 150 work hours, which may be completed at the same time you're enrolled in a full schedule of classes or when you're not taking classes (e.g., during summer term).

An advantage of an internship is that it enables college students to avoid the classic catch-22 situation they often run into when interviewing for their first career positions after graduation. The interview scenario usually goes something like this: The potential employer asks the college graduate, "What work experience have you had in this field?" The recent graduate replies, "I haven't had any work experience because I've been a full-time college student." This scenario can be avoided if you complete an internship during your college experience, which allows you to say, "Yes, I do have work experience in this field." We encourage you to participate in an internship while in college because it will enable you to beat the "no experience" rap after graduation and distinguish yourself from many other college graduates. Research shows that students who have internships while in college are more likely to develop career-relevant work skills and find employment immediately after college graduation (Pascarella & Terenzini, 2005).

Internships are typically available to college students during their junior or senior year; however, there may be internships available to first- and second-year students on your campus. You can also pursue internships on your own. Published guides describe various career-related internships, along with information on how to apply for them (e.g., *Peterson's Internships* and the *Vault Guide to Top Internships*). You could also search for internships on the Web (e.g., www.internships.com and www.vaultreports.com). Another good resource for possible information on internships is the local chamber of commerce in the town or city where your college is located or in your hometown.

Another option for gaining firsthand work experience is enrolling in courses that allow you to engage in hands-on learning related to your career interest. For instance, if you're interested in working with children, courses in child psychology or early childhood education may offer experiential learning opportunities in a preschool or daycare center on campus.

A co-op is similar to an internship, but involves work experience that lasts longer than one academic term and often requires students to stop their coursework temporarily to participate in the program. However, some co-op programs allow you to continue to take classes while working part time at a co-op position; these are sometimes referred to as parallel co-ops. Students are paid for participating in co-op programs (Smith, 2005).

The value of co-ops and internships is strongly supported by research, which indicates that students who have these experiences during college:

- Are more likely to report that their college education was relevant to their career;
- Receive higher evaluations from employers who recruit them on campus;
- Have less difficulty finding initial positions after graduation;
- Are more satisfied with their first career positions after college;
- Obtain more prestigious positions after graduation; and
- Report greater job satisfaction (Gardner, 1991; Knouse, Tanner, & Harris, 1999; Pascarella & Terenzini, 1991, 2005).

In one statewide survey that asked employers to rank various factors they considered important when hiring new college graduates, internship or cooperative education programs received the highest ranking (Education Commission of the States, 1995). Furthermore, employers report that if full-time positions open up in their organization or company, they usually turn first to their own interns and co-op students (National Association of Colleges & Employers, 2003).

Volunteer Service

Engaging in volunteerism not only helps your community, but also helps you by giving you the opportunity to explore different work environments and gain work experience in career fields that relate to your area of service. For example, volunteer service to different age groups (e.g., children, adolescents, or the elderly) and service in different environments (e.g., hospital, school, or laboratory) can provide you with firsthand work experience and simultaneously give you a chance to test your interest in possibly pursuing future careers related to these different age groups and work environments. (To get a sense of the range of service opportunities that may be available to you, go to www.usa.service.org.)

Author's Experience

As an academic advisor, I was once working with two first-year students, Kim and Christopher. Kim was thinking about becoming a physical therapist, and Chris was thinking about becoming an elementary school teacher. I suggested to Kim that she visit the hospital near our college to see whether she could do volunteer work in the physical therapy unit. The hospital did need volunteers, so she volunteered in the physical therapy unit and loved it. That volunteer experience confirmed for her that physical therapy was what she should pursue as a career. She completed a degree in physical therapy and is now a professional physical therapist.

I suggested to Chris, the student who was thinking about becoming an elementary school teacher, that he visit some local schools to see whether they could use a volunteer teacher's aide. One of the schools did need his services, and Chris volunteered as a teacher's aide for about 10 weeks. At the halfway point during his volunteer experience, he came into my office to tell me that the kids were just about driving him crazy and that he no longer had any interest in becoming a teacher. He ended up majoring in communications.

Kim and Chris were the first two students I advised to get involved in volunteer work to test their career interests. Their volunteer experiences proved so valuable for helping both of them make a career decision that I now encourage all students I advise to get volunteer experience in the fields they're considering for future careers.

Joe Cuseo

Volunteer service also enables you to network with professionals outside of college who may serve as excellent references and resources for letters of recommendation for you. Furthermore, if these professionals are impressed with your volunteer work, they may become interested in hiring you part-time while you're still in college or full time when you graduate.

It may be possible to do volunteer work on campus by serving as an informal teaching assistant or research assistant to a faculty member. Such experiences are particularly valuable for students intending to go to graduate school. If you have a good relationship with any faculty members who are working in an academic field that interests you, consider asking them whether they would like some assistance (e.g., with their teaching or research responsibilities). Your volunteer work for a college professor could lead to making a presentation with your professor at a professional conference or even result in your name being included as a coauthor on an article published by the professor.

Think About It	*Journal Entry* **13.13**

Have you done volunteer work? If you have, did you learn anything from your volunteer experiences that might help you decide which types of work best match your interests or talents?

_____

_____

_____

_____

_____

_____

Jobs that you hold during the academic year or during summer break should not be overlooked as potential sources of career information and as resume-building experience. Part-time work can provide opportunities to learn or develop skills that may be relevant to your future career, such as organizational skills, communication skills, and the ability to work effectively with co-workers from diverse backgrounds or cultures.

Also, work in a part-time position may eventually turn into a full-time career. The following personal story illustrates how this can happen.

Author's Experience   One student of mine, an English major, worked part-time for an organization that provides special assistance to mentally handicapped children. After he completed his English degree, he was offered a full-time position in this organization, which he accepted. While working at his full-time position with handicapped children, he decided to go to graduate school part time and eventually completed a master's degree in special education, which qualified him for a promotion to a more advanced position in the organization, which he also accepted.

— Joe Cuseo

It might also be possible for you to obtain part-time work experience on campus through your school's work-study program. A work-study job allows you to work at your college in various work settings, such as the Financial Aid Office, College Library, Public Relations Office, or Computer Services Center, and often allows you to build your employment schedule around your academic schedule. On-campus work can provide you with valuable career-exploration and resume-building experiences, and the professionals for whom you work can serve as excellent references for letters of recommendation to future employers. To see whether you are eligible for your school's work-study program, visit the Financial Aid Office on your campus.

Learning about careers through firsthand experience in actual work settings (e.g., shadowing, internships, volunteer services, and part-time work) is critical to successful career exploration and preparation. You can take a career-interest test, or you can test your career interest through actual work experiences. There is simply no substitute for direct, hands-on experience for gaining knowledge about careers. These firsthand experiences represent the ultimate career-reality test. They allow you direct access to information about what careers are really like, as opposed to how they are portrayed on TV or in the movies, which often paint an inaccurate or unrealistic picture of careers, making them appear more exciting or glamorous than they are.

In summary, firsthand experiences in actual work settings equip you with five powerful career advantages:

- Learn about what work is like in a particular field;
- Test your interest and skills for certain types of work;
- Strengthen your resume by adding experiential learning to academic (classroom) learning;
- Acquire contacts for letters of recommendation; and
- Network with employers who may refer or hire you for a position after graduation.

"Give me a history major who has done internships and a business major who hasn't, and I'll hire the history major every time."

—William Ardery, senior vice president, investor communications company (quoted in *The New York Times*)

Be sure to use your campus resources (e.g., the Career Development Center, Counseling Center, and Financial Aid Office), your local resources (e.g., chamber of commerce), and your personal contacts (family and friends) to locate and participate in work experiences that relate to your career interests. When you land an internship, work hard at it, learn as much as you can from it, and build relationships with as many people as possible at your internship site, because these are the people who can provide you with future contacts, references, and referrals.

Think About It ——————————————— *Journal Entry* **13.14**

1. Have you learned anything from your firsthand work experiences that may influence your future career plans?

_____

_____

_____

_____

2. If you could get firsthand work experience in any career field right now, what career would it be? Why?

_____

_____

_____

_____

Step 3. Awareness of What Best Fits You

When considering career options, don't buy into either of the following common myths about careers, which can lead students to poor career decisions.

Myth 1. Once you've decided on a career, you have decided on what you'll be doing for the rest of your life. This is simply and totally false. The term *career* derives from the same root word as *racecourse*. Like a racecourse, a career involves movement that typically takes different turns and twists, and as in any race, it's not how fast you start but how strong you finish that matters most. This ability to move and change direction is what distinguishes a professional career from a dead-end job. Americans average four careers in a lifetime; it's also estimated that today's college graduates will change jobs 12 to 15 times, which will span three to five career fields (U.S. Bureau of Labor Statistics, 2005). These statistics may be surprising because you're probably going to college with the idea that you're preparing for a particular career. However, these results become less surprising when you consider that the general education component of your college experience provides you with versatile, transferable skills that can qualify you for different positions in various career fields.

Myth 2. You need to pick a career that's in demand and that will get you a job with a good starting salary right after graduation. Looking only at careers that are "hot" now and have high starting salaries can distract you from looking at yourself and cause you to overlook a more important question: are these careers truly compatible with your personal abilities, interests, needs, and values? Starting salaries and available job openings are external factors that can be easily seen and counted; thus, they may get more attention and receive more weight in the decision-making process than qualities that are harder to see and put a number on, such as inner characteris-

tics. In the case of career decision making, this can result in college students choosing careers based exclusively on external factors (salaries and openings) without giving equal (or any) attention to such internal factors as personal abilities, interests, and values. This can lead some college graduates to enter careers that eventually leave them bored, frustrated, or dissatisfied.

The number of job offers you receive immediately after graduation and the number of dollars you earn as a starting salary in your first position are short-term (and shortsighted) standards for judging whether you've made a good career choice. Remember that there's a critical difference between career *entry* and career *advancement*. Some college graduates may not bolt out of the starting gate and begin their career paths with well-paying first positions, but they will steadily work their way up the career ladder and be promoted to more advanced positions than graduates who start out with higher salaries.

Criteria (Standards) to Consider When Evaluating Career Options

Effective decision making requires you to identify all important factors that should be considered when evaluating your options and determine how much weight (influence) each of these factors should carry. As we emphasize throughout this chapter, the factor that should carry the greatest weight in career decision making is the match between your choice and your personal abilities, interests, needs, and values.

Suppose you discover more than one career option that's compatible with these four dimensions of yourself. What other aspects of a career should be considered to help you reach a decision and make a selection? Many people would probably say salary, but as the length of the following list suggests, other important aspects or characteristics of careers should be factored into your decision-making process.

- **Work conditions.** Work conditions include such considerations as:
  - the nature of the work environment (e.g., physical and social environment);
  - the geographical location of the work (e.g., urban, suburban, or rural);
  - the work schedule (e.g., number of hours per week and flexibility of hours); and
  - work-related travel (e.g., opportunities to travel, frequency of travel, and locations traveled to).

- **Career entry.** Can you enter into the career without much difficulty, or does the supply of people pursuing the career far exceed the demand (e.g., professional acting or athletes)? If a career is highly competitive and difficult to gain entry into, it doesn't mean you should automatically give up on it; however, it does mean you should have an alternative career to fall back on until you can (or in case you can't) catch a break that will allow you to break into your ideal career.

- **Career advancement (promotion).** An ideal first job educates and prepares you to advance to an even better one. Will the career you're considering provide you with opportunities for promotion to more advanced positions?

- **Career mobility.** Is it easy to move out of the career and into a different career path? This may be an important factor to consider because careers may rise or fall in demand; furthermore, your career interests or values may change as you gain more work and life experience.

- **Financial benefits.** Financial considerations include salary—both starting salary and expected salary increases with greater work experience or advancement to higher positions. However, they also include fringe benefits, such as health insurance, paid vacation time, paid sick-leave time, paid maternity- or paternity-leave time, paid tuition for seeking advanced education, and retirement benefits.

- **Impact of the career on your personal life.** How would the career affect your family life, your physical and mental health, and your self-concept or self-esteem? Remember that your life should not be built around your career: your career should be built around your life. Your means of making a living and other important aspects of yourself need to be considered simultaneously when making career choices, because the nature of your work will affect the nature (and quality) of your life.

> "The French work to live, but the Swiss live to work."
> —French proverb

Remember

A good career decision should involve more than salary and should take into consideration how the career will affect all dimensions of your self (social, emotional, physical, etc.) throughout all stages of your adult life: young adulthood, middle age, and late adulthood. It's almost inevitable that your career will affect your identity, the type of person you become, how you will balance the demands of work and family, and how well you will serve others beyond yourself. An effective career decision-making process requires you to make tough and thoughtful decisions about what matters most to you.

> "Money is a good servant but a bad master."
> —French proverb

Think About It ——————— *Journal Entry* 13.15

Answer the following questions about a career that you're considering or have chosen:

1. What is the career?

   _____

2. Why are you considering this career? (What led or caused you to become interested in it?)

   _____

   _____

3. Would you say that your interest in this career is motivated primarily by intrinsic factors—that is, factors "inside" of you, such as your personal abilities, interests, needs, and values? Or, would you say that your interest in the career is influenced more heavily by extrinsic factors—that is, factors "outside" of you, such as starting salary, pleasing parents, meeting family expectations, or meeting an expected role for your gender (male role or female role)? Why?

   _____

   _____

   _____

4. If money was not an issue and you could earn a comfortable living in any career, would you choose the same career? Why or why not? What career would you choose?

   _____

   _____

   _____

   _____

Step 4. Awareness of the Process

Whether you're keeping your career options open or you've already decided on a particular career, you can start preparing for career success by using the following strategies.

Self-Monitoring: Watching and Tracking Your Personal Skills and Positive Qualities

Don't forget that *learning* skills are also *earning* skills. The skills you're acquiring in college may appear to be just *academic* skills, but they're also *career* skills. For instance, when you're in the process of completing academic tasks such as taking tests and writing papers, you're using various career-relevant skills (e.g., analyzing, organizing, communicating, and problem solving).

Many students think that a college diploma or certificate is an automatic passport to a good job and career success (Ellin, 1993; Sullivan, 1993). However, for most employers of college graduates, what matters most is not only the credential but also the skills and personal strengths an applicant brings to the position (Education Commission of the States, 1995). You can start building these skills and strengths by self-monitoring (i.e., watching yourself and keeping track of the skills you're using and developing during your college experience). Skills are mental habits, and like all other habits that are repeatedly practiced, their development can be so gradual that you may not even notice how much growth is taking place—perhaps somewhat like watching grass grow. Thus, career development specialists recommend that you consciously track your skills to remain aware of them and to put you in a position to "sell" them to potential employers (Lock, 2000).

One strategy you can use to track your developing skills is to keep a career-development journal in which you note academic tasks and assignments you've completed, along with the skills you used to complete them. Be sure to record skills in your journal that you've developed in nonacademic situations, such as those skills used while performing part-time jobs, personal hobbies, cocurricular activities, or volunteer services. Since skills are actions, it's best to record them as action verbs in your career-development journal.

The key to discovering career-relevant skills and qualities is to get in the habit of stepping back from your academic and out-of-class experiences to reflect on what skills and qualities these experiences entailed and then get them down in writing before they slip your mind. You're likely to find that many personal skills you develop in college will be the same ones that employers will seek in the workforce.

Author's Experience After class one day, I had a conversation with a student (Max) about his personal interests. He said he was considering a career in the music industry and was now working part-time as a disc jockey at a nightclub. I asked him what it took to be a good disc jockey, and in less than five minutes of conversation, we discovered many more skills were involved in doing his job than either of us had realized. He was responsible for organizing three to four hours of music each night he worked; he had to read the reactions of his audience (customers) and adapt or adjust his selections to their musical tastes; he had to arrange his selections in a sequence that periodically varied the tempo (speed) of the music he played throughout the night; and he had to continually research and update his music collection to track the latest trends in hits and popular artists. Max also said that he had to overcome his fear of public speaking to deliver announcements that were a required part of his job.

Although we were just having a short, friendly conversation after class about his part-time job, Max wound up reflecting on and identifying multiple skills he was using on the job. We both agreed that it would be a good idea to get these skills down in writing so that he could use them as selling points for future jobs in the music industry or in any industry.

Joe Cuseo

13.2   DO IT **NOW**

Personal Skills Relevant to Successful Career Performance

The following behaviors represent a sample of useful skills that are relevant to success in various careers (Bolles, 1998). As you read these skills, underline or highlight any of them that you have performed, either inside or outside of school.

advising	assembling	calculating	coaching	coordinating
creating	delegating	designing	evaluating	explaining
initiating	mediating	measuring	motivating	negotiating
operating	planning	producing	proving	researching
resolving	sorting	summarizing	supervising	synthesizing
translating				

In addition to tracking your developing skills, track your positive traits or personal qualities. While it's best to record your skills as action verbs because they represent actions that you can perform for anyone who hires you, it may be best to track your attributes as adjectives because they describe who you are and what personal qualities you can bring to the job. Do It Now! 13.3 gives a sample of personal traits and qualities that are relevant to success in multiple careers. As you read these traits, underline or highlight any of them that you feel you possess or will soon possess.

13.3   DO IT **NOW**

Personal Traits and Qualities Relevant to Successful Career Performance

broad-minded	cheerful	congenial	conscientious	considerate
courteous	curious	dependable	determined	energetic
enthusiastic	ethical	flexible	imaginative	industrious
loyal	observant	open-minded	outgoing	patient
prepared	persistent	persuasive	positive	precise
productive	punctual	reasonable	reflective	sincere
tactful	thorough			

Remember

Keeping track of your developing skills and your positive qualities is as important to your successful entry into a future career as completing courses and compiling credits.

Self-Marketing: Packaging and Presenting Your Personal Strengths and Achievements

To convert your college experience into immediate employment, it might be useful to view yourself (a college graduate) as a product and employers as intentional customers who may be interested in making a purchase (of your skills and attributes). As a first-year student, it could be said that you're in the early stages of the product-development process. Now is the time to begin the process so that by the time you graduate, your finished product (you) will be one that employers notice and become interested in purchasing.

An effective self-marketing plan is one that gives employers a clear idea of what you can bring to the table and do for them. This should increase the number of job offers you receive and increase your chances of finding a position that best matches your interests, talents, and values.

You can effectively advertise or market your personal skills, qualities, and achievements to future employers through the following channels:

- College transcript
- Cocurricular experiences
- Personal portfolio
- Personal resume
- Letters of application (a.k.a. cover letters)
- Letters of recommendation (a.k.a. letters of reference)
- Networking
- Personal interview

These are the primary tools you will use to showcase yourself to employers and employers will use to evaluate you. Here's how you can strategically prepare for and sharpen these tools to maximize their effectiveness.

College Transcript

A college transcript is a listing of all courses you enrolled in and the grades you received in those courses. Two pieces of information included on your college transcript can influence employers' hiring decisions or admissions committee decisions about your acceptance to a four-year college, graduate, or professional school: (1) the grades you earned in your courses, and (2) the types of courses you completed.

Simply stated, the better your grades in college, the better your employment prospects after college. Research on college graduates indicates that the higher their grades, the higher:

- The prestige of their first job;
- Their total earnings; and
- Their job mobility.

This relationship between college grades and career success exists for students at all types of colleges and universities, regardless of the reputation or prestige of the institution they attend (Pascarella & Terenzini, 1991, 2005).

The particular types of courses listed on your college transcript can also influence employment and acceptance decisions. Listed here the types of courses that should strengthen your college transcript.

- **Honors courses.** If you achieve excellent grades during your first year, you may apply or be recommended for the honors program at your campus and take more academically challenging courses. If you qualify for the honors program, we recommend that you accept the challenge. Even though A grades may be more difficult to achieve in honors courses, the presence of these courses on your college transcript clearly shows that you were admitted to the honors program and were willing to accept this academic challenge.

- **Leadership courses.** Many employers hire college graduates with the hope or expectation that they will advance and eventually assume important leadership positions in the company or organization. Although a leadership course is not likely to be required for general education, or for your major, it is an elective course that will develop your leadership skills and the impressiveness of your college transcript.

- **International and cross-cultural courses.** Courses whose content crosses national and cultural boundaries are often referred to as international and cross-cultural courses. These courses are particularly pertinent to success in today's world, in which there is more international travel, more interaction among citizens from different countries, and more economic interdependence among nations than at any other time in world history (Office of Research, 1994). As a result of these developments, employers now place higher value on employees with international knowledge and foreign language skills (Fixman, 1990; Office of Research, 1994). Taking courses that have an international focus, or that focus on cross-cultural comparisons, helps you develop a global perspective that can improve the quality of your college degree and increase the attractiveness of your college transcript to potential employers.

- **Diversity (multicultural) courses.** America's workforce is more ethnically and racially diverse today than at any other time in the nation's history, and it will grow even more so in the years ahead (U.S. Bureau of Labor Statistics, 2005). Successful career performance in today's diverse workforce requires sensitivity to human differences and the ability to relate to people from different cultural backgrounds (National Association of Colleges & Employers, 2003; Smith, 1997). College courses relating to diversity awareness and appreciation, or courses emphasizing multicultural interaction and communication, can be valuable additions to your college transcript that should strengthen your career preparation, placement, and advancement.

Co-Curricular Experiences

Participation in student clubs, campus organizations, and other types of co-curricular activities can be a valuable source of experiential learning that can complement classroom-based learning and contribute to your career preparation and development. A sizable body of research supports the value of co-curricular experiences for career success (Astin, 1993; Kuh, 1993; Pascarella & Terenzini, 1991, 2005). Strongly consider getting involved in co-curricular life on your campus, especially involvement with co-curricular experiences that:

- Allow you to develop leadership and helping skills (e.g., leadership retreats, student government, college committees, peer counseling, or peer tutoring);
- Enable you to interact with others from diverse ethnic and racial groups (e.g., multicultural club or international club), and
- Provide you with out-of-class experiences related to your academic major or career interests (e.g., student clubs in your college major or intended career field).

Keep in mind that co-curricular experiences are also resume-building experiences that provide solid evidence of your commitment to the college community outside the classroom. Be sure to showcase these experiences to prospective employers.

Also, the campus professionals with whom you may interact while participating in co-curricular activities (e.g., the director of student activities or dean of students) can serve as valuable references for letters of recommendation to future employers or graduate and professional schools.

Personal Portfolio

You may have heard the word *portfolio* used to mean a collection of artwork that professional artists put together to showcase or advertise their artistic talents. However, a portfolio can be a collection of any materials or products that illustrates an individual's skills and talents or demonstrates an individual's educational and personal development. For example, a portfolio could include such items as:

- Outstanding papers, exam performances, research projects, or lab reports;
- Artwork, photos from study abroad, service learning, or internships experiences;
- Video footage of oral presentations or theatrical performances;
- CDs of musical performances;
- Assessments from employers or coaches; and
- Letters of recognition or commendation.

You can start the process of portfolio development right now by saving your best work and performances. Store them in a traditional portfolio folder, or save them on a computer disc to create an electronic portfolio. Another option would be to create a Web site and upload your materials there. Eventually, you should be able to build a well-stocked portfolio that documents your skills and demonstrates your development to future employers or future schools. You can start to develop an electronic portfolio now by completing the Creating an Electronic Portfolio exercise at the end of this chapter.

Letters of Application (a.k.a. Cover Letters)

You write a letter of application when applying for a position opening or for acceptance to a school. When writing these letters, be sure that you demonstrate awareness and knowledge of:

- Yourself (e.g., your personal interests, abilities, and values);
- The organization or institution to which you are applying (e.g., showing that you know something specific about its purpose, philosophy, programs, and the position you are applying for); and
- The match or fit between you and the organization (e.g., between the skills and qualities you possess and those that the position requires).

Focusing on these three major points should make your letter complete and will allow the letter to flow sequentially from a focus on *you,* to a focus on *them,* to a focus on the *relationship* between you and them. Here are some suggestions for developing each of these three points in your letter of application.

13.4   DO IT **NOW**!

Constructing a Resume

Use this skeletal resume as an outline or template for beginning construction of your own resume and for setting your future goals. (If you have already developed a resume, use this template to identify and add categories that may be missing from your current one.)

Name (First, Middle, Last)

Current Addresses:	Permanent Addresses:
Postal Address	Postal Address
E-mail address	E-mail address
Phone no.	Phone no.

EDUCATION: Name of College or University, City, State
Degree Name (e.g., Bachelor of Science)
College Major (e.g., Accounting)
Graduation Date, GPA

RELATED WORK   Position Title, City, State   Start and stop dates

EXPERIENCES: (Begin the list with the most recent
position dates held.)

(List skills used or developed.)

VOLUNTEER (COMMUNITY SERVICE)
EXPERIENCES:

(List skills used or developed.)

NOTABLE COURSEWORK:
(e.g., leadership, international, or interdisciplinary courses)

CO-CURRICULAR EXPERIENCES:
(e.g., student government or peer leadership)
(List skills used or developed.)

PERSONAL SKILLS AND POSITIVE QUALITIES:
(List as bullets. Be sure to include those that are especially relevant to the position for which you're applying.)

HONORS/AWARDS: (In addition to those received in college, you may include those received in high school.)

- Organize information about yourself into a past-present-future sequence of personal development. For instance, point out the following:
  - Where you have been—your past history or background experiences that qualify you to apply for the position (academic, co-curricular, and work experiences).
  - Where you are now—why you've decided to apply for the position today.
  - Where you intend to go—what you hope to do or accomplish for the employer once you get there.

Taking this past-present-future approach to organizing your letter should result in a smooth, well-sequenced flow of information about you and your development. Also, by focusing on where you've been and where you're going, you demonstrate your ability to reflect on the past and project to the future.

When describing yourself, try to identify specific examples or concrete illustrations of your positive qualities and areas in which you have grown or improved in recent years. While it is important to highlight all your major strengths, this doesn't necessarily mean you should ignore or cover up areas in which you feel you still need to improve or develop. No human is perfect; one indication of someone with a healthy self-concept is that person's ability to recognize and acknowledge both personal strengths and areas in which further improvement or development is needed. Including a touch of honest self-assessment in your letter of application demonstrates both sincerity and integrity. It should also reduce the risk that your letter will be perceived as a "snow job" that pours on mounds and pounds of self-flattery without an ounce of personal humility.

- **Do some advance research about the particular organization to which you're applying.** In your letter of application, mention some aspects or characteristics of the organization that you've learned about, such as one of its programs that impressed you or attracted your interest. This sends the message that you have taken the time and initiative to learn something about the organization, which says something positive about you.

- **Make it clear why you feel there is a good fit or match between you and the organization to which you've applied.** When applying for a position, your first objective is to focus on what you can do for the organization rather than what it can do for you or what's in it for you. Point out how your qualities, skills, interests, or values are in line with the organization's needs or goals. By doing some research on the particular institution or organization that you're applying to, and by including this information in your letter of application, you also distinguish your application from the swarms of standard "form letters" that companies receive from other applicants.

Letters of Recommendation (a.k.a. Letters of Reference)

Personal letters of recommendation can be a powerful way to document your strengths and selling points. To maximize the power of your personal recommendations, give careful thought to:

- Who should serve as your references;
- How to approach them; and
- What to provide them.

Strategies for improving the quality of your letters of recommendation are suggested in Do It Now! 13.5.

13.5   DO IT **NOW**

The Art and Science of Requesting Letters of Recommendation: Effective Strategies and Common Courtesies

1. **Select recommendations from people who know you well.** Think about individuals with whom you've had an ongoing relationship, who know your name, and who know your strengths: for example, an instructor who you've had for more than one class, an academic advisor whom you see often, or an employer whom you've worked for over an extended period.

2. **Seek a balanced blend of letters from people who have observed you perform in different settings or situations.** The following are settings in which you may have performed well and people who may have observed your performance in these settings:
   - The classroom—a professor who can speak to your academic performance.
   - On campus—a student life professional for a co-curricular reference who can comment on your contributions outside the classroom.
   - Off campus—a professional for whom you've performed volunteer service, part-time work, or an internship.

3. **Pick the right time and place to make your request.** Be sure to make your request well in advance of the letter's deadline date (e.g., at least two weeks). First ask whether the person is willing to write the letter, and then come back with forms and envelopes. Do not approach the person with these materials in hand, because this may send the message that you have assumed or presumed the person will automatically say "yes." (This is not the most socially sensitive message to send someone whom you're about to ask for a favor.) Lastly, pick a place where the person can give full attention to your request. For instance, make a personal visit to the person's office, rather than making the request in a busy hallway or in front of a classroom full of students.

4. **Waive your right to see the letter.** If the school or organization to which you're applying has a reference-letter form that asks whether or not you want to waive (give up) your right to see the letter, waive your right—as long as you feel reasonably certain that you will be receiving a good letter of recommendation. By waiving your right to see your letter of recommendation, you show confidence that the letter to be written about you will be positive, and you assure the person who reads the letter that you didn't inspect or screen it to make sure it was a good one before sending it.

5. **Provide your references with a fact sheet about yourself.** Include your experiences and achievements—both inside and outside the classroom. This will help make your references' job a little easier by providing points to focus on. More importantly, it will help you because your letter becomes more powerful when it contains concrete examples or illustrations of your positive qualities and accomplishments. On your fact sheet, be sure to include any exceptionally high grades you may have earned in certain courses, as well as volunteer services, leadership experiences, special awards or forms of recognition, and special interests or talents that relate to your academic major and career choice. Your fact sheet is the place and time for you to "toot your own horn," so don't be afraid of coming across as a braggart or egotist. You're not being conceited—you're just showcasing your strengths.

6. **Provide your references with a stamped, addressed envelope.** This is a simple courtesy that makes their job a little easier and demonstrates your social sensitivity.

7. **Follow up with a thank-you note.** Thank your references at about the time when your letter of recommendation should be sent.

   This is the right thing to do because it shows your appreciation; it's also the smart thing to do because if the letter hasn't been written yet, the thank-you note serves as a gentle reminder for your reference to write the letter.

8. **Let your references know the outcome of your application** (e.g., your admission to a school or acceptance of a job offer). This is the courteous thing to do, and your references are likely to remember your courtesy, which could strengthen the quality of any future letters they may write for you.

Think About It ——————————— *Journal Entry* **13.16**

1. Have you met a faculty member or other professional on campus who knows you well enough to write a personal letter of recommendation for you?

_____

2. If yes, who is this person, and what position does he or she hold on campus?

_____

_____

_____

Networking

Would it surprise you to learn that 80 percent of jobs are never advertised? This means that the jobs you see listed in a classified section of the newspaper and posted in a Career Development Center or employment center represent only 20 percent of available openings at any given time. Almost one-half of all job hunters find employment through people they know or have met, such as friends, family members, and casual acquaintances. When it comes to locating positions, *whom* you know can be as important as *what* you know or how good your resume looks. Consequently, it's important to continually expand the circle of people who are aware of your career interests and abilities, because they can be a valuable source of information about employment opportunities.

Also, be sure to share copies of your resume with friends and family members, just in case they come in contact with employers who are looking for somebody with your career interests and qualifications.

Personal Interview

A personal interview is your opportunity to make a positive in-person impression. You can make a strong first impression during any interview by showing that you've done your homework and have come prepared. In particular, you should come to the interview with knowledge about yourself and your audience.

You can demonstrate knowledge about yourself by bringing a mental list of your strongest selling points to the interview and being ready to speak about them when the opportunity arises. You can demonstrate knowledge of your audience by doing some homework on the organization you are applying to, the people who are likely to be interviewing you, and the questions they are likely to ask you. Try to acquire as much information about the organization and its key employees as is available to you online and in print. When you know your audience (who your interviewers are likely to be and what they're likely to ask), and when you know yourself well (what about yourself you're going to say), you should then be ready to answer what probably is the most important interview question of all: "What can *you* do for *us?*"

To prepare for interviews, visit your Career Development Center and inquire about questions that are commonly asked during personal interviews. You might also try to speak with seniors who have interviewed with recruiters and ask them whether certain questions tended to be frequently asked. Once you begin to participate in actual interviews, make note of the questions you are asked. Although you may be able to anticipate some of the more general questions that are asked in almost any interview, there likely will be unique questions asked of you that relate specifically to your personal qualifications and experiences. If these questions are asked in one of your interviews, there's a good chance they'll be asked in a future interview. As soon as you complete an interview, mentally review it and attempt to recall the major questions you were asked before they slip your mind. Consider developing an index-card catalog of questions that you've been asked during interviews, with the question on one side and your prepared response on the reverse side. By being better prepared for personal interviews, you'll increase the quality of your answers and decrease your level of anxiety. You should also have a list of questions to ask at the interview. This shows that you are interested and did your homework. Finally, remember to dress appropriately for an interview. If you are unsure how to dress, consult a professional you trust on campus.

Lastly, remember to send a thank-you note to the person who interviewed you. This is not only the courteous thing to do, but also the smart thing to do because it demonstrates your interpersonal sensitivity and reinforces the person's memory of you.

Technology and Career Placement

Once you start looking for a job, internship, or co-op, it is very important to consider how you use technology:

1. **Your e-mail address.** Make sure it is professional and would not offend anyone.
2. **Your cell phone.** Consider your "ringback tone." If it is music that has offensive language, remove it. Also, make sure your voice mail message is short and professional. Time is precious and people don't want to listen to a two-minute voice mail message, no matter what it is about.
3. **Facebook, Twitter, etc.** Make sure anything you post would not turn off any potential employers. Even if your page is marked "private," employers are hiring people to get all the dirt on you!

It is important when you are looking for a job to put your best self out there; this includes your digital self.

Summary and Conclusion

Here is a snapshot of the points that were made in this chapter:

- Changing your educational goal is not necessarily a bad thing; it may represent your discovery of another field that's more interesting to you or that's more compatible with your personal interests and talents.
- Several myths exist about the relationship between college majors and careers that need to be dispelled:
  - **Myth 1.** When you choose your major, you're choosing your career.
  - **Myth 2.** After a bachelor's degree, any further education must be in the same field as your college major.
  - **Myth 3.** You should major in business because most college graduates work in business settings.

- **Myth 4.** If you major in a liberal arts field, the only career available is teaching.
- **Myth 5.** Specialized skills are more important for career success than general skills.

- You should be aware of two important elements when choosing your major: your form or forms of multiple intelligence (your mental strengths or talents) and your learning style (your preferred way of learning).
- Strategically select your courses in a way that contributes most to your educational, personal, and professional development. Choose your elective courses with one or more of the following purposes in mind:
  - Choose a major or confirm whether your first choice is a good one.
  - Acquire a minor or build a concentration that will complement your major.
  - Broaden your perspectives on the world around you.
  - Become a more balanced or complete person.
  - Handle the practical life tasks that face you now and in the future.
  - Strengthen your career development and employment prospects after graduation.

With higher education comes more freedom of choice and a greater opportunity to determine your own academic course of action. Employ it and enjoy it—use your freedom strategically to make the most of your college experience and college degree.

In national surveys, employers rank attitude of the job applicant as the number one factor in making hiring decisions; they rate is higher in importance than such factors as reputation of the applicant's school, previous work experience, and recommendations of former employers (Education Commission of the States, 1995; Institute for Research on Higher Education, 1995). Graduating from college with a diploma or certificate may make you a more competitive job candidate, but you still have to compete by documenting and selling your strengths and skills. Your diploma or certificate doesn't work like a merit badge or passport that you flash to gain automatic access to an ideal job. Your college experience will open career doors, but it's your attitude, initiative, and effort that will enable you to step through those doors and into a successful career.

Learning More through the World Wide Web

Internet-Based Resources for Further Information on Educational Planning and Decision Making

For additional information related to the ideas discussed in this chapter, we recommend the following Web sites:

www.mymajors.com

www.princetonreview.com/majors.aspx

www.eace.org/networks/liberalarts.html

www.internships.com

www.vaultreports.com

mappingyourfuture.org/PlanYourCareer/

www.monster.com

www.salary.com

13.1 Planning General Education

- Look at your college catalog. If you don't have a copy, you may be able to access it online or obtain a copy from your academic advisor or Registrar's Office. Use the index in the catalog to find the general education requirements at your college. You're likely to find that general education requirements are organized into academic divisions of knowledge that make up the college curriculum, such as humanities, fine arts, and natural sciences. Within each of these academic divisions, you'll see courses listed that fulfill the general education requirement for that particular division. In some cases, you'll have no choice about what courses you must take to fulfill the general education requirement, but in most cases, you'll have the freedom to choose from a group of courses. Read the course descriptions to get an idea about what each course covers, and choose those courses that are most relevant to your educational and career plans or to your interests in fields that you might consider choosing as a major.

- Record the courses you plan to take to fulfill your general education requirements on the following form. (Remember that courses you are taking this term may be fulfilling certain general education requirements, so be sure to include them on the form.)

General Education Planning Form

Academic Division: _____

General education courses you plan to take to fulfill requirements in this division:

(Record the course number and course title)

Academic Division: _____

General education courses you plan to take to fulfill requirements in this division:

Academic Division: _____

General education courses you plan to take to fulfill requirements in this division:

Academic Division: _____

General education courses you plan to take to fulfill requirements in this division:

Academic Division: _____

General education courses you plan to take to fulfill requirements in this division:

Academic Division: _____

General education courses you plan to take to fulfill requirements in this division:

13.2 Planning for a College Major and Transfer to a Four-Year College

In the preceding exercise, you made a plan for the general education component of your college experience. Now consider developing a tentative plan for a college major or specialized field of study. Even if you don't think you're going to transfer to a four-year college and complete a bachelor's degree, it's still a good idea to complete this exercise because it'll give you an idea about what it would take to get such a degree. It's possible that when you see it all laid out in a plan, you might be motivated to pursue a bachelor's degree—if not right now, then perhaps at a later point in your life.

1. Go to your college catalog and use its index to locate pages containing information related to the major you have chosen or are considering. If you are undecided, select a field that you might consider as a possibility. To help you identify possible majors, you can use your catalog or go online and complete the short interview at the www.mymajors.com Web site.

    The point of this exercise is not to force you to commit to a major now, but to familiarize you with the process of developing a plan, thereby putting you in a position to apply this knowledge when you reach a final decision about the major you intend to pursue. Even if you don't yet know what your final destination may be with respect to a college major, creating this educational plan will keep you moving in the right direction.

2. Once you've selected a major for this assignment, look at the catalog of the four-year college to which you plan to transfer to identify the courses that are required for the major you have selected. Use the form that follows to list the number and title of each course required by the major.

    You'll find that you must take certain courses for the major; these are often called core requirements. For instance, at most colleges, all business majors must take microeconomics. You will likely discover that you can choose other required courses from a menu or list of options (e.g., "choose any three courses from the following list of six courses"). Such courses are often called restricted electives in the major. When you find restricted electives in the major you've selected, read the course descriptions and choose those courses from the list that appeal most to you. Simply list the numbers and titles of these courses on the planning form. (You don't need to write down all choices listed in the catalog.)

    College catalogs can sometimes be tricky to navigate or interpret, so if you run into any difficulty, don't panic. Seek help from an academic advisor. Your campus may also have a degree audit program available, which allows you to track major requirements electronically. If so, take advantage of it.

College Major Planning Form

Major Selected: _____

Core Requirements in the Major
(Courses in your major that you must take)

Course #	Course Title		Course #	Course Title

Restricted Electives in the Major
(Courses required for your major that you choose to take from a specified list)

Course #	Course Title		Course #	Course Title

Self-Assessment Questions

1. Looking over the courses required for the major you've selected, would you still be interested in majoring in this field?

2. Were there courses required by the major that you were surprised to see or that you did not expect would be required?

3. Are there questions that you still have about this major?

13.3 Developing a Comprehensive Transfer and Graduation Plan

A comprehensive, long-range graduation plan includes all three types of courses you need to complete a college degree:

1. General education requirements

2. Major requirements

3. Free electives

In the preceding exercises, you planned for your required general education courses and required courses in your major. The third set of courses you'll take in college that count toward your degree consists of courses called free electives—courses that are not required for general education or your major but that you freely choose from any of the courses listed in your college catalog. By combining your general education courses, major courses, and free elective courses, you can create a comprehensive, long-term transfer and graduation plan.

Use the form on p. 377 to develop this complete educational plan. Use the slots to pencil in the general education courses you're planning to take to fulfill your general education requirements, your major requirements, and your free electives. Since this may be a tentative plan, it's probably best to use a pencil when completing it in case you need to make modifications to it.

Notes

1. If you have not decided on a major, a good strategy might be to concentrate on taking liberal arts courses to fulfill your general education requirements during your first year of college. This will open more slots in your course schedule during your sophomore year. By that time, you may have a better idea of what you want to major in, and you can fill these open slots with courses required by your major. This may be a particularly effective strategy if you choose to major in a field that has many lower-division (freshman and sophomore) requirements that have to be completed before you can be accepted as a transfer student in that major. (These lower-division requirements are often referred to as premajor requirements.)

2. Keep in mind that the course number indicates the year in the college experience that the course is usually taken. Courses numbered in the 100s (or below) are typically taken in the first year of college, 200-numbered courses in the sophomore year, 300-numbered courses in the junior year, and 400-numbered courses in the senior year. Also, be sure to check whether the course you're planning to take has any prerequisites—courses that need to be completed before you can enroll in the course you're planning to take. For example, if you are planning to take a course in literature, it is likely that you cannot enroll in it until you have completed at least one prerequisite course in writing or English composition.

3. To complete a college degree in four years, you should complete about 30 credits each academic year. Summer term is considered part of an academic year, and we encourage you to use that term to help keep you on a four-year timeline.

4. Check with an academic advisor to see whether your college and the four-year college to which you're planning to transfer have developed a projected plan of scheduled courses, which indicates the academic term when courses listed in the catalog are scheduled to be offered (e.g., fall, spring, or summer) for the next two to three years. If such a long-range plan of scheduled courses is available, take advantage of it because it will enable you to develop a personal educational plan that includes not only what courses you will take but also when you will take them. This can be an important advantage because some courses you may need for graduation will not be offered every term. We strongly encourage you to inquire about and acquire any long-range plan of scheduled courses that may be available and use it when developing your long-range graduation plan.

5. Don't forget to include out-of-class learning experiences as part of your educational plan, such as volunteer service, internships, and study abroad.

Your long-range graduation plan is not something set in stone that can never be modified. Like clay, its shape can be molded and changed into a different form as you gain more experience with the college curriculum. Nevertheless, your creation of this initial plan will be useful because it will provide you with a blueprint to work from. Once you have created slots specifically for your general education requirements, your major courses, and your electives, you have accounted for all the categories of courses you will need to complete to graduate. Thus, if changes need to be made to your plan, they can be easily accommodated by simply substituting different courses into the slots you've already created for these three categories.

Remember

The purpose of this long-range planning assignment is not to lock you into a rigid plan, but to give you a telescope for viewing your educational future and a map for reaching your educational goals.

Long-Range Transfer and Graduation Planning Form

STUDENT: ID NO.:

MAJOR: MINOR:

TERM:		Units	TERM:		Units	TERM:		Units	TERM:		Units
Course			Course			Course			Course		
TOTAL			TOTAL			TOTAL			TOTAL		

TERM:		Units	TERM:		Units	TERM:		Units	TERM:		Units
Course			Course			Course			Course		
TOTAL			TOTAL			TOTAL			TOTAL		

TERM:		TERM:		TERM:		TERM:	
Course	Units	Course	Units	Course	Units	Course	Units
TOTAL		TOTAL		TOTAL		TOTAL	

TERM:		TERM:		TERM:		TERM:	
Course	Units	Course	Units	Course	Units	Course	Units
TOTAL		TOTAL		TOTAL		TOTAL	

		CO-CURRICULAR EXPERIENCES	SERVICE LEARNING AND INTERNSHIP EXPERIENCES
Advisor's Signature	Date:		
Student's Signature	Date:		
Notes:			

Self-Assessment Questions

1. Do you think this was a useful assignment? Why or why not?

2. Do you see any way in which this assignment could be improved or strengthened?

3. Did completing this long-range graduation plan influence your educational plans in any way?

13.4 Conducting an Informational Interview

To learn accurate information about a career that interests you, interview working professionals in that career—a career-exploration strategy known as informational interviewing. An informational interview enables you to:

- Learn what a career is really like;

- Network with professionals in the field; and

- Become confident in interview situations and prepare for later job interviews.

Self-Assessment Questions

1. Select a career that you may be interested in pursuing. Even if you are currently keeping your career options open, pick a career that might be a possibility. You can use the resources cited on p. 353 in this chapter to help you identify a career that may be most appealing to you.

2. Find someone who is working in the career you selected and set up an informational interview with that person. To help locate possible interview candidates, consider members of your family, friends of your family members, and family members of your friends. Any of these people may be working in the career you selected and may be good interview candidates, or they may know others who could be good candidates. The Career Development Center on your campus may also be able to provide you with graduates of your college or professionals working in the local community near your college who are willing to talk about their careers with students. Lastly, you might consider using the Yellow Pages or the Internet to find names and addresses of possible candidates. Send them a short letter or e-mail asking about the possibility of scheduling a short interview. Mention that you would be willing to conduct the interview in person or by phone, whichever would be more convenient for them. If you do not hear back within a reasonable period (e.g., within a couple of weeks), send a follow-up message; if you do not receive a response to the follow-up message, then consider contacting someone else.

3. Conduct an informational interview with the professional who has agreed to speak with you. Consider using the following suggested strategies.

13.5 Suggested Strategies for Conducting Informational Interviews

First, thank the person for taking the time to speak with you. This should be the first thing you do after meeting the person, before you officially begin the interview.

Prepare your interview questions in advance. Here are some questions that you might consider asking:

1. How did you decide on your career?

2. What qualifications or prior experiences did you have that enabled you to enter your career?

3. How does someone find out about openings in your field?

4. What steps did you take to find your current position?

5. What advice would you give to beginning college students about things they could start doing now to help them prepare to enter your career?

6. During a typical day's work, what do you spend most of your time doing?

7. What do you like most about your career?

8. What are the most difficult or frustrating aspects of your career?

9. What personal skills or qualities do you see as being critical for success in your career?

10. How does someone advance in your career?

11. Are there any moral issues or ethical challenges that tend to arise in your career?

12. Are members of diverse groups likely to be found in your career? (This is an especially important question to ask if you are a member of an ethnic, racial, or gender group that is underrepresented in the career field.)

13. What impact does your career have on your home life or personal life outside of work?

14. If you had to do it all over again, would you choose the same career?

15. Would you recommend that I speak with anyone else to obtain additional information or a different perspective on this career field? (If the answer is "yes," you may follow up by asking, "May I mention that you referred me?") This question is recommended because it's always a good idea to obtain more than one person's perspective before making an important choice or decision, especially one that can have a major influence on your life, such as your career choice.

Take notes during the interview. This not only benefits you by helping you remember what was said, but also sends a positive message to the person you're interviewing by showing that the person's ideas are important and worth writing down.

If the interview goes well, you could ask whether it might be possible to observe or shadow your interviewee during a day at work.

Self-Assessment Questions

After completing your interview, take a moment to reflect on it and answer the following questions:

1. What information did you receive that impressed you about this career?

2. What information did you receive that distressed (or depressed) you about this career?

3. What was the most useful thing you learned from conducting this interview?

4. Knowing what you know now, would you still be interested in pursuing this career? If yes, why? If no, why not?

Dazed and Confused: General Education versus Career Specialization

Joe Tech was looking forward to college because he thought he would have freedom to select the courses he wanted and the opportunity to get into the major of his choice (computer science). However, he is shocked and disappointed with his first-term schedule of classes because it consists mostly of required general education courses that do not seem to relate to his major, and some of these courses are about subjects that he already took in high school (English, history, and biology). He's beginning to think he would be better off moving off the transfer track and getting a technical degree so that he could finish sooner, get into the computer industry, and start earning money.

Discussion Questions

1. What do you see as the potential advantages and disadvantages of Joe pursuing a technical degree instead of a four-year college degree?

2. Can you relate to Joe, or do you know of students who feel as he does?

3. Do you see any way Joe might strike a balance between pursuing his career interest and obtaining his college degree so that he can pursue both goals at the same time?

Career Choice: Conflict and Confusion

Josh is a first-year student whose family has made a great financial sacrifice to send him to college. He deeply appreciates the tremendous commitment his family has made to his education and wants to pay them back as soon as possible. Consequently, he has been looking into careers that offer the highest starting salaries to college students immediately after graduation. Unfortunately, none of these careers seem to match Josh's natural abilities and personal interests, so he's conflicted, confused, and starting to get stressed out. He knows he'll have to make a decision soon because the careers with high starting salaries involve majors that have many course requirements, and if he expects to graduate in a reasonable period, he'll have to start taking some of these courses during his first year.

Discussion Questions

1. If you were Josh, what would you do?

2. Do you see any way that Josh might balance his desire to pay back his parents as soon as possible with his desire to pursue a career that's compatible with his interests and talents?

3. What other questions or factors do you think Josh should consider before making his decision?

Chapter 13 Reflection

Reflect back on Chapter 13 and think about your ideal career. What is it? What would your work day be like? Make a **detailed** plan for how you can get to this career. What are some things you can utilize from this chapter to make it happen?

Vegan Deli

Wholesome Ethnic Fast Food

Joanne Stepaniak

Book Publishing Company
Summertown, Tenn.

Cover art: Linda Paul (www.lindapaul.com)
Cover design: Warren Jefferson
Interior art: Kim Trainor

Published in the United States by
Book Publishing Company
P. O. Box 99
Summertown, TN 38483
1-888-260-8458
www.bookpubco.com

ISBN 1-57067-109-5

09 08 07 06 05 04 03 02 01   1 2 3 4 5 6 7 8 9

Stepaniak, Joanne
    Vegan deli : wholesome ethnic fast food / Joanne Stepaniak
        p. cm.
    ISBN 1-57067-109-5
        1. Vegan cookery. 2. Delicatessens. I. Title
    TX837 .S765 2001
    641.5'636--dc21   00-067505

Calculations for the nutritional analyses in this book are based
on the average number of servings listed with the recipes and
the average amount of an ingredient if a range is called for.
Calculations are rounded up to the nearest gram. If two options
for an ingredient are listed, the first one is used. Not included
are fat used for frying (unless the amount is specified in the
recipe), optional ingredients, or serving suggestions.